Happy Birthday,

Mike!

Pat McManus

9-12-89

**They Shoot Canoes,
Don't They?**

Also by Patrick F. McManus

Kid Camping from Aaaaiii! to Zip
A Fine and Pleasant Misery

Patrick F. McManus

THEY SHOOT CANOES, DON'T THEY?

HENRY HOLT AND COMPANY   NEW YORK

Published by Henry Holt and Company, Inc.,
521 Fifth Avenue, New York, New York 10175.
Distributed in Canada by Fitzhenry & Whiteside,
195 Allstate Parkway, Markham, Ontario L3R 4T8.

Library of Congress Cataloging in Publication Data

McManus, Patrick F.
They shoot canoes, don't they?
1. Outdoor recreation—Anecdotes, facetiae,
satire, etc. 2. Camping—Anecdotes, facetiae,
satire, etc. 3. Fishing—Anecdotes, facetiae,
satire, etc. 4. Hunting—Anecdotes, facetiae,
satire, etc. I. Title.
GV191.6.M33   796.5'0207   80-24131
ISBN 0–8050–0165–4
ISBN 0–8050–0030–5 (An Owl book) (pbk.)

Designer: Joy Chu
Printed in the United States of America
20 19 18 17 16 15 14 13 12 11

All stories in this book originally appeared in Field &
Stream or its allied publications, Field & Stream Deer
Hunting Annual and Field & Stream Fishing Annual,
with the exception of "Meanwhile Back at the B Western,"
which first appeared in Colt American Handgunning
Annual 1979, Aqua-Field Publications, Inc.

ISBN 0-8050-0165-4 HARDBOUND
ISBN 0-8050-0030-5 PAPERBACK

TO DARLENE

CONTENTS

**They Shoot Canoes,
Don't They?**

All You Ever Wanted
to Know About
Live Bait but Were
Afraid to Ask

☞ ☞ ☞ **S**urprisingly, many anglers are ashamed to admit that they fish with live bait. You'll run into one of these so-called purists on a trout stream and ask him what he's using. He'll say, "A Number thirty-two Royal Coachman on a three-ounce leader." Then he'll get a bite, snap his line out of the water, and there will be a worm on his hook. "That's the problem with these tiny flies," he'll say. "You keep catching worms with them."

The truth is that live-bait fishing has a long and noble history. Live bait was totally unknown to the early cavemen, who had to make do with a rather limited assortment of dry flies, nymphs, and a few streamers. One day, whether out of exasperation or simple impatience, a caveman made a backcast with a gray hackle he had not bothered to remove from a sage hen. Instantly, it was taken by a brontosaurus. The caveman was elated by his discovery, even though it was several centuries before anyone learned how to take a brontosaurus off the hook.

The caveman reasoned that if you can catch a

brontosaurus with live bait, you can surely catch fish with it, and he immediately began conducting experiments. He tried live chickens, ducks, and geese, but he soon found these very undependable, particularly on casts that passed directly overhead.

When he was about to give up and go back to dry flies, the caveman decided to bait his hook with a worm. He cast out into a deep, dark pool and immediately received the surprise of his life. A five-hundred-pound wild boar charged out of the brush and chased him for eighteen miles, and he never did learn whether worms were good bait.

Thus the discovery of worms as fishing bait was left to a humble cook in the army of Genghis Khan. After a busy day of conquering the Civilized World, the Khan decided he would like fish for supper and dropped a casual hint to one of his lieutenants. The lieutenant, who had had considerable experience with the Khan's casual hints, nearly trampled three foot soldiers getting the news into the kitchen. Dismounting, he said to the cooks, "Guess what? Old G.K. wants fish for supper." Since fishing had been extremely poor and no one had had so much as a nibble in days, the kitchen staff immediately bought tickets and caught the first stage out of town, the single exception being a little hors d'oeuvre specialist, Leroy Swartz, who knew absolutely nothing about fishing. Leroy had never developed the knack for plundering and pillaging—though he wasn't bad at razing—and as a result his total loot for the campaign was a spade with a broken handle. For a reason known only to Leroy, he started digging up the ground with the spade. The lieutenant, assuming he was digging a grave, said, "If we can't get G.K. any fish for his supper, you might as well make that big enough for two." Then Leroy started picking up worms and stuffing them into his pocket, tomato cans not yet having been invented. He grabbed a fishing pole and went off to the nearest river, from whence he shortly returned with his limit, in those days as many as you could carry plus one fish. Everyone danced and shouted over Leroy's discovery that worms were excellent fishing bait. Even the Khan was beside himself with joy, a condition that caused Mrs. Khan considerable annoyance since they slept in the same bed. Leroy Swartz was henceforth known as the Father of Worms, a title he did not much care for, but it beat employment as a battering ram on the next fortress to be attacked.

Toward the latter part of the eighteenth century, grasshoppers were discovered to be exceptional live bait. Up until then they were thought to be good only for devouring grain crops and causing widespread famine. One day an angler was walking along a country road in search of a good place to dig a supply of worms. He happened to glance out into a field fairly alive with grasshoppers and noticed a man leaping about on all fours and slapping the ground with his hat. The angler thought the fellow must be crazy to behave in such a strange manner and walked over to see what he was up to. It turned out the man *was* crazy, but the angler didn't discover this until he had helped him catch a dozen grasshoppers. Since by then it was too late to dig any worms, the angler decided to bait his hook with grasshoppers—and the rest is history.

Up until the Industrial Revolution and the invention of tomato cans and the flat tobacco can, there were no suitable containers for live bait, and anglers had to carry their bait around in their hands, pockets, and hats. In the case of grasshoppers, wealthy fishermen would sometimes hire a boy to drive a herd of them along the bank. In later years worms were carried in pokes similar to those used for gold coins. There is at least one recorded instance in which a card-playing fisherman narrowly escaped lynching when he attempted to bluff with a poke of nightcrawlers.

So much for the history of live bait. We will now examine some of the various kinds of live bait, where to find it, how to preserve it, and assorted techniques for using it.

First off, there are only two kinds of bait: live bait and dead bait. Worms, grubs, grasshoppers, minnows, and the like are live bait, unless left unattended in a hot car too long, in which case they become dead bait. I have on occasion forgotten to remove a can of worms from my car on a blistering July day, a mistake that has led to attempts to bait hooks with little balls of worm paste, not to mention the necessity of driving with all the car's windows open until approximately the middle of February. On the other hand, I've carried around salmon eggs and pickled pork rind until they were showing definite signs of life.

My favorite method of preserving live bait is to store it in the refrigerator until it is ready for use. There are two schools of thought on the proper execution of this procedure. Some hold it is better to tell your wife first, and the others claim it is better to let her make the discovery for herself. I'm a member of the latter group and have been ever since my wife came across a jar of my hellgrammites while she was sorting through the refrigerator in search of some mayonnaise. The incident would probably have passed without any lingering ill effects had she not at the time been entertaining her church bridge club. It is difficult to describe the resulting commotion with any accuracy, but I learned later that cards from our bridge deck were found as far away as three blocks and one of the olive-and-avocado sandwiches served at the party turned up in a ladies' restroom halfway across town. Our dog was asleep on the front sidewalk when the ladies left, and it was weeks before we could get all the dents out of him left by their heels.

I have on occasion attempted to lay in a supply of worms during the spring months while they are still near the surface and one doesn't have to dig down to the aquifer to find them. I'll stash a couple of hundred of them in a washtub filled with dirt and feed them coffee grounds. The reason I feed them coffee grounds is that numerous people have told me that that is what worms like to eat. Whether they do or not, I'm not sure. In any case, I've yet to find a single worm when I dump out the tub later in the summer. I'm beginning to suspect that worms can't stand coffee grounds (or maybe coffee grounds like worms). When you stop to think about it, where would your average worm develop a taste for coffee anyway?

The beginning angler is often of the impression that there are only three kinds of worms: small, medium, and large. Actually, the size of the worm makes little difference. Temperament and character are everything. These two characteristics seem to be determined primarily by environment. For example, I've never found a worm raised in a manure pile who could earn his keep as fishing bait. Manure-pile worms are soft and pale and accustomed to easy living. To a worm, a manure pile is a suite in the Ritz, a villa on the Riviera. He never has to worry about where his next meal is coming from. (If he knew, he would probably worry, but he doesn't know.) Manure-pile worms don't have any street savvy. Now, you dig up a worm out of a garden, an individual who has been through a couple of rototillings, and that worm has been around. He's going to go out and put up a good fight. Nothing builds character in a worm like a good rototilling.

Some time ago a sporting-goods company sent me a package of freeze-dried worms. Honest. At first I thought it was some kind of veiled threat, but then I found a note saying that if I soaked the worms in water they would reconstitute into fishing bait. I stuck the package in my backpack with my other freeze-drieds and a couple of nights later at a mountain lake took it out and soaked the contents in some water. It turned out to be macaroni and cheese sauce. "That's funny," my friend Retch Sweeney said. "I thought we ate the macaroni and cheese sauce last night." The freeze-dried worms never did turn up.

The most troublesome of all live bait is the grasshopper. By the time you've caught enough of them you're usually too tired to go fishing. Furthermore, grasshoppers are not content simply to sit around in a bottle waiting to be fed to some fish. Once a worm is in the can, he pretty well knows his fate is sealed and will lie back and take it easy until his number comes up. Not so with grasshoppers. They are no sooner in the bottle than they're plotting their escape. Every time the lid is lifted to insert a new inmate, half a dozen of the others will try to make a break for it. While I was still a young boy, I learned that the only way to foil their escapes was to shake the bottle vigorously and then slip the new grasshopper in while the others were still dazed. What apparently happens is that the grasshoppers get high from the shaking and like it so much that after a while you can hardly chase them out of the bottle with a stick. They just lie on their backs, smiling. Of course this is confusing to the new grasshopper, who thinks he has been incarcerated with a bunch of degenerate insects who keep calling out, "C'mon, man, give us another shake!"

To my mind, the best live bait is the hellgrammite, an

insect that resides on streambeds and builds little cocoons for itself out of pebbles. Fish cannot resist them, in their shells or out. They are the salted peanuts of baits. Not long ago I was fishing a stream in Idaho and hadn't had a nibble all day. Then I discovered a nice patch of hellgrammites and within a half an hour had nearly filled my limit with plump cutthroat. There were a dozen or so other anglers on the stream, and they were so astonished at my success that they could not help expressing their awe by jovially threatening to slash my waders the next time I was in deep water. Finally, after I had creeled my final catch, a couple of them came over and demanded to know what I was using.

"These," I said.

"Jeez, those are ugly-looking things!" one of them said. "I almost hate to touch them."

"Trout love 'em," I said. "Here, take a couple of mine just to try them out." I thought it was the very least I could do.

As I was climbing into my car, I heard one of the other fishermen yell, "What was he using?"

"These nasty-looking things," the first fellow yelled back. "Big, red, white, and blue flies!"

I felt a little bad about the deception. On the other hand, you can never tell. There *could* be such a thing as patriotic fish.

The Green Box

☞ ☞ ☞ **T**he other day I came home and found my wife cleaning out the garage. She was covered from one end to the other with dirt and cobwebs. Beads of sweat were dripping off the tip of her nose as she came staggering out of the garage carrying a huge green box in the general direction of the garbage cans.

"You shouldn't be doing that," I scolded.

"I shouldn't?" she said, putting the box down and massaging the small of her back with both hands.

"No, you shouldn't," I said. "I'm saving the stuff in that box. Now you carry it right back to where you found it."

I could tell I had hurt her feelings, partly because her eyes got all teary and her mouth formed into this cute little pout, but mostly because of the way she sprang forward and tried to crush my instep with her sneakers. After she had calmed down a bit, I explained to her that the box she was attempting to commit to oblivion was filled with priceless relics of my sporting youth.

"You must be thinking of some other box," she said. "I checked, and this one is just filled with a bunch of old junk."

"Ha!" I exclaimed, thrusting my hand into the box and withdrawing an artifact at random. "And just what do you call this?"

"Junk," she said.

"Well, it just so happens that this little metal band is a 1950 deer tag. This is the tag of my very first deer."

"You shot your first deer in 1950?"

"No, my very first deer got away that year, but this was its tag."

The deer tag tripped the hair trigger of my reminiscence mechanism, and suddenly the last hour of daylight was flitting away on the last day of deer season, 1950. I was crouched behind a log at the edge of an abandoned apple orchard on the side of a mountain. A quarter of a mile away, my very first deer and several others were meandering down a brushy slope in the general direction of the orchard. My hope was that they would step out into the orchard while there was still light enough to shoot. The only sounds were those of my own nervous breathing and Olga Bonemarrow's impatient popping of gum in my ear.

"Jeez, I'm freezing," Olga said in a nasty tone. "I don't know why I ever let you talk me into this."

"Shhhh!" I said. I slipped out of my mackinaw and told her to put it on over her own coat, which she did. I myself was wondering why I had talked Olga into coming along. As a matter of fact, I hadn't had to talk that much. Olga had stopped by my place just as I was getting ready to go hunting. All I had said to her was, "Hey, Olga, how'd you like to take a little ride up into the mountains with me?"

She had given me a long look. "What for?"

I smiled mischievously, an expression I had been attempting to perfect in front of my bedroom mirror for the past few days. "You'll find out," I said. "It's something you ain't never done before."

"I wouldn't bet on it," Olga said. "But okay."

It turned out that this was indeed Olga's first experience with hunting. She tried her best to conceal her surprise under a veneer of rage. Despite my best efforts to keep her quiet as we waited for my first deer to step into the orchard, she continued to growl and complain and whine, her hands thrust deep into the pockets of my mackinaw. In the thicket on the far side of the orchard, my straining eyes picked up a movement. Then a buck stepped halfway out of the brush and ran an inventory on the orchard. This was it. Tensely, I slipped the safety off my Marlin .32 Special.

"Hey," Olga said suddenly. "How do you unlock this dumb cheap bracelet?"

I looked at her in horror. Snapped shut around her wrist was my deer tag!

I stood up, slipped the rifle safety back on, and jacked out the shells. My first deer vanished in a single bound.

"How come your eyes are watering?" Olga said.

" 'Cause I'm cold," I said. "Give me back my mackinaw."

The sound of my wife's voice snapped me back to the present. "I don't know what's so great about an old deer tag," she said. "Look, it's even been snipped in two. Why would you lock it and then snip it in two if you never used it?"

There are certain things the female mind is incapable of fathoming, so I ignored the question. Rummaging around in the box, I found the first dry fly I ever tied and held it up for my wife to view. She screeched and jumped back.

"It's just a dry fly," I told her.

"Thank heavens!" she said. "I thought the cat had killed another bird."

"So, you're interested in birds, are you?" I said, pulling from the box one of my most prized treasures. "This is the first grouse I ever shot. I mounted it myself."

"Why, that's just some feathers glued on a board."

"Actually," I explained, "I was a little close to the grouse when I shot. That's all that was left. Anyway, I *think* that's all that was left."

It happened like this. I had pursued the grouse into a swamp near my home and had just stepped over a deep drainage ditch, my old double-barreled 12-gauge at the ready, when I spotted the grouse on a limb a scant twenty feet away. He spotted me too, revved his engine, and took off. I pointed the shotgun and fired, thereby learning once and for all the valuable lesson of having the butt of the stock pressed firmly against one's shoulder, not six inches away from it, at the moment one squeezes the trigger. Even so, I probably would have survived the impact a good deal better had not both barrels fired simultaneously. Upon regaining my senses, I immediately assumed I would spend the rest of my life with my right shoulder wrapped around my back in approximately the shape of a taco shell. What really scared me though was that I was cold all over, my vision was blurred, and I couldn't breathe. Then I realized that I was a five-foot-eight person standing in a six-foot-deep drainage ditch filled with green slime. I scrambled out of the drain ditch with the alacrity of a person who has a profound dread of green slime, and went in immediate pursuit of the grouse. A few feathers were still drifting in the air, but there was no other sign of the grouse. "I couldn't have missed at that range?" I mumbled, scarcely able to bring myself to accept the obvious. It was almost too sad even to think about. *I had vaporized my first grouse.* Glumly, I picked up as many feathers as I could find, took them home, and glued them on a board, printing neatly underneath them with lead pencil the words MY FIRST GROUSE, 1948.

"Maybe you just plain outright missed the grouse," my wife said. "Did you ever consider that possibility?"

"No, I would never consider that possibility," I informed her. "Anyhow, if I missed, it wouldn't have been my first grouse, would it? How do you explain that?"

While she was still struggling with this flawless bit of logic I extracted another relic from the green box. "Now this lovely piece of material is what remains of what once was one of my finest fishing hats. I called it my lucky hat."

"Looks like an old grease rag to me," my wife said.

"That's just because you don't have any true sense of aesthetics and . . . uh . . . say, this *is* a grease rag! How'd it get mixed in with these valuables? I bet I had you fooled when I let on like it was my lucky hat. Heh, heh."

"Heh, heh," she said without enthusiasm.

The next item extracted from the green box evoked a memory of high school. It was a moldy plug of tobacco, with one sizable chaw taken from a single corner.

In the days of my youth I spent a great deal of time in the company of an old woodsman by the name of Rancid Crabtree. He was my idol. More than anything I wanted to be like Rancid, a man who owned himself, who spent his life roaming the woods, hunting and fishing and trapping, almost always enjoying himself. I tried to emulate him in every way, and even went so far one time as to try a chaw of tobacco.

On that memorable occasion, some of the guys and I

were discussing deer-hunting tactics in the back of the classroom while we waited for the teacher, Mrs. Axelrod, to come in and start haranguing us about the French Revolution, as if it had been our fault. I casually hauled out my plug of tobacco, took a good healthy chaw, then stuffed the plug back in my pocket. Not one of the guys so much as blinked, but I could tell they were impressed. At that moment Mrs. Axelrod sailed into the room and ordered us to our seats. Since she didn't even allow gum chewing in class, I decided I had better get rid of the tobacco fast. So I swallowed it.

A few minutes later, it became apparent to me that one does not actually get rid of a chaw of tobacco by swallowing it. The chaw, in fact, was traveling up and down my esophagus like a yo-yo on a short string, and was giving every indication that it was about to reenter society at any moment.

"Now, who can tell us the underlying causes of the French Revolution?" Mrs. Axelrod asked. She looked at me. "Pat."

I pointed a questioning finger to my chest, hoping to delay answering until the chaw was on the downstroke.

"Yes, you, the green person with the bloated cheeks!" Mrs. Axelrod snapped.

One second later I departed the room in a manner I hoped was not totally without dignity but which was later described to me by Peewee Thompson as a "sort of greenish blur."

Peering into the green box, I could scarcely refrain from emitting a shout of joy. There, nestled among such collector's items as gopher traps, a single warped bear-paw snowshoe, a rusty machete, a jungle hammock, a collection of spent cartridges, a collection of dried toads, a perforated canteen, a casting reel encased in a permanent backlash, a dog harness made out of nylon stockings, and other rare and priceless mementos of my sporting youth, was without doubt what had to be the world's most powerful hand-held slingshot. I had thought the slingshot lost to posterity.

The slingshot had been designed and built by me at about age ten. I describe it as hand-held because later I also had built a more powerful slingshot, one that consisted of two live trees and a series of bicycle inner tubes. That slingshot almost earned the distinction of putting the first human into orbit, a kid by the name of Henry, who, when a gang of us stretched the inner tubes back to the limit of our combined strength, failed to hear the order "Fire!" Henry reported later that the lift-off actually had been a lot of fun, but he had run into difficulty at the termination of reentry.

The fork of the world's most powerful hand-held slingshot consisted of a Y-shaped section of trunk from a birch tree that I hacked down with my machete. The bands were made of strips cut from a tractor inner tube. These strips were then woven together in such a manner as to greatly increase their firing power. The pouch consisted of a tongue cut from a leather boot. Whomper, as I called the slingshot, was a magnificent and awesome instrument. Originally, my intention in building Whomper had been to hunt elk with it. I was disappointed to discover upon its completion, however, that, strain as I might, I could no more stretch the bands than if they had been made of cast iron. I considered this only a minor defect, however, and took to carrying Whomper about with me in a special holster attached to the back of my belt. I also carried a regular slingshot for utilitarian and sporting purposes. It was this combination of elastic armaments that resulted in one of my more satisfying experiences as a youngster.

My old woodsman friend Rancid Crabtree had taken me to the Loggers Picnic, an annual event in which the loggers competed in eating, drinking, and feats of strength. Rancid said he figured he could hold his own in two of the categories but that he was too old and feeble for feats of strength.

"Ah'll leave the feats of strangth to you," Rancid told me.

Actually, I figured I might do quite well in some of the events, but I was immediately sent to humiliating defeat in arm wrestling by the strapping offspring of a logger.

Rancid tried to console me. "Don't fret about it," he said. "Some of them girls is a lot stronger than they look. You'd a probly won iffin she'd been a boy."

No doubt my defeat by Mary Jane Railbender would have gone unnoticed by most of the picnickers had it not been for the presence of a large, loud, loathsome fellow by the name of Whitey. Whitey, though ten years older than myself, was one of my most despised enemies and passed up no opportunity to torment me.

"Har, har, har!" he roared. "Got beat by a little snip of a girl, did you? Har, har, har!" He then rushed to spread the news among the loggers and their kin, who, while they didn't exactly find the news of my downfall sidesplitting, seemed at least mildly amused. To me, that constituted excessive mirth at my expense, and I stalked off beyond the reach of their har, har's.

While I was drowning my sorrow in a bottle of orange crush, I happened to notice a flock of crows flying over. As was my practice in those days, I sprang to my feet, drew my regular slingshot to its full capacity, and let fly at them with a rock. I missed the crows by a quarter of a mile, but suddenly somebody yelled out, "Holy cow! Who threw that rock? That's one heck of a throw!"

"That was just Pat," somebody else said. "But he done it with a slingshot."

"A slingshot!" shouted out Whitey. "Pat's got a slingshot? Must be made out of wishbone and a rubber-band if he can shoot it, anybody who lets himself get beat by a little girl in arm wrastlin'." Whitey took the little sounds of amusement from the other picnickers for encouragement. "Here, Shrimpy, toss me yore peashooter. I'll show you how a man does with a slingshot."

From deep inside me I could feel this great, evil, hysterical laugh welling up, but I fought it back down. Calmly, with just the right touch of nonchalance, I reached behind me and drew Whomper from its holster. The big slingshot landed with a solid *chunk* at Whitey's feet. He stared down at it: the massive fork, the woven rubber bands thick as a man's wrist, the boot-tongue pouch, all of it bound together with wrappings of baling wire. Even from where I stood I could tell he was impressed.

"C'mon, Whitey," shouted Rancid from the crowd of spectators. "Show us how a man does with a slangshot!"

"All right, I will," said Whitey, and he scooped up the slingshot, fitted a stone the size of a walnut in the pouch, and hauled back. Well, it was a terrible spectacle to have to witness, and I've always felt a little remorseful that I enjoyed it so much. Up to the part where the buttons started popping off the front of Whitey's shirt and flying about like shrapnel, I thought Whitey might actually stretch the sling an inch or two. But by the time the women and little children were sent away because of the horrible sounds he was making, I knew there wasn't a chance.

At last, quivering with rage and exhaustion, Whitey threw the slingshot to the ground. "Ain't nobody can pull that thing," he gasped. For a second, I thought I detected a wave of sympathy, even admiration, flowing from the spectators toward Whitey.

Then Rancid stepped forward. "Shucks," he said. "Let a feeble old man give thet thang a try." He grabbed up Whomper, hauled back until the woven tractor-tube bands hummed like guitar strings. He then shot the rock out of sight. His face split in a big grin, Rancid handed Whomper back to me. The loggers laughed and applauded and slapped both me and Rancid on the back. I never again had any trouble from Whitey.

When we were driving home, Rancid still had the big grin on his face.

"What's so funny?" I asked him.

"Ain't nuthin' funny," he said through his teeth.

"How come you're grinning like that then?"

"Ah ain't grinnin'," he said. "Ah thank Ah ruptured maw face pullin' thet dang slangshot!"

My wife kicked the green box with one of her sneakers. "All right, all right, I won't throw this junk out if it means so much to you that you have to reminisce for twenty minutes over every piece of it."

"What?" I said. "No, of course you're not going to throw it out. I won't let you. Say, look at this! Look at the stuff in this jar. It's some of my old bear grease!"

"Oh, good heavens," she said. "Now I suppose you're going to tell me how you used to grease bears."

That really burned me up. Who would have thought she would guess the punch line of one of my best stories?

Skunk Dog

☞ ☞ ☞ **W**hen I was a kid, I used to beg my mother to get me a dog.

"You've got a dog," she would say.

"No, I mean a real dog," I'd reply.

"Why, you've got Strange, and he's a real dog, more or less."

Strange was mostly less. He had stopped by to cadge a free meal off of us one day and found the pickings so easy he decided to stay on. He lived with us for ten years, although, as my grandmother used to say, it seemed like centuries. In all those years, he displayed not a single socially redeeming quality. If dogs were films, he'd have been X-rated.

I recall one Sunday when my mother had invited the new parish priest to dinner. Our dining room table was situated in front of a large window overlooking the front yard. During the first course, Strange passed by the window not once but twice, walking on his front legs but dragging his rear over the grass. His mouth was split in an ear-to-ear grin of sublime relief, and possibly of pride, in his discovery of a new treatment for embarrassing itch.

"Well, Father," Mom said in a hasty effort at distraction, "and how do you like our little town by now?"

"Hunh?" the pastor said, a fork full of salad frozen in mid-stroke as he gaped out the window at the disgusting spectacle. "Pardon me, what were you saying?"

During the next course, Strange appeared outside the window with the remains of some creature that had met its end sometime prior to the previous winter, no doubt something he had saved for just such a formal occasion. As he licked his chops in pretense of preparing to consume the loathsome object, Mom shot me a look that said, "*Kill that dog!*" I stepped to the door fully intending to carry out the order, but Strange ran off, snickering under his breath.

"More chicken, Father?" Mom asked.

"Thank you, I think not," the priest said, running a finger around the inside of his Roman collar, as if experiencing some welling of the throat.

Fortunately, the dinner was only four courses in length, ending before Strange could stage his grand finale. A female collie, three dead rats, and the entrails of a sheep were left waiting in the wings.

Mom said later she didn't know whether Strange was just being more disgusting than usual that day or had something against organized religion. In any case, it was a long while before the priest came to dinner again, our invitations invariably conflicting with funerals, baptisms, or his self-imposed days of fasting.

Strange was the only dog I've ever known who could belch at will. It was his idea of high comedy. If my mother had some of her friends over for a game of pinochle, Strange would slip into the house and slouch over to the ladies. Then he would emit a loud belch. Apparently, he mistook shudders of revulsion for a form of applause, because he would sit there on his haunches, grinning modestly up at the group and preparing an encore. "Stop, stop!" he would snarl, as I dragged him back outdoors. "They love me! They'll die laughing at my other routine! It'll have them on the floor!" I will not speak here of his other routine.

In general appearance, Strange could easily have been mistaken for your average brown-and-white mongrel with floppy ears and a shaggy tail, except that depravity was written all over him. He looked as if he sold dirty postcards to support an opium habit. His eyes spoke of having known the depths of degeneracy, and approving of them.

Tramps were his favorite people. If a tramp stopped by for a free meal at our picnic table and to case the place, Strange would greet him warmly, exchange bits of news about underworld connections, and leak inside information about the household: "They ain't got any decent jewelry, but the silver's not bad and there's a good radio in the living room." The tramp would reach down and scratch the dog behind the ears as a gesture of appreciation, and Strange would belch for him. Face wrinkled in disgust, the tramp would then hoist his bedroll and depart the premises, no doubt concerned about the reliability of food given him by a family that kept such a dog.

My friends at school often debated the attributes of various breeds of dogs. "I tend to favor black labs," I'd say, going on to recite the various characteristics I had recently excerpted from a *Field & Stream* dog column. Somehow my classmates got the impression that I actually owned a black lab and had personally observed these characteristics. While I was aware of the mistaken impression, I didn't feel it was my business to go around refuting all the rumors that happened to get started.

Sooner or later, however, one of these friends would visit me at home. Strange would come out of his house and satisfy himself that the visitor wasn't a tramp in need of his counsel. That done, he would yawn, belch, gag, and return to his den of iniquity.

"That your uh dog?" the kid would ask.

"I guess so," I'd reply, embarrassed.

"Too bad," the kid would say. "I always thought you had a black lab."

"Naw, just him. But I'm planning on buying me a black lab pup first chance I get."

"I sure would," the kid would say, shaking his head.

As a hunting dog, Strange was a good deal worse than no dog. Nevertheless, he clearly thought of himself as a great hunting guide. "Fresh spoor," he would say, indicating a pine cone. "We can't be far behind him. And for gosh sakes shoot straight, because I judge from the sign he'll be in a bad mood!"

Chances of shooting any game at all with Strange along were nil. He had no concept of stealth. His standard hunting practice was to go through the woods shouting directions and advice to me and speculating loudly about the absence of game. I would have had more luck hunting with a rock band.

Strange did not believe in violence, except possibly in regard to chickens. He couldn't stand chickens. If a chicken walked by his house, Strange would rush out in a rage and tell the bird off and maybe even cuff it around a bit in the manner of early Bogart or Cagney. "You stupid chicken, don't ever let me catch you in dis neighborhood again, you hear?"

Some of our neighbors kept half-starved timber wolves for watchdogs. Occasionally one of these beasts would come loping warily through our yard and encounter Strange. Since Strange considered the whole world as his territory, he felt no particular obligation to defend this small portion of it. He would sit there, figuratively picking his teeth with a match, and stare insolently at the wolf, who was four times his size, its lip curled over glistening fangs, hackles raised, growls rumbling up from its belly. After a bit, the wolf would circle Strange, back away, and then lope on, occasionally casting a nervous glance back over its shoulder. "Punk!" Strange would mutter. Probably the reason none of these wolves ever attacked Strange was that they figured he was carrying a switchblade and maybe a blackjack.

Despite the peculiar passive side to his character, Strange did commit a single act of violence that was so terrible my mother actually considered selling the farm and moving us all to town. At the very least, she said, she was getting rid of Strange.

The episode began one warm spring evening when my grandmother sighted a skunk scurrying under our woodshed.

"He's probably the one that's been killing our chickens," Gram said. "I wouldn't be surprised but that he has his missus under there and they're planning a family. We'll be overrun with skunks!"

"Well, we'll just have to get him out from under the woodshed," Mom said. "Land sakes, a person can scarcely get a breath of fresh air in the backyard without smelling skunk. Maybe we should get Rancid Crabtree to come over and see what he can do about it."

"He'd certainly overpower the skunk smell," Gram said, "but I don't see that's any gain."

"What I mean is," Mom said, "maybe Rancid could trap the skunk or at least get it to leave. It's worth a try."

"I don't know," Gram said. "It just doesn't seem like a fair contest to me."

"Because Rancid uses guns and traps?" I asked.

"No, because the skunk has a brain!"

Gram and Rancid were not fond of each other.

The next day I was sent to tell Rancid we needed his expertise in extracting a skunk from under our woodshed. His face brightened at this news.

"Ha!" he said. "Thet ol' woman couldn't figure out how to git a skonk out from under yore shed, so fust thang she does is start yelling fer ol' Crabtree! If thet don't beat all!"

"Actually, it was Mom who told me to come get you," I said.

"Oh. Wall, in thet case, Ah'll come. Jist keep the ol' woman outta ma ha'r."

When we arrived, Gram was standing out by the woodshed banging on a pot with a steel spoon and whooping and hollering. The old woodsman nudged me in the ribs and winked. I could tell he was going to get off one of his "good ones."

"Would you mind practicin' your drummin' and singin' somewhar else?" Rancid said to her. "Me and the boy got to git a skonk out from under thet shed."

If Gram could have given the skunk the same look she fired at Rancid, the creature would have been stunned if not killed outright. The glare had no effect on Rancid, however, since he was bent over laughing and slapping his knee in appreciation of his good one. It was, in fact, one of the best good ones I'd ever heard him get off, but I didn't dare laugh.

"All right, Bob Hope," Gram snapped. "Let's see how you get the skunk out from under there. Maybe if you stood upwind of it, that would do the trick!"

"Don't rile me, ol' woman, don't rile me," Rancid said. "Now, boy, go fetch me some newspapers. Ah'm gonna smoke thet critter outta thar."

"And burn down the shed most likely," Gram said.

"Ha!" Rancid said. "You thank Ah don't know how to smoke a skonk out from under a shed?"

Fortunately, the well and a bucket were close at hand and we were able to douse the fire before it did any more damage than blackening one corner of the building.

During these proceedings, Strange had emerged from his house and sat looking on with an air of bemusement. There was nothing he loved better than a ruckus.

"Maybe we should just let the skunk be," Mom said.

"Land sakes, yes!" Gram shouted at Rancid. "Before you destroy the whole dang farm!"

Rancid snorted. "No skonk's ever bested me yet, and this ain't gonna be the fust!"

After each failed attempt to drive out the skunk, Rancid seemed to become angrier and more frenzied. Furiously, he dug a hole on one side of the shed. Then he jammed a long pole in through the hole and flailed wildly about with it. No luck. He went inside the shed and jumped up and down on the floor with his heavy boots. Still no skunk emerged. At one point, he tried to crawl under the shed, apparently with the idea of entering into hand-to-gland combat with the skunk, but the shed floor was too low to the ground. Then he grabbed up the pole and flailed it wildly under the floor again. Next he dropped the pole and yelled at me, "Go git another batch of newspapers!"

"No, no, no!" screamed Mom.

"Leave the poor skunk alone," Gram yelled. "I'm startin' to become fond of the little critter!"

Rancid stood there panting and mopping sweat from his forehead with his arm. "Ah know what Ah'll do, Ah'll set a trap fer him! Should of did thet in the fust place. No skonk is gonna . . ."

At that moment, the skunk, no doubt taking advantage of the calm, or perhaps frightened by it, ran out from under the shed and made for the nearby brush.

"Ah figured thet little trick would work," Rancid said, although no one else was quite sure which trick he was speaking of. "And this way, there ain't no big stank, which is how Ah planned it."

Then Strange tore into the skunk.

The battle was short but fierce, with the skunk expending its whole arsenal as Strange dragged it about the yard, up the porch and down, into the woodshed and out, and through the group of frantically dispersing spectators. At last, coming to his senses, the dog dropped the skunk and allowed it to stagger off into the bushes.

Strange seemed embarrassed by his first and only display of heroism. "I don't know what came over me," he said, shaking. "I've got nothing against skunks!" Still, I couldn't help but be proud of him.

The skunk was gone, but its essence lingered on. The air was stiff with the smell of skunk for weeks afterwards.

"That dog has got to go," Mom said. But, of course, Strange refused to go, and that was that.

It was years before Strange was entirely free of the skunk odor. Every time he got wet, the smell came back in potent force.

"Phew!" a new friend of mine would say. "That your dog?"

"Yeah," I'd say, proudly, "he's a skunk dog."

Cold Fish

☞ ☞ ☞**S**how me a man who fishes in winter, and I'll show you a fanatic. Actually, I'll get the better of the deal, because for sheer spectacle a fanatic doesn't hold a candle to a man who fishes in winter.

I have often thought that if you could capture a half-dozen winter fishermen and put them in a circus sideshow you could make a fortune on them: "Step right this way ladies and gentlemen—no children please, we don't want to warp any young minds—and see the men who actually fish during the winter! They are amazing, they are absolutely astounding! Their skin is blue, their hair is blue, ladies and gentlemen, even their *language* is blue!"

Much as it pains me, I must confess that I too am a winter fisherman. It has been said that the first step toward recovering from this affliction is to admit that you are one, but I have been admitting it for years without noticeable effect. Actually, I take a certain pride in being a member of this select but compulsive group of hearty anglers. We even have a number of sayings: "No man is an icicle unto himself, but each a piece of the whole cube." And: "If one ice fisherman is defrosted, another will freeze to take his place." This goes to show that you can't expect memorable sayings from a bunch of demented fishermen.

Frequently I am asked why a man of my age and character persists in fishing right on through the most bitter months of winter. If I recall correctly, the exact wording of the question is: "Why does an old fool like you persist in going fishing in sub-zero weather?"

My answer is succinct and to the point. "Shut up and help me off with these *bleeping* boots. And be careful with my socks! I don't want my toes falling out and rolling under the chesterfield!"

There is a thin streak of sadism that runs through the directors of state fish and game departments. I have long suspected the requirements for fish and game directors include the following: "Must be outstanding citizens of their communities; must have demonstrated deep interest in outdoor sports and recreation; must have not less than three years experience as fiends."

How else explain their declaring certain waters open during the winter months? Indeed, I have no difficulty imagining the directors roaring with maniacal laughter as they debate the subject of which waters to open for winter fishing.

"Hey, fellows," says Milt Thumbscrew, "how about opening Lake Chill Factor during February?" He giggles wildly.

The other directors stomp their feet and pound on the table as they try to withdraw from fits of hysterical laughter.

"Oh dear, that's absolutely great!" says Adolf Wrinklebunn. "Can't you just see those poor devils up to their armpits in snow and ice, fighting their way to the lake!" He slides from his chair, shrieking.

"And they aren't even out of their cars yet!" screams the chairman. "Oh, stop, stop, you're killing me! Quick, somebody call for the vote!"

Now, even though I know that is basically how and why certain water is open for winter fishing, I find the enticement almost impossible to resist. Consider, if you will, a telephone conversation I had with my friend Retch Sweeney a while back.

"Speak up," I said. "The wind is howling so bad outside I can't hear you."

"I said," Retch shouted, "I tried to get through to you earlier, but the lines were down. I guess the ice got so heavy on them they broke. Anyway, I got this terrible urge to go fishing."

"Well, that's easily cured," I said. "Just go out in your backyard and stand in a bucket of ice water while your wife shovels snow down the back of your neck."

"I already tried that, but I still got the urge," Retch said.

"Have you talked to a psychiatrist?"

"As a matter of fact I did. I ran into Doc Portnoy over at the hospital. He was the one who told me about catching a five-pound rainbow up on the Frigid River. It's open in February, ya know."

"A five-pounder! Did he say what he caught it on?"

"Salmon eggs. That was all I could get out of him before the nurses rushed him into the furnace room in a last-ditch effort to thaw him out."

"I'll get my gear together and pick you up in half an hour," I said. Actually, it took me a bit longer than I had anticipated. I hadn't figured in the time it would take to stand in a bucket of ice water in the backyard while my wife shoveled snow down the back of my neck.

When I was a kid still in my single-digit years, I got my start in winter fishing under the tutelage of old Rancid Crabtree. Rancid was a man who believed in teaching a kid the basics.

"You know how to check fer thin ice, boy?" he would ask me. "Wall, what you do is stick one foot way out ahead of you and stomp the ice real hard and listen fer it to make a crackin' sound. Thar now, did you hear how the ice cracked whan Ah stomped it? Thet means it's too thin to hold a man's weight. Now pull me up out of hyar and we'll run back to shore and see if we kin built a fahr b'fore Ah freezes to death!"

Our usual practice was simply to hike out on the frozen surface of the lake or river, chop a hole in the ice, and try to catch some fish before either the hole or we froze over. One year, however, we built ourselves a luxurious fishing shack. It was made of scrap lumber, rusty tin, tarpaper, and other equally attractive materials. We put a tiny airtight heater inside with the stovepipe running out through the roof at a rakish angle. I always expected the stovepipe to set fire to the roof and was not often disappointed. Having the roof catch fire became so much a part of our fishing routine that Rancid would say to me, "Go put the fahr on the roof out, will ya? Ah thank Ah jist had a bite."

The truth is I was always glad for an excuse to step outside of the shack for a breath of fresh air. Rancid was a man who bathed only on leap years, and the previous leap year had escaped his notice. He smelled bad enough dry; wet, he could drive a lame badger out of its hole at forty yards. Sometimes in the warmth of the tiny shack he would actually begin to steam, and that was the worst. I'd sit there hoping the roof would catch fire so I'd have an excuse to step outside.

Sometimes when I knew I'd be cooped up in the

fishing shack with Rancid for several hours on the following day, I'd try to induce in him the desire to take a bath.

"You know what I like to do after a nasty chore like this," I'd tell him as we worked together at his place. "I like to climb into a nice hot tub of soapy water and soak and scrub and soak and scrub and soak and scrub. Doesn't that sound good?"

"Nope, it don't. Now watch what yore doin' thar! How many times I got to show you how to skin a skonk?"

Despite Rancid's aversion to bathing, the days we spent fishing together in the fish shack were among the best I've ever known. From the darkness of the shack you could peer through the hole in the ice clear down to the bottom of the lake and watch the fish move in to take the bait. And Rancid would tell me all the old stories over again, changing them just enough each time so that they always seemed fresh and new. He gave me little fishing tips, too. He said one good way to warm up bait maggots was to stick a pinch of them under your lower lip. I said I'd have to try that sometime when the need arose. After thirty years and more, the need has not yet arisen, but it's a good thing to know anyhow.

Another interesting thing he told me was about the time he went fishing in winter and it was so cold his line froze right in the middle of a cast. He said it was downright comical the way his line just stuck out in the air stiff as a wire from the end of his pole. He had to stand his line up against a tall snag and build a little fire near it. As the end close to the fire thawed out, the line just slid down the snag and formed itself into a nice little coil. Rancid knew all kinds of neat fishing lore like that.

The one problem with the fishing shack was that dragging it about the lake from one fishing site to another bore a striking resemblance to hard work.

Rancid said that he didn't have anything against hard work in principle and that if other folks wanted to indulge themselves in it that was all right with him and he certainly wouldn't hold it against them. He said that some folks were born with that flaw in their character and just couldn't help themselves. All a decent man could do, he said, was pretend that such folks were just as normal as anybody else and that they should never be looked down upon or ridiculed or in any way be made to feel inferior.

Rancid told me that what a normal man did when confronted with a task that bore a striking resemblance to hard work was to sit down and try to come up with an idea for avoiding it. That is exactly what Rancid did in regard to the fishing shack.

"Ah got a great idea," he said. "What we is gonna do is rig up a sail fer the fish shack! We'll let the wind blow the fish shack along the ice and we'll jist foller along behind and steer it whar ever we wants it to go."

In practically no time at all, Rancid had a tall, slender cedar pole bolted to the front end of the fish shack for a mast. A massive canvas tarp was converted swiftly into a sail. A confusion of booms, lines, and pulleys allowed the sail to be hauled up the mast, in which position its general appearance was not unlike some of the sails on the boats pictured in my geography book.

"Say, it looks just like a Chinese junk," I told Rancid, realizing at once that I had hurt his feelings.

"Ah don't care iffin it looks like a whole gol-durn Chinese dump," he snapped, "jist so it works."

Looking back through the corrective lens of time, I now realize that Rancid was one of those men who just can't let a good idea be but have to keep improving on it right up to the point where it turns into a catastrophe. I didn't know that back then, of course, and just assumed that what happened was one of those unavoidable mishaps that occurred with surprising regularity while I was in the company of Rancid.

Much to my surprise, the sail worked like a charm. The gentle breeze on the lake filled the billowing tarp and moved the little fish shack steadily if somewhat jerkily across the wind-burnished surface of the ice. We walked behind or alongside the shack, guiding the little vessel this way and that by pulling on various lines, much as one guides horses with a set of reins. Then Rancid came up with his improvement on the basic idea.

"Say," he said, "Ah got me a good notion to get inside the shack and jist ride along. Ah bet Ah kin steer it jist by pushing a stick along the ice through the hole in the floor. Iffin the critter gits to movin' too fast, Ah'll jist drag maw feet to slow it down."

The breeze had fallen off for the moment, so we made fast all the lines and Rancid climbed into the shack and made himself comfortable. Later Rancid was to accuse me of having dropped the spike through the latch on the outside of the door, thereby locking him inside; but if that was the case, the action was merely an absentminded reflex on my part and bore not the slightest hint of mischief. Besides, how was I to know that anytime he wanted out I wouldn't be there to pull the spike out of the latch?

I stood around outside the shack stomping my feet and rubbing my hands together, waiting for a breeze to come up and get us under way again. Every so often, Rancid would shout at me from inside the shack. "Any sign of wind out thar yet?"

"Nope," I'd reply. "It's pretty quiet." If I'd been more attuned to the weather, I would have known that the particular quiet we were experiencing was the kind known as "ominous."

I heard a distant rustling behind me. Turning, I observed a rather startling phenomenon. Clouds of snow were billowing up off the far side of the lake and moving in our direction.

"HOLY COW, RANCID, THE WIND . . . !"

"The wind's comin' up is she? Hot dang! Now yore gonna see . . ."

He never finished his sentence.

As soon as I got to my feet after being knocked down by the first blast of wind, I tried to track the fish shack as best I could. I felt I owed it to Rancid, since by then I had remembered dropping the spike through the latch. Rancid wasn't a person you wanted to have mad at you.

For a long ways, I could see the skid marks Rancid had made with his boots on the ice. After that I saw some scratches that looked like they had been made by two sets of fingernails. Then there were only the ski marks made by the sled and an occasional board or piece of tin from the fish shack. Over several long stretches, where the shack had become airborne, there were no signs at all.

After a while I came across two ice fishermen fighting against the wind on their way home. I asked them if they had seen Rancid go by in the fish shack. They said they had.

"I don't know what that durn fool will think of next," one of the men said, "but he was reachin' out a little winder with a hatchet, and it looked like he was tryin' to chop down the pole holdin' up that hay tarp. He went by so fast we couldn't rightly see what he was up to."

"Did you hear him say anything?" I asked.

"Nothin' I'd repeat to a boy your age," the man said.

A half-mile farther on, I ran into another fisherman. Before I could ask him anything, he said, "Land sakes, boy, you shouldn't be out alone in a blizzard like this! Why, I just saw some farmer's hay tarp fly by here.

Somehow it got hooked onto his outhouse and was draggin' it along too. Just tearin' that privy all to pieces. Strangest dang thing I ever seen! Anyway, come along with me and I'll give you a ride home."

I was about to refuse, when I glanced off across the lake and saw the figure of a tall, lean man striding purposefully in our direction through the clouds of driven snow. Even though he was downwind from me, I could tell it was Rancid. I could also tell he was carrying what looked like a piece of broken ski in one hand.

"I'll ride home with you on one condition," I told the fisherman. "And that is that you leave right now."

The Rifle

☞ ☞ ☞At least once a week from the fifth grade on, I made it a practice to stop by Clyde Fitch's Sport Shop after school. Clyde was always glad to see me, and we would josh each other.

"Hi, Clyde," I'd say as I came through the door.

"Don't handle the guns," Clyde would say.

"Yeah, there is a chill in the air," I'd respond. "Folks say it's gonna be an early winter."

"You got peanut butter on one of the twelve-gauges last time," he would retort. "I wish you'd find someplace else to eat your after-school snack."

I would nod appreciatively at Clyde's sharp wit and mark up a score for him in the air. Then, as he turned to wait on a customer, I would hear a soft sweet song beckoning me to the gun racks. It would be the rifles and shotguns singing to me:

"You drive me to distraction

When you work my lever action," sang a .30-30.

"When you give my stock a nuzzle,

You send chills down to my muzzle," trilled a .270.

"I lie awake nights
After you peer down my sights," moaned a .30-06.

I'll admit they weren't great lyricists, but they had nice voices and the melody was pleasant. Before I knew what was happening, a .30-06 would have leaped into my hands and I would be checking its action.

"DON'T TOUCH THE GUNS!" Clyde Fitch would yell, doing a fair impression of an enraged businessman.

"Good, Clyde, good," I would say as I set the rifle back in the rack and peered down at a sleek, inviting .300. Apparently displeased by my lack of enthusiasm for his performance, Clyde would rush over, grab me by the back of my coat collar and belt, and rush me out the door of his establishment. We kidded around with each other like that for about four years, occasionally working in new bits of dialogue but with Clyde always opening with his favorite line, "Don't touch the guns!" I suppose the reason he liked it so much was that it always got a laugh.

Just a few days short of eternity, my fourteenth birthday finally arrived. I had expected it to come bearing as a gift one .30-30 rifle, about which I had dropped approximately 30,000 hints to my family. No rifle! I could tell from the shapes of the packages. They were all shaped like school clothes. "Something seems to be missing here," I said, nervously ripping open a package of Jockey shorts. "You sure you didn't forget and leave one of my presents in the closet?"

"No," my mother said. "That's the whole kit and kaboodle of them right there."

"I was, uh, sort of expecting a, uh, thirty-thirty rifle."

"Oh," Mom said. "Well, if you want a rifle, you'll just have to get yourself a job and earn enough money to buy one."

It was not unusual in those days for parents to say brutal things like that to their children. There were no laws back then to prevent parents from saying no and, worse yet, meaning no. Life was hard for a kid. Still, I couldn't believe that my mother was actually suggesting that her only son go out and find a job.

"Surely you are jesting," I said to her.

"No," she replied.

Naturally, I had heard about work. My family was always talking about it within range of my hearing, and, as far as I could tell, seemed generally to be in favor of it. I didn't know why. Nothing I ever heard about work made it seem very appealing. My old friend Rancid Crabtree had told me that he had tried work once as a young man. He said that he was supposed to cut down trees for the man who had hired him, but when he picked up the ax and started to chop, his whole life passed before him. He gave up work then and there. He said that he knew some folks loved to work, and that was fine, but that he himself couldn't stand even to be near it. Of the two opinions about work, I favored Rancid's.

Still, if I wanted to hunt deer that coming fall, I would need a rifle. On the other hand, if I got a job, that would ruin my summer and leave me only mornings and evenings and weekends to fish. At best, I might be able to get in some more fishing on days I was too sick to work. I weighed my need for the rifle against a ruined summer and, after much long and painful thought, arrived at a distasteful decision: I would have to borrow a rifle.

Then, as now, people did not stand in line to loan out their rifles to beginning hunters, or to anyone else for that matter. Rancid Crabtree seemed to me to be the best prospect for the loan of a rifle.

"By the way, Rancid," I said to him casually one day, "how about loaning me your thirty-thirty for deer season this year."

Rancid's face erupted into that beautiful snaggletoothed grin of his. "Thet's a good-un," he said. "Make it up yersef or somebody tell it to you?"

"It's no joke," I said. "I need a deer rifle, and I don't see why you can't loan me your thirty-thirty."

"Wall, Ah would loan it to you except fer one thang," Rancid said. "An' thet is, Ah don't want to."

Rancid had only two defects to his character: He had never learned the art of mincing words, and you could never talk him into doing something he didn't want to do.

I shook my head in despair. "You're the only person I can think of, Rancid, who might loan me a rifle. I guess the only thing left for me to do is to get a job and earn some money."

"Now don't go talkin' like thet," Rancid said, as soon as he had recovered from the shock. "A young fella like you, got everthang to live fer, talkin' about gettin' a j-j-jo—throwin' away his life. No sar, Ah won't stand fer it! Now, hyar's what you do. You go ask the Inyun if you kin borry one of his rifles."

"Pinto Jack?"

"Why shore, ol' Pinto'd give you the hide offen his scrawny carcass iffin it had a zipper on it."

I found Pinto Jack puffing a pipe on the front porch of his cabin, and put my request straight to him.

Pinto Jack smiled only on rare occasions, and this was not one of them. "You want to borrow my rifle?" he said, studying me thoughtfully through a cloud of pipe smoke. "If I loaned you my rifle, what would I use when I raided the ranchers and burned their buildings and drove off their livestock, and like that?"

"Couldn't you use a bow and arrow for a few raids?" I said.

"You tell me, how am I going to drive my old truck and shoot a bow and arrow at the same time? No, I got to have my rifle for raiding the ranchers."

I looked crestfallen, having many years before learned that this was one of the best looks to use on Pinto Jack.

"Tell you what," he said after a moment. "I could maybe let you use the old rifle my father brought back from the Great War."

"First World?"

"Little Big Horn. It's a single-shot and kicks a bit, but you're welcome to it."

I rushed home lugging the monstrous firearm, pinned a target to a fence post backed by a sandbank, paced off a hundred yards, drew a bead on the target, and gently squeezed the trigger. Later I heard that all the livestock within a mile radius sprang two feet into the air and went darting about in all directions at that altitude. Apples rained down out of the trees in the orchards. Three lumberjacks swore off drink, and two atheists were converted to religion. My own interpretation of the event was that I had just been struck by lightning, a meteorite, or a bomb. When my vision cleared, I knew I was in trouble. Not only would my folks be upset about my shooting one of their fence posts in half, but the neighbors would be mad at me for destroying their sandbank. Nevertheless, I decided to try one more shot, this one left-handed. The second shot went off a little better, since by now I knew what to expect. It was easier for me to keep my nose out of the way, too, because the first shot had moved it up into the vacant area above my right eyebrow where it would be safe. By the time I had finished sighting in the rifle, I figured I'd be the only kid in the school talent show who could applaud behind his back with his shoulder blades.

My first deer managed to elude me that year. Even though I had opportunities for several good shots, by the time I had grimaced enough to pull the trigger, the deer was always gone. At the end of the season, I returned the rifle to Pinto Jack.

"Any luck?" he asked.

"Nope."

"Well, don't feel so bad about it," he said. "Come on in and have yourself an orange pop, and I'll show you how I can applaud with my shoulder blades. Bet you don't know anybody who can do that."

By the time the next summer rolled around, it had become apparent to me that the only way I was ever going to get a deer rifle was to earn the money for it. There was a dairy farmer by the name of Brown who lived nearby and whose reputation in the community was that of a kindly, if somewhat frugal, gentleman. Out of desperation for a deer rifle, I broke down and indentured myself to him at the rate of fifty cents an hour manufacturing postholes. Mr. Brown gave me the job after asking if I thought I could do a man's work. My ingenious reply was: "It depends on the man." The farmer said later that he supposed the particular man I had been referring to was an Egyptian mummy. For all his other drawbacks, Mr. Brown did not lack a sense of humor.

About his other drawbacks. It was only after going to work for him that I discovered that he wasn't a kindly gentleman at all but the former commandant of a slave-labor camp. Our mutual misfortune was that he had somehow missed the last boat to Brazil and had been forced to escape to Idaho, where he took up dairy farming as a cover.

"Vork, vork!" he would scream at me, slapping the leg of his bib overalls with a swagger stick. "Make die postholes, make die postholes, fahster, fahster!"

And I would streak about the landscape, trailing fresh-dug postholes. Sometimes, after glancing nervously around, I would step behind a tree to catch my breath. The farmer would drop out of the branches and screech at me: "Vot you do-ink? I not pay-ink you fifty zents an hour to breathe! Vork! Vork!"

At day's end, my mother would drive over to the farm to give me a ride home. She and the farmer would chat about my capacity for hard labor.

"I'm surprised you can get any work out of him at all," Mom would say.

The old farmer would laugh in his kindly way. "Actually, I have found him to be a bit slow, but he is doing better. Just today, while he was digging a posthole, I thought I detected some motion in one of his arms." Then he would give me a pat on my sagging, quivering back. "Off you go now, lad. See you bright and early in the morning!"

Odd, I thought. He seems to have lost his accent.

Bright and early the next morning the farmer would tell me: "Vork, vork, lazy Dummkopf! Make die postholes, fahster, fahster!"

At the end of the very hour in which I earned the last fifty cents I needed to buy the rifle, I resigned my position. When I told the farmer I was quitting, he tried to conceal his disappointment by leaping in the air and clicking his heels. There are few things, by the way, more disgusting than a dairy farmer clicking his heels in the air.

"I'll say this for you," he told me. "You have dug what I regard to be the most expensive postholes in the whole history of agriculture. If it was possible, I would gather them all up and put them in a bank vault rather than leave them scattered randomly about my property. Nevertheless, lad, should you ever find yourself in need of a job to buy yourself, say, a shotgun, why you just come to me. I'll be happy to recommend you as a worker to my neighbor, Fergussen, who, though I may say a harsh word about him now and again, is not a bad sort at all, particularly for a man who is stupid and greedy and probably a thief."

Naturally, I was flattered by this little farewell speech. I even changed my mind about his being a former commandant of a slave-labor camp. "Thanks," I told him, "but now that I've tried work and found it to be about what I expected, I think I'll avoid it in the future."

Mr. Brown said he thought that would be a good idea and that, as far as he had observed, I had considerable talent for that line of endeavor and was practically assured of success.

The very next day, with the money for the rifle wadded up in a pocket of my jeans, I sauntered into Clyde Fitch's Sport Shop.

"Hi, Clyde," I said.

"Don't touch the guns!" Clyde shouted.

I took out my wad of money and began to unfold it.

"Seriously though, my boy," Clyde said, "I was just asking myself why ol' Pat hadn't been in lately to fondle the guns. Yes indeed. Now, good buddy, I'd be much obliged if you would try out the action on this new thirty-thirty and give me your expert opinion of it."

They Shoot Canoes, Don't They?

☞ ☞ ☞**A** while back my friend Retch Sweeney and I were hiking through a wilderness area and happened to come across these three guys who were pretending to cling to the side of a mountain as if their lives depended on it. They were dressed in funny little costumes and all tied together on a long rope. Their leader was pounding what looked like a big spike into a crack in the rock. We guessed right off what they were up to. They were obviously being initiated into a college fraternity, and this was part of the hazing. Not wishing to embarrass them any more than was absolutely necessary, Retch and I just let on as if everything was normal and that scarcely a day went by that we didn't see people in funny costumes hammering nails into rock.

"We seem to have taken a wrong turn back there a ways," I said to them. "Could you give us some idea where we are?"

The three pledgies seemed both angered and astonished at seeing us. "Why, this is the North Face of Mount

Terrible," the leader said. "We're making an assault on it. You shouldn't be up here!"

"You're telling me!" I said. "We're supposed to be on our way to Wild Rose Lake."

"Say, it's none of my business," Retch put in, "but this thing you're makin', don't you think you would get it built a lot faster if you found some level ground? It's pretty steep up here."

That didn't seem to set too well with them, or at least so I interpreted from their flared nostrils and narrowed eyes.

"Say, don't let a couple of flabby, middle-aged men disturb you," I said. "We'll just mosey on past you and climb up to the top of this hill and get out of your way. Maybe we can get a bearing on Wild Rose Lake from up there."

Well, I was glad they were all roped together and the rope was fastened to one of the spikes they had hammered into the rock. Otherwise, I think they would have taken off after us, and that slope was so steep you could just barely walk on it, let alone run. They would have caught us for sure.

"Those guys certainly weren't too friendly, were they?" Retch said later.

"No, they weren't," I said. "The very least they could have done was offer to give us a hand with the canoe."

Upon later reflection, I came to the conclusion that it was probably the canoe itself that had disturbed the pledgies. There are people who can't get within fifteen feet of a canoe without turning psychotic or, as my psychiatrist puts it, "going bananas."

I've been around canoes most of my life and have high regard for them. They're versatile and efficient and serve the angler and hunter well. But I have no truck with the sentimental nonsense often associated with them. Some years back I wrecked an old canoe of mine that I had spent hundreds of happy hours in. When I saw there was no way to salvage it, I tossed it on top of the car rack and hauled it out to the city dump. That was it. There was no sentimental nonsense involved. Just to show you some of the strange things that can happen, though, a few days later my wife went out to clean the garage and found the canoe back in its old place.

I had to laugh. "Well, I'll be darned," I said. "The old thing must have followed me home from the dump! Well, if it cares that much about me, I guess we'll let it stay."

After babbling sentimentality, the next most prevalent form of irrational behavior evoked by canoes is raw terror (occasionally there is boiled terror or even fried terror, but usually it's raw). Take my neighbor Al Finley, the city councilperson, for example. I figured that anyone so adept at floating bond issues as Finley certainly wouldn't have any trouble floating a canoe—a duck to water, so to speak. I've taught him most of the paddle strokes and he is quite proficient at them, but he has never gotten over his fear of canoes.

"Careful!" he screams. "It's tipping! It's tipping! Watch that rock! Careful!"

The way he acts is absolutely pathetic. I don't know what he'd do if we ever put the canoe in the water.

Some canoe-induced behavior is so odd you can't even put a name to it. Take the time I was canoeing up in Canada with Dork Simp, a chap who had been a staunch atheist for as long as I could remember. When we saw that we had made a mistake and had to shoot the Good God Almighty Rapids (named by the first trapper to take a raft of furs down the river), Dork yelled out that he had recently had some serious doubts about the intellectual validity of atheism.

"Forget philosophy, for pete's sake!" I screamed at him. "It's getting rough! Get off that seat and kneel down in the canoe!"

"Amen to that," he yelled back. "You say the words first and I'll try to follow along!"

We smacked into a rock and broke several ribs, two of which, incidentally, seemed to be mine. As we slid sideways off the rock, Dork shouted out that he had just found religion.

A few seconds later, as we were paddling up out of the vortex of a whirlpool, he swore off smoking, drinking, and profanity, the last of which cut his vocabulary by approximately half. When we were at last forcibly ejected from the lower end of the rapids, Dork said that he had decided to enter the ministry.

"It's been a lifelong ambition of mine," he added.

"What!" I said. "Why, not more than fifteen minutes ago you were an atheist."

"Was it only fifteen minutes?" he said. "I could have sworn it was a lifetime!"

The weirdest reaction to canoes that I've ever observed took place in Kelly's Bar & Grill. I had just walked in and mounted a barstool next to Doc Moos, owner and operator of Doc's Boat Works, where I had Zelda, my old wood-and-canvas canoe, in for repairs. Doc was chatting with a new bartender Kelly had hired, a great dull slab of a man but pleasant enough, or so he seemed at first.

"How's my Zelda doing, Doc?" I asked.

"I got bad news for you," Doc said. "I couldn't save her."

"Oh no!" I moaned. "I can't get along without her."

The bartender gave me a sympathetic look. "Gee, I'm sorry fella," he said. "Here, have a drink on Kelly."

I thanked him brusquely, not wanting him to mistake my concern about Zelda for maudlin sentimentality.

"What went wrong?" I asked Doc.

"Well, first of all, as you know, she was cracked and peeling all over, but that was no real problem since we could have put a new fiberglass skin on her. But . . ."

"You can do that now, can you, Doc, put on a fiberglass skin?" the bartender asked.

"Sure," Doc told him. "It's quite a bit of work and expensive, but it wears forever."

"I bet it does," the bartender said. "But how does it look?"

"Just like new," Doc said. "Paint it a nice glossy red or green and it'll knock your eye out."

The bartender looked astounded. "I would've thought pink," he said.

"Pink!" Doc and I both shuddered. The man was totally without taste.

"Anyway," Doc went on, doing his best to ignore the bartender, "some of her ribs were busted up pretty bad. I was going to work up some new ones out of some oak boards I got in the shop . . ."

"What won't they think of next!" the bartender said. "Wood ribs!"

"But as I was saying," Doc continued, shaking his head, "that was when we found the dry rot."

"Oh no, not dry rot!" I moaned.

"Gee, dry rot," the bartender said. "I think my brother got that once from not washin' between his toes."

"Well, it was fatal for Zelda," Doc said.

"Here, have another drink on Kelly," the bartender said.

Up to this time the bartender had seemed like a decent enough fellow, if only slightly smarter than a grapefruit. Now he started to act a bit weird, particularly after I had said something about how much I enjoyed paddling Zelda, even when she was loaded down with all my camping gear. Then Doc asked me what I wanted to do with Zelda's remains. As I say, I'm not much on sentimentality so I told him just to keep them around the shop and use them for parts.

"It's about time I got myself a new one anyway," I said.

"So much for grief, hunh, fella?" the bartender snarled. "Beat the old thing, make her carry all your campin' junk, and then forget her, just like that!" He snapped his fingers so close to my face I jumped.

"What's with you?" I said. "All along I thought you were a canoeist."

That was when he tossed Doc and me out of the bar.

"Call me a canoeist, will you!" he shouted from the doorway. "Listen, fella, I may not be too smart, but I'm a lot more normal than you!"

I suppose these strange attitudes toward canoes are to be expected of persons who don't establish a meaningful relationship with them early in life. My own association with canoes began at age ten. That was when I built my first one. Even if I do say so myself, it was one of the most beautiful canoes I've ever seen.

I built it in a vacant upstairs bedroom out of some old lumber I found in the hog pen. The lumber was dirty and heavy, and I had great difficulty dragging it through the house and up to the bedroom. Most of the difficulty was caused by my mother and grandmother, who kept making nasty remarks about my character and trying to strike me with blunt objects.

It took me about three weeks to build the canoe. If you've never built a canoe, you probably don't realize that the hardest part is shaping the bow and stern just right. I came up with an ingenious solution to this problem that, if it had caught on, would have revolutionized canoe design. I put square ends on it. There were a couple of other minor modifications that also simplified construction—the bottom and sides were flat! I painted it with some red barn paint as a final touch, and the end result was a sharp-looking canoe. Everyone else in my family thought so, too, except Gram. She said it looked like a coffin for someone's pet boa constrictor. Gram, of course, knew next to nothing about boat design.

The canoe's one drawback was that it weighed just slightly less than a Buick, and since I was the only man in the family, we had to ask the old woodsman Rancid Crabtree to come over and help us carry it out of the house.

As Rancid was walking up the stairs, he sniffed the air and asked, "You been keepin' hogs up here? Smells like . . ."

"Never mind what it smells like," Gram snapped. "Just help us carry that contraption out of the house."

Mom, Gram, and I got at one end of the canoe and Rancid at the other, and with a great deal of shouting and groaning managed to lift it until it was resting on our shoulders. We carried it out of the bedroom to the head of the stairs, at which point Rancid gasped that he couldn't hold up his end a second longer. While he was looking around frantically for something to rest the canoe on, he accidentally stepped down backwards onto the stairs. We at the rear end of the canoe naturally assumed from this gesture that he had changed his mind about resting, so we charged forward. It was just one of those innocent misunderstandings. As it turned out, no one was seriously injured, but some of the language would have made the hair of a wart hog stand on end. The only ill effect I suffered was psychological. As we all galloped around the sharp turn at the landing, I caught a glimpse of the expression on Rancid's face, and it just wasn't the sort of thing a ten-year-old boy should be allowed to see. For years afterwards, it would cause me to wake up whimpering in the night.

When Rancid came into the kitchen for coffee after the ordeal was over, he complained that he felt two feet shorter. Gram pointed out to him that he was walking on his knees. Rancid was always doing comical things like that.

Beautiful as it was, my first canoe was never launched but sat for years in the yard at the place where it was dropped. My mother later filled it with dirt and planted flowers in it. Strangers sometimes got the mistaken impression from it that we were holding a funeral for a tall, thin gangster.

The first store-bought canoe with which I had a meaningful relationship was hidden in some brush on the banks of a creek near where I lived. During the spring of the year, the creek was deep and fast with some nice rapids in it, but I had enough sense to realize that it would be dangerous for me to attempt to paddle the canoe down it. The main reason it would have been dangerous was that the big kid who owned the canoe had threatened to put me in a sack and toss the sack in the creek if he caught me messing around with it.

The big kid's name was Buster, and he divided his time among eating, sleeping, and beating up people, although not necessarily in that order. Sometimes he would catch me down by the creek and practice his beating-up techniques on me. Although these sessions were more monotonous than painful, they were sufficiently instructive to make me realize that I didn't want Buster performing real beating-up on me.

Nevertheless, I could not force myself to stay entirely

away from the canoe, a lovely little fifteen-footer, mostly green but with a patch of white on the side where Buster had attempted to paint over the words PROPERTY OF SUNSET RESORT. Once, I even slipped the canoe into the water just to see how it floated. It floated fine. After giving considerable thought to the questions (1) how much fun would it be to paddle the canoe around a bit, and (2) how difficult would it be to swim while confined in a sack, I slipped the canoe back into its hiding place and wiped off my fingerprints.

About a mile from my home, the creek wound through a swamp that was full of dead trees, rotting stumps, quicksand, mud flats, snakes, frogs, slime—all the usual neat swamp stuff. Brook trout the size of alligators were said to inhabit the deeper waters of the swamp, and I would occasionally pole my log raft into the dark interior in search of them. It was on one of these excursions that I happened to come upon Buster's canoe, bobbing gently among the cattails that surrounded a small, brush-covered island. My heart leaped up.

"Well, I'll be darned!" I said to myself. "Ol' Buster's canoe has somehow slid itself into the crick and drifted into the swamp. Won't he be tickled pink when I bring it back to him—in a day or two or the week after next at the latest?"

My elation, however, was diluted by a sense of foreboding, even though there wasn't a sign of human life in any direction. I eased myself silently into the canoe and set the raft adrift, just in case someone might get the notion of using it as a means of pursuing me.

That the canoe had somehow drifted upstream and tied itself to a branch with a length of clothesline and a square knot were matters of no little curiosity to me, and I remember making a mental note to ask my arithmetic teacher what the odds of such an occurrence might be.

As I was untying the square knot, I happened to glance out from among the cattails. What I saw momentarily freeze-dried my corpuscles. Strolling right toward me, arm-in-arm from out of the brush in the middle of the island, were Buster and a girl by the name of Alvira Holstein. Even as it was locked in the grip of terror, my fertile mind groped with the question of what the two of them could be doing on the island, Buster never having struck me as much of a picnicker On the other hand, the occasion didn't seem appropriate for casual conversation. I did take some comfort in the fact that Buster did not appear to have a sack with him.

Upon seeing me crouched in his canoe, Buster let out a roar that is best described as approximating that of a grizzly bear having a bicuspid extracted without benefit of anesthetic. I had never paddled a canoe before, but at that instant, such was the inspiration of seeing Buster charging toward me, I instantly discovered that I had a talent for it bordering on genius. Within seconds I had the canoe moving at sufficient momentum to plane easily over half-submerged logs, mud flats, and flocks of waterfowl caught unawares. I looked back once, and Buster was still in hot pursuit, even though he was up to his armpits in swamp slime. He was screeching almost incoherently, something to the effect that he would make sweeping but imaginative alterations on my anatomy once he laid hands on it. Alvira Holstein was jumping up and down on the island, crying and screaming, and yelling out, "Don't kill him, Buster, don't kill him!" Even to this day it sets my nerves on edge to hear a woman yell something like that.

I paddled the canoe halfway to my house, which was remarkable only in that the water ended some distance short of that. My grandmother was in the kitchen when I burst through the door.

"Land sakes, what's after you?" she said.

"Never mind that now," I said. "Just tell me this. Is there really quicksand in the swamp?"

"There certainly is," she said. "And you just stay out of that swamp if you don't want to get swallowed up by it!"

I crossed my fingers. "Come on, *quicksand!*" I said.

Actually, it was Gram who finally saved me from the sack or, at best, going through life as a very odd-looking person. When she found out Buster was after me, she just scoffed.

"Buster ain't going to hurt you," she said, neglecting to mention why I should be an exception to the rule. "If he does, you just tell the sheriff on him. The sheriff's a tough man, and he don't stand for no nonsense."

"Yeah, he's tough all right," I said, pulling back the window curtain an inch to peer out. "But he don't bother about kids' fightin'. He says it's just natural."

"Oh, I don't know," Gram said. "Sheriff Holstein's a pretty sensible man, and I think if you just told him . . ."

"Holstein?" I said. "That's right, it *is* Sheriff Holstein, isn't it?" I walked away from the window, cut myself a slab of fresh-baked bread, and smeared on a layer of raspberry jam.

"Well, forget about Buster, Gram," I told her. "I got to go paddle my canoe."

My First Deer,
and Welcome to It

☞ ☞ ☞ For a first deer, there is no habitat so lush and fine as a hunter's memory. Three decades and more of observation have convinced me that a first deer not only lives on in the memory of a hunter but thrives there, increasing in points and pounds with each passing year until at last it reaches full maturity, which is to say, big enough to shade a team of Belgian draft horses in its shadow at high noon. It is a remarkable phenomenon and worthy of study.

Consider the case of my friend Retch Sweeney and his first deer. I was with him when he shot the deer, and though my first impression was that Retch had killed a large jackrabbit, closer examination revealed it to be a little spike buck. We were both only fourteen at the time and quivering with excitement over Retch's good fortune in getting his first deer. Still, there was no question in either of our minds that what he had bagged was a spike buck, one slightly larger than a bread box.

You can imagine my surprise when, scarcely a month later, I overheard Retch telling some friends that his first deer was a nice four-point buck. I mentioned to Retch afterwards that I was amazed at how fast his deer was growing. He said he was a little surprised himself but was pleased it was doing so well. He admitted that he had known all along that the deer was going to get bigger eventually although he hadn't expected it to happen so quickly. Staring off into the middle distance, a dreamy expression on his face, he told me, "You know, I wouldn't be surprised if someday my first deer becomes a world's-record trophy."

"I wouldn't either," I said. "In fact, I'd be willing to bet on it."

Not long ago, Retch and I were chatting with some of the boys down at Kelly's Bar & Grill and the talk turned to first deer. It was disgusting. I can stand maudlin sentimentality as well as the next fellow, but I have my limits. Some of those first deer had a mastery of escape routines that would have put Houdini to shame. Most of them were so smart there was some question in my mind as to whether the hunter had bagged a deer or a Rhodes Scholar. I wanted to ask them if they had tagged their buck or awarded it a Phi Beta Kappa key. And big! There wasn't a deer there who couldn't have cradled a baby grand piano in its rack. Finally it was Retch's turn, and between waves of nausea I wondered whether that little spike buck had developed enough over the years to meet this kind of competition. I needn't have wondered.

Retch's deer no longer walked in typical deer fashion; it "ghosted" about through the trees like an apparition. When it galloped, though, the sound was "like thunder rolling through the hills." And so help me, "fire flickered in its eyes." Its tracks "looked like they'd been excavated with a backhoe, they were that big." Smart? That deer could have taught field tactics at West Point. Retch's little spike buck had come a long way, baby.

At last Retch reached the climax of his story. "I don't expect you boys to believe this," he said, his voice hushed with reverence, "but when I dropped that deer, the mountain *trembled!*"

The boys all nodded, believing. Why, hadn't the mountain trembled for them too when they shot their first deer? Of course it had. All first deer are like that.

Except mine.

I banged the table for attention. "Now," I said, "I'm going to tell you about a *real* first deer, not a figment of my senility, not some fossilized hope of my gangling adolescence, but a *real* first deer."

Now I could tell from looking at their stunned faces that the boys were upset. There is nothing that angers the participants of a bull session more than someone who refuses to engage in the mutual exchange of illusions, someone who tells the simple truth, unstretched, unvarnished, unembellished, and whole.

"Even though it violates the code of the true sportsperson," I began, "I must confess that I still harbor unkind thoughts for my first deer. True to his form and unlike almost all other first deer, he has steadfastly refused to grow in either my memory or imagination; he simply stands there in original size and puny rack, peering over the lip of my consciousness, an insolent smirk decorating his pointy face. Here I offered that thankless creature escape from the anonymity of becoming someone else's second or seventh or seventeenth deer or, at the very least, from an old age presided over by coyotes. And how did he repay me? With humiliation!"

The boys at Kelly's shrank back in horror at this heresy. Retch Sweeney tried to slip away, but I riveted him to his chair with a maniacal laugh. His eyes pleaded with me. *"No, don't tell us!"* they said. *"Don't destroy the myth of the first deer!*" (which is a pretty long speech for a couple of beady, bloodshot eyes).

Unrelenting and with only an occasional pause for a bitter, sardonic cackle to escape my foam-flecked lips, I plunged on with the tale, stripping away layer after layer of myth until at last the truth about one man's first deer had been disrobed and lay before them in all its grim and naked majesty, shivering and covered with goose bumps.

I began by pointing out what I considered to be one of the great bureaucratic absurdities of all time: that a boy at age fourteen was allowed to purchase his first hunting license and deer tag but was prevented from obtaining a driver's license until he was sixteen. This was like telling a kid he could go swimming but to stay away from the water. Did the bureaucrats think that trophy mule deer came down from the hills in the evening to drink out of your garden hose? The predicament left you no recourse but to beg the adult hunters you knew to take you hunting with them on weekends. My problem was that all the adult hunters I knew bagged their deer in the first couple of weeks of the season, and from then on I had to furnish my own transportation. This meant that in order to get up to the top of the mountain where the trophy mule deer hung out, I had to start out at four in the morning if I wanted to be there by noon. I remember one time when I was steering around some big boulders in the road about three-quarters of the way up the Dawson Grade and a Jeep with two hunters in it came plowing up behind me. I pulled over so they could pass. The hunters grinned at me as they went by. You'd think they'd never before seen anyone pedaling a bike twenty miles up the side of a mountain to go deer hunting.

I had rigged up my bike especially for deer hunting. There were straps to hold my rifle snugly across the handlebars, and saddlebags draped over the back fender to carry my gear. The back fender had been reinforced to support a sturdy platform, my reason for this being that I didn't believe the original fender was stout enough to support a buck when I got one. My one oversight was failing to put a guard over the top of the bike chain, in which I had to worry constantly about getting my tongue caught. Deer hunting on a bike was no picnic.

A mile farther on and a couple of hours later I came to where the fellows in the Jeep were busy setting up camp with some other hunters. Apparently, someone told a fantastic joke just as I went pumping by because they all collapsed in a fit of laughter and were doubled over and rolling on the ground and pounding trees with their fists. They seemed like a bunch of lunatics to me, and I hoped they didn't plan on hunting in the same area I was headed for. I couldn't wait to see their faces when I came coasting easily back down the mountain with a trophy buck draped over the back of my bike.

One of the main problems with biking your way out to hunt deer was that, if you left at four in the morning, by the time you got to the hunting place there were only a couple of hours of daylight left in which to do your hunting. Then you had to spend some time resting, at least until the pounding of your heart eased up enough not to frighten the deer.

As luck would have it, just as I was unstrapping my rifle from the handlebars, a buck mule deer came dancing out of the brush not twenty yards away from me. Now right then I should have known he was up to no good. He had doubtless been lying on a ledge and watching me for hours as I pumped my way up the mountain. He had probably even snickered to himself as he plotted ways to embarrass me.

All the time I was easing the rifle loose from the handlebars, digging a shell out of my pocket, and thumbing it into the rifle, the deer danced and clowned and cut up all around me, smirking the whole while. The instant I jacked the shell into the chamber, however, he stepped behind a tree. I darted to one side, rifle at the ready. He moved to the other side of the tree and stuck his head out just enough so I could see him feigning a yawn. As I moved up close to the tree, he did a rapid tiptoe to another tree. I heard him snort with laughter. For a whole hour he toyed with me in this manner, enjoying himself immensely. Then I fooled him, or at least so I thought at the time. I turned and started walking in a dejected manner back toward my bike, still watching his hiding place out of the corner of my eye. He stuck his head out to see what I was up to. I stepped behind a small bush and knelt as if to tie my shoe. Then, swiftly I turned, drew a bead on his head, and fired. Down he went.

I was still congratulating myself on a fine shot when I rushed up to his crumpled form. Strangely, I could not detect a bullet hole in his head, but one of his antlers was chipped and I figured the slug had struck there with sufficient force to do him in. "No matter," I said to myself, "I have at last got my first deer," and I pictured in my mind the joyous welcome I would receive when I came home hauling in a hundred or so pounds of venison. Then I discovered my knife had fallen out of its sheath during my frantic pursuit of the deer. Instant anguish! The question that nagged my waking moments for years afterwards was: Did the deer know that I had dropped my knife? Had I only interpreted it correctly, the answer to that question was written all over the buck's face—he was still wearing that stupid smirk.

"Well," I told myself, "what I'll do is just load him on my bike, haul him down to the lunatic hunters' camp, and borrow a knife from them to dress him out with." I thought this plan particularly good in that it would offer me the opportunity to give those smart alecks a few tips on deer hunting.

Loading the buck on the bike was much more of a problem than I had expected. When I draped him crosswise over the platform on the rear fender, his head and front quarters dragged on one side and his rear quarters on the other. Several times as I lifted and pulled and hauled, I thought I heard a giggle, but when I looked around nobody was there. It was during one of these pauses that a brilliant idea occurred to me. With herculean effort, I managed to arrange the deer so that he was sitting astraddle of the platform, his four legs splayed out forward and his head drooping down. I lashed his front feet to the handlebars, one on each side. Then I slid up onto the seat ahead of him, draped his head over my right shoulder, and pushed off.

I must admit that riding a bike with a deer on behind was a good deal more difficult than I had anticipated. Even though I pressed down on the brake for all I was worth, our wobbling descent was much faster than I would have liked. The road was narrow, twisting, and filled with ruts and large rocks, with breathtaking drop-offs on the outer edge. When we came hurtling around a sharp, high bend above the hunters' camp, I glanced down. Even from that distance I could see their eyes pop and their jaws sag as they caught sight of us.

What worried me most was the hill that led down to the camp. As we arrived at the crest of it, my heart, liver, and kidneys all jumped in unison. The hill was much steeper than I had remembered. It was at that point that the buck gave a loud, startled snort.

My first deer had either just regained consciousness or been shocked out of his pretense of death at the sight of the plummeting grade before us. We both tried to leap free of the bike, but he was tied on and I was locked in the embrace of his front legs.

When we shot past the hunters' camp, I was too occupied at the moment to get a good look at their faces. I heard afterwards that a game warden found them several hours later, frozen in various postures and still staring at the road in front of their camp. The report was probably exaggerated, however, game wardens being little better than hunters at sticking to the simple truth.

I probably would have been able to get the bike stopped sooner and with fewer injuries to myself if I had had enough sense to tie down the deer's hind legs. As it was, he started flailing wildly about with them and somehow managed to get his hooves on the pedals. By the time we reached the bottom of the mountain he not only had the hang of pedaling but was showing considerable talent for it. He also seemed to be enjoying himself immensely. We zoomed up and down over the rolling foothills and into the bottomlands, with the deer pedaling wildly and me shouting and cursing and trying to wrest control of the bike from him. At last he piled us up in the middle of a farmer's pumpkin patch. He tore himself loose from the bike and bounded into the woods, all the while making obscene gestures at me with his tail. I threw the rifle to my shoulder and got off one quick shot. It might have hit him too, if the bike hadn't been still strapped to the rifle.

"Now that," I said to the boys at Kelly's, "is how to tell about a first deer—a straightforward factual report unadorned by a lot of lies and sentimentality."

Unrepentant, they muttered angrily. To soothe their injured feelings, I told them about my second deer. It was so big it could cradle a baby grand piano in its rack and shade a team of Belgian draft horses in its shadow at high noon. Honest! I wouldn't lie about a thing like that.

The Crouch Hop
and Other Useful
Outdoor Steps

☞ ☞ ☞ **W**hile going through my mail at breakfast the other morning, I noticed a picture on a magazine cover of what was purported to be a group of backpackers. The individuals portrayed were all neat, clean, and beaming with happy smiles as they came striding up over a grassy knoll.

"Those aren't backpackers, they're fashion models," I told my wife.

Always keen to assimilate my wisdom on such matters, she fixed me with an intense look. "Did you eat my piece of bacon? That last piece of bacon was *mine!*"

"Well, first of all," I explained patiently, "they're all neat, clean, and beaming with happy smiles, whereas backpackers are generally messy, grubby, and grunting. Second, they're climbing a grassy knoll instead of a forty-five-degree, rock-strewn snake path the Forest Service laughingly calls a trail. What really gives them away, though, is that they're *striding*. No self-respecting backpacker would be caught dead striding."

"You even ate my English muffin!" my wife shouted.

This enlightening exchange got me to thinking that there are probably many people like my wife who have waited in vain for someone to erase their ignorance concerning the various foot movements, or steps, as they are sometimes called, employed in the practice of outdoor sports. I herewith offer as a public service the following compendium of the basic forms of outdoor pedestrianism.

THE PACKER'S PLOD—Backpackers, being generally optimistic souls, will start off on an excursion at a brisk pace, which they maintain for approximately nine steps. They then shift into the standard packer's plod. One foot is raised and placed forward three inches on the trail. The backpacker then breathes deeply, checks his hip strap, wipes the perspiration off his face, takes a swig from his canteen, eats a piece of beef jerky, snaps a photograph of a Stellar's jay, and consults his map. Then he repeats the process. A good backpacker, if he had a table handy, could play a hand of solitaire between steps. His forward motion defies detection by the human eye. Nevertheless, his progress is steady and unrelenting, and during the course of a day he can eat up a surprising number of miles, not to mention several pounds of jerky.

It always amuses experienced backpackers to see neophytes of the sport go racing past them on the trail. The tale of the tortoise and the hare leaps instantly to mind. Last summer my old backpacking partner Vern Schulze and I took his two boys, Wayne and Jim, on their first overnight hike. Our destination was a lake high up in the mountains of Idaho. Vern and I set off at the standard packer's plod, while the boys tore off up the trail ahead of us, soon disappearing from view. After about an hour they came racing back down the trail.

"What happened?" they shouted. "When you didn't show up at the lake, we thought maybe you had fallen and hurt yourselves."

Vern and I just winked at each other. "Don't worry about us. You fellows just go on ahead. We'll catch up."

After the boys had charged back up the trail, I said to Vern, "You know, when Wayne and Jim are exhausted and we pass them up, it would be better if we didn't tease them too much. It's a bad thing to break a boy's spirit."

"Right," Vern said, munching a handful of beef jerky while he snapped a picture of a Stellar's jay.

A couple of hours later the boys came jogging back down the trail.

"Look," I whispered to Vern. "They're already starting to slow down."

"Hey, Dad!" Wayne shouted. "The fish are really biting great! We've already caught enough for supper!"

It was all we could do to suppress our mirth. Both youngsters were showing definite signs of burning themselves out.

"You guys better speed it up a bit," Jim said.

"We can take care of ourselves," Vern replied, giving me a nudge with his elbow that almost toppled me off the trail. "Say, if you guys want to sit down and take a rest, go right ahead. It's nothing to be ashamed of. Just because Pat and I never stop doesn't mean you shouldn't."

"I thought you were stopped right now," Jim said.

"No," Vern said, "as a matter of fact we have just quickened our pace."

"We'd better be going," Wayne said. "We've got the tent pitched and a rock fireplace made and want to finish gathering wood for the fire."

They made three or four more trips back to check on us, each time moving a little slower. Along about evening we came upon them sitting alongside the trail eating huckleberries, and they both looked plumb tuckered out. Vern and I passed them up without so much as a single unkind remark. When we had dumped our packs in camp, though, I couldn't help offering a bit of advice to Wayne, who was hunkered at my feet.

"Easy does it," I told him. "If you pull a man's boots off too fast it hurts his ankles."

A boy is never too young to start learning the basics of backpacking, I always say.

THE SIDEWINDER—Skilled anglers the world over are masters of this rather peculiar outdoor step. Essentially, it consists of sauntering sideways. While looking straight ahead as if wearing blinders, you attempt to give the impression that you are oblivious to what is taking place on either side of you. The situation in which it is used is this: Your partner has laid claim to a nice piece of fishing water twenty yards or so downstream from you. Suddenly he gets a strike and flicks his fly into the uppermost branches of a thorn apple. You know the fish was a big one because of the way your friend suddenly crouches down and scurries about like a hyperactive crab as he tries to untangle his line and stay out of sight of the fish at the same time. There is a great temptation on such occasions to be overwhelmed by your partner's desperate maneuvers and to laugh yourself senseless. A master angler, however, will maintain an expression that is not only sober but that conveys the impression he is totally unaware of anything but his own rhythmic casting. While maintaining this expression, he then performs the sidewinder, which carries him sideways along the bank to that portion of water where the monster trout has signaled its presence. Upon arriving at this position, the master angler must make a pretense of being in a trance of sufficient depth that it cannot be penetrated by the vile epithets screamed at him by his former friend. The former friend will at this point give up all caution and throw himself into all-out combat with the thorn apple in order to free the offending line. Catching and landing a fish under such trying circumstances is what qualifies one as a master angler, sometimes referred to by fishing partners as a "no-good *bleep* of a *bleep*." Good sportsmanship requires that one refrain from maniacal laughter after performing a successful sidewinder.

THE MOSEY—This is a walk that belongs almost exclusively to game wardens, and they reserve it for occasions when they are moving in to make a pinch. If you see a man moseying toward you while you are fishing or hunting, you had better make a quick study of your game regulations because you may be in trouble. If game wardens in your area are prone to being sneaky, a stump or a bush moseying toward you also may mean trouble. I myself have on occasion put the mosey to good use. Indeed, it is rather amusing to see how quickly other anglers can be cleared from a stream by the simple expedient of moseying toward them.

THE HEEL-AND-TOE—This is essentially the same step employed in the track event of the same name. It is characterized by quick, tiny steps, an exaggeratedly straight vertical posture, and a facial expression combined of equal parts of indignation and suffering. It is not unusual to see a whole party of elk hunters going about camp in this fashion after a twenty-mile horseback ride into the mountains.

THE CROUCH HOP—This is usually performed midway through the process of driving in a tent peg with a large flat rock. The individual will suddenly leap up, clamp one of his hands between his thighs, and, making strange grunting sounds, begin to hop madly about the camp. I have performed this exercise many times, and it does wonders for relieving the pain resulting from a finger caught between a rock and a tent peg. It is equally important to recognize the crouch hop for what it is when you see it being performed. Once in Yellowstone Park, blinded by tears, I accidentally crouch-hopped into the adjoining camp space where an hysterical lady tried to run me through with her wiener stick. Luckily for me, she didn't have sufficient foresight to remove the wiener and I escaped with a single bruise no larger than the business end of a Ball Park frank.

THE SAUNTER—The saunter is applicable almost exclusively to bird hunting. I can remember the very first time I used it. I was fourteen and grouse hunting with my friend Retch Sweeney. We were moving stealthily through a thick stand of evergreens where we knew a grouse to be hiding. Suddenly the bird exploded off a limb almost directly above us and roared away through the trees. Startled, I whirled, pointed my old double-barrel at a patch of sky as big around as a bread box, and fired. Out of sheer coincidence, the shot and the grouse arrived at that patch of sky simultaneously, and the bird landed with a dead thump ten yards away. All my instincts told me to race over, grab up the grouse, and clamp it to my throbbing chest, all the while exclaiming, "Holy cow! Did you see that shot? Holy cow! What a shot!" For the first time in my life, however, I defied my instincts. I s-a-u-n-t-e-r-e-d over, picked up the grouse, and nonchalantly deposited it in my game pocket. "That one sort of surprised me," I said to Retch, whose tongue still dangled limply from his gaping mouth.

Now, had I gone bounding and bawling after that grouse like a hound pup after a squirrel, Retch would have known the shot was an accident. Instead, my saunter filled the great empty spaces of his mind with the impression that I was a fantastic wing shot. He frequently commented afterwards that he didn't understand how anyone who was such a great shot could miss so often. I have found, in fact, that a properly executed saunter after downed game will sustain one's reputation as a great shot through an unbroken string of twenty-five misses.

If one hunts with a dog, by the way, the same effect can be achieved by teaching it to retrieve game in a manner that suggests unrelieved boredom. Personally, I haven't had much success in this area with my own dog, since I've never been able to break him of the habit of doing a histrionic double take every time I hit something. You just can't compensate for bad breeding, so there is nothing for me to do but saunter to make up for a stupid dog who aspires to be a stand-up comic.

The TRUDGE—Used primarily for returning to one's car after a cold, wet, windy day of hunting and you missed three easy shots and it's the last day of the season and you can't remember where you left your car.

The LOPE—Basically a fast saunter, in that it implies casualness. Say you're out fishing a remote mountain stream with your boy and along toward dusk the hair on the back of your neck, for no reason at all, rises. You have the distinct impression that you are being *watched*. You halt a cast in mid-air and reel in.

"What you doin'?" the boy says. "I just had a good bite."

"It's getting late," you say. "We'd better head home." You then take off at a lope.

"Well, shoot!" the boy says.

The SHAMBLE—What the boy does in the above situation.

The BOLT—What the lope is changed into if the feeling of being watched is followed by a low, rumbling growl and a crashing in the brush. Actually, a low, rumbling growl or a crashing in the brush are sufficient reasons in themselves to engage in a bolt.

THE TRAMPLE—What the boy does to you when he hears the low, rumbling growl and crashing in the brush.

There are literally dozens of other interesting and enjoyable outdoor steps, but those given above are basic. It might be well to practice them at home until you feel both comfortable and confident with them. As a matter of fact, my wife just crouch-hopped past the door of my study. I wonder what she was doing driving a tent peg with a flat rock when she was supposed to be hanging a picture.

Meanwhile,
Back at the
B Western

☞ ☞ ☞**F**ew people appreciate the great contribution the handgun has made to television and motion pictures. What would police shows, for example, be without .38 Specials and .357 Magnums? Imagine police detectives standing around the squad room in shirtsleeves, rifles dangling from under their armpits. Ridiculous!

The shows that would really suffer from an absence of handguns, though, would be the westerns. Without the pistol, there would be no fast draw, and without the fast draw, westerns would be a whole lot different. Consider, if you will, and if you have the stomach for it, a quick-draw scene with rifles. Matt Dillon clumps out into the street from the Long Branch Saloon to issue a warning to one of the quaintly named villains so characteristic of "Gunsmoke."

"Chester and I caught you red-handed stealin' buffalo humps up on the flat, Ick Crud," he says. "You be outta town by sundown if you know what's good fer ya. Folks here 'bouts don't take kindly to buffalo-humpers."

Ick Crud sneers. "Reach fer yer iron, Marshal!"

The camera zooms in for a close-up of Matt's low-slung Winchester, the tie-downs knotted around his ankle. Quicker than Dean Martin can sing "Old Man River," Matt draws . . . and draws . . . and draws. Ick Crud uses a frantic hand-over-hand draw on his Sharps-Borchardt. During the draw, Chester, Doc, and Miss Kitty go back into the Long Branch for a drink to steady their nerves.

"Three whiskeys and be quick about it," Miss Kitty snaps to the bartender. "Matt's drawin' out there in the street, and we ain't got much time before the shootin' starts."

"I don't know why Matt don't git outta the marshaling business," Doc grumbles. "I keep tellin' him, 'Matt, sooner or later a gunfighter's gonna shade your draw by just a minute or two, and that'll be it fer ya.'"

"We better git back out there," Chester whines. "They should be just about finished drawin', and I don't want to miss the shootin'."

No doubt about it, the handgun and the fast draw are essential to the true western, and any movie fan worth his hot-buttered popcorn not only expects them to be in the western but knows the ritual by heart. The ritual usually begins with the "call out." The villain stands in the street and calls out the hero—"C'mon out, Ringo, you yellow-bellied, chicken-livered, varicose-veined, spastic-coloned wimp!"

Upon hearing himself being called out, the hero immediately begins his preparations. He tosses down his shot of whiskey and grinds out his cigar on the greasy nose of the belligerent bartender. He slips his pistol out of its holster and checks the cylinder to make sure he reloaded after his last shoot-out. (There is nothing more disappointing than to beat the other fellow to the draw and then discover that you forgot to reload.) He then reholsters his gun and slips it out and in a few times to make sure it isn't sticking. (A stuck gun is just about as bad as an unloaded one.) Next he unstraps his spurs, his motive here apparently being that, should he change his mind about the fight, it is a lot easier to run when you're not wearing spurs. He pulls his hat low over his eyes, limbers up the fingers of his gun hand, and tucks his jacket back behind the butt of his revolver. One purpose of all this preparation may be the hope that the villain will get tired of waiting and go home. The villain never does, of course, although sometimes he gets a cramp in his lip from holding a sneer so long.

Back in the olden days when I was a kid, we had what were called the B westerns. The B stood for "best." These were movies starring Roy Rogers, Gene Autry, and Hopalong Cassidy. They weren't anything like the westerns nowadays starring Clint Eastwood, the ones where you have to buy a program to tell the good guys from the bad guys. In the B westerns, you always knew the good guys. They were neatly dressed, clean-shaven, and didn't cuss, smoke, drink, kiss, or do anything else that was bad for health or morals. Even the bad guys didn't do most of these things, but you could tell them anyway. For one thing, they all used the interrupted curse:

"What the . . . !"
"Well, I'll be . . . !"
"Why you . . . !"

They had real action in the B's too, not like the "modern" western where you spend half the movie watching Eastwood squint his eyes and ripple his jaw muscles. Clint holsters his gun like he was setting a carton of milk back in a refrigerator. Why, Roy, Gene, and Hoppy wouldn't even think of putting their guns back into their holsters without giving them a twirl or two first.

I don't recall seeing Roy, Gene, or Hoppy ever shoot anybody, but they probably did. Usually, they just shot the gun out of the villain's hand and let it go at that. Sometimes they would rope the bad guys, often getting a single loop of their lasso around the whole gang. Heroes knew their business in the B westerns.

One nice bit of business Roy, Gene, and Hoppy perfected was to leapfrog over the rumps of their horses and land smack in the saddle. They never landed on the saddle horn either, although once I think I heard the Lone Ranger cry out in a shrill voice, "Hii *owwww* Silver away!"

My cousin Buck, who was several years older than I and knew everything, told me he was an expert at getting on horses like that and that there really wasn't anything to it. I said I couldn't believe that. He said if I had a horse handy he would show me. I said I didn't have a horse but I had a cow. Would a cow work? He said sure. We went out to the pasture and found a cow engaged in licking a salt block. Buck said that one would do just fine. I suggested that we warn the cow of what to expect, but Buck said that wouldn't be necessary. As it turned out, Buck was wrong about that and the rest as well. I still think the cow probably would have cooperated and even entered into the spirit of the thing had we just let her know what to expect. As it was, Buck got back twenty yards or so and made a dash for her. At the exact instant he got his hands on the cow's rump and his legs had crossed over his arms in mid-vault, the cow let out a frightened bellow and bolted forward. As the cow disappeared over a nearby hill, Buck was still perched on her tail bones in a strange variation of the lotus position and screaming, "Whoa, you stupid cow, whoa!"

"Well, I'll be . . . !" I said.

The B western heroes were big on tricks. Say the

villain got the drop on Roy in a little cabin out in the middle of the desert. Just as the baddy was about to plug him, Roy would shout "Watch out!" and point over the other man's shoulder. The villain would spin around, and Roy would jump him and thump his head to a fare-thee-well. These villains were *dumb!* Otherwise, why would they expect the guy they were about to gun down to warn them of a surprise attack? They were slow to learn. Roy, Gene, and Hoppy would catch them with this little trick movie after movie. Maybe the reason they were so dumb was from getting their heads thumped so often.

Eventually, however, they did start catching on to the trick. "You ain't foolin' me with that old trick, Rogers," the bad guy would say, as if he had seen some of these movies before himself. But this time Gabby Hayes would actually be sneaking up behind him and would thump his head a good one. Again, one might wonder why Roy thought it necessary to warn the villain when his comical sidekick was in fact sneaking up behind the man. The reason, of course, was to complicate matters for the villain when this particular situation arose in future movies. Roy, Gene, and Hoppy all worked half a dozen different ploys of this same routine, always with success. After a while the villain could scarcely get the drop on one of them without instantly becoming a nervous wreck from wondering whether or not he was about to be jumped.

The B western villain was a sucker for pebbles, too. Anytime the hero wanted to draw the baddy's attention away from himself, he would toss a pebble. The villain would whirl around and empty his six-gun into the pebble. Then he would see that it was only a pebble and would get this worried, expectant look in his eyes, which said, *"Head, get ready for a thumping!"*

Counting shots was a favorite tactic of B western

heroes. They would wave a hat around on a stick or perform some other trick to draw fire, all the time counting shots. Then, suddenly, they would walk right out in the open and announce, "Six! That was your last bullet, Slade!" Villains liked to try this trick too, but having the IQ's of celery, they could never get it straight. There was scarcely a villain in B westerns who could count to six without making a mistake. "Six," the bad guy would say, walking out from behind his rock. "That was your last bullet, Autry!"

BANG!

If the movie patron wondered what it was the villain was muttering as he lay sprawled in the dust, it was probably, "Let's see now, two shots ricocheted off the rock, two went through my hat on the stick, that makes five . . ."

Even among the B western audiences there were those who counted shots. They counted the number of shots the hero fired without reloading. I hated these wise guys. Right in the tense part of the movie, they would guffaw: "That's nine shots without reloading! Roy must be using a nine-shooter!"

"Why you . . . !" I would say under my breath. If there was anyone who couldn't appreciate a B western, it was a nitpicker.

The last B western I ever saw in a theater was in a small college town in Idaho. It starred Randolph Scott, and in the big scene the baddies had ganged up on Randolph in the saloon. When they started blazing away at him, Randolph jumped behind a cast-iron stove and, if I recall correctly, used the stove lid as a sort of shield while he returned their fire. The theater was filled with college kids and, as is the nature of college kids, they began whooping and jeering and laughing at Randolph's plight. Seated just behind me were an old farmer and his wife who had paid their hard-earned $1.50 for an evening of serious entertainment. As the slugs were spanging off the stove like lead hail and the college kids were whooping it up, I heard the old woman whisper nervously to her husband. The farmer, in a gruff but gentle voice, reassured her. "Don't worry, Mother," he said, "Ol' Randolph, he'll figure a way to git hisself out of this mess."

You bet! The farmer and his wife were my kind of people.

Looking back, I now realize it was a good thing Hollywood stopped turning out B westerns when it did. I was grown up and had a job by then, and folks were beginning to ask, "What's that big fellow doing down there, sitting in the front row with the kids?"

The Education
of a Sportsman

☞ ☞ ☞The letter came in the spring of my eighteenth year, telling me when to report in, and later that summer I packed my few belongings in my rucksack and an old battered suitcase and prepared to depart my home in the mountains of Idaho. Little did I know what lay in store for me during the months ahead, but my mother and grandmother offered plenty of warnings.

"Don't try to be a hero," Gram said.

"You don't have to worry about that," I consoled her.

"I know," Gram said, "but in the off chance the urge comes over you, don't try to be one."

"Right," I said.

"Those people are savages, many of them," Mom said. "They're not like us. I remember the atrocities your father used to tell about when he was in . . ." Her voice trailed off.

"I can't believe it's that bad," I said. "Lonny Henderson went, didn't he, and he came back okay."

Mom shook her head. "No, there's something wrong

with Lonny. Folks say he talks strange now. I don't want that to happen to you."

"Look, don't worry," I said. "I'm going to come back all right. After all, it's not as if I'm going off to war. College is different than that."

Mom and Gram helped me with my packing, and there was considerable discussion over what a young college man should take or leave behind.

"Let's see now," Mom said, surveying my assembled belongings. "You have your fishing rods, your tackle box, your twenty-two, your thirty-thirty, your shotgun, your hunting knife, your hunting boots and wool socks, your lucky hunting hat, your good pair of pants, and your good shirt. Since you're going to be gone for almost a whole year, do you think you might need a change of underwear?"

"Wouldn't hurt," I said. "Why don't you throw in a set?"

"How about the dictionary?" Gram asked.

"Naw," I said. "It'd take up the space of at least four boxes of shells. I know most words, anyway."

"Of course you couldn't think about leaving behind these hides you tanned and the deer head you mounted yourself," Mom added.

"Yeah, I thought my dorm room might need a little decoration, something to make me feel at home." I did wonder a bit about the head, since it had turned out with this stupid grin on its face.

Gram pointed to the big tangle of rusty traps. "You think you might actually have time to run a trap line between classes and studying?"

"There's lots of streams and wild country near the college," I said. "And muskrat hides are probably going to get up to near three dollars this winter."

"Why didn't I think of that?" Gram said.

As it turned out, college was not nearly so dangerous as Gram and Mom had led me to believe. The campus was located in the middle of a vast farming region bordered on one side by a fairly decent range of mountains. The surrounding countryside was dotted with lakes and laced with streams ranging from rivers to creeks to cricks with an occasional swamp thrown in for good luck. From my dorm window, pheasants could be seen strutting the wheat fields and deer were abundant in the mountains. It was my kind of place.

Originally an agricultural school, the college now enjoyed a reputation for research and scholarship in dozens of different academic areas. The chairman of my major department was himself a scholar of international reputation, to which was added the honor of having me as one of his advisees. Later in my college career, after I knew him better, Dr. Osgood revealed to me the peculiar circumstance under which he became my faculty adviser, once and for all clearing up the mystery of how great universities arrive at decisions that will forever influence the future life of a student. "I drew the short straw," he said.

Even now I remember our first meeting. A secretary showed me into an office, where Dr. Osgood, his great mop of white hair seemingly suspended in mid-explosion, sat staring intently at a file folder on his desk. He looked up, smiling.

"From a brief study of your academic record, young man, I see a great future ahead of you as a scholar."

"Gosh," I replied, hanging my head and digging at the carpet with my toe. "I don't know about that."

"Now now now," Dr. Osgood said. "You have amassed a wonderful academic record and are obviously a brilliant student. There's no need for false modesty, Heinzburger."

"*McManus*," I corrected.

"Oh, *McManus?*" Dr. Osgood picked up another file folder and perused it, occasionally allowing himself a slight shudder. "*Harumph!* Well, now, perhaps I spoke too soon, McManus. It appears from your record that you have every reason for legitimate modesty."

I laughed, not wishing to embarrass him, even though I didn't find his little joke particularly funny.

"By the way, McManus, what happened to the top of your head there, an auto accident?"

"That's my lucky hunting hat, sir."

"Oh. Is it removable or permanently attached?"

"I almost always take it off when I go to bed," I said. "Unless I happen to forget."

"That's most admirable," he said. "One must always strive to cultivate the little niceties." As far as I know, that was the first and only compliment I ever received from Dr. Osgood.

Then we got down to a serious discussion of my academic career, during which Dr. Osgood at times raved incoherently and at other times appeared on the verge of physical violence. Finally, he sat up very straight in his chair and began to perform what I later learned were deep-breathing exercises. Afterwards, for a while, he seemed calmer.

"Let's take a different tack," he said, forcing a small smile that trembled at the corners. "Let's concentrate for a moment on your future, presuming you have one. Now think about this very carefully. All other things aside, what is your ultimate goal in life? When you're as old as I, what single achievement would you like to look back upon, the one great shining accomplishment?"

I could see that we had now got down to serious business, and I sorted through all my vague hopes and desires and finally selected one that stood out among all others, the impossible dream.

"I have it," I said.

"Yes? Yes?" Dr. Osgood implored.

"I'd like to shoot a world's-record trophy moose!"

Dr. Osgood appeared at that moment to have suffered an infarction of some sort. He rose slowly from his chair, his face twisted in anguish, leaned forward across the desk, and croaked, "Moose? Moose? What do you mean, MOOSE!"

I must admit that my first meeting with Dr. Osgood made me a bit uneasy, but in our later sessions over the years I was able to relax and banter with him about my grades and various other trifles. Often I would leave his office in a state of high good humor, slinging one last witty retort over my shoulder, while Dr. Osgood would put on a show of weeping uncontrollably, at which he was very good. The man could have made his fortune as an actor.

Life in the dorm was not nearly so bad as Mom and Gram had predicted. Oh, sure, occasionally some of the guys would commit a minor atrocity, but nothing out of the ordinary as atrocities go. There were the usual panty raids, water fights, short-sheeting of beds, and dropping of stink bombs into the ventilation system, that sort of innocent fun.

During the first semester of my freshman year I had extremely bad luck with roommates. My first roommate, Wilson Fawfush, flipped out after a few weeks and finally insisted upon being moved to another dorm. The dorm director told me confidentially that Wilson had been suffering from hallucinations, even to the extent of claiming he saw snakes crawling all over the floor of our room.

"Poor Wilson," I said.

"Yes, it's too bad," the director said. "Sometimes the human mind can play strange tricks on us."

"No question about it," I said.

The next roommate assigned me was a real dilly. His name was Lester T. Lillybridge III. It immediately became apparent that Lester had been spoiled rotten as a kid, one result of which was that he had just been expelled from a classy private college back East. His lips seemed to be curled in a permanent sneer of superiority. Scarcely had he dropped his leather-trimmed luggage on the linoleum of our room than we had our first exchange of hostility.

"What are all the guns doing in here?" he asked.

"I'm a hunter," I said.

"Figures," he said. "My parents have arranged this as a punishment for me. What's that ugly thing on the wall?"

His words momentarily crippled my ego. No sooner had I learned I possessed an ego than some fool had to come along and cripple it. "That," I said indignantly, "is a deer head. I mounted it myself."

"Why does it have that stupid grin on its face?"

"That question just goes to show you know nothing about deer," I snapped. "In their natural state, all deer wear stupid grins like that."

Lillybridge laughed evilly. He walked over and kicked a crate I had built in the corner of the room. "What's in there?"

"Snakes," I said.

"Don't be a wise-elbow," Lillybridge said, opening the lid on top and peering in. He slammed down the lid and jumped back. "There *are* snakes in there!"

"Yes."

"Can they get out?"

"Well, they did one night a few weeks ago. That's why I built the crate for them. They can't get out now."

"Geez!" Lillybridge said. "My parents have really done it to me this time!"

Lillybridge found some of the other guys in the dorm more to his liking and spent most of his free time with them, planning and executing various atrocities. When not in class, I spent most of my time in the museum of natural history, where I had a part-time job assisting the curator in various chores. I was thinking of becoming a naturalist. The work was so much fun I would sometimes take it home with me.

"Where's that last batch of snakes we caught?" the curator would ask me.

"I took them home to study," I'd say.

"Well, bring them back!"

Occasionally, the curator would let me try my hand at taxidermy, but the results were never up to his standards. "You didn't do too badly on that ground squirrel," he'd say, "but why does it have that stupid grin on its face?"

During the day, when there were people milling about, the museum was quite pleasant. But at night, when I was there late sweeping the floors or cleaning up a mess of some kind, not always of my own making, the place was downright creepy. The live rattlesnakes in their glass cages, for example, would strike at me, popping the glass with their noses as I walked by. I knew that the snakes couldn't strike through the glass, but my adrenal glands, being ignorant of that fact, would pump a quart or so of adrenaline into my system every time a rattler struck at me. Pretty soon my nerves would be jangling, and shadows would seem to dart and dance among the displays. The huge, mounted timber wolf would blink his eyes as I scurried by with my dust cloth. The mounted cougar would lash its tail. The bobcat would twitch its whiskers.

There was one particularly loathsome room that I had to venture into in order to empty the various waste receptacles, some of which occasionally held startling surprises. This was the dissection room, where dead animals were prepared for whatever purpose the curator had in mind for them. One large glass case contained a kind of carnivorous beetle, thousands of them, used for cleaning the flesh off bones, leaving them shiny clean. I would imagine I could hear the beetles at their work, performing a grim symphony with their infinitesimal *chomp-chomp-chomps*. Between the rattlesnakes and the beetles, my late night chores in the museum would often leave me in a state of barely controlled terror.

The dissection room contained a dingy gray freezer about the size and shape of a coffin, only somewhat deeper. I often wondered what it might hold. One night when I was there alone, my curiosity overpowered my terror sufficiently for me to peek in. Ever so carefully I raised the lid, feeling the beat of my heart in every single goose bump on my body. Bit by bit, with cold sweat flooding off of me, I raised one eyelid. Nothing! The freezer was empty.

At that moment I thought of an atrocity to commit.

I had happened to mention to Lester, as we lay in our bunks one night, that my nerves were a bit frazzled from my work at the museum. He had laughed in his nasty, evil way and expressed the opinion that I was "just chicken." Confiding my fear to a person like Lilly-bridge had been nothing less than a lapse of sanity on my part. He had soon told all the other guys on our floor, most of whom up to that moment had regarded me with a certain amount of trepidation. Now they began to feel that I was a safe subject upon which to perform their practical jokes. This was a theory in need of puncturing.

I set my trap for Lillybridge with great care. First I wrote on a sheet of paper the message, "Dr. Smith, please finish with the dissection of this cadaver as soon as possible. It's beginning to spoil."

Then I waited until late one night when Lillybridge and I were in our bunks exchanging a few nasty barbs with each other before going to sleep.

"Let's be serious for a moment, Lester," I said.

"I am being serious, worm wit," he replied.

"Naw, come on, I mean it. I've got to tell somebody about this. It's really getting to me. I may even have to quit my job in the museum because of it."

"So, what is it, mussel mouth? You can tell your old Uncle Lester anything in complete confidence. Har! Har! Har!"

"Well, you see, there's this freezer in the dissection room at the museum. It's about the size and shape of a coffin. And I'm dying to look into it. I just have this uncontrollable compulsion to see what's inside. But I'm scared of what I'll find. I'm torn between my fear and my curiosity. I just can't stand it any more!"

"Har har har har har har har har!" Lester said. "Har har har."

"And what I was wondering, Lester, is if maybe you and I could sneak out to the museum right now and open that freezer. I've got a key."

"Sure!" he said. "Sounds like fun!"

"No kidding, Lester? You promise you won't chicken out? That no matter what, you'll open the freezer? I'd hate to have to tell the guys that you were afraid to open the freezer!"

"Let's go," Lester said, bounding out of his bunk.

After checking to make sure the campus security police were nowhere in sight, I unlocked the door to the museum and we slipped inside. I told Lester we couldn't turn on any lights because that would alert campus security to our presence. We'd just have to make do with the lights from the display cases, which cast an eerie glow about the room.

"You're not getting nervous are you, Lester?" I asked, as we worked our way through the museum.

"Har! Har! Har!" Lester laughed.

I led him up alongside the rattlesnake case. Lester stared dully at the snakes. Then, *buzzzzz-buzzzzz pop! pop! pop!* The snakes hit the glass a few inches from his face.

As soon as he had stopped dancing up and down, Lester said, "You should have told me they were alive! How was I to know they would strike at me!" I could see the level of adrenaline rising through his eyes.

We moved on a ways. "What's that behind you?" I asked suddenly. Lester spun around to stare the timber wolf in the fangs. Even in the soft glow of the display lights, I thought I could see outward signs of Lester's heart ricocheting around his rib cage. "Oh, just an ol' timber wolf," I said. "Nothing to be afraid of." By now, I calculated that Lester's circulation system was pumping about 80 percent adrenaline. And I hadn't even shown him the carnivorous beetles yet.

When we reached the door of the windowless dissection room, I told Lester to wait outside until I had gone in and turned on the light. He didn't argue. I slipped in and placed my note on top of the freezer, then flipped the wall switch. The lights came on in a blinding glare. Then I opened the door and motioned Lester in.

"Here's something you might find interesting, Lester," I said, in the manner of a tour guide. "These beetles are used to clean all the flesh off skeletons. Gee, I wonder what they are working on now."

Lester stared at the quivering black mass of beetles, his eyes widening in horror.

"Hear their tiny little *chomp-chomps?*" I asked.

"Yeh," Lester said weakly.

I turned and pulled Lester stumbling along behind me. "Now over here we have the freezer. Looks sorta like a coffin, doesn't it? Maybe now you can see why it gives me the creeps. Can't tell what might be in there, but I've got this terrible compulsion to find out! How about you, Lester?"

"Hunh?"

"Boy am I glad you came along to open up the freezer for me, Lester. But what have we here? Seems to be a note. Dang! I forgot my spectacles! Read it for me, will you, Lester?"

Lester's eyes fastened on the note like a matched set of vises. "*Good jumpin' gosh almighty,*" he hissed through his teeth, something that's not that easy to do even in the best of times.

"Well, forget the note, we're wasting time," I said. "Go ahead and pop her open, and let's see what's inside."

"N-no!" Lester said.

"C'mon!" I said. "Quit kidding around! Flip up the ol' lid there!"

"Un-unh," Lester said, shaking his head.

"You mean you're too chicken to open the freezer?" I asked.

"Un-hunh," Lester said, nodding affirmatively.

"Har! Har! Har!" I replied. "Too chicken to open a measly old freezer! Wait till the guys hear about this! I guess I'll just have to open it myself!"

I grabbed the lid and flipped it up, watching Lester's face all the while in order to record every detail of his reaction so I'd be able to provide the guys in the dorm with an accurate report. There was, for instance, this little popping motion of his eyeballs as he stared into the open freezer. Then there was the way his jaw sagged and a bit of drool rolled over his lower lip. Overall, there was the general response of someone accidentally sticking a finger in an empty light socket. The effect was even better than I had hoped for.

"Har! Har! Har!" I laughed. "There, you see, it's empty!" I turned to point into the freezer. "Har! Har! HAAAAAAARRRRRR!"

Ol' Lester may have been a spoiled brat, but he sure knew how to run. I counted at least three times that he passed me on our way back to the dorm.

Later, I learned that, unbeknownst to me, the curator had stored a dead black bear in the freezer, its skin partially peeled off.

Lester and I went on to become good friends, and that winter I even taught him how to trap muskrat, just in case he ever ran short of money. He changed into as nice a guy as you would ever want to meet. It seemed as if the scare at the museum had purged all the meanness and smugness and arrogance out of Lester. Heck, I was even a little purged myself.

The Gift

☞ ☞ ☞ Christmas is an uneasy time for me. Maybe it's because my father was a practical joker. When I was small he would tell me that if I didn't behave myself Santa would fill my stocking with kindling sticks and rotten potatoes. I would try to behave myself but could never seem to get the hang of it. Christmas thus became a matter of great apprehension to me, because even though I couldn't behave I wasn't stupid, and I figured Santa Claus had to have my name on some kindling and rotten potatoes. Sure enough, come Christmas morning I would creep out of bed, peek around the corner at my stocking, and there would be some kindling sticks protruding from it, along with a few sprouts from rotten potatoes.

"AAIIIGHHHHHHH!" I would exclaim.

"Ho, ho, ho!" my father would laugh.

Then, of course, he would show me that under the kindling sticks and rotten potatoes were a ball, a top, some dominoes, a tin soldier, and maybe some candy orange slices. I would punish him by playing all day with kindling and potatoes. We didn't have psychology in those days; otherwise, I might have been emotionally scarred for life by my father's little trick. As it is, I become uneasy at Christmastime.

One of the reasons I become uneasy is the cost of things I put in my own kids' stockings: digital watches, rock-concert tickets, skiing lessons, and the like. Fortunately, the kindling sticks and rotten potatoes don't cost much and never fail to give me a good laugh. There's nothing funnier than teenagers dumping out their stockings and exclaiming, "AAIIIGHHHHHHHH!" They exclaim that when they discover the stocking doesn't contain a set of keys to a new car.

Probably the main reason for my unease, however, is the gifts I receive for Christmas. Whenever the kids ask my wife what to get Ol' Whosis for Christmas, she tells them, "You know how he loves outdoor sports. Why don't you get him something outdoorsie?"

"Good idea," they cry in unison. "How much can he afford for us to get him?"

Let me state here that there should be a law prohibiting any person who uses the term "outdoorsie" from dispensing advice about what kinds of presents to buy an outdoorsman. A few years ago, after my spouse advised her I would like something outdoorsie, one of my wealthy aunts gave me something called the Ultimate Fishing Machine. As near as I could make out from the operational manual, you stayed at home and watched TV while the UFM went out and caught the fish, cleaned them, cooked them, and ate them. When it got back home, you asked the UFM what kind of luck it had and it told you lies.

The manufacturer claimed in his literature that the Ultimate Fishing Machine had been made possible through the miracle of miniaturization. I would have preferred a miracle that assembled the machine before passing it on to me. At the very least, the company could have miniaturized an engineer and enclosed him in the package to help put the UFM together. I never even attempted to assemble the Ultimate Fishing Machine and so cannot report on its competence at fishing. Bothersome as it may be, I'd just as soon go to the trouble of catching, cleaning, cooking, and eating my own fish. If I work at it, I can probably even learn to tell fishing lies.

Nothing gladdens the heart of a sporting-goods store proprietor more than to be approached by a lady who says something like, "My husband is the outdoorsie type. I wonder if you might suggest a suitable Christmas gift for him."

The proprietor grins evilly and rumples his hair so as to conceal the horns protruding just above his temples. Here is his chance to revenge himself on one of the arrogant sportsmen who have snorted derisively and even guffawed openly at certain items of the proprietor's stock.

"Here's something fishermen are absolutely crazy about," he says. "The musical fishing creel! Every time a fish is inserted, it plays Beethoven's Fifth Symphony. If they go over their limit, Elvis Presley sings 'I Ain't Nothin' but a Hound Dog.'"

"Marvelous!" the wife exclaims. "I'll take it! Any other suggestions?"

"Now here's a nifty item—a pair of sleeping-bag warmers for backpackers."

"They look like bricks."

"That's what they are—but not just your ordinary bricks. No ma'am. These are special high-density bricks —just feel how heavy they are. The way they work, the backpacker heats them in the campfire and then inserts them in his sleeping bag. Keep him toasty warm all night."

"What a nice idea," the wife says. "I'll take a set."

"How about a gag gift for the fellow who likes to go out exploring by himself in the wilds—a trick compass. See, every time you look at it, North shifts to a different direction. Ha! Ha! It comes with maps that instantly dissolve when they come in contact with cold sweat. The compass and maps together are sold as The $8.95 Do-It-Yourself Divorce Kit."

"It's tempting," the wife says, "but I'd better not."

"Here's a nice gift for the man who has nothing," the proprietor tells her. "A tiny inflatable vest for grasshoppers. Keeps them afloat, and with this little harness to fasten them to the hook, they can be used over and over until a fish takes them or they die of old age."

"That is absolutely *darling!*" the wife exclaims. "I'll take two."

"Did I show you the grasshopper water skis . . . ?"

There are other reasons for my unease at Christmas. After my father died, Christmas was a rather bleak occasion at our house for a number of years. I got a foreshadowing of just how bleak one Christmas was going to be when my mother warned me, "If you don't behave, all Santa is going to put in your stocking is kindling sticks."

"What about the rotten potatoes?" I asked.

"He can't afford them this year," she said.

Santa always seemed to come through with something though, even if it was pre-owned, as they say. I would get some used clothes, used books, used toys, used candy. It was my sister, the Troll, who gave me the used candy.

"This Snickers bar has teeth marks on it," I said.

"I know," the Troll said. "I forgot, I don't like caramel."

"You didn't lick it all over, did you?" I asked, examining the bar carefully for lick marks.

"No," she said. "What kind of a person do you think I am?"

Thinking that she was the kind of a person who would lick a Christmas present, I worried for weeks after eating the candy bar that I would come down with some terrible disease carried by sisters.

Even back when I was nine or ten I was known as an outdoorsie type among the relatives. Rich Aunt Maude wrote my mother and asked what kind of outdoorsie present I would like for Christmas. My mother wrote back that I would "just love something related to fishing." We speculated for weeks whether Maude would send me a fine fishing rod or a fine reel or a tackle box filled with tackle. I thought possibly she might even come through with a boat, motor, and trailer. When the gift arrived though, the boat, motor, and trailer were instantly ruled out because of the package's minuscule dimensions, so minuscule in fact that they also ruled out the fine fishing rod, reel, and tackle box. I figured all it could be was a fly book filled up with expensive flies. Christmas morning we all got up and rushed down to the Christmas bush, and the family waited with bated breath—mouthwash being unknown to us in those days—as I tore open the package from rich Aunt Maude. Even to this day I can recall my response upon unveiling the present:

"AAIIIGHHHHHHH!"

There, lying in state before me in a monogrammed box with glittering foil wrapping and soft crinkly tissue paper were . . . *two silk neckties . . . with pictures of fish on them!*

"Don't be so upset," my mother pleaded, pulling me down off the wall. "You can wear them with your new suit—whenever you get a new suit."

"And whenever you get a neck," the Troll added. "Now open my present!"

"What is it?" I said, my bitterness ebbing.

The Troll smiled sweetly. "Gum."

I must say it was pretty good gum, too. There was still a lot of flavor left in it.

My mother always used to say that we should be grateful for whatever we received. "Just think," she would admonish us, "there are millions of people all over the country living in poverty, who can't even afford popcorn to decorate their Christmas bush with."

I tried not to think of the poor people as I decorated the bush. "How does this look?" I would ask as I stepped back to study my placement of the popcorn.

"Why not put it right up on the tip?" the Troll would suggest. "That way it'll look like a little tiny white star."

The only poor person I knew at that time was Rancid Crabtree, the old woodsman who lived at the foot of the mountain about a mile from our place. I spent a large part of my early life following Rancid around and studying him and learning all sorts of interesting things. But Rancid was poor. He didn't seem to know that he was poor, however, and I never had the heart to tell him, because he was the happiest person I'd ever met. If he had known he was poor, of course, then he would have been sad and miserable all the time. As it was, Rancid was able to live out his whole life in blissful ignorance of the fact that he was poor.

A few days before Christmas one year, I wandered over to Rancid's cabin to see what he was up to. He was carrying an armload of firewood into the cabin and

invited me in. I looked around, expecting to see a
Christmas bush with some presents under it. There was
nothing but the rumpled bed, the old barrel stove, a table
and some broken chairs, rusty traps, a shotgun and some
rifles on wall pegs, and a few other odds and ends.

"Where's your Christmas bush?" I asked him.

"If Ah was to have anythang, it 'ud be a Crimmas
tree. But Ah don't see why Ah got to brang a tree into the
house when all Ah's got to do is look out the winder and
see all of 'ems Ah want."

"But what do you put all your presents under?" I
persisted.

Rancid stared at me for a long moment, then
snorted. "Ah use to git all kinds of presents. They'd be
piled up n'ar to the ceilin' and Ah be kickin' an' stumblin'
over 'em all the time. So finally Ah just up an' tells folks
to shet off givin' me all them presents. Ya know, Ah ain't
missed 'em one bit. A man jist outgrows presents, Ah
guess."

I hoped I'd never outgrow presents, and while I was
thinking about that, a great wave of sorrow crashed down
upon me and poured right down into the insides of my
feet and filled up my toes and then came welling back up
again into my throat.

"What's wrong with you, boy?" Rancid said.

"Your stove is smoking," I choked. "I better get some
fresh air," and I bolted out the door.

Rancid came out on the porch and watched me as I
gasped cold air into my lungs.

That was when the great idea occurred to me.

"Say, Rancid," I said, "why don't you come have
Christmas dinner with us at our house?"

"Naw, Ah couldn't do thet. You know yer ol' granny
an' me don't git along."

"Why, it was her who told me to invite you," I lied. "She said to me, 'Now you go give Rancid Crabtree an invite to Christmas dinner!'"

"Wall, dad-gum maw hide! Shore! You tell her Ah'd be happy as a hawg at a hangin' to shar' yer Crimmas vittles with y'alls."

When I told Mom that I had invited Rancid to Christmas dinner, she said she didn't know if we could afford the extra expense.

"Heck, he won't eat that much," I said.

"The expense I'm talking about is repairing the hole in the roof when your grandmother goes through it."

Gram didn't go through the roof when she heard the news about Rancid. She took it rather well as a matter of fact, as soon as she got done hopping up and down in the middle of the kitchen and saying "AAIIIGHHHH!"

"Good gosh almighty, boy, do you know what you've done? That Rancid Crabtree ain't took a bath since he fell in the crick in '27. Folks pay him just to walk by their farms so the smell will drive the ticks off their critters. And you invite him to Christmas dinner! Well, all we can do is put the extra leaves in the table and set you and him down at the far end!"

"Hoooray!" I shouted. "I'll even help get things ready. How many extra leaves we got for the table, Gram?"

Gram shook her head. "Not nearly enough, boy, not nearly enough!"

Personally, I didn't think that Rancid smelled all that bad, but there was a story told that his approach from an upwind direction had once raised an alarm that the stockyards had caught on fire. In any case, there was a great deal of moaning and groaning among the women-folk that Rancid's presence at Christmas dinner would be a lingering one. The Troll practiced eating with her nose pinched together, and Gram and Mom debated whether we should eat with all the windows open and hope a blizzard would come up and provide a strong cross draft.

All of this carrying on began to worry me, because I didn't want to ruin Christmas dinner for the rest of the family. So, the day before Christmas I hastened through the snow to Rancid's cabin with the notion of persuading him that coming to dinner might not be such a good idea after all. Upon approaching the cabin, however, I noticed great white clouds rising from the doors and windows and cracks in the roof. I thought the place was on fire, and ran yelling for Rancid to get out of the cabin.

Rancid stuck his head out of a steam cloud. "What in tarnation is all the ruckus about?"

I peeked past him into the cabin. There was a great tub on top of the barrel stove, which was belching out smoke and flames on all sides, and the clouds of steam were boiling up from the tub.

"Whatcha got in the tub?" I asked.

Rancid shuddered. "Water. Ah'm gonna do somethin' Ah ain't did since '27. It's a torture to me, but Ah'm gonna do it jist fer you. Ah hope you appreciate it. An' don't never ast me to do it ag'in, 'cause Ah ain't!"

"Oh, I won't, I won't never ask you to do it again, Rancid." I turned to sprint happily back to my house. "See you at Christmas dinner tomorrow!"

When I burst into the kitchen, Gram was just removing from the oven a batch of cinnamon rolls.

"You don't have to worry about eating with the windows open at Christmas dinner tomorrow," I told her.

"Oh? Rancid ain't comin'?"

"He's coming all right, but this very moment he's fixing us up a nice surprise."

"A gift! Land sakes alive, we didn't think to get that dirty ol' rascal anything!"

"Well, it's not exactly . . ."

Gram slapped a hot cinnamon roll out of my hand. "Don't tell me exactly. I'll just wrap up these cinnamon rolls for him. Ain't nobody gives us a present we don't give him a present back!"

"But . . ."

"No but's!"

Christmas day, as we waited for Rancid to show up for dinner, Mom said, "I'd feel better about this if we already had all the windows open when he came. That way we wouldn't be so likely to hurt his feelings."

"That's the way I feel about it, too," Gram said. "And we should of put the extra leaves in the table."

Suddenly, the Troll, who had been looking out the window, shouted, "Here he comes! And wow! You're not going to believe this!"

There was a knock on the door, and Mom called out, "Come right on in, Rancid!"

In burst Rancid with a big snaggletoothed grin. "Surprise!" he shouted.

And were we surprised? Why, you could have knocked every last one of us over with a feather!

As soon as Mom had recovered from her astonishment enough to speak, she said, "Rancid, why don't you throw open a few of those windows over there and let in some fresh air while we put the extra leaves in the table. Then I want to get a better look at those skis."

"Steamed the curve into the tips mawsef," Rancid said proudly. "Put a couple birch boards in a tub of water on top of maw stove and them ol' tips bent up jist as purty as you please. Ain't made a pa'r of skis since '27."

"A mite wider on that window, if you please,

Rancid," Gram said. "My, don't that blizzard feel good! Now let me feast my eyes on them skis."

"Thar fer the boy," Rancid said. "But Ah made them big nuff y'all can use 'em if ya wants."

That was one of the finest Christmas gifts and one of the finest Christmas dinners I have ever known. As Mom said as we sat shivering happily around the table, "It's a chill wind that blows no warmth."

The Sensuous Angler

☞ ☞ ☞ There would be a lot less divorce in this country if more husbands and wives fished together. Spouses that fish together stay together.

My wife, Bun, for example, used to absolutely detest fishing. Whenever I dragged her out on the lake, she would sit there in the boat with her eyes fixed on me in an unblinking stare that I often imagined to be almost murderous. From time to time I'd even speak a few kind words to her in an effort to break the spell: "Row a bit faster along here, will you, Bun? I don't want my lure to get snagged in the weeds." Of course, there are some people who just don't respond to kind words, and Bun seemed to be one of them.

Besides my compulsive interest in fishing, what complicated our marital situation even more was that women find me extraordinarily attractive. "Irresistible" would not be too strong a word. I sometimes have to laugh to myself at the great show they put on to make me think they're totally unaware of my existence. Just recently I was sitting next to a beautiful woman on the uptown bus. I could tell she was flustered by the way she rummaged around in her purse, finally dug out a compact, and started fixing her face. It was absolutely hilarious, particularly when she wiped off some excess eye shadow with the tip of my tie. I mean, there are no lengths to which women will not go in their pretense of ignoring me!

Bun, quite forgivably, used to be terribly jealous. I'd try to kid her out of it. When we would come home from grocery shopping, I'd say, "Did you see how that cute blonde at the store was pretending to ignore me? I nearly laughed out loud!"

"There's only one can of tuna here," Bun would say. "I could have sworn I bought two cans of tuna."

That's how bad it was. Mad, uncontrollable jealousy was practically destroying our marriage.

The combination of my obsession with fishing and my irresistible appeal to women took a more extreme turn for the worse one day when Bun discovered a reddish smudge on the collar of one of my white dress shirts.

"Aha, I've got you now, you rascal," she snarled. "What's this red smudge on your shirt collar?"

How had I ever managed to overlook that smudge? My mind raced, feverishly searching for a plausible lie.

"It's probably just a lipstick smudge from one of the girls at the office," I tried.

"Ha!" Bun snapped. "I wasn't born yesterday, you know! This is salmon-egg juice! Here I think you're down at the office working, and actually you're sneaking off to go fishing. You've probably rented a secret apartment where you keep an extra set of fishing gear!"

"But there's this other woman . . ." That's as far as I

got. If there's one thing I can't stand about Bun, it's the way she expresses her jealousy by laughing uncontrollably.

Actually, there *was* another woman. Her name was Jennifer, and she worked in the same advertising agency I did. There was something about her that made it almost impossible for me to keep my eyes off of her. As with most women, she made a great show of ignoring my existence. There was that time, for instance, when I was standing by the coat rack and she tried to hang her coat on me. Of course she had laughed in an embarrassed way, but not until she had made repeated efforts to keep her coat from slipping off my shoulders.

My job at the agency was to invent benevolent lies about a client's product. So distracted was I by Jennifer that one day I allowed a truth to slip into my copy and was nearly fired. Naturally, I was upset by the mishap, and as soon as the boss had gone down to the shop to resharpen his reamer, I whipped out my portable fly-tying outfit and began to tie a few Royal Henchmen to soothe my nerves. Suddenly I felt a pair of eyes on me. At first I thought it was Charley Fife, playing another one of his grotesque practical jokes. Then I realized it was Jennifer watching me. She came over to my desk.

"Hello," she said, holding out a hand. "I'm Jennifer. You must be new here."

"Oh, I've been here awhile," I replied suavely.

"How long?"

"Four years."

"Strange that I've never noticed you before. Our desks are only twenty feet apart."

"Yes, well *I've* noticed you, Jennifer."

"You have? Anything in particular."

"Is there ever!" I breathed. "For one thing, there's the way you read *Field & Stream* so avidly at lunch while the other girls are gawking at *Glamour*. Then I saw the way you took that casting reel apart and put it back together when you were supposed to be typing the annual report."

"Oh dear!" she cried, tittering. "You caught me in the act, did you? I was just cleaning my Protron Ninety Double-Widget Power-Glide Pro-Caster."

"You're telling me!" I said. "You have about the prettiest little Pro-Caster I've ever laid eyes on."

A flush of embarrassment filled Jennifer's cheeks, reminding me of the red-bellies I used to catch in the creek behind our house when I was a kid. As she bent over to whisper in my ear, I detected the faint, lingering fragrance of OFF! "Did you notice anything else?" Her voice was husky.

"You mean . . . the way you rewrapped the split bamboo rod during your coffee breaks last February? Of course I noticed! It nearly drove me wild!"

She smiled. "You're really a very attract . . . You're not that bad look . . . I like large ears a lot, I really do."

I chuckled. The poor girl was practically tongue-tied.

"What attracted me to you most, though," she continued, "was your little portable fly-tying outfit. It's lovely! Say, I've got an idea. Why don't you stop by my place tonight and we'll . . . well, you know?"

"I know!" I said. "I know!"

After I had slipped into Jennifer's apartment that evening, she poured us each a glass of wine and turned on the stereo. Then we got right down to business. I was amazed, I must tell you, at what that woman knew. In fifteen minutes she taught me more about how to cure fresh steelhead eggs for bait than all the grizzled old anglers I've ever known. Such was our mad frenzy of curing steelhead eggs that some of the juice apparently splashed on my collar. That was the spot my wife detected.

"No one must ever find out about us," I told Jennifer as we shook hands at the door of her apartment as I was leaving.

"Oh, I know, I know," she said. "But next ume, next time . . ."

"What?" I gasped. "Tell me what, Jennifer!"

"Next time . . . I'll show you how to filet perch!"

I was puzzled. "But, Jennifer, I know how to filet perch."

She gave me a lascivious smile. "Not the way *I* do it."

My imagination did a wild dance, raising goose bumps on my flesh the size of bongo drums. "When can we do it?" I asked. "When can we filet perch together?"

"Maybe next Tuesday night. Call me after eight. But if a man's voice answers, hang up."

"A man's voice?"

"Yes, my husband's. He is very big, with a short temper. And he hates fishing and fish. It would be most unfortunate for you if he caught us—you know—fileting together."

I shuddered at the image conjured up by her warning.

It was a long week. Every time I looked up, I saw Jennifer typing reports a few yards away. I could scarcely tear my eyes away from her flying fingers, those very fingers which, but a few days before, I had watched . . . had watched knead alum into a sinewy mess of steelhead eggs. Once a man, an angler, has experienced that with a woman, there is no turning back. And she had this lovely way of tossing her head. It reminded me of the way a fly fisher, hands filled with rod and line, will toss his head in order to shake a deer fly off his nose. It was beautiful.

At home during supper, I found myself staring absently at my plate. All I could think about was fileting with Jennifer.

"What's wrong with Pop?" one of the kids asked one evening. "How come he doesn't tell us those stupid stories about his childhood any more?"

"Don't complain," their mother said. "Your father has important things on his mind."

"We ain't complaining!" the kids said in unison. "We ain't complaining!"

"Have some respect!" I shouted at them. "I never once talked to one of my parents like that! Why, one time when I was only eight years old and had just walked the fifteen miles home from school in knee-deep snow . . ."

"Forget I mentioned it," the first kid said.

After supper Bun followed me into my den, also jestingly referred to as "the hole under the stairs." She put her hands on my shoulders and said, "Something's wrong. I know something's wrong. You get upset over the smallest things. I saw the way your eyes became all teary when you couldn't stab that last pea with your fork at supper. You can tell me! What's wrong?"

"Nothing's wrong," I said. What made me feel so bad about my affair with Jennifer is that Bun's a great wife. Sure, she has her faults. There was that time she screamed as if she had found Jack the Ripper in our refrigerator instead of merely a mayonnaise jar containing live hellgrammites. Heck, Jennifer would never have screamed at the sight of a few crummy live hellgrammites.

The truth was that Jennifer didn't really stand a chance of coming between my wife and me. Ol' Bun and I had just been through too many things together. She had stuck with me through thin and thin. The only thing to do, I told myself, was to try to forget Jennifer. But I couldn't.

When Tuesday night rolled around, I slipped out to a pay phone and called Jennifer's number. Jennifer answered.

"Is it all right?" I asked.

"Yes," she said, breathlessly. "Hammer is flying out of town on a business trip tonight and won't be back until tomorrow."

"Great!" I said. "I'll sneak right over."

I told Bun I was going to spend the evening with the boys down at Kelly's Bar & Grill and not to expect me home too early. She said fine, that she would leave the key under the cushion on the porch swing. I was halfway over to Jennifer's before it occurred to me that there isn't a cushion on the porch swing. We don't even have a porch swing. We scarcely have a porch. I wondered if Bun suspected anything.

A sudden thought jolted me: *Hammer? Her husband's name is Hammer?*

When Jennifer met me at the door, I was disappointed to find her dressed in a low-cut, filmy negligee.

"You're early," she said. "Mix yourself a drink while I slip into something a little more comfortable." Presently she returned from the bedroom dressed in baggy, patched fishing pants and a plaid wool shirt sprinkled with fish scales.

"Hey hey hey!" I said. "Now that's more like it!" I thrust a package into her hands. "By the way, here's a little something for you."

Her hands tore eagerly at the wrappings. Nervously, I wondered if maybe I had made a mistake, giving her such a personal gift so soon in our relationship.

"Oh!" she cried, clapping her hands together in

delight. "They're beautiful! You shouldn't have! They must have cost you a small fortune!"

"Nope," I said, smiling modestly. "I caught them myself. Off the old Grand Street fishing pier. Do you really like them?"

Jennifer wiped her joy-streaked cheeks on her shirt sleeve. "Oh, I love them! They are absolutely gorgeous perch! All Hammer ever gives me are long-stemmed red roses and dumb furs."

It was obvious her husband was either a thoughtless clod or totally insensitive. Some men just don't know how to treat a woman!

Overcome by the excitement of the moment, Jennifer and I rushed into the kitchen and began to filet madly. Never have I known a woman who could filet like Jennifer! Perch after perch fell under her flashing knife. I became mesmerized by her very motions, the way she whacked off the heads, stripped away the skins, and sliced off the filets. Time ceased to exist for me, and all space seemed confined to Jennifer's laminated maple chopping block.

Then the earth moved.

"Did the earth move for you, Jennifer?" I asked.

"Yes yes yes yes yes!" she cried. "And do you know what made it move?"

"What?"

"Hammer! He always trips on that last step at the top of the stairs!"

"HAMMER?" I yelled. "I thought you said he was away on business!"

"Maybe he missed his flight! Maybe he suspects something! But that is Hammer coming down the hall!"

Now I could feel the earth move with every step Hammer took down the hallway. The steps sounded angry.

"What'll we do?" I hissed at Jennifer.

"What do you mean 'we,' you burglar you!" she snapped.

Somehow I felt that Jennifer had chosen that moment to break off our relationship. Very soon I expected her husband to break off more than that.

"Look at the evidence!" I hissed, as Hammer rattled his key in the lock. "He'll know we've been fileting together. No matter what you tell him, he'll know a burglar didn't break into the apartment and force you to filet!"

Jennifer scooped up all the evidence and flung it into the freezing compartment of the refrigerator.

"Jen?" called out Hammer, his voice rumbling into the kitchen like a slow freight.

A second before Hammer's shadow fell upon us, Jennifer lunged across the kitchen, threw her arms around me, and planted a big, wet, utterly disgusting kiss on my mustache. And then Hammer filled the doorway.

"Who dis?" he demanded, pointing at me with a finger the size of a zucchini.

"Oh," said Jennifer, "this is just one of my professors from night school who heard you were going to be out of town tonight and thought he'd sneak by."

"You 'spect me to buy a cock'n'bull story like dat? It smells fishy in here! You two been up to somethin' wid fish, ain'tcha? Filetin'! I'll bet the two of you have been filetin' behind my back. Or maybe even, even—I can't stand the thought of it—curin' steelhead eggs for bait! As soon as I leave town to do a little job for the Godfather . . ."

"No, no, Hammy, it wasn't anything like that," Jennifer cried. "Please don't kill him!"

"Repeat that last part, would you, Jennifer?" I whispered to her. "I don't think Hammy heard it."

At that moment Hammer blinked, giving me the opportunity to leap out the kitchen window and sprint to safety down the alley. When I finally stopped to catch my breath, I made up my mind right then and there that never again was I going to filet with another man's wife, particularly one whose apartment was higher than the ground floor. For one thing, it's so darn hard to sprint to safety with your legs protruding from your armpits.

I had learned my lesson about other women and decided that the thing to do was to give my own wife more instruction in the art of fileting. That way she might even learn to enjoy the sport. And the very next weekend I started her lessons.

"All right, Bun," I instructed, "just remember that balance is everything. There, you've nearly got it. Raise your right arm a bit more. Good. Now you've got the idea! Heck, you could carry the canoe all day like that if you had to. Get started toward the lake now, and I'll grab my fly rod and be right along behind."

Bun still isn't too enthusiastic about fishing yet. As a matter of fact, just the other day when we were out on the river she said if I would forget about the idea of making her my fishing pal, she wouldn't complain about another woman or two.

Not a chance! "Listen, Bun," I said, "you're the only woman for me, and I'm going to make you love fishing if it's the last thing you do."

I could have sworn that she was so touched by this remark that a single tear trickled down her cheek. It was hard to tell for sure, though, because of the cloud of mosquitoes around her.

And Now Stay Tuned for "The Camp Chef"

☞ ☞ ☞ **A** friend of mine, Fred Flim, is a television producer, and at lunch a while back I suggested to him that what the tube needs now is a show about camp cookery. Scarcely able to conceal his enthusiasm for such a show, Fred pretended to be totally absorbed in an effort to suck the pimento out of a martini olive.

"Great concept, hunh?" I said.

"Fantastic," Fred said. "Hey, man, can you believe those Yankees! What a team! After those first two games, I would have . . ."

"You really like the idea that much?" I said, almost overcome by excitement. "You're not just putting me on? Wow! I hope you're not just saying this because we're such good friends."

Fred turned serious, his gravity only slightly lessened by his having clenched a large, pitless green olive grotesquely in his eye. "May I have this dance, Miss?" he asked me, hunching his neck down into his shoulders and reaching out with two bread sticks protruding from his sleeves. People who are not friends of Fred's often have difficulty telling when he's being serious.

I chuckled appreciatively at his little performance and told him that it reminded me of the time his wife thought he was on a three-day fishing trip with me but wasn't and what a kick she'd get out of the story.

Fred plucked the olive from his eye and put the bread sticks back in their basket. "What are you thinking of calling this show of yours?" he asked.

" 'The Camp Chef,' " I replied. "It will be kind of an outdoorsie 'The French Chef' but with me as the star instead of Julia Child."

"Fantastic," he said. "Really fantastic. It sort of gets a person right here."

"How come there?"

"Well, I was never very knowledgeable about anatomy. Tell you what, you work up a script and get the necessary props together and be down at the studio at ten sharp Monday morning and we'll shoot a pilot of 'The Camp Chef.' "

"Fantastic!" I said, just to show Fred I was already picking up on the technical jargon.

"By the way," he said, "you don't happen to know any reliable hit men, do you?"

"No, I don't," I replied. "Anyway, the hit-man concept has been worked to death on television. I'd scrap that idea if I were you."

Fred smiled thinly and drummed his fingers on the table. I could tell he was already calculating the Nielsen ratings on "The Camp Chef."

I was a little late getting to the studio on Monday. For some unknown reason, my brakes failed just as I was approaching the steep, winding stretch of highway between my home and the television studio. The mechanic at the garage said it looked as if my brake line had been sabotaged, but I told him that was ridiculous. Then, while I was hoofing back to the house to get my camper truck, some idiot in a big black sedan nearly ran over me—twice!—which was odd, since I was walking across a cow pasture at the time.

Anyway, I was late getting to the studio, and I guess Fred had just about given up on me, because he seemed more than a little astonished when I showed up carrying all my props.

"Boy," I told him by way of explanation, "you just can't hire competent help anymore."

"You're telling *me!*" Fred interrupted.

"Yeah," I went on, "I had this guy do some repair work on my car last week, and the incompetent fool accidentally filed my brake line nearly in half. Lucky I wasn't killed."

"Hmmmmmmm," Fred said. "What's all that junk you got in the gunnysack there, anyway?"

"These are the props for my show, 'The Camp Chef.' "

Fred shook his head. "Gee, I'm really sorry, but I forgot that we were going to do a pilot of your show today. All the studios are being used."

"That's all right, Fred, ol' buddy," I said. "Think nothing of it. Danged if it doesn't remind me of that time you were supposed to be on a three-day fishing trip with me but . . ."

Fred picked up a phone. "Clear Studio Five," he snarled. "We need it for a show on camp cookery. . . . That's right—*camp cookery!* Are you deaf or something!"

Just as we were stepping into the studio, a concrete block dropped from the darkness above us and crashed at my feet. It was a close call, and I must say I've never seen Fred more upset. Glaring up into the shadows, he screamed, "Not *here*, you meathead, not *here!*" I could tell this wasn't one of Fred's better days either.

Knowing that time is money in the television business, I immediately dragged my sack of props out to a lighted platform in front of the cameras and started to get everything arranged. I had studied Julia Child's technique for many years and consequently was quite familiar with the format, as they say, of cooking shows.

I quickly organized my cooking ingredients, utensils, and props, using as a table a piece of television equipment that didn't seem to be in use at the moment. My friend Retch Sweeney showed up about then, dragging several dried-up Christmas trees and a red-faced receptionist.

"You can't haul that junk in here," the receptionist whined.

"Where do ya want these trees, Pat?" Retch asked.

"Arrange them around the set," I said. "It's all right, Miss," I told the receptionist. "He's with me."

"Who are you?" she asked.

"I'm with Fred," I explained.

"Gee, I dunno," she said. "I better call the guard."

"Ha! Ha!" I laughed. "That reminds me of a funny story. One time Fred was supposed to be on a three-day fishing trip with me . . ."

"Oh, no!" she responded. "I remember you now! Yeah, come to think of it, Fred did tell me about your idea for a show."

"I bet he said to take good care of me, too, didn't he?"

"Gosh, I dunno. I thought he said he had arranged for somebody else to take care of you."

"Good ol' Fred," I said. "It would be hard to find a more considerate guy."

Even though dried out, Retch's trees gave a nice woodsy effect to the set.

Two cameramen came into the studio, yawning and scratching themselves, and started pushing the television cameras into position. I could see Fred in the director's booth arguing with a couple of technicians who kept shaking their heads. Finally Fred's voice came over a speaker: "You ready?"

"Yes," I said. "But there are only two cameramen here. I thought we'd use at least three cameras."

"Julia Child uses only two cameras," Fred said.

"In that case," I said, "I'm ready."

"Is your friend going to be on the set with you?" Fred asked. "We wouldn't want viewers confusing your show with 'The Incredible Hulk.'"

"Yeah, I'll need his assistance," I said.

"What'd he say?" Retch said.

"Nothing," I said.

"Okay, you're on!" Fred said.

I had no sooner gone into my introductory remarks than I detected a technical difficulty. The red light that indicates a television camera is on wasn't functioning on either camera. As soon as I had called Fred's attention to the problem, he corrected it, and I got my show under way again.

Looking back, I wish I hadn't tried quite so many complicated dishes on my first show. Otherwise, I don't think matters would have gotten out of hand.

I opened with my Whatcha-Got Hunters' Stew. As I explained, this stew derives its name from the situation of a group of hungry hunters meeting at night at the end of a mountain road and deciding to cook up a hearty meal before undertaking the long drive home.

"What we gonna cook?" one hunter will ask.

"How about a stew?" another hunter will say.

"What we gonna put in the stew?" still another hunter will inquire.

Then the hunter who suggested the stew will say, "Well, whatcha got?"

At that point the hunters will start rummaging around in their lunch sacks and food boxes and game pockets and trunks of their cars, tossing whatever they find into the stew pot. No one knows exactly what the ingredients of Whatcha-Got Hunters' Stew are because there is a firm rule against anyone shining a light onto it. I am told that once a hunter broke this rule and as a result had to be placed under a doctor's care for treatment of hypergagging.

Of course, I couldn't concoct an authentic Whatcha-Got Hunters' Stew in the television studio, but I came fairly close, or so I judged from the fact that when one of the cameramen zoomed in for a close-up shot of it he dropped to the floor, curled up in the prenatal position, and jammed a thumb in his mouth.

"One thing about camp cooking," my commentary went, "you can't be too picky about a few gnats, mosquitoes, ants, or even an occasional deerfly that happens to land in your stew. Since there are no live insects flying about the studio, ha, ha, I have to make do with some dried ones my kids gathered up for me in the garage. They are by no means as good as fresh insects but . . ."

At this point I was distracted by the sound of running footsteps headed for a restroom at the far end of the studio. I wondered in passing if television cameras can be operated by remote control, since cameramen seem to be such a temperamental lot. Still, there was nothing to do but continue with the show.

My Chipped Beef on a Shingle was a real smasheroo, judging from its impact on the individuals in the control booth.

My one moment of embarrassment came when I started to prepare Creek Mussels in Marshmallow Sauce and discovered that the piece of equipment on which I had placed the ingredients had heated up and the marshmallows had melted and dribbled down inside the thing. I was shocked, of course. You know how much marshmallows cost these days?

I had counted on Retch's assistance in the show, but early on a rather distinguished-looking lunatic in a pinstripe suit tried to rush onto the set. The guy probably would have ruined the whole show if Retch hadn't been able to get a half-nelson on him and wrestle him to the floor. There are some people who will do just about anything for a chance to clown around in front of a TV camera.

My most spectacular dish was the Flaming Bacon. It also provided me with the opportunity to demonstrate the proper procedure for extinguishing a small forest fire. I explained to the viewing audience that a shovel should always be carried for the purpose of smothering forest fires since one can't always expect to find the jacket of a pinstripe suit out in the woods.

Just as I was finishing up "The Camp Chef," my closing comments were practically drowned out by the sounds of sirens. As I told Retch while we were slipping out a back exit, you'd think television executives would wise up. Viewers are tired of all the violence on crime shows.

Several days later I happened to stumble across Fred as he was crawling under the front of my car with a hacksaw.

"Any idea when 'The Camp Chef' might be aired?" I asked him.

"Hoo hooo heeee haa hooo," he replied.

I could tell ol' Fred had been under a lot of strain

lately. That television business can really take it out of a person.

"Listen," I told him, "what you need is a good three-day fishing trip with me. Some of my camp cooking will straighten you out in nothing flat."

Oh, I tell you, the look of gratitude Fred gave me would have wrenched your heart!

The Heartbreak
of Astigmatism

☞ ☞ ☞When I was about fourteen the world turned fuzzy. I wasn't particularly concerned with the phenomenon at first, attributing it to the lateness of spring that year or possibly the Communists. It was a history teacher, Mrs. Axelrod, who finally diagnosed my affliction. She asked me to step to the front of the room and, with a long wooden pointer, indicate on the wall map the region occupied by Gaul. Not knowing Gaul from my left elbow, I decided to take a random stab at it anyway, since I figured the whole world, including the map, had become so blurred that no one would know the difference anyway. Also, my walk to the front of the classroom would give me an opportunity to display the attitude of debonair nonchalance I had been attempting to perfect. Arriving at the front of the room, I directed the pointer to a likely little fuzzy blotch. This drew a good laugh from the other kids, which I immediately capitalized on by doing a Gene Kelly soft-shoe routine on the way back to my desk.

"All right, Fred Astaire!" the teacher snarled. "I

want to see you dance yourself right back into this classroom immediately after school tonight!"

I was miffed. How could anyone mistake my Gene Kelly for a Fred Astaire? On the other hand, ever since the world had turned fuzzy, I myself was having trouble distinguishing the two of them even when they were forty feet high on the showhouse screen. Perhaps, I told myself, her *faux pas* was excusable.

I was hoping that by the time school was out, Mrs. Axelrod's rage would have withered a bit, but I found it still in full bloom. There was a rumor going around that the history teacher could kill flies in mid-air with her sarcasm, but I doubted there was any truth to it. Sure, a few flies may have been stunned but certainly not killed.

"Ah!" Mrs. Axelrod exclaimed as I entered the classroom. "The master of comic impersonations arrives!"

"Uh, I'm really sorry about that little dance," I apologized. "It was Gene Kelly, by the way."

"Oh, I should have known!" she replied. "I do hope you will forgive me!"

I flicked a stunned fly off my shoulder. "No problem," I said. "Anybody can make a mistake."

"Has anyone ever told you how obtuse you are?" she asked.

"No," I said, blushing, "but thank you very much. You're not so bad yourself, no matter what the kids say."

"Indeed!" she said, attempting to conceal her pleasure under a veil of wrath. "Well, now that the exchange of compliments is over, we are still left with the problem of Gaul."

"Actually," I confessed, "I didn't have the foggiest notion of where Gaul was, so I just took a flying guess. What country did I get?"

"Oh, you didn't get a country," she said with what I

thought I detected as a softening of tone. "You are apparently unaware that I also teach hygiene in this classroom. What you got was the bladder on an anatomical diagram of the human body!"

"Gee," I said, stunned. "It's a good thing you didn't ask me to point out Rome. We all would have been embarrassed."

"No doubt," she replied. "Are you by any chance having some trouble seeing clearly?"

"Not at all," I replied, gallantly scooping her folded coat up off her desk and helping her on with it. "Why do you ask?"

"Just a woman's intuition," she replied. "And little observations, such as the way you just now helped me on with the American flag."

"I did?" I said. "Well, to tell the truth, you look pretty good in stripes. Besides, it's so blurred that nobody would even guess it's a flag. Surely, you've noticed how fuzzy the world has become lately. I think it's the Communists doing it."

"My dear young man," she said. "I have some news for you. The world has not become fuzzy. Only *you* have become fuzzy. *You need glasses!*"

I was stunned. People had said a lot of bad things to me in my day, but this was the worst. I hadn't expected even Mrs. Axelrod to stoop this low, mean as she was. Didn't she know that I was famous for my vision, that my friends all called me Hawkeye. My gosh! Glasses! Spectacles! What was she saying? My mind reeled; my body beaded with sweat. If what Mrs. Axelrod said was true, that the world was not blurred, then my whole career was finished. No professional big-game guide could wear glasses! Jeez, could you imagine what one of my clients would think if I told him, "All right, we know the rhino's wounded and is going to charge as soon as we go in after him. But don't worry, I'm backing you up with my double-barreled elephant rifle. Before we start in, though, let me wipe the dust off my spectacles because I want to be able to see him real good."

And my squint! All the years I'd been practicing my squint, and now it was down the drain. A squint just doesn't look right behind a pair of glasses.

I tried to swear Mrs. Axelrod to secrecy, but she would have none of it. You probably have never met a person as mean as Mrs. Axelrod, so you may find it hard to believe the next thing she did. She called my parents and told them I needed glasses.

My folks wasted no time in hauling me down to an eye doctor to get me outfitted with spectacles. I did not go easily. My rage was such that it even worried the doctor. At one point he said to my mother, "Would you check his ropes again please? I think he's starting to work them loose."

Well, as I always said, you can buy a kid spectacles, but you can't make him wear them. I wore them only when my folks were around, and the rest of the time I carried them stuffed in my pocket where they stood a good chance of being broken. Then one day I was out in our pasture target practicing with my .22 rifle. After I had put ten successive shots right in the bull's-eye, the thought occurred to me that maybe if I wore my glasses I could hit a smaller bull's-eye, one less than three feet across. First, I made sure that no one was in the vicinity, a precaution I accomplished by shouting out "Hello! Anybody around!" Then I slipped the glasses out of my pocket and put them on.

The world snapped into focus. I could see mountains, trees, barns! I could see flowers and blades of grass and even ants crawling on the blades of grass. I hadn't seen ants in a year. I thought they had become extinct. It was . . . fantastic!

So after that whenever I went out into the great outdoors I wore my glasses, but only when alone. The real problem came when I was with the other guys. When we would go fishing, for example, I always had to pretend that I was clowning around.

"Hey, look at ol' Pat, he keeps casting his fly across the crick onto the sandbar! Ho, ho! That ol' Pat, he'll do anything for a laugh!" So then I'd have to go along with the gag and put on my hyena grin and wear my hat upside down. It was a real pain.

One day when my friend Peewee Thompson and I were sitting in my bedroom, I decided to sound him out on what he thought about people who wore glasses.

"Say, Peewee," I said. "You know that kid in the school band, Marvin Phelps, the one with the glasses, what do you think about the way he looks? He's a pretty good-looking kid, don't you think?"

Peewee gave me a nervous, sidelong glance. "I got to go home," he said.

"No, you idiot, what I mean is, do you think wearing glasses makes him look, uh, kinda funny?"

"Heck no. He's always worn glasses. He would look funny if he didn't wear them. He wouldn't even look like Four-Eyes Phelps if he didn't wear glasses. Why do you ask?"

"No reason," I said. "Just forget it."

"I'll tell you though," Peewee went on. "I sure wouldn't want ol' Four-Eyes Phelps backin' me up if I was goin' into the bush after a wounded rhino."

"I SAID FORGET IT!"

My greatest dread was that Rancid Crabtree would find out about my spectacles. If there was one thing

Rancid respected in another outdoorsman, it was keen vision. His own eyesight was superb. He was always the first to spot deer on a hunting trip. Pointing to a line of dots moving through the snow on the side of a mountain, he would say simply, "Deer." Then, while the rest of the hunters were straining to make out the dots, Rancid would say, "Mulies." The other hunters would stare at each other in disbelief. "Looks like they's all does, though. No, by gosh, one of 'em's a little spike buck!"

Rancid was the last person in the world I wanted to find out that I wore glasses. He wouldn't have any use for me after that.

One day we were in Rancid's old pickup truck on our way out to do some fishing, and, in his usual fashion, the old woodsman was pointing out distant sights to me. "Look up thar on thet side hill! Huncklebarries! Two or three of the little buggers are startin' to tarn color. Won't be long till they's ripe!"

I stared morosely off in the general direction he was pointing and tried to penetrate the green blur. "Yup. They sure do look like they're ripening up."

"Say, look at the size of them deer tracks crossin' the road. The deer thet made them was a biggun. Come fall, you 'n' me, we's gonna come up hyar an' look fer him, Ah kin tell you thet!"

"Yup," I said.

"What's wrong with you?" Rancid said. "You sound about as happy as a badger in a bees' nest."

"Nothin'," I said.

It was shortly after we got started fishing that Rancid began acting peculiar. Right at first he suggested that I fish upstream and he fish downstream.

"That's no fun," I told him. "We always fish together."

"Yeh," he said sheepishly. "Oh, all right, c'mon!"

The only good thing about my impaired vision was

that I could see perfectly up to a range of two feet. I therefore had no difficulty tying on the tiniest flies in my book, which I instantly deduced were the only flies likely to take trout in that particular time and place.

In the next twenty minutes or so I caught half a dozen fish. Rancid didn't get a single bite. "How come you don't change over to one of these little white flies?" I kept asking him. "That's what they're taking."

"Shoot," Rancid said. "Ah got this big ol' Grasshopper already tied on. Ah'll fish it."

Now this was totally unlike Rancid. I knew he didn't care all that much for work, but changing a fly didn't require any great effort. Usually he would have tried a dozen different flies by the time we got our feet wet. Then a whooper cutthroat (one that causes you to whoop, as distinguished from a mere whopper) smashed into my white fly. It took me a couple of minutes to land the fish.

"Wow, it's a beaut!" I whooped, thrashing my way across the creek to show Rancid the fish. When I was close enough, within two feet of him, I could see that his little eyes were bugged out in their comical fashion, as was their habit whenever he got excited.

"Gol-dang, thet's a purty fish!" he said, almost trembling. Instantly, he became stern. "You got any more of them itty-bitty white flies? All I brung with me was these big ones."

"Sure," I said, and handed him a couple.

Then Rancid did a remarkable thing. He reached into his pants pocket and hauled out a pair of spectacles, the kind you buy off the counter in a variety store. He put the glasses on, snipped the big fly off his tippet, and tied on the tiny one. Then he leveled a fierce glare at me.

"Wipe thet smirk off yer face," he snarled. "If you so much as open yer yap, I'll . . ."

I stepped back and thrust my hand into my pants pocket, took out my own glasses, and put them on. The stubby whiskers on Rancid's face snapped into focus. They quivered for a moment, then rippled out into the great crescent-shaped waves of his grin.

Neither one of us in all the years after that moment ever said a word about glasses. There was no need.

If a man like Rancid could wear glasses, I figured there couldn't be any shame in my wearing them. So the very next time I went out fishing with the guys, I showed up with my glasses on. The guys were all lifelong friends of mine, fellows I'd suffered with on a hundred camping trips. We had shared each other's triumphs and defeats, happiness and sorrows, the sweet and the bitter. When they saw me for the first time wearing my glasses, I learned once and for all the true meaning of friendship. It is that you don't thrash your friends within an inch of their lives if they laugh themselves silly when you show up wearing spectacles.

"What the heck," Peewee said later, after he had stopped pounding his thighs and had wiped away the tears of his mirth. "We ain't likely to run into a wounded rhino in this part of the country anyway."

Sneed

☞ ☞ ☞ **B**ack in the shadows of time when I was a youngster, a man by the name of Darcy Sneed lived in our county. I don't think I ever heard anyone say a kind word for Sneed, and I'm sure nobody ever heard me say one. He was always showing up without notice when and where he wasn't wanted and causing folks grief. Several times he scared the daylights out of me, catching me alone out in the woods, but except for one time I always managed to escape. As far as I know, Sneed never smiled nor cracked a joke. He was cold and hard and tight-lipped and generally unlikable. Besides that, he was the game warden.

Now, the truth is I seldom broke the game laws, not because I had any love for rules and regulations but because it seemed unsporting. Once, though, my friend Retch and I did sneak down to the creek early one morning three days before the opening of fishing season. We hid in some deep brush along the bank and at the first hint of dawn cast our salmon eggs out toward a logjam, where we knew some cutthroat had to be waiting. But I was so filled with dread and guilt that I couldn't enjoy fishing, and I knew that if I caught anything it would just compound the existing dread and guilt. Retch, on the other hand, didn't seem burdened by any doubts and was intently working his line so the eggs would drift under the logs. Somehow, I had to impress upon him that what we were doing was wrong. I searched for the right words, the kind of words that would convey to him the deep moral and ethical implications of our action. Then I thought of them.

"Sneed's comin'!" I hissed at him.

Retch instantly grasped the deep moral and ethical implications and reeled in his line so fast only its being wet saved it from instant combustion. We stashed our rods under a log and beat it out of there, hurrying down the creek trail. Retch was in front. As he rounded a bend, he turned his head slightly and said out of the corner of his mouth, "Good thing you seen him comin'."

"Who?" I said, already having forgotten the lie.

"Sneed," he said.

And there was Sneed, striding purposefully toward us down the trail.

"Howdy, Mr. Sneed," we said politely.

Sneed didn't say anything for a moment. He just let his glare rove over our quaking carcasses. The seconds passed, ticked off by the sound of our dripping sweat.

"What you boys doin' here?" he demanded finally.

We answered simultaneously: "Lookin' for a cow." "Pullin' up thistles."

Sneed didn't smile at these contradictory explanations. He was not a fun-loving man.

"I'm going to ask you boys one more time, what you *doin'* here?"

By now I had forgotten who had told him what, so I nudged Retch to go ahead and answer, he being the more experienced and polished liar. But Sneed's glare had penetrated Retch's brain and tangled his speech mechanism.

"We was just pullin' up cows," he said.

Sneed replied with another long silence. Then he said, "Let me see if I've got this straight. You two were down here on the crick at five in the morning pullin' up cows, is that correct?"

Right then I figured Sneed was going to throw us in jail, and for what? Not being able to think of a decent lie when we had to.

Sneed reached out and thumped a bony finger on Retch's chest. "I know and you know that you boys were down here fishin', gettin' a jump on the season. I'd arrest you both, but I didn't catch you at it. Next time I will."

Sneed knew how to put fear into a person. If he didn't manage to keep people from breaking the game laws, he at least kept them from enjoying it. He never forgot me after that morning on the creek, having filed me away in his memory bank as a person who took the game laws lightly and who bore watching.

Sneed was not one of those game wardens who come semi-attached to the seat of a pickup truck; he knew how to walk and was infamous for suddenly materializing in remote and roadless places. There was a friend of our family who was widely regarded as the best trapper in our part of the state. During the winter he would snowshoe far back into the high country to work his trap line. "It's real nice to be up there alone in the winter," he told me once. "There's just you and the silence and the snow and Sneed."

Numerous theories were set forth regarding the game warden. One was that there were actually three Sneeds. This was based on multiple sightings of Sneed in different parts of the county at the same time. Men would shake their heads and say, "There's something unnatural about Sneed."

One time I was sitting in the kitchen of a chronic poacher, and he told me how he had outsmarted Sneed once.

"I strapped my heels down on my snowshoes and walked backwards with the deer over my shoulder. Funniest thing you ever seen. I hid in some trees at the top of a rise to watch, and pretty soon Sneed hits my trail. He looks one way and t'other, and then he takes off followin' my tracks toward where I been." The poacher nearly split his sides laughing at the memory of his little trick.

His wife glared at him. "Now, Otis, you tell the boy the rest of the story, you hear?"

Otis sobered up and reluctantly finished the tale. "Well, when I got the deer back to my truck and started scrapin' the frost off the winders, there's ol' Sneed sittin' inside, smokin' a cigarette calm as you please."

"Cost us a hunnert dollars!" the wife snarled. "Ain't no deer worth no hunnert dollars!"

"Durn that Sneed," the poacher muttered, glowering into the coffee grounds at the bottom of his cup.

Another time, three men poached a deer close to the bottom of a rocky gorge and waited until after dark to sneak it up to their car parked on a road a half-mile up the mountain. The going was rough, and as they fought their way upwards over logs and rocks and through brush, one of the poachers plopped down on the ground for a rest and gasped, "Man, this is hard! It's a good thing there's four of us to drag this here deer, 'cause otherwise I don't think we'd make it."

One of the other poachers looked around, counting heads in the darkness. "Ain't *s'posed* to be but three of us draggin' this deer," he said nervously.

"Ain't s'posed to be nobody draggin' it!" Sneed said.

Over the years, I heard dozens of such tales about Sneed, some true, some imaginary, but their net effect was to leave me with the impression that the game warden was possessed of powers not generally found among the psychic accessories of ordinary human beings. I never went afield with rod or gun that I didn't feel Sneed's presence. One of my great fears was that I would sometime lose count and catch one fish over my limit, and Sneed would nab me. Then I'd be fined a hundred dollars and since neither my family nor I had ever seen a hundred dollars altogether at the same time, I would have to go to jail. Well, I wouldn't be able to stand being in jail, so I'd have to break out and steal a car and escape in a hail of gunfire. After that I'd probably kill a bank guard and be fatally wounded myself. And while I was sprawled on a sidewalk breathing my last, a reporter would come up to me and ask, "What made you do it, son?" And I'd tell him: "I caught one fish over my limit." It was easy to see how it all would work out, so anytime I got anywhere near my limit I practically wore my fish out counting them. It was a heavy burden for a kid, especially for one who didn't have any better grasp of mathematics than I did.

In the light of this background, it will be clear that my decision to fish the forbidden waters of the creek that fed the town reservoir was not arrived at casually. Despite all my fears and misgivings, I was simply over-powered by the logic that led me to the conclusion that that creek had to be crammed full of giant eastern brook. I should mention here that water pollution as such was unknown at the time. It was simply referred to then as "dumpin' stuff in the cricks." A few enlightened and farsighted individuals would occasionally speak out in the cause of pure water. "I wish folks would stop dumpin' stuff in the cricks," they would say, thereby branding themselves forever after as wild-eyed eccentrics. The only creek that was sacrosanct was that of the town reservoir, the townspeople being in unanimous agreement that they didn't want anyone dumping stuff in their drinking water. My reasoning, however, was this: (1) a dry fly wouldn't dirty the water; (2) I would be providing a civic service by removing trout that certainly had to be dirtying it; and finally (3) my family got its water out of a well. There was only one flaw in this logic: Sneed.

My plan of attack seemed foolproof, however. I would sneak into the reservoir under cover of predawn darkness, follow the creek up into the dense woods that would provide me cover through the day, then do my fishing and return after nightfall. I would carry a few carefully selected flies, a length of leader, and some line, and cut myself a willow pole when I reached the spot where I wanted to start fishing. The night before I launched my assault on Reservoir Creek, I went to bed early, chuckling evilly over the boldness of the plan, beautiful even in its very simplicity. Ol' Sneed, as I told myself, had finally met his match.

Thus it was that I found myself returning home late the following evening with a fine catch of brook trout. The fishing had been just as fantastic as I had known it would be. Nevertheless, I was filled with fear and remorse and a dark sense of foreboding about what the future held for me. Part of the reason for these feelings was that I knew I had deliberately and maliciously broken the law, discovering too late that I possessed neither the temperament nor the taste for crime. The rest of the reason was that I was sitting alongside of Sneed in the front seat of his dusty old Dodge sedan.

As I had come sneaking up over the edge of a logging road on my way out of the reservoir basin, there was Sneed, sitting in his car with the lights off. True to his fashion, he didn't say a word. He just leaned over, pushed open the door on the passenger side, and motioned for me to get in. For an instant I thought of running, but then decided against it. You just can't move all that fast when you're paralyzed.

While Sneed drove along in his usual silence, I tried to appeal to his sympathy, even though from all the reports I'd heard no one had ever detected a smidgen of it in him.

"Look, Mr. Sneed," I said, "maybe it don't matter none to you, sending a kid to jail, but don't you care nothin' about that poor bank guard? What's his little children gonna do without him?"

"What bank guard?" Sneed said.

Before I could explain, a voice from the back seat said, "Ain't no use pleadin' with him, boy. When he was born, they heated him white hot and tempered him in oil, and he's been hard ever since."

This dismal report had issued from a tall, lean young man sprawled across the back seat and chewing on a match. He was covered with dirt and bits of grass and brush, apparently acquired in an attempt to escape from Sneed.

"What did he get you for?" I asked my fellow criminal, feeling an instant kinship with him.

"Nothin' a-tall. I was just up there on the mountain tryin' out my new jacklight. It must have riled up this ol' buck deer, 'cause first thing I know he come chargin' at me out of the brush. I had to shoot him to save my life!"

"Shut up, LeRoy," Sneed said. "You can tell it all to the judge."

About that time we drove up in front of my house. Sneed stopped the car and motioned for me to get out.

"You mean you ain't arresting me?" I said.

"What for?" Sneed said. "It ain't my responsibility to keep folks from fishin' that reservoir; it's the Water Department's. They own the water, and they own the fish in it. Besides, I get my drinkin' water from a well."

The game warden went on to tell me, in his tone of cold certainty, that he would turn me over to the Water Department for appropriate punishment if he ever caught me within a mile of the reservoir again. I nodded solemnly, even though inside I was chuckling silently to myself. Ol' Sneed did have a soft spot after all, and I, with my boyish charm, had touched it. No doubt I had reminded him of his own son or perhaps even of himself as a boy. Even before the sound of Sneed's old Dodge had faded off in the distance, my resolve to retire from a life of crime had vanished and I was already plotting my next raid on the reservoir. Even if he did catch me, I knew the game warden wouldn't have the heart to turn me in to the Water Department.

What changed my mind was an item my grandmother read in the newspaper the following week.

"I see by the paper where a fellow by the name of LeRoy Sneed was fined a hundred dollars for poaching deer," she said. "When are folks ever gonna learn to obey the law?"

One folk learned right then, and I'm happy to report that I've never intentionally violated so much as a single game regulation since. Oh, I've been tempted several times, but even though Sneed has been dead for fifteen years now, you just never can tell about a man like that.

The Hunter's Dictionary

☞ ☞ ☞**M**any persons who have just started hunting mistakenly assume that they understand the specialized terminology and jargon of the sport. As a result, they spend years in a state of befuddlement, wondering at the perversity of fate and cursing the contrariness of experienced hunters.

The problem is that they simply don't grasp the true meaning of the terms, phrases, and casual utterances as used by the hunting fraternity. I have therefore compiled *The Hunter's Dictionary,* published below in its entirety. It will do nothing to improve the beginning hunter's skills but should go a long way toward preserving his mental health.

It has long seemed to me to be an affectation of the overeducated to insist that dictionaries be printed in alphabetical order. If during my years spent in first grade I had succeeded in learning the alphabet, I might now feel more kindly toward it. In fact, I am rather fond of that portion of it that runs up to the letter *G*; beyond that point my feeling is largely one of hostility. So much for the explanation of why this dictionary is presented in a random and, to my mind, more meaningful order.

One further note: For the purpose of conciseness, "beginning hunter" and "experienced hunter" are abbreviated "BH" and "EH," respectively.

Without further display of my mastery of lexicography, I herewith present *The Hunter's Dictionary.*

FIVE MINUTES—This refers to a period of time ranging from five minutes to eight hours, generally speaking, but has been known to run as long as five days. It is used in this way: "Wait here. I'll be back in five minutes." What happens is that the EH who makes the statement will step off into the brush to check for tracks or possibly for some other business. While there, he will catch sight of a deer fifty yards or so up the slope, but the deer's head will be behind a tree. The hunter crouches down and sneaks up to a little rise off to one side to get a better look and determine the sex of the deer. It turns out to be a nice buck, which is just stepping over the ridge of the hill. The hunter, still in his crouch, scurries silently up the hill, expecting an easy shot. Cresting the hill, he catches a glimpse of its tail as the deer rounds the bend of an old logging road. The hunter will be occupied with this pursuit for the next few hours. His companion, if he too is an EH, will wait no longer than it takes to consume half a sandwich and a cup of coffee. By then he knows that the "five minutes" is a period to be measured in hours, and he will immediately proceed with his own hunting. A BH, on the other hand, assuming that "five minutes" means five minutes, will remain rooted loyally to the waiting place until lichens begin to form on him. When the EH finally returns, the lichen-covered hunter will yell at him, "I thought you said you'd be back in five minutes!"

The EH, somewhat puzzled by this display of wrath, will glance at his watch and say, "Well, here I am, ain't I? I left at ten-thirty, and now it's only five-fifteen! If I was going to be gone longer than five minutes, I would've told you!"

HUNTING VEHICLE—The BH assumes that what is meant by this phrase is any vehicle used to transport persons on a hunting trip, preferably a four-wheel drive of some sort. What the EH means by a "hunting vehicle" is *any* vehicle so long as it isn't his. If a BH is along on the trip, it means the BH's vehicle specifically. It matters not that the EH owns an outfit capable of swimming rivers and climbing trees or that the BH owns a sports car. The EH will merely glance at the sports car and observe: "Nice little hunting rig you have here."

FUNNY NOISE—A sound the EH reports the engine of his vehicle to be making any time the subject arises as to whose rig should be used for the hunting trip.

IMPASSABLE ROAD—Any road that gives indications it might mar the paint job or muddy the hub caps, provided the vehicle under consideration belongs to the EH.

PRACTICALLY A FOUR-LANE HIGHWAY—Any terrain slightly less hazardous than a streambed at flood stage, provided the vehicle under consideration does not belong to the EH.

BUILT TO TAKE IT—Describes any hunting vehicle not the EH's.

OOOOOOOOOEEEEE-AH-AH-AH!—If there's one thing I hate, it's putting on cold, wet pants in the morning!

PNEUMONIA—What the EH claims to have whenever it's his turn to climb out of a warm sleeping bag and build the morning fire. Between spasms of hideous coughing, the EH may also request that someone say some kind words over his remains if he drops dead while returning from starting the fire.

MIRACULOUS RECOVERY—What the EH experiences as soon as he hears the morning fire crackling cheerily and smells coffee perking and bacon frying.

CAMP COOK—The guy who draws the short straw.

OVERDONE—Used by camp cooks to mean "burnt to a crisp."

BURNED—At some point the meal was totally engulfed by flames. The meal is still regarded as edible provided the hunting trip has been under way for at least three days.

RARE—The wood was too wet to start a cooking fire.

HASH—What all hunting-trip breakfasts appear to be. There is yellow hash, brown hash, gray hash, black hash, and green hash. Only a fool eats green hash.

STEW—Basically the same as green hash.

BLEEPING BLEEP-OF-A-BLEEP!—Phrase used by EH to announce he has just stepped out of a boat three feet short of the duck blind in the darkness of a cold December morning.

IMPOSSIBLE SHOT—What the EH has made anytime he downs game farther away than fifty feet.

FAIR SHOT—Any impossible shot made by someone other than the EH.

DID YOU FEEL THAT EARTH TREMOR JUST NOW?—Question asked by EH immediately after missing an easy shot.

A BIT—A lot.

SOME—All. As in, "I ate some of those little cheese-flavored crackers you had hidden in the bottom of your pack."

LEG CRAMP—What the EH insists is killing him and which requires that he get out of the hunting vehicle and "walk it out" on any occasion that a treacherous stretch of road appears up ahead.

TO MAKE A LONG STORY SHORT—The EH is about to

relate a story approximately the length of the history of mankind since the Creation.

I'M ABSOLUTELY CERTAIN THIS IS THE RIGHT TURN— There's one chance in ten this is the right turn.

IT AIN'T GONNA RAIN—Pitch tent on high ground and begin work immediately on a log raft.

AAAIIII!—The hash has become too hot for the camp cook's stirring finger.

BAFF MAST PIME IG BEAD FEAS MID MIFF PIFE!—That's the last time I try to eat peas in the dark with my hunting knife!

WHAT'S THAT? DID YOU HEAR SOMETHING PROWLING AROUND OUTSIDE THE TENT JUST NOW?—Questions hissed to arouse snoring tent partner and keep him awake for the rest of the night, listening.

DEER STAND—What the BH is placed on to keep him out of the way of the EH.

JAMMED RIFLE, DAMAGED GUNSIGHT, BLINDING HEADACHE, BAD KNEE, FOGGED SPECTACLES, ACUTE IRREGULARITY, SPONTANEOUS REGULARITY, and GREEN HASH—Any one or all of these are given as reasons the BH got a deer and the EH didn't.

CONSUMMATE SKILL—Why the EH got a deer and the BH didn't.

MEETING PLACE—An imaginary point in space that hunters are supposed to converge upon at a particular time. It is sometimes referred to as The Big Snag, The Old Apple Orchard, The Car, and Camp. The EH knows that such a place is merely a figment of the imagination and that the proposed meeting will never occur. It is hard for an EH to keep a straight face whenever a meeting place is spoken of.

A TRUE STORY—A collection of the most outrageous, preposterous, and unmitigated lies ever assembled.

DRESSED OUT AT 140 POUNDS—Dressed out at eighty pounds.

A RUNNING SHOT AT OVER 200 YARDS—I don't know how those powder burns got on its hide.

FLAT TRAJECTORY—Describes the movement of a hunter leaving his sleeping bag one hour after having eaten green hash for supper.

DID ANYONE THINK TO BRING—I left it sitting on my kitchen table.

MY CARDIOLOGIST—A mythical person casually referred to by the EH whenever it is suggested that he help haul a dead elk up the side of a steep mountain.

A HUNTING TIP—What the EH pays his hunting guide to keep his mouth shut and not to regale the boys back at the camp with an amusing account of what happened.

LEAVE THE LANTERN ON; IT'LL ATTRACT THE INSECTS AND KEEP THEM OFF OF US—I have trouble getting to sleep without a night light.

I SCOUTED OUT A LOT OF REAL NICE COUNTRY ON THE OTHER SIDE OF THE MOUNTAIN—The EH was lost for most of the day.

DON'T WORRY—Worry.

WIND, SNOW, COLD; THIS IS THE MOST MISERABLE DAY I'VE SPENT IN MY LIFE—Had a great time.

NEXT TIME, KID, TRY NOT TO MAKE SO MUCH RACKET, TROMPING THROUGH THE BRUSH THE WAY YOU DO. BOY, I'VE NEVER SEEN SUCH A CASE OF BUCK FEVER AS THAT ONE OF YOURS! ALSO, YOU'VE GOT TO LEARN NOT TO SHOUT, "THERE'S A BUCK!" JUST AS I'M SETTIN' THE CROSS HAIRS ON HIM. HA! AND THOSE TRACKS YOU THOUGHT WERE FRESH? WHY, YOU COULD HAVE GATHERED THEM UP AND SOLD THEM TO A MUSEUM AS FOSSILS! GEEZ!—You did all right, kid.

Tenner
Shoes

☞ ☞ ☞ **"W**hy don't you throw out some of these shoes?" my wife shouted from inside the closet.

"Are you crazy, woman?" I replied. "I *need* all those shoes—my bowling shoes, my jogging shoes, my hiking shoes, my canoeing shoes, my sailing shoes, my black dress shoes, my brown dress shoes, my brown casual shoes, my black casual shoes, my white casual shoes, my moccasins, my hip boots, my waders, my canvas wading shoes, my hunting boots, my mountain-climbing boots, my down booties, my camp shoes, my sandals, my . . ."

"Stop! Stop!" my wife screamed. "I give up! You can keep them! What I wish, though, is that somebody would invent a pair of shoes that could be used for everything."

Well, as a matter of fact, somebody once did. I wore them every summer when I was a kid. The shoe's inventor, I believe, was a Mr. Tenner. At least that's what we called them—Tenner shoes.

Once a rich kid moved to our town and tried to tell us that the shoes we were wearing were not called Tenner shoes at all but tennis shoes. We'd never seen anyone as ignorant as that kid. He didn't even wear Tenner shoes, so we wondered why he thought he knew so much about them.

"You tryin' to tell us these shoes weren't invented by a Mr. Tenner?" Retch Sweeney said to the kid. "How come everybody calls them Tenner shoes, then?"

"Only illiterates call them Tenner shoes," the kid shot back. Naturally, that got us all riled up, and we started yelling at him and pushing him and trying to get him to fight one of us.

"Listen," Peewee Thompson said. "We're all just as normal as you are, except for maybe Birdy—he's a little weird."

"No, no!" the rich kid shouted. " 'Illiterate' means you don't know how to read and write." Well, as soon as we found out that we hadn't been insulted, everybody cooled down and started patting the kid on the back and telling him he was all right after all, and we hoped he wouldn't harbor any hard feelings against us because of a little misunderstanding.

"Just the same," Retch said, "I ain't never heard of anybody by the name of Tennis."

"I did once," I said. "I think his son was one of them English poets, but I doubt either one of them knew anything about shoes."

Tenner shoes were made out of black canvas and had rubber soles and little round patches over the part that covered your anklebones. They were ugly. Tenner designed them that way on purpose so girls wouldn't want to wear them.

You got your pair of Tenner shoes each spring about the time the snow began to recede from the lowlands. There was an interesting little ritual that went with the purchase of each year's Tenner shoes. My mother would take me down to Hobbs's dry goods store, where Mr. Hobbs himself waited on the shoe customers.

"Howdy," Mr. Hobbs would say. "By golly, I bet you brought that young colt in to get him shod." Mr. Hobbs and my mother would cackle at monotonous length over this witticism. Interestingly enough, when I was very young and first heard the little joke, I thought Hobbs had said, "to get him shot." My fright was such that I behaved myself for the better part of the day and wondered long afterwards in what manner my sentence had been commuted.

Hobbs's arsenal of wit seemed to consist of the single joke, and as soon as he had spent that round on his customers he seemed to revert immediately into his natural self, perhaps best described as peevish.

"Siddown and take off your shoes," he would order. The shoes he referred to were generally some kind of clodhopper boots well along into the first stage of oblivion, heels and tongue missing, soles flopping loose, seams gaping, the laces a Chinese puzzle of knots and frayed ends. As I peeled off the boots, Mr. Hobbs and my mother would both leap back and gasp.

"I thought I told you to wash your feet!" my mother would screech, more for Mr. Hobbs's benefit than my own. "I've never seen the likes of it."

Mr. Hobbs would mutter under his breath about having seen the likes of it, something about hygiene films in Navy boot camp.

"How's that?" my mother would say.

"Nothing," Mr. Hobbs would snort. "Nothing."

He would then lock one of my feet in a measuring device, all the while doing his impression of a person removing a long-dead rat from a trap. The measurement taken, Hobbs would get up and return shortly with a box of Tenner shoes, which he would drop in my lap and order me to try on.

Even to this day I recall with ecstasy the pure sensual delight of slipping my feet into a brand-new pair of Tenner shoes, my ol' toes up in the forward part wiggling around, checking out their new quarters, the ankles swelling boastfully under the protective cushions of the rubber patches as the fat clean laces snugged tight the embrace of canvas and rubber. After a winter of wearing the clodhopper boots, I felt like I was strapping on a pair of wings.

"I better go try them out," I would say.

"Stay in the store!" Mr. Hobbs would shout. "Don't take them out of the store!"

But it would be too late. I would be out on the sidewalk, and the Tenner shoes would be carrying me in free soaring flight around the block. The test completed, I would brake to a screeching stop and reenter the store.

"Maybe just a half-size larger," I would tell Mr. Hobbs. "Gosh, I don't know why anyone would let their dog run loose on the sidewalk, but I washed these Tenner shoes off good as new in a mud puddle and as soon as they dry . . ."

"Dog?" Mr. Hobbs would say. *"Dog!* Nothing doing! Those are your size! That'll be ninety-eight cents, Missus."

"Ninety-eight cents!" my mother would say. "My land, I don't know what folks are going to do if prices keep going up the way they are."

"Terrible," Mr. Hobbs would mutter. "Don't know these young whelps are worth it anyways." He always sounded as if he meant it, too.

To my mind, the Tenner was the ultimate shoe. You could use it for running and hiking and jumping, for playing football and basketball, hunting and fishing, mountain climbing, rafting, spelunking, swimming, bicycling, horseback riding, cowback riding, pigback riding. Whatever the activity, the Tenner shoe adapted itself to the task in noble and admirable fashion.

The one area in which the Tenner shoe may have fallen a bit short was as a dress-up shoe. Suppose, for example, that you had to go to some social event where all the youngsters were dressed up in their best clothes. You showed up wearing your good pair of pants, your good shirt, your good socks, and your Tenner shoes, which by now may have been showing the strain of hunting, fishing, pigback riding, etc. Now, as soon as you got within hearing distance of some of the other mothers at the affair, your mother would look down at your feet, conjure up an expression of absolute horror, and say, "I thought I told you to wear *your brown oxfords!* My land, you'll mortify me to death! Just look at those filthy old Tenner shoes."

Now of course all of the other mothers would look at your mother and smile and shake their heads in an understanding way as if to say, "What can you expect of little boys?" What was truly shrewd about this charade was your mother's use of the phrase "your brown oxfords." This not only implied that you *had* brown oxfords but also black ones and possibly white ones. Maybe one of the reasons the ruse worked so well was that most of the other guys had protruding from the cuffs of their good pairs of pants the unmistakable rubber noses of Tenner shoes. If there was a poor kid present at one of these social functions, by the way, his mother would look down at his feet and say, "Land sakes, Henry, didn't I tell you to wear shoes!" Of course, all of us guys knew that Henry didn't have any shoes. Otherwise, why would he paint his feet to look as if he were wearing Tenners? It made you kind of sad if you thought about it.

The great thing about Tenners was their almost unlimited versatility. They were great for wearing inside a sleeping bag, for example. Nowadays, of course, there are little down booties especially designed for wearing inside of sleeping bags. The one problem with these booties is that they really aren't designed for outside wear, and if you have to get up in the night for any reason, they're not much good for wandering around over rough ground in the dark. Of course, when you're camping out as a kid, there is only one thing that can make you get up in the middle of the night, and that is the necessity of running for your life. And if ever there was a shoe designed for running for your life, it was the Tenner. Many was the dark night that a troop of us young campers made our way home, trailing in our wake the distinct odor of smoldering Tenners.

Tenners made great fishing waders. Mr. Tenner, who must have been an absolute genius, had designed them without any insulation so that when you waded out into an icy spring stream it took only a few minutes for your feet to turn numb. From then on you could fish in complete comfort. The numbness also prevented you from feeling any pain when your Tenners slithered into narrow and odd-shaped openings between slippery rocks. You could continue fishing in blissful comfort up above while down below the rocks committed various acts of depravity on your feet, rearranging the bones in imaginative ways, doing trick shuffles with your toes, and playing football with your ankles. We would often return from a fishing trip with an affliction known technically as cauliflower feet. Fortunately, we had the good sense never to remove our Tenners until they had dried, thereby preserving our feet in the shape, if not exactly of feet, at least of Tenners. Indeed, I was often afraid to remove my Tenners after a fishing trip for fear of what I might find inside them. I have always had a weak stomach.

There was considerable controversy among us about how often Tenners should be taken off. The conservatives argued for once a week, the liberals for three or four times a summer, and the radicals for never, preferring to allow decay and disintegration to take their natural course. Although I was one of the conservatives, I shared the radicals' curiosity over whether, when their Tenners finally self-destructed, there would be any feet left inside.

I frequently shared space in small tents with Tenner radicals, and the idea occurred to me more than once to take a caged canary in with me so that its sudden demise could warn me when the gas escaping from the radicals' Tenners had reached a lethal level. To my knowledge, there were never any human fatalities from this cause, although large numbers of flying and crawling insects in the tent died mysteriously.

There were many other theories concerning the proper use of Tenner shoes. These theories were passed on from the older fellows to the younger ones and were usually taken at face value. One of these theories was passed on to me by my cousin Buck, several years my senior, who told me that little slits should be cut in the canvas of new Tenner shoes so that in an emergency you could thrust some of your toes out through the slits and get better traction. This seemed to me to be a good idea, even though I could never bring myself to cut a brand-new pair of Tenners. It was just as well. In fact, I'll never forget the day I saw this theory put to the test.

Buck had taken me on a little hiking trip in the

mountains for the purpose of instructing me in wood-craft. He was one of those people who loved to teach but can never be bothered learning anything. What Buck taught me was any odd thought that happened to pop into his head, and some of the thoughts were pretty odd. He taught me, for example, that woodpeckers were tapping out code on the trunks of dead trees, warning other woodpeckers of our approach. He even let me in on the secret that he had cracked this code and knew what they were saying. Sometimes, he said, the wood-peckers even made jokes in code, and Buck had to laugh when he heard them.

"What did that one say?" I would ask Buck when he laughed.

"Oh, you're too little for me to repeat a joke like that to," he would say. "But I can tell you this—them woodpeckers is pretty funny birds!"

It turned out that Buck's theory about slitting Tenners to stick your toes out of was on a par with his knowledge of ornithology. After what happened that day on the mountain, I never again had any use for Buck's teachings. What happened was this: We were walking along single file, with Buck, of course, in the lead, reciting all sorts of incredible nature lore to me. The weather was chilly and the earth on the mountain frozen hard, with patches of snow still lingering here and there. As we were making our way down the unexplored back side of the mountain, we came to a huge slab of rock approximately fifty feet square and slanting down to a drop-off. The surface of the rock was smooth and covered with frost. Buck started walking straight across the rock. I stopped.

"Whatcha stop for?" Buck asked, turning around about halfway across the slab. "Tenner shoes don't slide on rock. The little suction cups on the soles, they grab right onto the . . ."

Buck was sliding.

"Well, this frost makes it a little slick," he said. "I better . . ."

By now Buck was *really* sliding. He gave up all efforts at further conversation and devoted his full attention to scrambling back up the rock. The problem was that no matter how fast and furious Buck's scramble was, his downward rate of slide seemed to be greater by about an inch per second. I had no idea how much of a drop awaited him at the brink of the slab—a hundred feet, half a mile? I remembered all the mountain-climbing movies I'd ever seen where a climber loses his grip and plummets downward until he is just a tiny, noisy speck hurtling toward the patchwork farmlands below. From the look on his face, I knew Buck was remembering the same movies. Then I noticed that Buck had forgotten to stick his toes out through the slits in his Tenners.

"Stick out your toes, Buck," I screamed at him. "Stick out your toes!"

Buck's toes suddenly emerged from the slits like little pink landing gear, and I have to admit that he did some marvelous things with his toes—in fact, just about everything it is possible to do with toes and not get arrested. But nothing worked.

Buck shot backward right off over the edge of the cliff. His drop was accompanied by a long, horrible, slowly diminishing scream.

I was a bit puzzled by the scream, since Buck was standing there on a wide ledge just three feet down from the brink of the slab, his whole top half still in full view of me. Later, he tried to tell me he was just doing his imitation of Tarzan's ape call. Well, I'd heard his imitation of Tarzan's ape call numerous times, and it had never before made my hair stand on end. Buck was finished as a mentor. I was just happy that I hadn't followed his advice and violated a perfectly good pair of Tenners by cutting slits in them for an emergency.

As with all good things, Tenners did not last forever. Spring eased into summer and summer wore on, and the Tenners would begin to fade, the dark rich black of the canvas turning to pale dirty gray. Then the seams where the rubber was glued to the canvas would start to peel loose. The eyelets for the laces would begin popping out. The laces themselves would break and have to be knotted; their ends would fray out into tiny pompoms. The round rubber ankle patches would fall off. The canvas at the balls of the feet would wear through. Then a tear would move back along the instep. By September the Tenners would be done for.

On the first day of school, your new clodhopper boots felt good. Their weight gave you a sense of security, of substance, of manhood, and the will to face another year of school. But there would be a note of sadness, too, because Henry, the poor kid, would be there, his feet painted to look like new boots. You tried not to think about it.

My wife's muffled voice came from inside the closet. "How about this pair of shoes? Can I at least give these to the Salvation Army?"

"Those old tennis shoes? Sure, go ahead," I said. "Hell, I never play tennis, anyway."

Reading Sign

☞ ☞ ☞**B**ack when I was a kid, the mark of a true woodsman was his ability to read sign. Knowing this, many persons trying to pass themselves off as woodsmen would make a great show of staring at sign for a few minutes and then offering up profound remarks about it:

"I'd judge from this broken twig that we're about ten minutes behind a herd of mule deer, most of them yearlings or does, but there's one big fella I'd guess to be a trophy buck. You'll know him when you see him 'cause he favors his left front leg when he's running flat out and . . ."

The only way to deal with a person like that was to walk over, look down, and say, "For heaven's sake, so that's where I dropped my lucky twig! The amazing thing is, I broke it three months ago and it still works!" You then picked up the twig, put it in your pocket, and strolled away.

My cousin Buck was one of these impostors. Even though I was several years younger than Buck, sign was

serious business to me and I spent long hours reading
about it and studying it first-hand and trying to find out
what it meant and whether it was sign at all or maybe just
an accident. Buck, on the other hand, couldn't concentrate on any subject longer than fifteen seconds unless it
wore a dress and smelled of perfume, which sign seldom
if ever did. Still, ever so often I had to endure his hauling
me out to the woods to instruct me on how to read sign.

"Hey, looky here," he would hiss at me. "Elk sign!"

Now, any fool could see that the sign was not that of
an elk but the handiwork of a mule who stood nearby
with a smile on his face and a snicker in his voice. If I
hadn't been smarter than I looked, I would have pointed
that fact out to Buck. But not wishing to have my head
thumped, I said, "Yes! Elk! Elk! I can see now they were
elk!"

Thumping your head was Buck's way of proving to
you that he could read sign.

If I, on the other hand, happened to discover some
fresh deer sign, Buck would always dismiss my find with a
shrug of his shoulders and the profound bit of wisdom:
"You can't eat sign."

He lived to regurgitate those words.

One frosty November morn Buck had dragged me
out deer hunting with him. I wasn't old enough yet to
carry a rifle, but Buck needed someone along to brag to
about how he could read sign. We were cruising down a
back road in Buck's old car, listening to Gene Autry on
the radio and looking for deer. (Buck believed the way to
hunt deer was to drive up and down roads; that's the sort
of woodsman he was.) For breakfast I had brought along
some chocolate-covered peanuts in my jacket pocket, and
ever so often I'd sneak one into my mouth so Buck
wouldn't see it and demand a share. There was some fool
notion in those days that if someone saw you with

something good to eat, all he had to do was yell "divvies" at you and then you had to share with him. If you didn't share with somebody when he yelled "divvies" at you, he got to beat you up and take it all—but only if he was bigger than you were. If he was smaller, he could yell "divvies" till the sun went down and you didn't have to share with him. In that way, I suppose, it was an equitable system. But I digress.

So anyway, there we were driving down the back road, and all at once Buck hit the brakes and yelled out, "Deer tracks!" Sure enough, even from where I now sat, wedged up under the dashboard, I could see that sometime during the past six months a deer had come sliding and bounding through the soft dirt of a high bank above the road. As soon as the car had slid to a stop, we jumped out, Buck breathlessly thumbing cartridges into his rifle, and rushed over to examine the tracks. All the while, Buck was making sure he got full credit for spotting the tracks.

"I told you they was deer tracks, and you didn't believe me, did you?" he whispered, his voice shrill with excitement.

"I believed you, Buck."

"Hell, we musta been drivin' past fifty miles an hour and I looks out and I says to you, 'There's some deer tracks!' Now didn't I say that?"

"That's what you said, Buck."

We looked at the tracks. Buck got down on his knees and felt the edges of the tracks, apparently to see if they were still warm. Then he bent over and sniffed them! It was almost too much to bear for a serious student of deer tracks. Any fool could see those tracks were so old they could have been classified as fossils. The deer who made them no doubt had since known a long and happy life and finally expired at a ripe old age.

"They fresh, Buck?" I asked.

Buck stood up and tugged at his wispy beard as he studied the tracks. "I'd say he went through here, oh, about a half-hour before daylight."

"Gee," I said, stifling a yawn. "We just missed him, hunh? Dang. If we had just been a few minutes earlier, hunh, Buck?"

"Yep," Buck said. "Well, win some, lose some."

While I was racking my brain trying to think of some that Buck had won, a terrible idea occurred to me. And the instant the idea occurred, I implemented it. Even after thirty years and more I am still ashamed of pulling it on Buck. That I am still convulsed with laughter upon recalling the expression on his face is even more despicable. Only the desire to ease my conscience compels me to confess the deed. What I did—oh, I shudder still to think of it—was to take a handful of the chocolate-covered peanuts and sprinkle them on the ground by my feet.

"Hey, Buck," I said, pointing. "Sign. Looks fresh, too."

Buck looked at me in disgust and shook his shaggy head. "How many times I got to tell ya: Ya can't eat sign!"

At that, I reached down, picked up a chocolate-covered peanut, snapped it into the air, and caught it in my mouth.

Buck's jaw dropped halfway to his belt buckle.

For years afterwards, Buck couldn't stand the sight of chocolate-covered peanuts. Offer him one and his upper lip would flutter like a broken window shade. Sure, when ol' Buck figured out the trick I'd played on him, he thumped my head until both of us were worn out, but that didn't change the obvious truth: He just wasn't a proper woodsman.

Much of my early knowledge about sign was gained

from reading books and magazine articles. These usually included drawings of the tracks of various wild animals, and all you had to do was memorize the shape and the number of toes and so on to be able to identify the track out in the wilds. I spent endless hours at this sort of study, but it was well worth the effort. For one thing, it taught me about true friendship. If you were out with one of your friends in the woods, you could point to a set of tracks and say, "Look, lynx tracks."

"Gee," the friend would say in a properly appreciative tone. If he didn't say that or an equivalent expression, he wasn't your friend.

Now, if you followed the lynx tracks and at the other end of them found a skunk waddling along, you would say to your friend, studying him closely, "Sometimes skunks make lynx tracks, did you know that?"

"No, I didn't," he might reply. "That's really interesting." Such a reply could mean only two things: This guy was impossibly stupid, or he was a *really* good friend.

Strangely enough, many of the magazine articles on sign were written by a lady. Her underlying principle was that wild animals were actors on the stage of the great outdoors. If you could read the scripts, namely their tracks in the snow, you could decipher the plot. A typical plot would go like this: Rabbit tracks are crossing the snow from one direction and coyote tracks from another. The two sets of tracks intersect at the base of a tree. Only the coyote tracks continue on from the tree. Hmmmmmmmmmmmm. How did the the rabbit get away from the tree without making any tracks? Did he climb the tree? The mystery was almost mind-boggling. The author of these articles could take an hour's walk through the snow and encounter a dozen fascinating little dramas, none of which, I might add, were ever comedies.

I hate to admit it, but at a certain age I was intrigued by these articles and was forever searching the snowy countryside for evidence of little wildlife dramas. Unfortunately, most of the dramas I encountered went about like this: Rabbit tracks emerge from thicket, go under barbwire fence, mess around in a patch of blackberry brambles, cross a creek over thin ice, go under another barbwire fence, mosey back across the thin ice, meander through the blackberry brambles again, pass under another barbwire fence, and go back into the thicket. That would be it. Although the drama itself might be deadly dull, following the "script" around the countryside could be fraught with pain, danger, and excitement. Several times I nearly froze to death in my wet clothes while rushing home to bandage my scratches and cuts and to dig out the stickers.

Where I really learned to read sign was from the old woodsman Rancid Crabtree. Rancid didn't care a hoot about reading little woodland dramas. To him, sign was not a form of entertainment but an essential element in a complex scheme that he had devised to make working for a living unnecessary. About the only things Rancid needed money for were a few clothes, rifle and shotgun shells, salt and pepper, some gas for his old truck, chewin' tobacco, and his medicine, which a local pharmacist, a Colt .45 stuffed in the waistband of his pants, delivered at night in quart-sized Mason jars. These commodities required cash, particularly the medicine. Rancid acquired his cash by running a little trap line each winter. And successful trapping required a rather extensive knowledge of sign. The intensity and seriousness with which Rancid studied sign can be fully appreciated only by realizing that to him it was virtually the same thing as tobacco and medicine. To Rancid, sign was a matter of ultimate concern.

A stroll with Rancid through the woods was a course in post-graduate study in reading sign. "B'ar," he would say, pointing to the ground as we walked along. "Porky-pine . . . bobcat . . . skonk . . ." And so on. One day we were going along in this fashion and he pointed down and said, "Snake."

"Snake?" I said to myself, glancing down. "This is a new . . . SNAKE!" My bare foot was descending toward the fat, frantic reptile. Despite my precarious posture, I managed to execute a successful lift-off before coming into actual contact with the creature. While involved in this effort, I left my vocal cords unattended and they took advantage of their moment of freedom to get off a loud and startling shriek. Upon hearing this, Rancid leaped to the conclusion that he had misjudged the snake as being a member of a benevolent sect and immediately began to curse and hop about and flail the earth with his walking stick. It was all pretty exciting, and Rancid was more than a little annoyed when he found out the snake hadn't taken a bite out of me after all.

"Gol-dang," he said, "don't never scream like thet ag'in fer no reason. Let the thang at least git a taste of you 'fer you starts hollerin' like you's bein' et. Now tarn loose maw ha'r and neck and git down offen maw shoulders!"

Over the years, my wife has become quite an expert on reading sign, ferreting out clues here and there and matching up odd bits of trivial information from which to deduce an ingenious conclusion that couldn't make the slightest difference to anyone. I like to call her the Sherlock Holmes of sign. Just recently she came in and reported that the reason the grass in an orchard up on the hill was matted down was that a herd of elk had been sleeping there.

"Ha!" I said. "Probably just cows. What makes you think it's elk?"

"Alimentary, my dear Watson," she said. "Alimentary."

There are, of course, worse things than a smart-aleck woman. A fellow even told me what they were once, but I can never remember.

Campgrounds are my wife's favorite places for sleuthing. As soon as we arrive at a campsite, she's out of the car in a flash, reading the sign. "Party of four camped here last. Spent at least three days, I'd say from the amount of ash in the fireplace. At least one of them was a slob."

"How do you know that?"

"Threw the pull-tabs from his beer cans all over the place—boy, that's really disgusting. You'd think he'd care what kind of example he was setting for his kids."

"His kids?"

"Yeah, there are three wiener sticks leaning against the tree over there. You can see the remains of toasted-coconut-covered marshmallows on two of the sticks. Only kids can eat burnt toasted-coconut-covered marshmallows and live. Boy, if I were married to that lazy slob!" she said, holding up the third wiener stick. "Look, the wife's stick has a fork on the end of it. That's so she could cook a wiener for the old man while she was doing her own! Well, I never!"

"The guy sounds like a real slob, no doubt about it," I said. "Hey, don't throw that forked wiener stick away. You never know when something like that might come in handy."

One good thing about forked wiener sticks: It's difficult to run a person through with them.

I myself don't have much opportunity to read sign

anymore. To tell the truth, my reading tastes have changed a good deal over the years and I'd just as soon curl up with a good book or magazine. Also, books and magazines are nicer to keep around the house and you're much less likely to get dirty looks if you read them in public waiting rooms.

Tying
My Own

☞ ☞ ☞Someday there will be a how-to-tie-flies book written for people like me. It will read something like this: "While holding the tying thread between two thumbs of your left hand, take a hackle feather between the big and little thumbs of your right hand . . ."

I am a person who is just naturally thumby. My eyesight isn't all that good either. When I read in a fly-tying book that I should "wrap each successive turn of tinsel next to the preceding one, edge to edge without overlapping," I can only shriek with delight and hope the author can sustain this level of humor through the rest of the book. I am seldom disappointed. Here's a line that really split my sides: "Wind the two hairs around the hook, keeping the darker one to the left." *Keeping the darker one to the left!* Oh what I wouldn't give to be able to come up with gems like that!

Contrary to the rumor spread by some of my alleged friends, I started fishing with artificial flies several years *after* the invention of the real ones, not *before*. Back when I was a kid, you could buy a good fly for fifteen cents.

And I mean a *good* fly. One Black Gnat would last you a whole season, providing you were willing to retrieve it from such receptacles as stumps submerged in rapids, thorn bushes on the sides of cliffs, and rotting logs balanced over the edges of precipices. I was always willing to retrieve it. After all, fifteen-cent flies didn't grow on trees (although a casual observer of my casting technique might assume they did). Sure, by the end of the season there would be some signs of wear and tear: the body would be on the verge of coming apart; the head, lumpy and gouged; and the general appearance, one of having been mauled and chewed on. The fly, on the other hand, would still look pretty good.

My friends and I kept count of the fish taken on each fly. Truly great flies were given names like Killer or Ol' Griz, unless, of course, they failed to attract fish on a given day, at which time they might be called simply Harold or Walter. It was not unusual for us to become quite attached to a fly. Equally common was for a fly to become attached to us. Since none of us enjoyed the prospect of having a fly surgically removed from whatever part of our anatomy it had become attached, we would occasionally pretend we were starting a new fad: wearing a fly on an ear, a shoulder blade, or an elbow. Lest the reader think we were sissies, let me hasten to add that the "surgeon" who excised the wayward fly was more often than not a burly miner (thus the expression "miner surgery"), who would haul out his pocketknife, run the flame of a kitchen match up and down the big blade a few times, order the women and children from the arena, and then say something like, "All right, you men grab hold of him and I'll have that fly out of his hide in a jiffy!"

When you found yourself in this predicament, the better part of valor if not of wisdom was simply to grab the embedded fly and remove it with a quick jerk and a muffled cry of pain, the latter sometimes causing all the cows in the vicinity to "go dry" for a month. This tactic not only saved you from "miner" surgery but for a brief period also enabled you to bait fish and fly fish simultaneously with a single hook.

The fifteen-centers were the expensive flies. The cheap flies cost about thirty-five cents a dozen and came in a little cellophane packet labeled "World's Greatest Fishing Bargain" or something like that. Neither fish nor entomologists have ever seen an insect bearing the slightest resemblance to any members of the world's greatest fishing bargain. Nevertheless, these eccentric flies served an important function: They filled up the empty space in our fly books. This function was important because the first thing you did when you and your fishing companions arrived at a fishing spot was to scoop a dead insect from the surface of the water—any bug would do—and studiously compare it with the contents of your fly book. After a couple minutes of such careful scrutiny, you would say, "By golly, I think what we have here is a hatch of black gnats." You would then take out your venerable fifteen-cent Black Gnat and tie it on. All the other guys would usually go along with this assessment unless, of course, the fifteen-center belonging to one of them happened to be a Silver Doctor or a Royal Coachman, in which case this individual would take exception to the verdict and argue heatedly that the hatch consisted of silver doctors or royal coachmen.

I must confess that if there were still good fifteen-cent flies on the market I'd hop naked on a pogo stick through a feminist picnic before I'd tie my own. But flies have gone up in price. Last summer I heard about a new pattern that was supposed to be good. My plan was to buy one, dissect it, and from the anatomical knowledge thus obtained, counterfeit a few copies. When the clerk told me the price of the fly, I was not only shocked but embarrassed. Unable to bring myself to ask if I could purchase the fly on an installment plan, I said, "Maybe I should have a look at some of your other flies."

"Oh, you mean the expensive ones," he said. "I'm sorry, but our new order hasn't come in yet."

As near as I could make out, either Lloyd's of London had refused to insure the shipment or the armored car service was late in making the delivery. It was all I could do to keep from sticking my hand in my jacket pocket, thrusting it toward the clerk, and saying, "This is a stickup! Give me all your dries, nymphs, and streamers, nothing larger than a six. And no funny stuff—this finger is loaded!"

A number of years ago—about the time investors started buying up fishing flies as a hedge against inflation —I decided that once and for all I'd better learn how to tie my own. After all, I'd been giving out advice on fly-tying for years, so I reasoned that it shouldn't be that difficult to learn how to construct the little buggers. Since I was a fly fisher of consummate skill, word spread that I knew absolutely everything there was to know about flies, including how to tie them. It beats me how a rumor like that got started, but no matter. Pretty soon, fishermen from all over came seeking my advice, and, not wishing to appear rude and secretive, I dispensed it to them freely. Although innocent of such fundamentals as how one got all those feathers and stuff to stay on a hook, I felt competent to offer consultation on the finer aspects of the art.

"I want to make some of my nymphs sink faster," a fellow said to me once. "Got any suggestions?"

"That's simple," I replied. "All you have to do is make them heavier."

"Gee, I wonder why I never thought of that," he said, and walked away shaking his head, no doubt at his own stupidity.

When the time came for me to learn how to tie my own flies, I couldn't very well ask the same people I'd been advising what tools and materials I would need to get started. If nothing else, I might have shaken their confidence in all the tips I had given them over the years. I decided the best approach would be to seek out an establishment specializing in fly-tying paraphernalia and located in an area of town where I was not likely to be recognized. I soon found just such a shop, the proprietor of which turned out to be an attractive lady of approximately my own youthful age.

"Say, don't I know you from somewhere?" she asked, scarcely before the bells on the shop's front door had ceased jangling the news of my arrival.

I smiled modestly. "Possibly you're confusing me with the actor Robert Redford, for whom I'm often mistaken despite his being of somewhat slighter build and a smidgen younger."

"No, no," she said, studying me curiously. "Now I've got it! There used to be this fellow who went fishing with my husband—Farley Quartze? I think his name was Pat or Mac or something like that, a roly-poly guy with thinning gray hair."

I was instantly overcome by pity for the frumpy wretch. Not only was the poor soul suffering from seriously impaired eyesight, she was married to a notoriously loud-mouthed know-it-all whose presence I had in fact endured on a fishing trip or two. Unless, of course, there were two Farley Quartzes, which seemed unlikely. In any case, it would not do for word to get back to *the* Farley Quartze that I had shown up at his wife's shop to buy a beginner's fly-tying outfit. There was nothing to do but pull the dubbing over the lady's lovely but afflicted eyes.

"Well, so much for chit-chat," I said, kindly. "Here's what I need. My fly-tying outfit has become such a mess, after twenty years or so of turning out thousands and thousands of flies, that I've decided to replace the whole shebang with a totally new outfit, something of professional caliber, of course. Why don't you just go ahead and whip me up one, all the usual feathers and stuff, you know?"

"Wow!" she said, staring at me in a way that I could only attribute to a momentary return of visual acuity. "That's really something! First, let me show you a really nifty little vise."

"Perhaps some other time," I replied. "Right now I think we should confine ourselves to matters related to fly-tying." The poor dear was struck speechless with disappointment by my rejection of her overture, and I couldn't help but feel sorry for her, particularly considering that she was married to an insensitive lout like Farley Quartze. Noting that she had absentmindedly extracted from a display case a tool I instantly recognized as an instrument of fly-tying, I tried to change the subject by calling her attention to it. "I see you have a hook-clamper there in your hand. I'm going to need one of those for sure, and that certainly looks like a good one."

After a moment she asked, "How long have you been tying flies?"

"You wouldn't believe me if I told you."

"Probably not," she said, and immediately began removing materials from boxes, bins, jars, and cases and stuffing them into clear plastic bags for me. I was happy to note that she was attaching to each bag a label that identified the contents, few of which I could otherwise have told from the plumage of a yellow-crested cuckold, ornithology not being one of my strong points. Having depleted the inventory of the store to her apparent satisfaction, Mrs. Quartze began computing my bill on an electronic calculator, her fingers dancing happily over its buttons. For some reason, this simple exercise in digital dexterity seemed to improve her mood just short of total delight, and I thought the moment an appropriate one to impress upon her that I was not only an experienced, nay, an expert, tier of flies but also one possessed of certain ethical standards.

"By the way," I said, surveying the mountain of packages stuffed with furs and feathers. "I hope none of these materials are derived from threatened or endangered species."

"Like what?" she said.

"Well," I said, picking up a package and reading the label, "like these chenilles."

Not only was Mrs. Quartze afflicted with poor vision, but she also had the rather distasteful mannerism of allowing her mouth to gape open every time a question was addressed to her. "Why, no," she said presently, regaining control of her jaw muscles, "there are plenty of chenilles left. They reproduce faster than lemmings."

"Good to hear it," I replied. "They're such colorful little beggars, it would be a shame if they became a threatened species."

"Yes," she said smiling. "You'll probably be happy to learn that the flosses are doing fine too. And the tinsels . . ."

Well, that conversation took place many years ago. I have since learned a good deal about the fundamentals of fly-tying, not that I ever really believed there were such creatures as chenilles and flosses and tinsels. That was just a little joke for the benefit of Mrs. Quartze. I don't think she got it, though, because a few days after our transaction somebody sent me a book in the mail —*Fly-tying Made Easy Even for Imbeciles*. Talk about your nerve! On the other hand, it turned out to be a pretty good book, once I got past the hard parts.

Psychic Powers
for Outdoorsmen

☞ ☞ ☞ **E**ven as a child I possessed psychic powers. For example, I once was fighting with my sister, the Troll, and, as she sat on my chest braiding my fingers into a potholder, I suddenly had this vision of a snake slithering happily about in the dresser drawer where the Troll stored her fresh underwear. Naturally, I immediately dismissed the vision as preposterous. How could a simpleminded snake manage to climb the sheer side of the dresser, open a drawer, crawl inside, and finally pull the drawer shut behind? Why would a snake even want to do this? What could its motive be? The very next day, however, the Troll announced the discovery of a snake in her underwear drawer. Her announcement was made simultaneously with the discovery and had a certain operatic quality to it, beginning with a rather elaborate inhalation, which was followed by a series of staccato sounds similar to aborted sneezes, then culminated in a long, quavering, sirenlike screech, the whole performance lasting not more than twenty seconds and concluding with several loud thumps, these last caused by the

Troll's rebounding off the wall in an effort to get a clear shot at the bedroom door. As pure entertainment it left something to be desired, but I found the routine not to be without a certain psychological interest. As with most psychic phenomena, the mystery of the snake in the drawer and my precognition of its being there never yielded to logical inquiry, although for years afterwards the Troll insisted upon advancing a pet theory of her own as to the unknown cause of the event. No one, of course, pays much attention to the theories of a person who goes through life forking her underwear out of a drawer with a long stick.

Quite often in those days our house would be invaded by strange odors. "Smells like something died," my grandmother would say, giving me a look heavy with accusation. I would then perform an age-old rite of exorcism, which consisted of removing from a secret storage place and burying outside by the light of the moon a bait can of deteriorating worms, a collection of more-or-less drying sunfish, or possibly a box of ripening freshwater mussels. Shortly after I had performed the rite, the mysterious odor would begin to diminish in power and soon be gone altogether. My family should have been grateful that they had me around to exorcise odors, but they were generally unappreciative.

I have managed to achieve true levitation only twice. In the first instance, I not only raised the person several feet off the ground in a prone position but propelled him over a fence, across the countryside, and into his own house, where his abrupt entrance through a locked screen door caused his mother to spill a cup of hot cocoa on the cat and his father to blurt out a word that nobody supposed he even knew—or so the subject of my feat of levitation reported to me upon returning to his senses several days later.

What happened was this: A kid by the name of Lester was spending the night with me, and we were sleeping on an old mattress out in my backyard. I had complained of an earache the previous night, and my grandmother suggested that I wear something around my head to keep the cold night air from my ear. Although I possessed half a dozen stocking caps, a search of the premises unearthed not a single one of them. Finally, my grandmother said she would find me something of hers to wear. She went to a trunk in the attic and fished out one of her old bonnets, a thing made out of bearskin and which she claimed once to have worn on hayrides. At some point prior to the bonnet's being stored in the trunk for reasons of sentiment, a dog had apparently attacked it, either out of anger or fright, and had managed to tear loose several large hanks of hair, leaving in their place grotesque patches of naked skin. It fastened under the chin with two cords. Naturally, I didn't want Lester to see me wearing such a monstrosity, since he might spread rumors about me around the schoolyard, a place where rumors about me were already rampant.

I concealed the hairy bonnet inside my shirt until Lester had dozed off, rather fitfully it seemed to me, even though I had entertained him for several hours with true accounts of the numerous grisly murders that had taken place in our neighborhood and which remained unsolved. I then whipped out the bonnet, put it on, knotted the cords under my chin, and slid down under the blankets, being careful not to disturb Lester and hoping that I would be the first to awaken in the morning in order to remove the headpiece before my bedmate saw it.

Sometime during the night, as luck would have it, the bearskin bonnet became twisted around my head in such a manner that it was leaking cold air to my faulty ear and shutting it off altogether from my nose and mouth. I awoke in a panic of suffocation and tore at the knots under my chin, but to no avail. There was only one thing to do. I lunged for Lester, hoping the moon was bright enough that he could see to untie the knots. *"MOW WAAAA OOOD AAAAAAHHH!"* I shouted at him. Through a ripped seam in the bearskin, I glimpsed one of Lester's eyelids lift tentatively. Then both eyes popped open. Without further ado, Lester levitated.

After Lester's departure, I groped my way into the house to my mother's bedroom and shook Mom awake to have her untie the cords of the hairy bonnet. That's when the second levitation occurred. It was less spectacular than Lester's but every bit as good as what one might see performed on stage by the average professional magician, although, on the whole, considerably less dignified.

I also possess considerable talent for rainmaking, although only in collaboration with my friend Vern Schulze. When we were still kids, Vern and I discovered that we could produce rain any time we wished simply by going on a camping trip together. Our sleeping out in the backyard would produce a steady drizzle for most of the night. A camping trip away from home for a couple of days would call forth a series of cloudbursts that would awaken new interest in arks and set people to arguing about the meaning of "cubits." Once when we were about sixteen, we even managed to work up a major blizzard in the middle of June by going camping in the mountains for a week. We learned from that experience that the severity of the weather is in direct but inverse proportion to the warmth of the clothes we wear camping. Our light attire, appropriate to the normal weather of late June, had in that instance brought on a blizzard. If we had gone naked, we probably would have launched a new ice age.

This past summer we had not a drop of rain for nearly two months in the region where I live, and forest fires were erupting all over the place. I called up Vern.

"Vern," I said, "this drought has gone on too long. The whole country may burn up if we don't do something about it. Get your gear ready. Any questions?"

"Yeah," he replied. "Who is this?"

"You know who it is! Don't try to pull that wrong-number routine on me, Vern!"

"You must have the wrong number," he said. "There's no Vern here."

"I told you not to try that routine on me," I snapped. "Do you want to be responsible for letting the whole country go up in flames?"

"I suppose not. What's your plan?"

"Well, I figure a week-long backpacking trip into the Hoodoo Mountains would do the job."

Vern gasped. "Are you crazy? Think of the floods, man! No, three days would be more than enough! A few roads may wash out, but a three-day backpacking trip shouldn't cause any more damage than that. And it will certainly produce enough rain to put out all the forest fires."

As soon as the word got out that Vern and I were going backpacking, the local television weatherpersons began qualifying their announcements: "The official forecast is for continued hot, dry weather; however, Pat McManus and Vern Schulze are going backpacking for three days, and rains ranging from severe to torrential should be expected." Farmers, whose crops had been dying on the vine, hoisted their children to their shoulders to catch a glimpse of Vern and me as we drove by on our way to the mountains. Their wives, cheeks wet with tears of joy, waved handkerchiefs in the still air and blew us kisses. Upon being notified that our backpacking trip was under way, forest service officials began pulling in their firefighting crews. Long lines of weary, smoke-blackened firefighters cheered our two-man relief team as we passed, and fire-retardant bombers flew low over us and dipped their wings in salute. We drove on, our jaws set in grim determination.

"I sure wish they'd discover a less extreme way of making rain," Vern said. "I'm getting too old for this sort of thing."

"Me too," I said. "It wouldn't be quite so bad if they paid us to go backpacking, but when we do it for nothing, that's a lot to ask."

"Yeah," Vern said. "Say, the bridge over that dry streambed we just crossed looked a little low to me. On the way back, watch out that it's not washed away."

"Right," I said.

By the time we had hiked the first mile up the trail, we could already hear the thunder.

Materialization is one of the more difficult of the psychic arts. To perform this, I need to hike fifteen miles up a canyon to fish a stretch of water generally supposed to be barren of fish and which hasn't been visited by *Homo sapiens* since the beginning of the last century. I'll climb over giant logs, battle brush, slog through swamp, and tunnel through clouds of mosquitoes and gnats. At last I'll arrive at a long, beautiful pool at the base of a waterfall, tie on a fly, and cast out into the pool. Crazed cutthroat slightly larger than French bread boxes will rush for the fly. I'll try to set the hook too soon, and my line will whip back over my head and become one with a fifteen-foot-high bush embellished with thorns the size of ice picks. The fly will dangle down in front of my face. At that instant, three other anglers will materialize out of thin air, gather around my dangling fly, and say, "Too bad, fella. Look Fred, what he got that strike on is one of them with hackle from unhatched pterodactyl, wings of gossamer, and body wrapping from the hair of the tooth fairy. Lucky we happen to have plenty of them along."

I'm also good at dematerialization. Once, using only a map and a compass for props, I made myself and two companions vanish for three days in a Montana wilderness area. I have attempted to repeat this feat several times since and have succeeded.

Generally, however, I like to practice my dematerialization in a really wild place—Kelly's Bar & Grill. I simply say aloud the magic words, "Speaking of big fish, that reminds me of the time . . ." At that point, half of Kelly's customers will disappear with a suddenness that leaves half-filled schooners of beer suspended in mid-air.

I'm not bad at hypnosis, either. All I need to do is finish expounding on my recollection and the rest of Kelly's customers will fall into a trance or, as Kelly puts it, "stupor." (Well, one man's trance is another man's stupor.)

Even Kelly, ignorant of the psychic arts as he is, can't help but admire my powers. Quite often he will point me out to a new customer and warn, "Stay away from that guy. He's a great psycho!"

"*Psychic!*" I correct him. "A *psychic!*"

Kelly will just chortle. If there's one thing I hate more about Kelly than his abuse of words, it's his asinine chortling.

The Fishing Lesson

☞ ☞ ☞ **O**ver the years, I've introduced several dozen people to the pleasures of outdoor sports. So what that some of them didn't want to be introduced! They might otherwise have ended up as criminals or drug addicts or golfers. I like to think I've had some small part in saving them from such dismal fates.

My neighbor Al Finley, the city councilperson, is a good example of what can be accomplished if you put your mind to it. Up until a few years ago, Finley had never been fishing in his life. One day he happened to mention that fact to me, and I couldn't help but feel sorry for him.

"Al," I said to him, "nobody's perfect. All of us have our faults. Want to talk about it?"

"Talk about what?" he said.

"Your degeneracy," I said.

Then he called me one of those nasty anatomical names so popular with guys who like to pretend they're tough.

"Listen, you dirty no-good elbow," he said, "just because I don't fish doesn't mean I'm a degenerate!"

"Somebody call me?" said Retch Sweeney, who had just walked in.

I explained to Retch that Finley had never been fishing. Retch, as a way of expressing amazement, has the irritating quirk of repeating the same rhetorical question over and over.

"You never been fishing, Al?" he asked.

"No," Finley said, irritably.

"I'll be darned, you never been fishing, hunh?"

"No!"

"That's really something! You never been fishing?"

Finley's eyes looked as if they were going to pop out of his head.

"NO!NO!NO!NO!NO!" he screamed. "I HAVE NEVER BEEN FISHING, NOT ONCE IN MY WHOLE BLINKETY-BLANK LIFE, YOU FRACTURED KNEE-CAP!"

"Well, that's probably what makes you so irritable," Retch said.

After I had helped pry Finley's thumbs off of Retch's windpipe and they had both calmed down, I suggested that the three of us take a little fishing trip together. Neither one of them was too happy with the idea at first, but I eventually brought them around.

"Hell, Finley," I said, "take a few days off from City Hall. The taxpayers can use the rest. Besides, learning to fish will open up a whole new way of life to you."

Once he sets his mind to do something, Finley goes all the way. He rushed out and bought himself rods, reels, lines, leaders, hooks, creel, waders, fishing vest, etc. He practically cleaned out the local sporting-goods stores. What made me mad wasn't that he put together a better fishing outfit than mine but that the city's rate for garbage collection went up in direct proportion to what he spent. If I had suggested an African safari to him, we wouldn't have been able to afford garbage anymore.

The night before we were to leave on the fishing trip, Retch and I went over to Finley's place to make sure he was properly outfitted and to make last-minute arrangements. Finley was flitting about getting his stuff ready, and it was enough to make a petrified toad smile.

He had everything arranged in neat little piles according to function, size, color, etc. His tackle box alone was so neat and orderly it was pathetic.

Retch looked at it and grinned. "This will never do, Finley."

"Why not?" Finley growled.

"It just don't look right," Retch said. "It ain't got any character. What you need is a good snarl of leader in there with sinkers and hooks and maybe a dried worm still attached. And it ain't very efficient either. With my lures, I just keep them all dumped together down in the bottom of the box. Then all I got to do is grab one of them and they all come out in a big clump. I just turn the big clump around till I find something that looks good and pluck it off. You gonna waste a lotta time pokin' around through all them compartments."

Finley was obviously embarrassed by his own ineptness in organizing a tackle box. Still, that was no reason for him to refer to Retch as an "ingrown toenail." Retch may not be smart, but he has feelings just like anyone else.

Retch and I did everything we could to help Finley get his stuff into some kind of respectable condition so we all wouldn't be embarrassed if we ran into other anglers on the river. But Finley said he liked for his stuff to look neat and clean and brand new. He wouldn't even let me

smear some salmon-egg clusters on his fishing vest or
leak some dry-fly dressing on his shirt.

Finally, Retch could stand it no longer. He grabbed
Finley's hat, threw it on the floor, and jumped up and
down on it.

"Now, that looks more like a fishing hat," he said,
holding it up for approval.

"I can see that, you shinbone," Finley said. "Too bad
it isn't my *fishing* hat!" Turned out it was his politicking
hat.

Retch and I had a good chuckle over the little
misunderstanding, and even Finley was mildly amused
by it, although not until several years later.

To make amends, Retch offered to let Finley stomp
on *his* fishing hat. Finley said all right but only if Retch
would agree to leave his head in it.

I could see that Finley was becoming irritated, since
he had acquired a rather severe twitch in his left eye and
was pacing back and forth popping his knuckles. It was
apparent that all those years without fishing had taken
their toll on his nervous system. I tried to be as gentle as I
could in giving him the last few bits of essential information about our fishing trip.

"I've got some bad news and some good news for
you, Al," I said.

"What? Tell me. I can hardly wait."

"First, the bad news. The road into the Big Muddy,
which is where we're going to fish, is pretty treacherous—
steep, winding, narrow, washouts, logging trucks, that
sort of thing."

"The good news?"

"We're taking your car, and you get to drive."

"What's so good about that?"

"Well, there are several high old wood bridges where
Retch and I have to get out and walk across just to make

sure they're safe for you to drive over. Then there's the stretch of road along the top of Bottomless Canyon, where we have to get out again and guide you along just to make sure your outside tires don't hang so far out in space they might slip off. Hell, all that walking would sap your energy, and we want you to save it for fishing."

"I see, I see," Finley said, twitching and popping.

The plan we worked out was for Finley to pick us up at three in the morning. Finley, not knowing anything about fishing, expressed some amazement at the early hour for getting started. We explained that it was necessary if we were to catch the first feed on the Big Muddy.

"And don't be late," Retch said. "The one sin I can't forgive is for a guy to be late for a fishing trip."

The resulting foul-up was probably my fault. I should have taken into account the fact that Finley knew absolutely nothing about fishing and its practitioners, and I should have explained the nuances more thoroughly to him. Right in the middle of the night, I was awakened from a deep sleep by a horn blaring in my driveway. I got up and staggered over to a window to look out.

"What is it?" my wife mumbled.

"I don't know," I said. "Some maniac is down in our driveway honking his fool horn off. What kind of a person honks his horn in front of your house at three A.M.?"

It was Finley, of course. As I stuffed my gear into the back of his station wagon, I tried to be as kind as possible.

"Al," I said, "when a fisherman says he is leaving on a fishing trip at exactly, absolutely and positively, three A.M., he means five-thirty at the earliest. If he's leaving at three, he says midnight."

After we had honked Retch out of bed, he staggered to the car looking like something put together by an inept taxidermist.

"Wha-what is it?" he said. "The dam bust? We gonna be flooded?"

By four we were on the road, pumping hot coffee into our veins from the thermos Finley had had the good sense to bring along. In a little while, we felt good. There is nothing better than to be headed into the mountains on a clean fresh day with the sun rising through the trees and good company and good talk and the sense of ease that comes from the knowledge that you are in somebody else's car and it is not your transmission that is going to get torn out on a big rock. Even Finley seemed to be enjoying himself. Then we came to the road that leads up to the headwaters of the Big Muddy.

"Hang a left there," I told Finley.

"A left where? All I see is that rock slide coming down off the mountain."

"That's it, buddy," I said. "By the way, Al, how do you feel about transmissions? You don't strike me as the sort of man who would develop an attachment to them."

I am happy to report that Finley is a superb driver and negotiated the Big Muddy road without the slightest damage to his car. In fact, the only incident worth reporting was when the car started to teeter on the edge of a washout and Finley became confused and jumped out of the car at the same time Retch and I did. When we explained to him that we had merely had a sudden urge to check the huckleberry crop along the road, he climbed back in and drove around the washout, by which time Retch and I had pretty well exhausted our interest in the huckleberry crop and were able to rejoin him.

"Why is it that every time we come to a bad stretch of

road, you two are overpowered by an urge to leap out and study the local flora?" Finley asked, mopping the sweat off his brow so it wouldn't drip into his twitching eye.

"Must be just a coincidence," I said. "Say, isn't that a beautiful specimen of Birdwell's lichen on those rocks up ahead there?"

"You mean up there where the road seems to be cracking off from the side of the cliff?"

"That's it, buddy," I said, opening the door. "Remind me sometime to show you my extensive collection of lichen."

As I say, we arrived at the Big Muddy without incident, and aside from the fact that Finley went about for some time afterwards with his hands shaped as though they were still gripping a steering wheel, we were all in fine fettle and high spirits. Finley even commented that he didn't know how he had managed to get through forty-three years of life without fishing, he was having so much fun.

"You ain't seen nothing yet," Retch told him. "Just wait till you actually start fishing."

"I can hardly contain myself," Finley said.

Retch and I helped Finley rig up his tackle, and then we all cut down through the brush toward the Big Muddy. It was rough going, and the mosquitoes came at us like mess call at a fat farm. I led the way and did the best I could to point out the obstacles to the other two, but apparently I stepped right over one beaver hole without noticing it. Suddenly I heard a strange sound and turned around to see what it was. I was shocked. There was Finley's head resting on the ground, its eyes still blinking in disbelief! It was about as horrible a thing as I've ever seen. Then the head spoke to me.

"You *gluteus maximus,*" it said. "Why didn't you tell me about this hole?"

"I didn't see it, head," I replied. "It looks pretty deep though—we better warn Retch about it."

"Ha!" Finley said. "Whose shoulders do you think I'm standing on?"

That was about the only real catastrophe to befall us. The rest of the day was pretty much your routine fishing trip. Oh, Finley did lose his sack lunch and made quite a fuss about that, but it was nothing really. As far as we could figure out, the lunch apparently washed out of the pocket in the back of his fishing vest. There was a pretty strong current at the place where he was trying to swim to the north bank of the Big Muddy, and that was probably when his lunch washed away. Actually, I had thought there were good odds that Finley would make it all the way across that high log over the river, even if he was running. But before Retch and I could shake hands on our bet, he ran right off into space and dropped like a shot into the river. Of course, I hadn't taken into account the fact that he was holding up his pants with one hand and had all those yellow jackets swarming around him. I had told Finley that yellow jackets sometimes hole up in old brush piles and don't like to be disturbed, but he didn't listen. I won't go into how he was disturbing them or why he was holding up his pants with one hand, because it isn't especially interesting. Anyway, to hear Finley tell it, you would think he was the only fisherman to have such an experience. You would think Retch and I had personally put those yellow jackets under that brush pile.

"Look, Finley," I told him, "it's no big deal. Fishermen lose their lunches all the time."

I dug a sandwich out of my own fishing vest and gave

it to him and patted him on the shoulder. He stared down at the sandwich. "Looks like peanut butter and jelly," he said.

I didn't have the heart to tell him it was supposed to be just peanut butter, even though I could have put those salmon eggs to good use. He didn't seem to notice, anyway.

One of the most difficult things about introducing a guy to the sport of fishing is determining whether it has taken hold on him. Finley had done so much complaining all day, I couldn't be sure. As we were driving back into town, I decided to ask him.

"I'm of two minds about it," he replied. "One bad and one good."

"What's the bad?"

"I won't be able to get out of bed for a week."

"What's the good?"

"Next time we're taking *his* car."

"Whose car?" Retch said.

"Yours, armpit, that's whose," he said.

I could see Finley was hooked. Already he had picked up one of the most important techniques.

The Hunting Camp

☞ ☞ ☞ The guys and I were practicing our lies down at Kelly's Bar & Grill the other night, and before I knew it Fred Smits had got started on a long and boring tale about one of his hunting trips. Something of an expert on long and boring tales, I can usually spot one and snuff it out while it is still in the larval stage. On this occasion, however, Mavis, Kelly's barmaid, had just leaned over my shoulder to replenish the beverages at our table. At that instant I noticed something flutter into my drink. At first glance it appeared to be an emaciated centipede. Since Kelly's is not exactly a showcase of the County Health Department, it was only natural for me to assume that the creature had lost its grip while being pursued across the ceiling by a pack of cockroaches. I shrank back in disgust from the loathsome creature and began to stab at it with a pepperoni stick in the hope of either flipping it out of my glass or drowning it before it drank too much.

Without warning, Mavis grabbed the pepperoni stick

and, trying to wrench it away from me, hissed in my ear, "It's mine, you idiot! Give it back!"

Mavis not seeming the type to own a starving centipede, I quite logically leaped to the conclusion that she was referring to my pepperoni stick. "It is not yours," I snapped. "It's mine, I bought it, and I'm going to eat the darn thing!"

This simple assertion seemed to touch off a burst of maniacal strength in Mavis, and, gasping with rage, she twisted my wrist back in such a manner that she was able to remove from the tip of the pepperoni stick the sodden centipede. She then stalked off, sniffling something about my trying to eat her eyelash!

Her eyelash, for pity's sake! It should be easy for anyone to understand how a man of my sensitivity would be upset by such a bizarre assault on his person and character, not to mention his pepperoni. I relate this dreadful experience only by way of indicating the magnitude of event necessary to distract me sufficiently that someone is allowed to get a long and boring tale under way without having it instantly snuffed. By the time I tuned in, Fred had covered the first couple hours preceding the hunt, leaving no detail unturned, no matter how lacking in relevance or consequence. The other guys at the table had already been poleaxed by trivia and were staring catatonically at Fred as he droned on: "So a couple of minutes after Ralph knocked the ash off his cigar, we pulled off the road and made camp, and then me and Ralph starts up the trail to look for deer sign and I steps on a twig but it don't make no noise 'cause it's wet—did I say it rained the night before? Anyway . . ."

"Hold it right there, Fred," I said, noticing how barren of detail was the reference to making camp. "Did you say 'made camp'?"

"Yeh. Now where was I? Did I tell you the part about the wet twig?"

"C'mon, Fred, don't try to weasel out of it," I said. "Admit that all you did was turn off the ignition on your camper truck and set the hand brake. That doesn't constitute making camp."

"We had to let down the camper jacks, too," he said sheepishly, looking about the circle of faces, which had suddenly filled with accusation.

I shook my head. "You know the rules, Fred. It's all right to lie about unimportant things as long as it's entertaining. Add a few points to your buck, a few inches to your trout, a few miles to a trail—but don't ever say you *made camp* when you didn't."

"I'm sorry, I'm sorry!" he cried. "I don't know what came over me. It just slipped out."

"All right," I said, patting his hand. "We'll forgive you this time. Just don't ever let it happen again." Snuffing out a long and boring tale can sometimes be cruel, but it has to be done.

Then Fred made his second blunder of the evening. He looked at me and, in a penitent tone, asked, "Say, Pat, just what does constitute making camp on a hunting trip?"

Well, if that didn't create an uproar! Everyone started jumping up and down and shouting threats at Fred, and the situation looked as if it might turn ugly. Then Kelly got out his baseball bat from behind the bar and charged over. By the time the fellows had got him calmed down and made him promise not to try to hit Fred with the bat, I had managed to scribble out an outline and a few rough notes on a napkin.

"I'm glad you asked that question," I said. "I can certainly tell you what constitutes making a hunting camp, but it may take a while, so you fellows might just as well sit down and relax."

They sank into their chairs, muttering.

"I'll have to ask you mutterers to be quiet," I said.

"Watch da language," Kelly said. "Dis is a nice bar."

Since he was still fingering the bat in a psychotic manner, I resisted the impulse to retort and got my lecture started. It went something like this.

The first hunting camps were invented by prehistoric man, who divided his time equally between hunting for wild meat and having wild meat hunt for him. Interestingly, if a man made a hunting camp when he should have made a hunted camp, he was thereafter referred to as "et." (As in: "How come I never see Iggy around anymore?" "Got et.")

The hunting camp consisted of nothing more than a few branches thrown on the ground for a bed, whereas the hunted camp utilized but a single branch, one attached to the upper part of a tall tree, where the hunted would spend the night standing on it. Occasionally, a fun-loving catamount would climb the tree and send the men fleeing wildly among the branches. From this activity arose the expression "tearing limb from limb." Usually, however, the hunted camp provided adequate security, not to mention a cure for sleepwalking.

These prehistoric hunters were the first to come up with that boon to camping, the shelter. The first shelters, simple affairs made of rock, eventually came to be called caves, after the cavemen who lived in them. Unlike the hunted camp, the caves provided protection from wind and rain as well as from wild beasts, but they made for a heavy pack on a long trip.

Since matches and camp stoves had not yet been invented, primitive man was forced to carry his campfire right along with him from place to place. Archeologists believe this may explain why hunting camps in those days were located only ten yards apart. These early firebearers are thought to have contributed to mankind the ten-yard dash and also the expressions "Ow!" "Ouch!" "Yipe!" and *"Bleeping bleep-of-a-bleep!"*

Harsh as these early camps may have been, they probably had a great many similarities to the hunting camps of today. Indeed, it is not hard to imagine the following conversation occurring around one of their prehistoric campfires.

"All right, who forgot to bring the salt? If there's one thing I hate it's pterodactyl wing without salt!"

"Squatty was supposed to bring it."

"The heck I was. I carry the cave, remember? It's Pudd's job to bring the salt."

"Ow! Ouch! Yipe! No sir! I carried the *bleeping bleep-of-a-bleep* fire!"

There is some evidence that early man very nearly invented the interior-frame umbrella tent. Apparently, a hunter one day got the idea of stretching dried skins over a framework of poles he had lashed together. The contraption aroused a great deal of curiosity among his fellow hunters, who up to that time had thought the man an imbecile.

"What is it?" they asked him.

"A brontosaurus trap," he replied.

His fellow hunters concluded that the man was indeed an imbecile. Because of his quick-witted reply, however, the anonymous inventor saved countless generations from the agony of pitching interior-frame umbrella tents, and he thus came to be regarded as one of the great benefactors of mankind.

Before the invention of sleeping bags, the hides of hairy mammoths and saber-toothed tigers provided cozy warmth through the long nights of the approaching ice age, but, unfortunately, only for hairy mammoths and saber-toothed tigers. Early cave paintings, however, indicate that one group of prehistoric hunters devised a clever substitute for a sleeping bag. They would lure a saber-toothed tiger into their cave, where one of the hunters would knock it out with a club. Then the hunters would all lie down in a row and tug the tiger up over them for warmth and try to get a few hours of sleep before the beast regained consciousness. The little band of hunters is thought to have vanished suddenly and mysteriously. The only theory for their disappearance that archeologists can offer is that one night the man in charge of the club forgot to put the cat out.

At this point in my lecture, Kelly began to shout incoherently and had to be wrestled back into his chair and disarmed of the baseball bat.

"All right," I said. "So much for the history of hunting camps. I will now move right along to my analysis of the phenomenon known as the modern hunting camp." And I did.

First off, as I told the boys at Kelly's, I don't consider anything that's comfortable a camp. I know one guy who goes hunting in a $50,000 motor home that has everything but a front lawn and a basement. Driving a hunting camp fifty-five miles an hour down a freeway goes against everything I believe in, and I simply won't stand for it. A hunting camp, after all, is not so much a thing as a state of mind.

Mention the phrase "hunting camp" to any hunter worth his fluorescent-orange vest and the picture that immediately leaps into his mind is this: A classic cabin-style tent, suspended from a framework of slender, unpeeled saplings that have been lashed together by the hunters, is situated on a flat, stoneless, grassy piece of ground with a backdrop of evergreens, tastefully splotched here and there with patches of autumn color. The pipe of a wood-burning stove pokes up through the roof of the tent. A small, pure, ice-cold mountain stream tumbles among boulders off to one side. From a stout tree limb dangles the standard fourteen-point buck. One of the hunters is splitting the evening's firewood from blocks that are miraculously dry, straight of grain, and the right length. The other hunter is pouring himself a steaming cup of hot coffee from the pot hung over the near-smokeless campfire. There are no insects in the picture, and the only snow glistens on a distant peak, made rosy by the sun setting gloriously in the west.

This picture, of course, represents the ideal of the hunting camp, which is seldom if ever achieved. The average hunting camp, infinite in its variety, falls somewhat short of the ideal. Here are but a few versions of it:

THE NO-FRILLS CAMP—This is the camp that is resorted to upon arriving at the hunting site very late on a cold and rainy night. One of the hunters will suggest something like this: "Hell, why don't we just sleep in the car. It's only five or six hours until dawn." A curious aftermath of the no-frills camp is that the hunter who suggested it is not spoken to again by any of the other hunters for approximately six months. The no-frills camp may be injurious to your health, but only if you should greet one of the occupants of it too cheerfully on the following morning.

THE FLAT CAMP—This is the camp that is resorted to after someone asks, "Okay, where are the tent poles? Who put them in the car?" And nobody answers.

THE SLANT CAMP—The commonest of all camps used in the mountains, the slant camp is the source of several interesting phenomena, one of which is that anytime something is dropped, it falls horizontally. Several times I myself have seen men encased in sleeping bags shoot out through the side of a slant camp tent like a burial at sea. One of the drawbacks of the slant camp is that by the middle of the night all the sleeping hunters are stacked on one another at the low side of the tent. And the guy on the bottom is always the one who drank a beer before turning in.

THE HANG-GLIDER CAMP—This camp results from the suggestion, "Let's pitch the tent right on top of the peak. That way the wind will blow the insects away from us."

THE HORSE CAMP—Where everyone except the packer eats standing up.

THE DOUBLE-BARREL CAMP—Where . . .

At this point, my lecture was interrupted by Mavis, who had returned sullenly to replenish our beverages. As luck would have it, her eyelash plopped into my drink again. I fished it out with a toothpick and handed it to her. You've never heard such screaming. I told Kelly afterwards, "Either fatten up these centipedes or make Mavis get rid of the false eyelashes. Otherwise, I'm not going to give any more lectures in this establishment."

So far, he has failed to heed my warning.

If You Don't Mind, I'll Do It Myself!

☞ ☞ ☞ **A**ll together, I was off the stuff for nearly six weeks. Did it cold turkey, too. Then I couldn't stand it any longer and sneaked down to the basement for a quicky, just a little something to steady my nerves. But one of the girls caught me at it and rushed upstairs to tell her mother. I could hear her in the kitchen, sobbing out the news of my relapse.

"I just found Dad hiding in the coalbin, and he's at it again."

"Oh dear! I was afraid of this!" my wife exclaimed. "I thought I had gotten rid of them all, but he probably had one stashed away under the coal."

Another kid wandered into the kitchen. "What's all the ruckus?"

"Your father's hitting the kits again."

"Figures. What is it this time?"

"Looks like another muzzleloader," the informer said.

My wife moaned. "I tried to get him to take the cure."

"Actually, there's no cure for do-it-yourselfism," Big

191

Mouth said. "Our school brought in a do-it-yourself addict to tell us kids how he got hooked on the habit. He said a friend of his got him tying his own fishing flies. Then he started refinishing his own split-bamboo rods. Before he knew it, he was into the hard stuff—making his own surf-casting rods, mountain tents, muzzle-loaders . . ."

"Oh, don't I know!" my wife said.

"The really terrible thing," the kid went on, "was that while this guy was talking to us, he rewired the teacher's reading lamp, overhauled the pencil sharpener, and was starting to sand the desk tops when his attendants dragged him off."

Well, everybody's got to have a hobby of some kind, I always say. And the next time I go on the wagon, I'm going to make it myself. I've never built a wagon before.

There's a lot of prejudice against us do-it-yourselfers. Most of it derives from jealousy. Take my neighbor, Al Finley, for instance. He had to give up headaches because he couldn't figure out how to get the tops off the new child-proof aspirin bottles. But do you think he would admit his incompetence? Not a chance.

"I prefer to buy my stuff ready-made," he told me a couple years ago. "If I wanted to waste my time doing it myself, I certainly could. I'm pretty good with tools, even though I just keep the basic ones around the house—a pounder, a screwturner, and one of those cutters with the sharp little points . . ."

"A saw?"

Finley sniffed. "You do-it-yourselfers just love to toss that technical jargon up at a fellow, don't you?"

"Not especially," I replied. "But now that you mention it, I'd appreciate your returning the squeezer you borrowed from me. You're never going to get the top off that aspirin bottle anyway."

Usually, I can just shrug off the nasty cracks hurled at us do-it-yourselfers, but once in a while they get to me. When I built my kids a sleek little soap-box racer, Finley leaned over the fence and asked me why I was putting wheels on a packing crate. That was bad enough, but when I built my dog a new house, employing some of the most advanced designs and technology of modern architecture, Finley called up on the phone and hissed into my ear:

"Don't make a sound! Some kind of huge, squat, brown, ugly creature has landed in your backyard! And that's not the worst!"

"What's the worst, Finley?"

"The worst is, I just saw it eat your dog! Har, har, har!"

Three questions instantly crossed my mind: Is it possible to cement a man's mouth shut while he is sleeping? Would it be considered a crime or, in Finley's case, a public service? And finally, would he be awakened by the sound of a pre-mix truck backing up to his bedroom window?

I must admit that do-it-yourselfism may be getting a bit out of hand in this country. There are do-it-yourself baby deliveries, do-it-yourself marriages, do-it-yourself divorces, and do-it-yourself funerals. If there were a kit and a set of instructions, there are probably people who would undertake do-it-yourself brain surgery. In fact, I once gave myself a haircut that was commonly mistaken for brain surgery.

Although I will tackle just about any do-it-yourself project, my specialty is outdoor gear. Nowadays I prefer to work with store-bought kits, but back when I was a youngster and just getting started on do-it-yourselfism, there weren't any kits on the market. You had to make your own kits.

The way you made a kit was to wander around gathering up the necessary parts as you found them. You then threw the parts into a large, handy container, often referred to as your bedroom. This procedure usually presented no problem if you were putting together a simple kit, like for a slingshot. On the other hand, if you were putting together a more complex kit, like for a four-wheel-drive ATV, family relations could become strained. I recall one particularly ugly scene with my mother, grandmother, and sister. To have heard them rave and carry on you would have thought there was something abnormal about a kid's bedroom leaking crankcase oil.

I have since read in child psychology books that parents are supposed to give their children "positive reinforcement" as a means of stimulating their creative urges. My family never gave *me* any positive reinforcement. The following account is an example of their narrow-minded and negative attitudes.

The peaceful quiet of a warm fall afternoon was suddenly shattered by a shrill scream from my sister. "There's something decaying in his bedroom! I know there is!"

"Nonsense!" I exclaimed. It was a pretty good word for a ten-year-old, and I exclaimed it every chance I got.

My mother and grandmother appeared at the bottom of the stairs. They conferred a moment and then, without warning, charged. I tried to bar the door but was too late. Gram got her foot in the crack, and they started forcing their way in.

"Most likely he caged some poor animal in there and let it starve to death," Gram said, reaching around the door and trying to swat me out of the way.

I ducked. "I wouldn't do anything like that."

"How about the worms, young man?" Mom snarled. "You remember the can of worms you left under the stairs last July?"

Then they burst in upon me, their fierce feminist eyes sweeping over the various kits in progress.

"There it is," Gram shouted. "Land sakes, what did I tell you? Just look what he's done to that poor creature!"

Horrified, my mother sucked in her breath. Even I could have told her that it's unwise to suck in one's breath in close proximity to a deer hide being tanned by a ten-year-old boy in a closed bedroom during an unseasonably warm fall. Her reaction was impressive and well worth observing from a scientific viewpoint. Nevertheless, I'm almost certain that there have been longer and more sustained fits of gagging, and for her to claim a record was sheer nonsense, as was her charge that she had suffered permanent damage to her olfactory system. I proved on several later occasions that her sense of smell was fully intact.

My reason for tanning the deer hide, a donation from a hunter I knew, was to put together a kit for making myself a suit of buckskins. I had used an old Indian recipe for my tanning solution, but I should have known that the old Indian was pulling a fast one on me because of the way he kept wiping smiles off his face. Some of the ingredients seemed pretty ridiculous to me at the time, but lots of things seem ridiculous to a ten-year-old, so I couldn't go by that. Probably it would have served Pinto Jack right if I had told Mom that he was the hunter who had given me the deer hide in the first place.

"You ever get your hide tanned?" Pinto Jack asked me some time later.

"Darned near did," I said. "But it's hard for a woman

to run and gag at the same time, particularly when she's carrying a rake handle."

Over the years I put together kits for bows and arrows, dogsleds, snowshoes, packframes, tents, caves, log cabins, canoes, a forty-foot sportfisher, and dozens of other neat things I can no longer recall. The kits eventually flowed out of my bedroom, through the house, into the yard, filled up the outbuildings, and started spreading over the fields. The neighbors considered me an unnatural disaster and worried that their own lands would soon be inundated by my kits. One old neighbor lady complained to my mother that she and her husband lived with their bags packed and in fear that my kits would break loose without warning and flow over them in the middle of the night before they could flee. Another neighbor accused me of stunting his potato crop, which was absurd. A forty-foot sportfisher just doesn't shade that much ground, except possibly in the late afternoon. Nevertheless, tiring of the constant stream of complaints and periodic attempts on my life, I finally curtailed my output of kits and construction projects in general and took up with girls as a means of filling in my spare time. Girls eventually turned out to be almost as interesting as kits, and they didn't take up so much space.

Over the years, I have learned a good deal about putting together do-it-yourself kits, and I herewith pass on to the reader a few helpful hints.

Never buy a beginner's kit. It is much more interesting to jump in at an advanced stage and strike out from there. After you have mastered a particular skill, you can always go back and pick up the basics. Nothing stimulates a high level of interest like a good dose of desperation.

After you have put together a firearm of any kind,

be sure to take the following safety precautions when you test fire it. First, it is absolutely essential to carry a pair of sunglasses with you when you drive out to the firing range. Never test fire a homemade firearm when you are alone; always take a friend along. Then, load the firearm in strict accordance to the standard procedures. Finally, hand the firearm to your friend and say, "Here, why don't you fire off a few rounds? I forgot my sunglasses in the car and have to go back and get them."

Over the years, I've learned that it never pays to publicly put a name to the results of one of my do-it-yourself projects. For example, when I made myself a really superb goose-down hunting jacket, other hunters I happened to meet in the woods would ask me why I was wearing a red sleeping bag. Actually, it isn't at all difficult to come up with a good many sound reasons for wearing a red sleeping bag, particularly if you give the subject a little thought.

Another good strategy is just to make up an appropriate name. Say, you've just put together a mountain-tent kit, but it didn't turn out quite right. Now if your friends happen by and ask what it is, you're going to be subjected to a lot of ridicule, or worse yet, sympathy, if you identify the object as a mountain tent. So what you do is call it a flamph.

"A flamph?" they will say.

"Yeah, a portable flamph."

"What's it for?"

"For sleeping in up in the mountains."

"Hey, man, that's pretty neat, kind of like a mountain tent, hunh?"

The final precaution is this: Never encourage do-it-yourselfism among your immediate neighbors. I know this because Finley finally caught the do-it-yourself bug from me. One day I saw him out in the backyard working away feverishly with his pounder and cutter and my squeezer.

"What are you doing?" I asked, forgetting to restrain a contemptuous laugh.

"Building a boat," he replied matter-of-factly.

"A toy boat?"

"No, a real boat."

I must say his antics provided me with a good deal of amusement. When he finally had it finished, I couldn't resist one final little jab at him.

"Tell me this, Finley, what kind of boat is that?"

"A flumph," he said.

Well, he had me there. There's just no way you can say a flumph doesn't look like a flumph. The one thing that I can say about the damn thing is that it has stunted the growth of my potatoes. A forty-foot flumph shades a lot more ground than you might think.

Useful
Outdoor Comments

☞ ☞ ☞ **E**very year thousands of sportspersons suffer unnecessary ridicule because they don't know the proper comments to make in particular outdoor situations. Merely extracting one's self from a predicament is insufficient; one must do so with grace and style. The proper comment not only enables one to prevail over embarrassment but, in many instances, even to survive.

Consider the following case: When my nephew Shaun and his friend Eddie were about twelve, they considered themselves to be master woodsmen. They demanded to be hauled out to a remote campsite and left to survive for four days with nothing but a handful of matches, their sheath knives, sleeping bags, a small tent, and forty pounds of food. I drove them to the campsite and dropped them off, giving each a firm handshake and a manly look in the eye to let them know how much I respected their courage and that I never expected to see either of them again.

On the second day of their adventure, Shaun's

mother, my sister, had to be repeatedly and forcibly detached from the walls she insisted upon climbing. That day, too, one of the worst rainstorms in the history of our county struck and continued on through the night. The next morning my sister argued persuasively that the time had come for me to retrieve the boys, which I set about doing the very instant I pried her thumbs off my Adam's apple.

As I arrived at the campsite, an ominous feeling settled over me. The rain had scarcely subsided to a downpour, and the clouds of mist hung in the trees. There was no sign of the boys, except for the soggy remains of a campfire and the pitiful little tent. They had pitched the tent in a low area, and the waves of a shallow lake now lapped its walls. I waded into the lake, pulled back the entrance flap, and peered hesitantly inside. Shaun and Eddie, encased in their sleeping bags and awash in a foot of water, peered back. Both looked embarrassed. Several seconds passed before Shaun spoke.

"Well, so much for woodcraft," he said.

Right then I knew that Shaun was a master woodsman and that there was nothing more I could teach him—except possibly the feasibility of pitching one's tent on high ground. He had said the perfect thing for the situation and, in so doing, had triumphed over it. Even his posture and facial expression were exactly right: body prone, limp, waterlogged; eyes telling mutely about the other side of despair; pale lips moving just enough to deliver the appropriate comment in a matter-of-fact tone: "Well, so much for woodcraft." Perfect!

Since then I have found countless opportunities in which to use a paraphrase of his comment:

"Well, so much for mountain climbing."

"Well, so much for scuba diving."

"Well, so much for flying lessons."
"Well, so much for seven-X leaders."
"Well, so much for sex."
"Well, so much for shooting rapids."
"Well, so much for sex while shooting rapids."

As a service to my readers, I have put together a compendium of situations and appropriate responses. It is my hope that these recommendations will be studied carefully and will enable you to comport yourself properly in the outdoors and in a manner worthy of a sportsman.

SITUATION—You have climbed into your mummy-style sleeping bag, wiggled around to sort the rocks under your Ensolit pad according to size and shape, and finally are about to drift into peaceful sleep. Then you detect what appears at first to be a minor problem—the wool sock on your left foot has become partially pulled off.

A partially pulled-off sock does not pose a threat to one's continued existence. On the other hand, it is not the sort of thing that can be totally ignored. It gives one the feeling that all is not right with the world, that everything is not in its proper place, performing its designated function in the prescribed and traditional manner. A partially pulled-off sock is an irritation, perhaps not one of the magnitude of, say, a mosquito walking around inside one's ear or nostril, but an irritation nevertheless.

After twisting and turning in your sleeping bag for some time, telling yourself that the sock is of no consequence, you at last arrive at the conclusion that it will drive you absolutely mad if you allow it to continue its insubordination for another minute. The simplest way in which to settle the matter is to unzip your sleeping bag, sit up, and pull the sock back on with a firm and reprimanding jerk. The problem is that unzipping the bag will invite in a blast of cold air, which will then require turning your metabolism back on to get everything warmed up again, and that in turn will result in your staying awake until you are once more nice and cozy. Another problem is that your previous twisting and turning have relocated the sleeping bag zipper between your shoulder blades at the top and your *peroneus longus* at the bottom. You therefore decide to try pulling up the sock without unzipping the bag.

Your first thought is that you can simply raise your leg high enough so that you can reach the sock. But no, your leg wedges against the sides of the bag, keeping the sock just a few inches out of reach of your clawing fingers. This effort has caused you to become turned at right angles to your Ensolite pad, but no matter; the contest with the sock has now engaged your honor. Since there is more room in the top of the bag, you now reason that by tilting your head forward onto your chest, you should be able to double over enough to get a grip on the sock. As you execute this maneuver, the nylon bag squeaks from the strain and squeezes your shoulders in against your ears. You are now locked into a semi-prenatal position inside the bag, presenting a spectacle that an outside observer could not help but compare to a defective German sausage in need of recall. But at last you have the offending wool in hand and pull it back on your foot with a pained but satisfying grunt. All that remains to be done now is to extract yourself from your compressed posture. Alas, the gentle slope you selected for a bedsite begins to take an active and aggressive role in compounding your plight. You topple over onto your side. With herculean effort and gasped curses that would provoke envy in a Marine drill sergeant, you manage to roll onto your knees. This is immediately determined to be a mistake, since it leads to a series of flopping somersaults down the incline, which becomes increasingly steeper. You come to rest jammed under a fallen tree fifty feet or so away from your starting point.

In the morning your companions get up, stare with some puzzlement at your vacated Ensolite pad, shrug, and begin preparing breakfast. Eventually you are discovered under the tree and extricated. At this moment you can either suffer ridicule or you can make the appropriate comment and earn your companions' everlasting respect and esteem. ("Everlasting" nowadays means approximately two weeks.)

What, then, is the proper response in this situation? Whining and inane jabber about a partially pulled-off sock simply won't cut it, particularly if you insist upon hobbling about in the posture of a chimpanzee with lumbago. Here's what you do: Smile, yawn, stretch luxuriously, and, as soon as your vertebrae cease their popping and pinging, say with a slightly lascivious chuckle, "Boy, I didn't think they made dreams like that anymore!"

SITUATION—The bush pilot returns to pick up you and your companion after a week of fishing on a wilderness lake. "Now you fellas are about to enjoy some real sporty flying," he says. "Did you notice how on my takeoff from here last week I had to flip this old crate over on her side when I went between those two tall pine trees and then how I stood her right up on her tail to get over that ridge?" He now doubles over with laughter and pounds his knee as you and your partner exchange glances. "Well," the pilot continues, "with the two of you and your canoe and all your gear on board, the takeoff is gonna be a little tricky this time. What I was wonderin' is if maybe I could get each of you fellas to straddle a pontoon, and if we come up a little short on the ridge there, maybe you could just sort of walk us right on over the top. How does that strike you?"

Naturally, it will be difficult for you and your partner to contain your joy at the prospect of being allowed in this way to assist in the takeoff. Since it is considered bad form to jump up and down and clap your hands in glee, you must restrict yourself to a few lip tremors and an eye twitch or two.

The important thing to keep in mind in selecting just the right response in this situation is that the pilot is probably joshing you. Therefore, you just shrug and say, "Which pontoon do you want me on?" If he isn't joshing, remember to walk really fast as you go over the ridge.

SITUATION—Back when I was about fifteen, my stepfather, Hank, and I drove out to the neighboring county to fish a stream that meandered through a series of dilapidated farms, none of which showed any visible means of support. After the day's fishing, we returned to our car to find that someone had stolen our battery. My stepfather was a gentle man of great kindness and understanding, and he said that the person who had taken our battery probably did so only because he was too poor to buy one. Therefore, Hank said, he would not place a curse on the thief that would strike him instantly dead but merely one that would make all his skin fall off. Suddenly. All at once. While he was square dancing Saturday night. And just as he was winking at the prettiest girl at the dance. As we trudged along the dusty road, Hank kept adding to and improving upon the curse until it seemed to me that the kinder thing would be to have the thief struck instantly dead.

Presently a car came by headed in the direction of town, and we waved it down. The driver was an elderly lady with a little flowered hat on her head. She asked if we would like a ride, and we said yes, but there seemed to be a problem. The lady had two large dogs in the car with her, and they were carrying on as if we were the first decent meal they had seen in months. Hank suggested that maybe he and I could just stand on the running boards, one of us on each side, and that way, "heh, heh," we wouldn't disturb her dogs. The lady said that would be just fine. "Hold on good and tight," she warned.

We immediately discovered that she had not offered this bit of advice frivolously. She took off so fast our fishing lines came loose and cracked like whips in the air behind us. We were a quarter-mile down the road before our hats hit the ground back at the starting point, not that either Hank or I were concerned with such minor details at the moment.

The lady seemed to think she needed to explain the sudden start. She rolled down her window and shouted out, "Bad clutch!"

Hank arched what he called his "vitals" back from the snapping jaws of a dog. "All right!" he yelled. "Perfectly all right!"

As the lady rolled the window back up, Hank and I dug our fingernails deeper into the rain gutters on the roof of the car and clutched our fishing rods with our armpits. By then we were traveling sufficiently fast that grasshoppers were splattering on our clothes. And still the car seemed to pick up speed. Again the driver rolled down her window and the dogs competed with each other to see which would be first to get a bite of Hank's belly.

"Bad gas pedal!" she shouted out, by way of explaining the speed with which we were hurtling down the road.

"All right! All right!" Hank cried.

She rolled the window back up.

A grasshopper exploded on the left lens of my spectacles. The air was being sucked from my lungs. My fingers were paralyzed, and I wasn't sure how much longer I could hang on. Then the situation took a sharp turn for the worse. A deputy sheriff's car sped by in the opposite direction. Upon seeing us about to break the world's record for fastest ride on running boards, the deputy whipped a bootlegger's turn in the road and came roaring up behind us with red light flashing and siren going. Hank released one hand and pounded on the glass to get the little old lady's attention. When she looked at him, he pointed back at the deputy sheriff. She smiled and nodded and pushed the faulty accelerator pedal to the floor. The deputy stayed right on our rear bumper. Every so often he would try to pass, but the old lady would cut over in front of him and force him to drop back. Then the driver rolled down her window again and grinned up at Hank. "What'd you think of that? Pretty fancy bit of driving for an old lady, huh?"

"All right! All right!" Hank said, as one of the dogs clipped a button off the front of his pants.

"Wait till you see the way I handle my rod!" she yelled, cackling wildly as she rolled the window up.

"What'd she say?" I yelled at Hank.

"She said, 'Wait till you see the way I handle my rod!'" Hank screamed back at me over the roof of the car.

"That's what I thought she said. What do you make of it?"

"I think she's going to shoot it out with the *bleeping* deputy," Hank screeched.

"I thought that's what you'd make of it," I yelled back. "She must be some kind of criminal!"

"Yeah, the crazy kind!"

At that instant the old lady whipped the car over to

the edge of the road and braked to a stop in a cloud of dust. Hank and I dropped from the running boards, coughing and gasping, and wiped our eyes with our deformed fingers. The deputy slid to a stop on the opposite side of the road, and both he and the old lady jumped out of their cars and went into gunfighter crouches, the deputy's hand hovering over the butt of his revolver.

"Oh my gosh!" Hank moaned.

Then the dogs went for the deputy. Both of them leaped simultaneously for what I thought would be the jugular, but he caught them both in his arms and staggered backwards as they licked his face and wagged their tails.

"Heeeee heeeee!" the deputy laughed.

"Heeeee heeeee!" echoed the old lady. Then she pointed at the deputy and said, "That there's my son, Rod! Ain't he somethin'? I can still handle the big bugger, though!"

"Caught you again, Ma!" the deputy squealed.

"Only 'cause I had to be careful these fellas didn't fall off the running boards, that's the only reason!" Ma shouted back.

"Somebody stole my battery," Hank said to the deputy.

"You don't say," the deputy said. "Well, I got to be going. Lots of crime in these here parts. Y'all be careful now, ya hear?" And he took off in pursuit of crime.

The old lady ordered the dogs back into the car, and they obeyed instantly, scarcely bothering to take a snap or two at Hank.

"Well, hop back on the running boards and hold on good and tight," she said to us, "and I'll haul you fellas on into town."

"Thanks anyway," Hank said, "but we can walk from

here. Can't be much more than five miles to the nearest town."

"Fifteen," the old lady said.

"Shucks, is that all?" Hank said. "Why that's even better than I figured. Thanks again for the lift."

That's the sort of comment that not only saves the outdoorsman embarrassment but enables him to survive.

Journal of
An Expedition

☞ ☞ ☞ **R**ummaging through my files some time ago, I happened across the journal I kept as leader of the expedition to Tuttle Lake during the winter of '75. I was immediately struck by the similarity the record of that momentous and heroic struggle bore to the journals of earlier explorers of the North American continent, and, lest it be lost to posterity, I immediately began editing the material for publication.

The other members of the expeditionary force consisted of my next-door neighbor, Al Finley, and my lifelong friend, Retch Sweeney. Neither man was particularly enthusiastic when I first broached the idea of a mid-winter excursion to Tuttle Lake.

"You must be crazy!" Finley said. "Why would we want to do a stupid thing like that?"

"Well, certainly not for fame or fortune," I said. "We'd do it for the simple reason that Tuttle Lake is there."

"Hunh?" Retch said. "Ain't it there in the summer?"

"Of course it's there in the summer," I told him

irritably. "What I mean is that it would be challenge for the sake of challenge."

Finley pointed out that there were two feet of snow on the ground.

"We'll use snowshoes," I told him. "We'll start early Saturday morning, snowshoe into Tuttle Lake, spend the night in my mountain tent, and snowshoe back out Sunday. It'll be a blast."

"Gee, I don't know," Finley said. "I've never been on snowshoes before. I better not go."

"That's a wise decision, Finley," Retch said. "A man your age shouldn't take any more chances than he has to."

"What kind of snowshoes should I buy?" Finley said.

Thus it was that the three of us found ourselves at trail's head, preparing for the assault on Tuttle Lake. The journal of the expedition begins at that point.

History of the Tuttle Lake Expedition
Under the Command of Patrick F. McManus

JANUARY 18, 1975—9:22 A.M. The weather being fair and pleasant, the men are in high spirits as they unload our provisions and baggage from the wagon for the trek into the mountains. The drivers of the wagon, a Mrs. Finley and a Mrs. Sweeney, offered to wager two of the men that they would "freeze off" various parts of their anatomy. I warned the men against gambling, particularly with wagon drivers, who are a singularly rough and untrustworthy lot. The throttle-skinners hurled a few parting jibes in our direction and drove away, leaving behind a billowing cloud of snow. This cloud apparently concealed from their view the man Retch Sweeney, who raced down the road after the departing wagon, shouting "Stop, Ethel, stop! I left the fifth of Old Thumbsucker under the front seat!" It was truly a heartrending spectacle.

9:45 A.M. I have assumed command of the expeditionary force. The men informed me that this is a false assumption, but I will not tolerate insubordination, particularly at such an early stage in the journey. I threatened both of them with suspension of rations from my hip flask. They immediately acquiesced to the old military principle that he who has remembered his hip flask gets to command.

11:00 A.M. The expedition has suffered an unexpected delay. I had directed two of the men to take turns carrying the Snappy-Up mountain tent, but it made them top-heavy and kept toppling them into the snow. We have now solved the difficulty by obtaining an old toboggan from a friendly native, who seemed delighted over the handful of trifles he requested for it. On future expeditions I must remember to bring more of those little green papers engraved with the portrait of President Jackson, for the natives seem fond of them.

All of our provisions and baggage are lashed to the toboggan, and I have directed the men to take turns pulling it. I myself remain burdened with the heavy weight of command. Rations from the hip flask cheered the men much and, for the time being, have defused their impulse to mutiny.

12:05 P.M. We have been on the trail for an hour. Our slow progress is a cause of some concern, since by now I had expected to be out of sight of our staging area. Part of the delay is due to Mr. Finley, who is voicing a complaint common to those who travel for the first time on snowshoes. He says he is experiencing shooting pains at the points where his legs hook on to the rest of him. To use his phrase, he feels like "the wishbone of a turkey on the day after Thanksgiving." I counseled him to keep tramping along and that eventually the pains would fade away. For the sake of his morale, I did not elaborate on my use of the term "eventually," by which I meant "in approximately three weeks."

1:10 P.M. We have stopped for lunch. Tempers are growing short. After kindling the propane camp stove, I had to settle a dispute between the men about who got to roast a wiener first. I narrowly was able to avert a brawl when Mr. Sweeney bumped a tree and dumped snow from a branch into Mr. Finley's Cup-a-Soup. Mr. Sweeney claims the mishap was unintentional, but his manner of bursting out in loud giggles gives me some cause for doubt. I have had to quick-draw the hip flask several times in order to preserve order.

I sent one of the men ahead to scout for a sign to Tuttle Lake. He returned shortly to the main party, very much excited, and reported a large number of fresh tracks. I went out with him to examine the tracks and to determine whether they were those of hostiles. Upon close study of the imprint of treads in the tracks, I concluded that a band of Sno-Putts had passed through earlier in the day. Upon our return to camp, the band of Sno-Putts appeared in the distance, and, sighting our party, came near and gunned their engines at us. After the exchange of a few friendly taunts, they went on their way.

For the last half-mile, Mr. Finley has been snowshoeing in a manner that suggests he is straddling an invisible barrel. We attempt to distract him from his discomfort with copious ridicule.

We are now about to begin the last leg of our journey—a two-mile ascent of Tuttle Mountain. The weather has turned raw and bitter.

5:05 P.M. After a lengthy and difficult climb, we have at last arrived at our destination—Tuttle Lake. During our ascent of the mountain, I found it prudent to order frequent rest stops, since I feared the excessive wheezing of the men might bring avalanches down upon us. Indeed, such was the extreme state of my own weariness that I at first did not grasp the obvious fact that we had arrived at Tuttle Lake. Mr. Finley was the first to make the discovery.

"This is Tuttle Lake," he gasped.

"I don't see no lake," Mr. Sweeney said.

"This is Tuttle Lake!" Mr. Finley shouted. "We make camp here!"

It took but a moment for me to perceive that Mr. Finley was correct in his assessment of the situation; the lake is frozen over and blanketed with a good three feet of snow. We are no doubt standing above its very surface. I am filled with wonderment, not only that we have finally triumphed in achieving the noble purpose of the expedition, but that Tuttle Lake should cling at an angle of forty-five degrees to the side of a mountain.

Snow is now falling with an intensity that beggars the imagination; either that, or we are caught in an avalanche. We are unable to see more than a yard before our faces. It is imperative that we get the Snappy-Up tent erected immediately.

7:15 P.M. The [obscenity deleted] Snappy-Up tent is not yet up. We are taking a rest break, whilst Mr. Sweeney, employing a cigarette lighter, attempts to thaw his handlebar mustache, which he fears might snap off if bumped. Mr. Finley went behind the tent to bury a snow anchor, whereupon he discovered a precipice. The drop was not great, or so we judged from the brief duration of his scream. The rest of the party were about to divide his share from the hip flask when they detected sounds of someone or something ascending the slope. We assumed it to be Mr. Finley, since few men and even fewer wild beasts possess the ability to curse in three languages. We celebrated his return with double rations from the hip flask.

9:30 P.M. We are now ensconced in our sleeping bags in the tent, after devouring a hearty stew, which I myself prepared. Darkness and the considerable violence of the snowstorm prevented me from reading the labels on the packages of dried food, which I emptied into the cooking pot. I then supplemented these basic victuals with a can of pork 'n' beans, several handfuls of spaghetti, four boiled eggs, six onions, half a head of cabbage, six wieners, a package of sliced salami, one wool mitten (recovered from the pot after dinner), and a sprig of parsley. The men were full of compliments about the tasty meal, although not until after I served dessert —each a cupful from the hip flask.

Strangely, I have been unable to find my package of pipe tobacco, which I had stashed in the provisions sack for safekeeping. It seems to have been replaced by a package of freeze-dried shrimp curry. Since smoking shrimp curry may be injurious to one's health, I have denied myself the pleasure of an after-dinner pipe. The disappearance of the tobacco is a matter of no little curiosity to me.

Upon preparing to enter his sleeping bag, which is of the style known as "mummy," Mr. Finley discovered that the snowshoeing had bowed his legs to such an exaggerated degree that he was unable to thrust them into the bag. The alternative of freezing to death or allowing Mr. Sweeney and me to straighten his legs was put to Mr. Finley. He pondered the alternative for some time and finally decided upon the latter course. I administered to him from the hip flask a portion commonly referred to as a "stiff belt," and, whilst Mr. Finley clamped his teeth on a rolled-up pair of spare socks, Mr. Sweeney and I bent his legs back into a rough approximation of their original attitude and inserted Mr. Finley into his bag, he now being capable only of drunken babbling. Now, to sleep.

JANUARY 19, 1975—1:30 A.M. Have just been startled awake by a ghastly growling seeming to originate from just outside the tent. After failing to frighten off the creature by the subterfuge of breathing rapidly, I regrouped my senses and immediately determined that the growling was gastronomical in nature and was emanating from the expeditionary force itself. I was suffering from a monumental case of indigestion, an affliction that comes upon me every time I succumb to eating parsley. My men, who seemingly possessed no greater immunity to that treacherous herb than I, moaned dreadfully in their sleep. In the knowledge that the growling is caused by something we've eaten rather than something we might be eaten by, I shall once again retreat into deep but fitful slumber.

6:15 A.M. The day dawned clear and cold. The men arose early, kindled the propane camp stove, and huddled around it for warmth. I have no notion of the temperature but have deduced from the fact that frost keeps forming on the flames that it is considerably below the freezing mark. The men complain bitterly over the loss to the cold of various parts of their anatomy, and I could not help but remind them of my advice pertaining to betting the wagon drivers against that possibility. They failed to express any gratitude, choosing instead to make threats on my life.

It is becoming increasingly clear to me that the hardships encountered on this expedition have taken a great toll on the men. They both say they have no appetite for breakfast and claim to have a strong taste of tobacco in their mouths, even though neither has been smoking. This sort of delusion is common among members of expeditions, and it is only with a great act of will that I force myself to the realization that the bits of pipe tobacco stuck in my teeth are only imaginary. When I try to encourage the men to down a few bites of frozen shrimp curry, they can only shudder and make strange gagging sounds that are scarcely audible over the chattering of their teeth. I realize now that time is of the essence, and that we must prepare for the return journey with the greatest expedience. The men realize this also, and without waiting for the command, rip the Snappy-Up tent from its icy moorings, wrap it around the baggage and leftover provisions, and heave the whole of it onto the toboggan.

I dispense to each man a generous ration from the hip flask. The retreat from Tuttle Lake begins.

7:35 A.M. We have descended the mountain much sooner than expected and, indeed, much faster than the main body of the party deemed either possible or agreeable. In the event that I fail to survive this expedition and so that the offending party may be suitably disciplined, I offer this account of the affair: Upon realizing that my hip flask was either empty or contained not more than a single shot which would not be wasted on him, Mr. Finley mutinied. He refused to take his turn at pulling the toboggan. He sat down in the snow alongside the craft and displayed a countenance that can only be described as pouting. After arguing with him briefly, Mr. Sweeney and I went off down the mountain without him. It was our mutual judgment that Mr. Finley would pursue and catch up with us, as soon as he came to his senses. We had progressed scarcely two hundred yards down from the campsite when we heard a fiendish shout ring out from above us. Upon turning, we could hardly believe what we saw, and it was a fraction of a second before we realized the full import of the mutinous madman's folly. He was perched atop the mound of baggage on the toboggan and hurtling down the slope toward us at a frightful speed. Before we could externalize the oaths forming on our tongues, he had descended close enough for us to make out quite clearly that he was grinning maniacally. "How do you steer one of these things?" he shouted at us. Dispensing with any attempt at reply, the main party broke into a spirited sprint that would have been considered respectable for Olympic athletes even if it had not been executed on snowshoes. All was for naught. The flying toboggan caught us in mid-stride, flipped us in the air, and added us to its already sizable load. We descended to the foot of the mountain in this unsightly fashion, clipping off saplings, blasting through snowdrifts, and touching down only on the high places. The ride, in retrospect, was quite exhilarating, but I was unable to overcome my apprehension for what awaited us at its termination. This apprehension turned out to be entirely justified. Indeed, some of the finer fragments of the toboggan are still floating down out of the air like so much confetti. Immediately upon regaining consciousness, Mr. Sweeney and I took up clubs and pursued the unremorseful villain across the icy wastes, but the spectacle of Mr. Finley plunging frantically through the snow, even as he laughed insanely, struck us as so pathetic that we were unable to administer to him the punishment he so justly deserved.

12:30 P.M. The wagon drivers rendezvoused with us at the appointed time, and we are now luxuriating in the warmth of the wagon's heater. The mutineer Finley has been pardoned, perhaps too soon, since he has taken to bragging monotonously of his exploits on the expedition to Tuttle Lake.

"I wouldn't mind doing that again," he said. "How about you fellows?"

"Perhaps," I replied, "but only for fame and fortune. I've had enough of just-because-it's-there."

"I'll tell you one thing," Mr. Sweeney said to me. "The next time I go on one of these winter expeditions, I'm going to get me a hip flask just like yours. Where do you buy that two-quart size, anyway?"

Before I entrust him with that information, I shall have to assure myself he is fit for command.

Praise for the *Make Your Brain Smarter* Approach

"After partnering with Dr. Chapman, it was an eye-opener to see how easily brain health can be measured, and how important it is to maintain it at every age. Maximizing our cognitive functioning is attainable and an important step in making good decisions over the entire lifespan."

—John Migliaccio, AVP and Director of Research and Gerontology at MetLife Mature Market Institute

"I've had annual physicals for over thirty years, so it made sense to check the top third of the body also. Taking the BrainHealth Physical gave me a sense of peace knowing that I had a baseline of my brain function and could measure any issues that arise in the future."

—Lyda Hill, a philanthropreneur

"When I learned of the research of Dr. Sandi Chapman, I immediately realized her work could be transformational in accelerating the brain performance of employees at all ages. As the global leader of human resources, I am always looking for ways to expand the diverse talents of the different generational age groups that all too often go underdeveloped. Both companies and the individuals will be the beneficiaries of better brain health."

—Cynthia Brinkley, Vice President of Global Human Resources, General Motors

"The profoundly effective program outlined in *Make Your Brain Smarter* uses relatively simple and straightforward strategies to empower learners. The program allowed my son to believe in himself, created a level playing field for him to pursue his dreams, and utilized his talents without barrier deficits. We have seen a dramatic improvement in his brain performance, and I know the strategies will continue to have a positive impact on his life and continued success for years to come."

—David Waldrep, entrepreneur and father whose son
participated in teen high-performance brain training

*f*P

MAKE YOUR BRAIN
SMARTER

Increase Your Brain's Creativity,
Energy, and Focus

SANDRA BOND CHAPMAN, Ph.D.
with Shelly Kirkland

Free Press
New York   London   Toronto   Sydney   New Delhi

Free Press
A Division of Simon & Schuster, Inc.
1230 Avenue of the Americas
New York, NY 10020

First Free Press hardcover edition January 2013

FREE PRESS and colophon are trademarks of Simon & Schuster, Inc.

For information about special discounts for bulk purchases, please contact Simon & Schuster Special Sales at 1-866-506-1949 or *business@simonandschuster.com*.

The Simon & Schuster Speakers Bureau can bring authors to your live event. For more information or to book an event contact the Simon & Schuster Speakers Bureau at 1-866-248-3049 or visit our website at *www.simonspeakers.com*.

Designed by Carla Jayne Jones

Manufactured in the United States of America

10 9 8 7 6 5 4 3 2 1

Library of Congress Cataloging-in-Publication Data
Chapman, Sandra Bond.
   Make your brain smarter : increase your brain's creativity, energy, and focus / Sandra Bond Chapman with Shelly Kirkland.—1st ed.
      p. cm.
   Includes bibliographical references and index.
   Thought and thinking. 2. Cognition. 3. Brain. 4. Neurosciences. I. Kirkland, Shelly. II. Title.
BF441.C3633 2013
   153—dc23   2012024798

ISBN 978-1-4516-6547-5
ISBN 978-1-4516-6549-9 (ebook)

Chart on page 172: Used with permission, MetLife Mature Market Institute 2012. All rights reserved.

To Don: one of the smartest and most compassionate men ever

To Noah: for showing me the evolution of smart in the younger generation

Without brain health, you do not have health.

CONTENTS

CONTENTS

FOREWORD

One of my most recent motivating and exciting adventures has been honoring my commitment to enhance brain performance in Navy SEALs—a select group of military service members dedicated to being at the top of their game in all areas of performance. When I received the letter below from Morgan, I thought what better message to open my book than words from an elite performer. I hope they inspire you to take the challenge of achieving higher brain performance this very day and every day forward.

Advances in modern medicine, science, and exercise physiology have taken our athletes to accomplishments that ten years ago were considered impossible. Usain Bolt ran faster than any human alive at the Olympic games. Mark Inglis climbed Mount Everest on two prosthetic legs. We are growing stronger, and going faster, longer, and higher than ever before.

Do you realize that the winner of a contest whether it is physical or mental is the one that has endured the most pain in training? The champions of the world are the ones that accept the idea that no matter the cost they will sacrifice everything to win. Champions want to be champions, and winners are winners no matter what they are doing at the time. How far can we take the ability of our brains if we actually focused on training it like we do our bodies?

My visit at the Center for BrainHealth taught me many things. One, that anyone can think smarter. Two, you can join the fight sharper than before. Three—none more important than this—I will not fail, and I can be better, stronger, and smarter. Why? Because it's up to me, and I will succeed.

—Morgan Luttrell, Navy SEAL

INTRODUCTION

When I say, "You can increase your brain performance," people stare at me, doubtful that this could be true. It is not surprising that many would challenge the claim and believe it to be false hype.

New brain science discoveries show that individuals, young and old, can, indeed, increase their intelligence.[1-7] As a cognitive neuroscientist and founder and chief director of the Center for BrainHealth at The University of Texas at Dallas, I strive to uncover how the brain best learns and reasons, rebounds and repairs after injury, and builds resilience against decline. The goal: to maximize the amazing potential of our most vital organ—the brain.

My research and scientific discoveries have shown that most everyone can increase their intellectual capital and maximize their cognitive potential.[8-15] What does that mean for you? Simply put, you can control the destiny of your brain. You can mold your brain's frontal lobe, the epicenter of your intelligence, to grow your brainpower.

Do you want to:

- start thinking smarter today?
- learn to avoid habits that drain your cognitive potential?
- strengthen your fluid intelligence continually?
- recognize that memory lapses may not be the chief thief robbing you of your highest level of mental productivity and cognitive creativity?
- advance your capacity to be an agent of change?

The answer to each of these is—a Know Brainer. By learning how to incorporate new brain science into your daily life, you can develop the mental agility necessary to help solve the complexities of the issues you face today and the unknown ones of the future. I will guide you to improve cognitive capacity and increase your peak performance and intellectual capital.

The Limitless Frontier of Cognitive Discovery

For the past thirty years, my life has been dedicated to discovering ways to optimize brain health by applying rapidly emerging innovations to make a difference in people's lives. Through my ongoing research with a host of populations—including but not limited to healthy teens and adults; people who have suffered traumatic brain injuries such as a concussion or stroke; those with brain diseases such as Alzheimer's and other forms of dementia; and children diagnosed with autism and ADHD—I have been struck by two key findings:

- The brain's frontal lobe unequivocally contributes to building resilience, to regaining cognitive function, and to retraining the brain to maximize its extraordinary power.
- It typically takes twenty to forty years or more for scientific discoveries to trickle down to meaningfully benefit human life.

And this is why I am writing this book.

None of us can afford to let our brains decline—not even for a day. You would not accept that for your heart, eyes, or lungs, so why allow such slippage for your most valued internal asset?

If you fail to harness the incredible potential of your brain, you are inhibiting your success. You are, in essence, going backward instead of forging a blazing trail to increased productivity and boundless performance.

Our life span only continues to grow as the twenty-first century proceeds. A health-care policy journal predicts an average American life span of eighty-six years for a man and ninety-three years for a woman by mid-century[16]—more than a decade longer than today's life expectancy—a mere forty years from now. This poses numerous ethical questions. When asked, people tend to respond that they desire to live as long as they have a healthy mind, since a robust and high-functioning brain is considered the very cornerstone of a satisfactory quality of life. Surprisingly, though, the steps to improve cognitive brain function are at least a generation and a half behind what has been achieved for heart health. Significantly more needs to be done to achieve a brain health span that more closely aligns with our body's new life span. This is why brain fitness should become your personal goal.

I have dedicated my life to discovering how the brain best absorbs complex information, learns to think strategically, and innovates at its optimal level. I am determined to help people increase and maximize their brainpower.

Why the Frontal Lobe?

This book will revolutionize how you think and use your brain's frontal lobe to solve the complexities you meet each day. Your frontal lobe is the part of the brain responsible for planning, decision making, judgment, and other executive functions. You will become keenly aware of new brain discoveries regarding which frontal lobe brain habits might obstruct clear thinking and which ones could facilitate your capacity to think smarter rather than harder, day in and day out. You will learn how to build a more robust cognitive capacity, how to process information deeply and insightfully, and how to develop strategic thinking to continually upgrade your realized potential.

One is never too young or too old to commit to a brain health plan that challenges the brain's capacity to think smarter. It requires concerted and continual efforts to achieve robust frontal lobe function since each generation comes to the table with different strengths and vulnerabilities. And while there is almost no area that one cannot improve with repeated practice and proper use, the choice of what to focus on may make a difference.

Our cognitive brain health declines because we let it. We are complicit in our own brain decline by failing to keep our frontal lobe as fit as we can and should, by not adopting and incorporating healthy brain habits that daily promote dynamic and flexible thinking, and by not taking full advantage of all our brains have to offer. It is unsettling how much brain potential is lost due to neglect and improper maintenance. **When your brain-power decreases it costs you dearly. Habitual low brain performance costs an estimated $100 trillion to our gross domestic product.**[17]

The hopeful part is that science is revealing that certain brain functions, such as problem solving, synthesizing big ideas, and innovative thinking, can actually improve with advancing age,[18-22] but only if we keep these functions fine-tuned. You can play a role in slowing the rate of deterioration of many cognitive brain functions—such as difficulty with new learning brought about by lack of confidence and practice—regardless of your age.

What brain value are you willing to lose this year? Or will you take the necessary steps to experience brain gain? Become a master of your own cognitive destiny. Increase your productivity, enhance your success, maximize your potential, and boost your bottom line. Don't overthink it—there is no downside to thinking more efficiently, more clearly, and smarter.

For additional tools and tips visit www.makeyourbrainsmarter.com.

SECTION I

DISCOVER THE FRONTAL LOBE FRONTIER

CHAPTER 1

YOUR BRAIN, YOUR PRODUCTIVITY

Imagine you are a nine-year-old having difficulty in school. You cannot concentrate for extended periods of time. You have trouble staying on task and, frankly, you are bored in the classroom.

You take an IQ test and are branded "average." At the early age of nine, your potential is impacted, squelched by mere words, and you are labeled as mediocre and not smart. How do you feel? Limited? Uninspired? Hopeless?

For years, this label haunts you, and your worries of being a failure grow stronger and stronger. Until one day in your twenties, you realize that you are most certainly not average—you are actually smart, and even more capable than most colleagues around you. Fast-forward thirty years, and you are a successful, innovative executive who exudes creativity and brilliant entrepreneurial skills. Despite your extraordinary achievements and unparalleled accomplishments, you still see the ghost of the early label; you think again of yourself as that nine-year-old who was deemed destined for mediocrity. Millions worldwide share this same story.

The idea that intelligence is innate—something that we are born with that cannot be altered or changed—has been deeply ingrained in conventional wisdom for almost a hundred years. Intelligence Quotient (IQ) testing remains a chief basis to determine different levels of education, potential for jobs and leadership positions, and roles in the military. The only thing that has not changed with time is the definition of intelligence. Until now.

Sadly, when it comes to issues of the brain, many of our thoughts and ideas are outdated and backward.

The brain is our most important and widely used organ, yet it is the most neglected. You do not have to feel as if nothing can be done to improve your brain function and productivity. Your brain can be changed; it is up to you. Your brain's ability to grow and rewire itself is referred to as neuroplasticity in the science community. This means that your brain is essentially plastic, moldable, transformable, pliable, flexible, resilient, and shapable. You can strengthen cognitive brain function and brain reserves at every stage of life—even into late life.[1-3] My goal is to inspire **you** to invest in your greatest **asset** and natural **resource**—your own brain—continually.

Your brain is the most modifiable part of your whole body, and you can rewire your brain by how you use it every single day.

How important would you say *your* brain is to your productivity? We can agree that we could not do much without our brainpower, but, admittedly, much that we are doing (and failing to do) may actually take a detrimental toll on our capacity to achieve our maximum brain potential.

People often ask me, "So what should I be doing to keep my brain healthy?" When I tell them my recommendations, they do not always like what they hear. There are three reasons for this:

1. **There is not a simple formula.** We always want something easy to do, like a certain number of puzzles to complete each day or a magic pill to take, to make us think smarter and keep our brain healthy. But a simple formula or exercise does not have a substantial and lasting impact on such a complex organ as our brain.

2. **We are creatures of habit.** We routinely rely on automatic, lower-level ways to take in, understand, and recall new information instead of using the amazing synthesizing capacity of our brains. We pride ourselves when remem-

bering information near perfectly in its original form when we should be thoughtfully processing and reshaping it to be creative thinkers. When we perform tasks by rote, our brain's connections are not continually strengthened. In fact, rote behavior is rotting our brain potential.

3. **It takes effort.** Our brain has to work hard to transform ideas from content we're absorbing . . . into novel concepts and approaches. The good news is that the more you practice deeper thinking, the easier and more efficient your brain operates when taking on more effortful thinking.[4-7] When you challenge your brain, you will be motivated to achieve new heights.

We each want to live a long life, but only if we still have our minds functioning and are able to make our own decisions. And to do so requires commitment to proper brain workouts—not brain burnouts! To think smarter, you need to learn brain habits to pursue.

Brain science is one of the fastest growing and most prolific fields of discovery, largely because there is so much to learn. Advances in new brain imaging technology are making it possible to view brain changes in real time. However, brain science is still at least twenty years behind heart health. We even know more about space travel and the universe than we do about the brain. Typically, once discoveries are made about the brain through scientific research, it can take at least twenty to forty years before the findings trickle down to change medical practices, advance policy, and improve lives. But our own brains cannot wait that long. Our brains cannot wait even a day. The losses will continually accrue, and may one day be too great to overcome. I am determined to change that. In truth, you can ramp up your mental capacity and build your brain to think smarter than it does today. I will show you how.

> New brain science discoveries show that individuals, young and old, can indeed increase their intelligence.

> We've learned more about the brain in the past ten years than in all previous years combined.

There are two critical pieces of information that are the foundation of this book. I briefly introduced the first—neuroplasticity—but want to expand upon that term here. The term "neuroplasticity" is derived from the root words "neuron" and "plastic." A neuron refers to the nerve cells in our brain. The word "plastic," as defined by Merriam-Webster's dictionary, means capable of being molded or modeled, capable of adapting to varying conditions. Neuroplasticity refers to the potential that the brain has to reorganize and rewire by birthing new neurons and creating new neural pathways.

Several decades ago scientists still widely believed that each individual was born with all the brain cells he or she would ever have and that the potential to develop new brain connections ended in adolescence. Recently neuroscientists have disproven both of these widely held beliefs. Every person can positively influence their brain's capacity to generate new brain cells and build connections in his or her own brain.[8–12]

Understanding neuroplasticity has transformed the scientific field. During the earliest stages of my career, I was intrigued and baffled by the idea that intellectual functioning was fixed. Over and over again, I have seen individuals who have manifested gains with training—healthy individuals, individuals with a brain injury, or individuals who had been diagnosed with brain disease. These individuals defied what I was first taught early in my career. The notion that brain change or brain repair is limited by age, the amount of time since injury, disease, and scale of severity has been proven false thanks to neuroplasticity.

> The brain can grow, change, rewire, repair, and heal itself continually. What hope!

The second pivotal piece of this book is the significant emphasis placed on the brain's frontal lobe. You'll learn more about the importance of this critical brain region in the next chapter, but I have discovered specific ways to expand our brain's cognitive potential by capitalizing and challenging our brain's frontal lobe. We are often complicit in our own brain decline because we don't keep our frontal lobe as fit as we can and should; we do not adopt and incorporate healthy brain habits, and we fail to take full advantage of what our brains have to offer.

The key to investing in your brain now and your cognitive reserve for the future lies largely within your remarkable frontal lobe and its deep connections to other brain areas, as well as ceasing many of the brain habits that work against healthy frontal lobe function. It is critical to adopt habits that **engage** rather than **engulf** your frontal lobe, helping you establish strong mental reserves that allow you to rethink and revamp your environment to better support your brain's health.

What happens today is a paradox: we are working longer hours in school, at home and at the office; yet, qualitatively, we are less mentally productive than we

> Overuse of Brain = Underutilized Potential

should be—a clear case where more is not better. As a society, we deeply value a strong work ethic and associate hard-charging, nonstop working with greater productivity. This incongruity between time worked and output seems like a contradiction and is hard to fathom. In reality, the news should be a relief.

What matters is the quality of the product that emanates from a brain in the "zone," not an exhausted brain that is battling through piles of endless to-dos. Think about an athlete who trains and trains to run a marathon. He runs in the mornings and trains again in the evenings. He believes the harder he runs, the better shape he will be in to complete the 26.2-mile race. But the body, like the brain, has its limits. Several weeks into training, the athlete experiences severe pain. A doctor diagnoses the problem as a stress fracture due to too much strain from exercise on the particular body part. Too much of a good thing is not a great thing. The brain can be overworked, just as the body can. With the brain there is always a trade-off, a balance to be reached.

To capture the linkage between our cognitive brain potential and productivity and our financial wherewithal, I coined the term "brainomics"; this addresses the:

- high economic costs of low brain performance.
- immense economic benefits from maximum brain performance.

Brainomics represents the attainable benefit of your richest natural resource—for personal, professional, and global gain. Increasing brainpower by even small degrees will produce immense tangible and rewarding intellectual returns on investment. For example, economists have determined that the high economic burden of stalled or low brain performance (low educational attainment) currently costs an estimated $100 trillion to our national gross domestic product (GDP) bottom line.[13]

Failing to close the gap between your brain potential and your actual performance costs you personally; it costs you professionally; it costs your family; it costs your company; and it is detrimental to your overall brain health. In short, habitual low brain performance takes its toll on your capacity to perform and maintain a high level and has a significant negative impact on your bottom line.

> You will see the greatest return on investment for the attention you give to your greatest natural resource—your brain.

Put yourself in the shoes of the following individuals who revealed important brain lessons that contradicted previously widely held views. These lessons significantly benefited their own personal and financial bottom lines, as well as those whose lives depend on them and the companies for which they work.

Myth Buster Case 1: Once memory starts to slip, a career is near its end.

Phil was afraid that he should be winding down his medical practice—not because he wanted to, but because he felt his brain was telling him he needed to. At sixty-two, he felt that he could not keep all the relevant information about his patients in his head from visit to visit—a skill in which he had always prided himself for decades. His self-doubts were put to rest when he had a BrainHealth Physical, a unique comprehensive assessment that establishes an individualized profile of cognitive performance in pivotal areas of higher-order mental functioning (you will learn more about this in chapter 3). Reassuringly, when tested, he performed extraordinarily high on intellectual skills of synthesizing, constructing abstracted meanings, and generating innovative solutions to problems—skills that are vital to providing quality medical care, skills that rely heavily on healthy frontal lobe functions. Phil's immediate memory was average but nothing else about his cognitive status was average. He demonstrated astute insights and deeply reasoned thoughts that were more vital to his professional cognitive demands. His *extraordinary frontal lobe function, not just his memory,* provided the fuel needed to ensure sound life-and-death medical decisions that he had to make daily for excellent patient care.

Brainomics: Abstract thinking and problem solving are core intellectual processes that reflect a robust mind, more so than simple straightforward memory. If Phil had retired at sixty-two, it would have been a devastating loss to his practice and to the beneficiaries of his practice—his patients. Some five years later, he is still at the top of his game, staying abreast of new treatment offerings,improving his brain health by his continuous complex thinking, and boosting both his community's and his own personal well-being and financial bottom line every day.

Myth Buster Case 2: Medications alone are the best first-line treatments to help students with attention deficit/ hyperactivity disorder (ADHD) to improve their learning.

Fourteen-year-old Todd had always been successful in elementary school, but in middle school his test and homework scores began to drop with no relief in sight. His declining performance was not due to lack of effort but because of his maladaptive strategies to overcome his attention deficit/hyperactivity disorder (ADHD).

"I would spend hours trying to help him complete his homework assignments," his mother said. "It wasn't that he didn't want to learn, but he quickly became overwhelmed by the massive amounts of information. He was trying to remember so many facts."

"I struggled with reading problems and writing out my answers," Todd said. "I needed something to change in order to improve my test-taking abilities and reading comprehension."

After ten sessions of brain training, where he learned how to engage in top-down processing by pursuing bigger concepts instead of bottom-up learning, which focuses on rote fact memorization, Todd began to construct abstract meanings from lessons and generate innovative solutions to problems. Soon he completed his homework assignments in one-fifth the time, and his grades returned to his A-level potential.

"With the training, Todd felt empowered and equipped to more effectively assimilate, manage, and utilize information," his father said.

"After training, I thought of my assignments in a different way. Todd said. "I approached homework more inspired, seeing how I could think bigger thoughts myself and break down assignments step by step. Learning became easier, and I was able to write more creatively. To top it off, my grades got better in all of my classes."

Brainomics: Strategic reasoning that involves transformed ideas rather than rote learning may enhance attentiveness for students with ADHD beyond what medication can attain alone. For some individuals, *medication may become unnecessary*. Indeed, Todd was able to stop the medication as his study skills improved, and he no longer needed the medication to help him focus. Just imagine the cost savings from elevating educational attainment level, controlling tutor costs, and reducing the need for medication costs. Most of all, some four years later, Todd has regained his confidence as a learner and innovative thinker and has set high expectations for himself as he prepares for college and a career as a statesman.

Myth Buster Case 3: The more exacting our memory, the more brainpower we will experience/exhibit.

Susan, a twenty-two-year-old, mostly A student through school, was hired right out of college as a project coordinator tasked with managing minute details and orchestrating schedules. After three years she was stuck in the same position and was never given an opportunity to advance her career. Why? She was consistently valued and rewarded for her keen attention to details. She was never challenged to exercise her innovative mind to offer fresh ideas and directions. She was being trained to be a perfect robot of ideas—taking in and spitting back data like a computer. Her creative mind was not stimulated so that it could grow.

In Susan's case, her remarkable ability to master details and information led to a great starting opportunity at a wonderful company. Unfortunately, without being intellectually challenged to create novel ideas and see the big picture, she was left bored and frustrated. Her position required prioritizing key decisions to be made, but because all the details and steps seemed equally important, she could not weed out and pare down the data to the essentials. Since Susan was not privy to the bigger goals, she was not learning how the pieces fit into the whole, leaving her feeling stuck, inadequate, and not integral to the overall mission of the company.

Brainomics: Young professionals are burning out and not able to contribute to futuristic paths because they are continually stuck in habitual rote learning. They are *building a brain that retains high volumes of data, but not a brain that can think critically, get out of status-quo mentality, and figure out new paths and solutions.* Educational systems across the country reinforce the importance of memorization and fact learning. Corporations must now provide the proper training environment where young professionals can learn to properly acquire and expand their creative potential, otherwise their potential will stagnate as it did in Susan's case.

> Quality over quantity. It is not how much knowledge capacity you have, but how you use what you know to solve new problems and chart new directions.

There is massive turnover in young top talent, and the costs associated with hiring and training a replacement are not economical. Turnover also drains potential high performers, whose talent is underdeveloped because of inadequate opportunities and brain challenges that engage higher-level strategic thinking, weighed discernment, and dynamic problem solving.

Myth Buster Case 4: The more we use our brains, the stronger they will be.

Forty-year-old Ben, a vice president of a major corporation, was feeling taxed. He constantly pushed his brain, overloading it with information by continually exposing himself to new courses and the latest leadership books and forcing it to complete an impressive litany of tasks at one time. With a packed schedule of back-to-back meetings and a constant open-door policy, Ben felt responsible for putting out all the fires at his company. "I always thought that the harder I worked my brain, the better," he said when I first met him.

Brainomics: In fact, the conventional wisdom of "use it or lose it" has become so oversubscribed that many of us are counterproductive. We are using our brain ("overusing" may be a better word for it) in such an unruly, rampant, and superficial way that we are failing to build and strengthen a mind that intentionally determines what to pursue and what NOT to pursue. Trying to solve every problem, rather than discerning which problems to focus on and which to put aside, leaves us distracted and increases brain drain. *Overuse of your brain is progressively detrimental.* There are major trade-offs to a brain that is constantly firing on all cylinders, diminishing intellectual growth.

Your brain builds deeper connections across ideas when you can take a step back and rest; letting your brain have downtime leads to greater insights, more fruitful pursuits of the important, and deeper-level thinking.[14-15] Efficiently using your brain equals increased mental productivity and richer intellectual resources.

Myth Buster Case 5: The aging brain has lost its potential for brain plasticity—where plasticity means capacity to be modified to rebound from injury.

Aaron was CEO of his own thriving business that he'd started some fifty years before. At eighty-one he had a stroke, which resulted in aphasia—problems expressing his ideas fluently due to damage to the language hemisphere. Aaron was told that he would never be able to go back to work, due mostly to his age but also his difficulty talking, the cognitive residual from his stroke. When I saw him one and a half years later as part of my dissertation work, Aaron was severely depressed and "stuck" due to minimal mental stimulation.

I asked him what his aims were for himself, and he answered that he desperately wanted to go back to work but was told that he did not have the cognitive capacity. After assessing his ability to synthesize and absorb content meaning, I was astounded by his astute intellectual capacity to draw abstract ideas from complex information, although he conveyed this in choppy language. How was this high level of performance possible given a severe stroke at his advanced age? After all, I had learned that the aging brain had little, if any, potential to recover. His high performance belied current thinking on brain plasticity in the older brain. He absolutely had the cognitive capacity to go back to work!

With two months of training, he was back at work part-time and continued to show recovery until he passed away some five years later. His son reported that Aaron got his life back and was certainly able to make sound decisions for the company to keep it thriving.

Brainomics: Our brain retains its ability to rebound from injury later in life—especially if we remain mentally active. Think of the cost burden of keeping Aaron disabled because of age, the perceived residuals of stroke, and the belief that the brain could not continue to recover one year after it had been damaged. This is not about incurring increased rehabilitative costs; instead, it's about taking advantage of the real-life cognitive repair that can take place in familiar life-work stimulating environments. Clearly, the positive brainomics of boosting brainpower into late life can have major cost savings. Aaron was likely able to return to work after his stroke because he'd built formidable cognitive reserves by challenging his brain through complex thinking all his life.

Aaron and his story inspired me to take a strong stance against the negative view of brain repair based on chronological age; I was so encouraged by his robust brain health that one of my first published papers shared his story. Aaron personified the immense potential of the aging mind to regain cognitive function despite a brain injury.

When people ask me where I think we will make the greatest impact in brain research, I quickly say it will not only be in people *with* brain injury or

The impact of subpar brain performance (and even brain decline) can be felt most dramatically on your personal bottom line and sense of well-being.

brain disease; we will make even more positive strides in normal, healthy individuals from teens to twentysomethings, to baby boomers, and for sure into late life for those nearing one hundred years of age. Only recently have scientists, physicians, and the general public begun to address brain fitness in healthy people. Why? Because we only thought brain issues were related to losses that emerged from brain injuries or brain diseases. In the absence of disease, it's essential to detect your own cognitive vulnerabilities, accept what cannot be changed (such as the speed with which you learn new information at older ages), and boost your brainpower in core areas to achieve optimal mental profitability that will powerfully benefit every aspect of your life.

The issue of how your brain thinks (cognition) at all ages is so vital to our nation that you cannot put off your brain's health any longer. But conventional wisdom says "If it ain't broke, don't fix it," leading many to believe if something is working adequately well, leave it alone. **For your brain, mediocrity and status quo are hurting your quest to think and be smarter, longer.**

Your brainpower can be harnessed to increase creativity and mental productivity.

With healthier brain function, you will remain productive longer and continue to make significant contributions to the well-being and productivity of your family, your community, and our nation. Time is of the essence.

Failure to reach your brain potential and declines in brain capacity grow increasingly worse with advancing age. It is up to you to take control of your mental command center and make improved thinking an attainable mission.

Investing in your brain's future, and specifically your brain's frontal lobe, is critical because this elaborate system is the control center for your thinking potential.[16-21] Your complex frontal lobe network, as you will learn in the next chapter, serves as your brain's unimpeachable commander in chief. Your frontal lobe must be efficient, productive, and dynamically flexible to maximize your brain potential and your personal potential.

What robs you of your mental productivity? I suspect you might respond as many do:

- Too many emails to get through
- Too much information to absorb
- Massive demands from others
- Too long a to-do list
- Constant interruptions
- No downtime
- Lack of sleep
- Rampant distractions
- Mindless and unfocused meetings
- Fast pace of changes
- Too many late night events
- A mind that will not turn off

Become an executive to your own brain health and you will reap decreases in illness and absenteeism, reductions in stress and brain fatigue, and increases in your profitability. The United States has recently witnessed a notable decline in innovation, and it is facing stronger economic competition from other nations. But any country can dramatically raise its gross domestic product as the brainpower of its citizens increases.

The math is simple: even the most marginal rate of individual improvement in brain capacity will have exponentially positive impacts when multiplied across populations. The upside of brainomics focuses on increasing personal and society brain net worth, thereby making the world a more innovative, thought-filled, dynamically visionary, and profitable place. Are you up to the challenge? There is no limit to your brain's potential.

Know Brainers

1. Brainomics: incremental increases in brainpower will have an exponential impact on your bottom line.
2. We have learned more about the brain and its

capability to be strengthened and repaired in the past ten years than in all previous years combined.

3. Increase or decrease your brainpower: You decide. Your brain changes from moment to moment depending on how you use it.

4. Maximizing human cognitive potential requires regular investments from an individual.

5. Age can be an asset for brain gain in keystone cognitive capacities.

6. The conventional wisdom of "use it or lose it" is driving down the net worth of our brains.

CHAPTER 2

FRONTAL LOBE FITNESS RULES

Why does frontal lobe power make you think smarter—not harder?
When were you the smartest?
How would you define being smart?
What do you worry about the most in terms of brain function?
Why is synthesizing meaning more vital to solving the complex everyday
*   life problems than remembering specific facts?*
What cognitive habits do you need to break to become a flexible
*   thinker?*
Why is novel thinking greater fuel for robust cognitive function than
*   thinking in routine ways?*
What is fluid intelligence, and is it the same as IQ?
What are the limitations of the saying "use or lose it" when applied to
*   your brainpower?*
Why is complex thinking good for your brain's neurons?

One of the greatest accomplishments of the past century is the doubling of the human life span. Unfortunately, our brain span has not been increased at all. When do you think your brain was operating at its peak performance? It is important for you to pause for a moment to think about the age you felt you were in your optimal mental zone. Write that age down. I want you to write it down before continuing to read on because you will be asked to look back on this age as you learn more about how you can think smarter—longer.

> I was sharpest at age _____.

I ask this question frequently because it always amazes me how people respond. Invariably, they throw out ages at least ten to twenty years younger than they are currently. "When I was fifty," say some, while others say, "When I was twenty-five," and still others, "When I was six years old"—all are frequent ages that I hear.

The typical reaction reflects the assumption that our best brain years are behind us:

- I was smartest twenty years ago, when I could remember phone numbers without a second thought.
- I was smartest when I was in college, when I could absorb facts like a sponge.
- I was smartest when I was in my thirties, with intellectual energy that never waned.
- I was smartest when I was three years old; every day my knowledge increased dramatically.

> Most people believe their best brain years are in the past. Grim thought!

Then I ask people, if you think you were smarter back then, could you perform what you are doing today, say, some twenty or thirty years ago? Not likely. Then why do we think we were sharper back then and not now?

It is appalling that in a world where more people are living to be older than ever before, aging is still seen as a form of disease. We have grown to fully expect that cognitive decline is an inevitable consequence of aging, even though the majority of seniors aged eighty-five and older manifest a potential for well-preserved intellect, capacity for new learning, and sound decision making.[1-3] We live believing our best brain years are in the past. What a depressing thought.

People often ask: How do I know if I am thinking sharper or if my thinking is stilted or stalled? How do I know if I am just plain losing it? Do annoying memory glitches mean I am losing my brainpower?

Ask yourself these questions to help you determine if your brainpower is where it should and could be:

1. Am I able to weigh the risks and benefits of decisions?
   For example: Would you feel comfortable weighing the pros and cons of taking a new job?

2. Am I able to come up with creative solutions to problems?
   For example: Do you know where to go to find the information needed to creatively solve a problem? And do you know when you have enough information to come to a workable resolution?

3. Am I a flexible thinker?
   For example: Are you comfortable departing from traditional modes of thought—from the known to the unknown?

If you answered no to any one of these questions, it is time to tune up your frontal lobe capacity.

Imagine a day without the ability to recognize the need for and embrace change, without the facility to reflect from a broader perspective and manage stressful situations, without the understanding of friendship and managing one's emotions, without being capable of identifying meaningful personal goals and making sound decisions to achieve them. A day without the ability to reason, execute plans, or imagine different options. Sound impossible?

To me, this seems to be a day without the use of efficient, functional frontal lobes—at least the prefrontal cortex and its intricate connections.

Take Jeremy, an extremely bright, talented, and creative fiftysomething who was struggling to manage his workload, his stress level, and his emotions. At first glance, he seemed to excel at being a dedicated worker with a positive and upbeat attitude, pursuing excellence. His career thrived on those admirable characteristics, but after further conversations, he confessed that he struggled to stay on task—any task, big or small. When given an assignment from his boss, Jeremy could rarely complete it to the level of his potential, instead getting bogged down by not knowing where to begin or what to pursue. In the end, he would shut down and turn in mediocre work just to get the assignment off his plate.

Upon assessment, it was clear that Jeremy was not struggling with motivation or ambition. Instead, his frontal lobe was failing him: it was performing inadequately, which led to even more stress, more brain drain, and lower performance.

Your frontal lobe is your higher-order cognitive command center responsible for novel thinking. It represents nearly a third of our entire brain and is intimately involved in orchestrating our capacity to reason, think abstractly, solve novel problems, flexibly deploy mental resources to update information, and generate insightful ideas.

Car rental companies knew what they were doing when they refused to loan cars to those younger than age twenty-five; raw statistics exposed the fact that young adult brains were not making rational and sound driving decisions. Brain science has now revealed that the frontal lobe is not fully developed until the late twenties.[4-6] From early adolescence to young adulthood, the frontal lobe, and the intricate connections between it, are undergoing dramatic functional and structural changes that remodel the brain's complex connectivity and advance its capacity to engage in integrated, reasoned, and high-level thinking.[7]

Anatomically, the frontal lobe, as illustrated below, sits in the front of the brain, just above your eyes in your skull. I adopt the practice of using the term "frontal lobe," as do many cognitive neuroscientists, when discussing higher-order cognitive functions commonly linked to the prefrontal cortex and its complex connections.

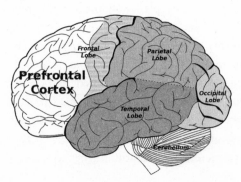

When engaged, frontal lobe brain functions serve to integrate various processes that are essential to independent thinking and decision making.[8–12] Even seemingly simple tasks rely heavily on the frontal lobe working in tandem with other brain networks—interpreting the message from a book or a movie, conveying important ideas in an email, planning and orchestrating a holiday party, or even mapping a route to a new destination. Complex frontal lobe connections are essential to helping us thrive personally and professionally in a rapidly changing world.

New research findings reveal that the road to thinking *smarter* appears to lead to the brain's intricate frontal lobe networks. The dynamic power of the frontal lobe is what allows you to think smarter and deeper every year of life. So much of what you need to accomplish daily is complex and new, requiring heavy lifting by your frontal lobe. Because of its unique abilities, many refer to the frontal lobe as the *sedes sapientiae,* the "seat of wisdom."[13–14] The power of your frontal lobe integrity is what separates you from all other life forms. **Harnessing that power will lead to increased brain potential, maximized brain efficiency, enhanced productivity, and enriched creativity and innovation.**

High-level thinking skills that you so often take for granted, such as figuring out what investment to make, what home to buy, or what job to pursue, emanate from the power of your frontal lobe functions. Those who study cognition often refer to these complex mental challenges as "fluid intelligence"—how dynamically and flexibly individuals use what they know and how they apply learning to new contexts. Fluid intelligence is manifested through the ability to deal with new and uncertain situations and to plan futuristically to solve problems in systematic ways. In contrast, "crystallized intelligence" refers to how much one knows and how much experience one has—that is, how much knowledge has been accrued.

Fluid intelligence relies heavily on the integrity of the prefrontal cor-

> Achieve your brain's potential to solve the most complex problems you face daily.

> Your prefrontal cortex serves as your personal CEO.

tex, and many cognitive neuroscientists refer to fluid intelligence skills as executive functions.[15] The core executive functions are: inhibition[16-19] (e.g., blocking distractions), switching[20-21] (e.g., toggling back and forth between tasks), working memory (e.g. active maintenance and manipulation of information), and flexibility (e.g., changing and updating old knowledge). The integration of these specific processes works in concert to achieve the complex and multidimensional cognitive functions of problem solving, reasoning, planning, and abstracting.[22-24] Fluid intelligence allows you to organize your day and successfully manage the large volumes of information confronting you each moment.

> Novel thinking keeps your brain thriving to support the cognitive demands of a fast-changing culture.

Exploring the best path to increase your brain's net worth—whether you are in your thirties, fifties, or eighties—requires continually strengthening your fluid intelligence. But how do you do that? You will learn more in later chapters, but achieving this goal boils down to **constantly** and dynamically managing, monitoring, and problem solving when faced with new situations, context, ideas, or issues. Fluid intelligence allows you to assimilate and reconcile disparate pieces of information, which you have acquired over your lifetime—perhaps some even this very day—in novel ways to create something **new.** Fluid intelligence skills are called upon when you engage in the ability to manipulate, monitor, and change your thinking in order to deal with stressful contexts or uncertain futures.[25-32] The goal is to repeatedly improve plans, ideas, or actions based on up-to-the-minute information. For example: Will you flexibly apply this book's new recommendations to your life? It is challenging and requires consistent effort to consciously tap into and train the power of your frontal lobe to change your ways.

So, how do you know if you are enlisting and challenging your novel-thinking potential? Ask yourself which side of the fence you stand on these questions:

Do you have the same dinner guests repeatedly?	Do you invite an unexpected guest to change up the conversation?
Do your regular gatherings with colleagues, friends, or family discuss the same predictable topics?	Do your gatherings always have an interesting new topic to discuss?
Do you express the same ideas to convey your stance on issues over and over?	Do you continually attempt to see things from a new perspective when you discuss a topic?
Do you adamantly resist using new technology, such as a new cell phone?	Do you stay open to moving from old to new technology?
Do your emails sound the same? Do you send cards following predictable traditions?	Do you think of creative ideas and unique timing to convey personal messages?
Do you stop short and only complete the task asked of you by your spouse, relative, or boss without reflecting on the process?	Do you add your own thinking to the task at hand or even try to offer new approaches to improve the outcome or solve an unexpected problem?

If you answered yes to the questions on the left, then you are not harnessing the power of your frontal lobe to achieve your greatest potential. But you can.

It is becoming increasingly important to strengthen your fluid intelligence and integrative frontal lobe functions to deal with an unknown future. The ability to succeed at every stage of life—whether in school, in the workplace, in retirement, or in marriage—largely depends on fluid intelligence rather than on how much you know or what your IQ score was at some point in time.

Success = flexible mental resources

Think about it. Success is highly related to the ability to dynamically draw upon and flexibly deploy mental resources to solve new problems, recognize aspects that need to be changed, know when to act on new insights or serendipities, and discern how to resist temptation to do something that would be irrelevant or regrettable. Your frontal lobe and its complex networks have far-reaching influences on almost all major complex mental activities,[33–35] including how to use the latest technology, learn the skills required for a new job or promotion, or develop an impressive presentation or organize a memorable birthday celebration. Those are just a few examples.

Central Command

Your frontal lobe sits in a privileged position as the brain's central command headquarters, linking information back and forth across other brain regions. This elaborate brain communication network guides behaviors by managing incoming information and associating it with existing knowledge stored across brain regions. Your frontal lobe has the vastest neural network and the most reciprocal interconnections with other brain structures.[36–40] This underscores its superiority in controlling our most complex and abstract higher-order thinking capacity. In other words, your frontal lobe power allows you to monitor, manage, and manipulate how you successfully coordinate your day, acquire and apply new things you've learned, and think futuristically.

> Executive functions are more important for everyday life performance and independence than your IQ or intelligence quotient.

Paradoxically and intriguingly, recent brain imaging studies show that frontal lobe functions are the last to develop in the brain and the first to decline.[41–43] The intricate neural circuitry of the prefrontal cortex is *the* control center for complex cognitive functions,[44–45] and it is vitally important to focus on frontal lobe development.

Frontal lobe functions are integral to managing and orchestrating the complex matters of everyday life during all stages of life. For the most part, individuals only think of being concerned about brain health in terms of injury or disease, where you can certainly see more vividly the detrimental impact of impaired frontal lobe functions. However, strong frontal lobe

> Everyone needs to invest in his or her own brain health as early and as long as possible.

functions are crucial in healthy development from adolescence until late life. When people learn what I research—how to maximize human cognitive potential—they say, "I don't need that [aka brain health] yet!"

Much research has focused on the enormous importance of frontal lobe functions in developing youth. But principles gleaned from frontal lobe development in youth are applicable to our brains even as we grow very old. Take the principles from the groundbreaking work of Drs. Adele Diamond and Kathleen Lee's research lab[46] at the University of British Columbia and BC Children's' Hospital in Vancouver, showing that:

- increasing frontal lobe cognitive functions elevates the brain potential of youth at greatest risk for academic failure; e.g., those from lower-income families and those with ADHD.
- in order to maintain gains, frontal lobe skills must be continually utilized and challenged.
- proper cognitive training increases frontal lobe fitness without medication.
- training to utilize complex frontal lobe functions is linked to more generalized benefits in additional untrained areas, whereas training of specific cognitive processes leads to narrow gains and minimal, if any, transfer.
- also intriguing is that stress, loneliness, and lack of physical fitness are associated with low frontal lobe functioning.

Diamond and Lee's work perfectly captures the relationship between frontal lobe functions and the real world: "As go frontal lobe EFs [executive function skills]—so goes school readiness and academic achievement."

I could modify their statement to read: "If frontal lobe executive function skills increase or decrease—so does job performance, family and home management, and personal discernment and decision making for the rest of our life."

Your frontal lobe prowess requires molding in youth with increasingly more disciplined sharpening for the rest of your lives.

Indeed, the above statement applies at every stage of life, yet adults all too often stop thinking of their brains after academic training is over, typically in their twenties. How could you neglect your brain from your twenties on? The answer is you cannot.

The current dilemma, however, is that a mature level of frontal lobe thinking is not a given, regardless of numerical age. Many young people today are failing to develop the full potential of their frontal lobe and critical thinking capacity, as you will learn later. If not given proper training, or allowance to experience some risks, or adequate opportunities to stretch thinking, the ability to perform sound decision making may stall and even fail to develop.

Combine this news of late-developing brain maturation with scientific discoveries that the brain's complex connectivity begins to decline in the forties with the first losses in the frontal brain regions. This paints a pretty dim picture revealing only, at most, twenty years of prime brain function. Can you imagine only having prime thinking for a mere twenty years? I can't. **Adults are living too long without developing, strengthening, and maintaining our amazing frontal lobe potential.** You can have the luxury of utilizing your frontal lobe power longer and building cognitive reserves, if you exercise the core capacities continually. Remember: the brain can continue to grow and change throughout your life.

> The more your cognitive function declines, the faster you slide. Apply the brakes!

Cognitive decline is not a given but is due, in large part, to your own behavior. The adoption of the pervasive laissez-faire attitude of putting your brain on automatic pilot increases the likelihood of mental slippage. Are your days mundane, filled with routine? The failure to pursue being a change maker sentences you to uncontrolled brain losses. Wouldn't you like to avoid this slippery slope?

Fortunately, large degrees of decline in certain cognitive areas may be avoided if you proactively target strategic thinking, especially if you strengthen your mental capital in areas of passion and expertise.[47] Doing so promotes continued stability and the growth of the key pillars needed to enhance frontal lobe brain functions.

> Be empowered: You can mold your brain to think sharper to increase your brainpower.

You'll learn how to adopt and practice strategic thinking, **to enhance your brain potential.**

If the mantra "use it or lose it" is true of your brain, then today you are likely using your brain so much that you should be in a place that is beyond smart. Are you constantly pushing your brain, overloading it with information, and asking it to complete many tasks at one time? Does your brain feel like Grand Central Station during rush hour? Recall Ben from chapter 1 whose brain was constantly exposed to interruptions. What if, like Ben, you are using your brain in a detrimental way and to such an exhaustive degree that you are actually making it less efficient, less creative, and perhaps even burning it out?

Take another case of a single, forty-five-year-old communications executive with whom I recently worked. He made an appointment for an assessment to establish a benchmark of his cognitive abilities and monitor his brain and memory degeneration. He reported that as a function of his job, he is "always on" and works "twenty-four hours a day, seven days a week for 365 days a year." He never loses touch with his BlackBerry, emails during breakfast meetings, texts during lunch outings, and rarely delegates tasks to other team members. In other words, he constantly multitasks, always dividing his attention and rarely, if ever, practices gatekeeping. He overuses his brain! But he can regain control of his mental workstation and increase productivity.

> Multitasking is toxic to your brain and your health.

Multitasking, a common practice for the populace at large, is definitely robbing us of frontal lobe brainpower and reducing its fitness. It is one of the most toxic things you can do to your brain and its health. Multitasking may be a chief culprit in destroying brain cells. We have all become addicted to technology and multitasking.[48–50] But it is not a healthy addiction (learn more in chapter 4). Science demonstrates that the human brain is not wired to perform two tasks at once. Multitasking requires that the frontal lobe quickly switch back and forth between chores. This high-performance demand to

> Age is just a number. With brain age, older should be better.

smoothly switch back and forth fatigues the frontal lobe, slows efficiency, and decreases performance.[51–52]

A client of mine proudly celebrates her age and continually relies on her thinking to maximize her cognitive potential each day. At eighty-three, she is actively involved in strategic business decisions at a financial services company. Undeterred by her numeric age, she is involved in professional projects and community programs that maintain and strengthen her brain's fitness. Whereas most people set themselves up to go on automatic pilot during their last work days and retirement years, this is a bad state of affairs for the brain. **The longer we stay actively engaged in complex thinking and meaningful work, the more energized the brain is and the more cognitive reserves are being built.**

Fine-tuned brain performance is integral to a fine life. The possibilities of increasing your intellectual potential are unending in the absence of disease. Who would have ever thought that you could engineer your brain and help mold how long your mental sharpness would thrive? Of course, genetic, environmental, and social factors are also in the mix in determining your mental sharpness, but brain science reveals that neurons are literally *born* in response to complex thinking and problem solving.[53–59] Complex thinking keeps neurons healthier and more fit—just like physical exercise keeps your muscles more fit.

> Brain neurons live longer when learning is taking place.

Truly remarkable! Just think, you engineer your brain's own health by actively learning. Who said college is for the young? We need to expand our vision of education or at least promote lifelong learning courses.

Previous science writings led scientists, health professionals, and the public, in general, to believe that the brain's life span is associated with insidious and substantial declines year after year. As previously stated, **cognitive decline is happening as a result of nonaction.** Cognitive decline affects your personal and the national economic bottom line. Now is the time to spend effort on building your human cognitive capital to boost your brainomics.

> Complex thinking builds cognitive reserves and increases mental capacity.

And you can do it. If you continually challenge your frontal lobe skills, your best brain years are ahead of you. Truth is, you should be your sharpest now—if you are keeping your brain fit. Your brain has incorporated a lifetime of learning and resonant experiences that can fuel it with the additional flexibility, insight, and judgment it needs to compute effectively in today's hectic world. Prior reports that documented significant age-related declines in fluid intelligence—the ability to think flexibly, engage in abstract reasoning, and solve novel problems—are being reversed. Recent research shows that fluid intelligence is significantly modifiable, despite numeric age, for the better.[60-62]

Brain aging is not, in fact, a vexation to be avoided; rather, it is a developmental process that adds valuable perspective to the brain's existing higher-order thinking abilities. Your brain may be getting older, but if continually fine-tuned, it should also be getting more efficient. And smarter, too. In healthy brain aging, your goal should not be to look for the fountain of youth mythical elixir to return to our younger brain state. Rather, the goal should be to maintain and strengthen your brain's robustness. Keep reminding yourself, if you do not work to improve your brain, you will go backward. For your brain's well-being, you want to keep progressing. If I were to take ten or twenty years off your brain, you would beg me to have the years back because they are packed with such rich developments, that is, if you properly fostered your brain fitness. If you think brains are optimally performing in thirtysomething-year-olds, have them make a decision or two for you.

> Your best brain years can be in the future.

This is not to ignore the fact that as we age, certain cognitive processes show inevitable decline.[63-68] As you age, your brain:

- is slower to learn new things, such as technology; although it is still able to learn, it just takes more time,
- becomes less efficient at storing enormous volumes of new facts,
- experiences increasing numbers of annoying memory access glitches, and
- has increasing difficulty blocking out background noise.

The hopeful news is that even these declining processes can be slowed with effort and practice.[69–74]

The power behind building stronger brain connections is driven largely by how you use your brain to engage in complex and innovative thinking.[75–77] Conversely, you weaken or even lose connections when you think

> Your cognitive capacity can increase with each decade.

superficially. Consider the superior brainpower of some of the great thinkers— Albert Einstein, T. Boone Pickens, Sandra Day O'Connor, Diane Sawyer, Stephen Hawking, and Alan Greenspan. At a general level, these brainy people are thought to be the exception rather than the rule.

These magnificent minds are curious, creative, extraordinary problem solvers and futuristic thinkers. Much can be done to increase these unique abilities in all individuals, especially you, by reframing your thinking to embrace your brain's fullest intellectual potential. In thinking smarter, you can become the rule rather than the exception. Still not convinced of the immense potential you have to neuroengineer, rewire, and build your

> The potential to think broader, deeper, and from a higher perspective increases as you age— thanks to your frontal lobe functions.

brain? Your brain changes moment to moment, depending on how you use it every day—to think, learn, create, problem solve, imagine, love, decide, and plan. And the truth is, you *can* think smarter.

Even more exciting is the news that brain aging can have some clear advantages when compared to the young adult brain. There are more decisive pieces to your brain puzzle as you age

than speed and amount of fact recall. Certain pivotal brain functions do not have to get slowly worse and can even get better.[78–83]

I would go so far as to say that the benefits of more strategic-thinking capacity outweigh the speed and volume of a vast memory for numbers and/or facts. Sound like the lesson conveyed in "The Tortoise and the Hare"? The

> Full frontal: Engage your frontal lobe to increase brainpower.

lifelong lesson of this ageless fable holds true—slow is often a good thing, especially when it comes to pondering critical life issues.

I recently worked with two women both in the same field but with very different frontal lobe thinking patterns. Both were intelligent, hardworking, and goal oriented. The younger, with less experience, a thirty-year-old, demonstrated quick but fixed rote thinking. She did not challenge herself to develop new ideas that were not already stated or in practice based on the training materials we were reviewing. On the other hand, the fifty-year-old constantly explored, was curious about different perspectives, and made new recommendations, taking longer to ponder the major issues. The latter individual demonstrated powerful integrated reasoning capabilities and robust cognitive reserve.

Interestingly, as a society we desperately want flawless memory and are fixated on memory glitches, which are frustrating, for sure, but, as you will see in later chapters, memory remains one of the easiest skills to compensate for in the absence of injury or disease. Indeed, memory recall slows with increasing age. You will find in chapter 4 why the information that was on the tip of your tongue but eluded you when you most needed it comes to you when you are no longer searching.

> Mine your greatest natural resource—your brain.

It fascinates me how wrong we have been about the brain for so many years. Point in fact: all the aggravations of age-related memory loss, as well as losses associated with brain diseases such as Alzheimer's, were equated with brain-cell decline or failure. Up until just recently, scientists believed that brain cells were dying from birth. Now, as Caleb Finch states

> Move beyond memory as your chief brain concern.

so eloquently in the cover article for the 2001 spring edition of *USC Health* magazine,[84] "Now, it is really clear that if you don't have a specific disease that causes loss of nerve cells, then most, if not all, of the neurons remain healthy until you die." These findings change the conversation and the future for brain health. They should inspire you to take advantage of your brain's potential. They inspire me!

Your frontal lobe integrity is what allows you to live independently lon-

> Live independently longer
> with intact brain health.

ger, not the strength of your memory capacity. My father is a perfect example of someone with an impressive memory who could not function independently at ninety years old. Dad's memory was commendable, but his frontal lobe was letting him down. He could not decide what bill to pay or what piece of mail to keep or discard. He knew exactly where every dollar he owned was in his many accounts, each with limited assets—even rainy-day funds that he kept holed away in a filing cabinet for emergency purposes. When we moved my dad from his house to an adult residence, he asked what happened to the $832 that was in the back folder in his file cabinet. He had not touched the money for more than five years, but amazingly, when we counted it, he knew down to the dollar what amount was there. He had an intact and incredible memory but was unable to manage stressful situations or his household bills and upkeep.

Memory ≠ smart

A near perfect memory is not the definition of a robust brain.

I have worked with many people with stellar memory capacities who nonetheless are not highly innovative, insightful, creative, or, for that matter, mentally productive. In fact, memory appears to work independently of strategic frontal lobe functions rather than synergistically. Would you still want a photographic memory if you knew it could hamper your higher-level thinking capacity? It can. And it does.

One of the most vivid illustrations of the link between frontal lobe capacity and everyday life success and independence was documented by the dramatic changes in cognitive facility in Phineas Gage.[85] Gage's situation dates back more than a hundred and fifty years. Gage was struck in the frontal lobe with an iron tamping bar as a result of an accidental explosion at a railroad construction site in Vermont. He regained simple cognitive functions, including memory, for his job responsibilities, enough to be able to physically return to work, but he was a changed man. Gage was unable to successfully engage in the necessary higher-order thinking skills to manage his own life, much less others he had previously overseen as their boss. He could not make simple and sound decisions or stick with plans he made. He had changed so much that the railroad company where he had previously been a model foreman refused to hire him back.

Research has shown that when regions within the frontal lobe or regions connected to the frontal lobe are damaged or not working properly, simple life tasks are difficult despite relatively intact intellectual function.[86–89] Some of the key difficulties are described as:

> Impaired frontal networks are an impediment to independent living.

- Poor insight and ability to take perspective
- Unsound judgment
- Irresponsibility
- Unreliable problem-solving skills
- Marked limitation in abstract thinking and creativity
- Rigid mental flexibility
- Fragile ability to manage emotions
- Poor management of stressful situations

My scientific discoveries[90–94] show that the clues to higher-level cognitive brain performance reside in how you engage, build, and strengthen your frontal lobe functions, including:

- Thinking strategically and futuristically
- Creating novel solutions and products
- Assimilating and reducing complex material to its absolute essence
- Constructing interpretations to improve information absorption
- Priming flashes of insight
- Updating and revising out-of-date goals and knowledge
- Identifying potential problems
- Tackling problems before they appear
- Dealing with new, uncertain circumstances
- Dynamically and flexibly shifting between information to create solutions

More attention is required to build complex strategy-based thinking, which is driven largely by your frontal lobe connections. New brain science reveals strategy-based skills are the foundational pillars that will enhance your brain edge every day and expand our own intellectual capital.[95–100]

> High-performance brain training increases frontal lobe power.

What I have found through my research is the identification of three key frontal lobe processes that are responsible for higher-order brain function: *strategic attention, integrated reasoning,* and **mental flexibility.**[101–4] In truth, very few individuals are indeed reaching their maximum cognitive potential—even executives who feel at the top of their game can improve. I challenge myself daily. I am always pursuing new ways to improve my research because each day offers a gift of new brain potential.

Making a conscious effort to properly engage complex frontal lobe functions will help you attain a higher performance level. As I delve into these pivotal areas, you will begin to understand why these multidimensional cognitive capacities are the keys to building robust frontal lobe function that will promote mental independence throughout life. Then in subsequent chapters, you will learn how to practice ways to build these prime cognitive skills.

> You can build cognitive reserves that will add years to your brain's life.

I will take you through a newly discovered, scientifically proven course designed to increase high-performing frontal lobe capacity in order to elevate your brain's control center in whichever arenas you spend your time and energy—whether you work at home, in the corporate world, or in the community. **You will come to see why frontal lobe fitness rules, no matter your generation, no matter your life's work.** You will learn ways to properly engage your frontal lobe networks to build cognitive brain reserves needed to support a long productive life. Train yourself to increase your dynamic thinking capacity by harvesting the natural integrative abilities of your frontal lobe.

> My goal: To match your brain health span to your life span.

Now I want you to revisit the question we started with and fill in the blank, hoping you will now conceive that your sharpest brain age is not in the past, but now or yet to come.

> I was/am/will be sharpest at age _____.

In the next chapter, you will learn how to get a good vantage point into the health of your brain and become aware of how to strengthen your frontal lobe function, harness your brainpower, and increase your mental productivity while reducing preventable brain fatigue and losses at the same time. You will see how to take a good look at the condition of your own brain. You accumulate large savings in your brain account from preventive actions if you commit to building stronger brainpower. Challenge your brain's frontal lobe capacity. If you do, you will help to extend your brain span to more closely match your extended life span. Now that is a great gap to close.

Know Brainers

1. Your frontal lobe functionality powers your ability to thrive personally and professionally.
2. Frontal lobe fitness becomes increasingly more indispensable as you age.
3. Executive functions are more important for everyday life performance and independence than your IQ or intelligence quotient.
4. Your best brain years can be ahead of you, if you challenge your brain properly.
5. High-performance brain training can increase frontal lobe power.
6. You can build cognitive reserves that will add years to your brain's life and help build intellectual capacity in injury or disease.
7. Frontal lobe fitness rules, no matter your generation, no matter your life's work.

CHAPTER 3

A CHECKUP FROM YOUR NECK UP

Is cognitive decline inevitable? If so, when does it begin?
What are the essential cognitive brain capacities to benchmark and
*   monitor?*
Why get a brain benchmark when you are not worried about how your
*   brain is working?*
What age is prime for getting the first brain health benchmark?
How can intellectual capital (cognitive reserves) be built and stored?
Why is enhancing your brain edge a process rather than a product?

Each year you most likely have an annual checkup with your family practice physician or internal medicine doctor. Weight is noted, blood pressure taken, and cholesterol checked. All routine measures to keep your physical body in tip-top shape. The appointment is brief, and your doctor reminds you to exercise and eat right before sending you on your way. This annual routine establishes a benchmark of your physical health, one by which the next year's visit will be measured. What is not taken into consideration is your brain health, otherwise known as your cognitive fitness level.

> As life expectancy increases, so does risk for cognitive decline.

The Centers for Disease Control and Prevention reports the estimated life expectancy for this decade is seventy-eight. As I mentioned earlier, a health-care policy journal predicts that a mere forty years from now the average American life span for a man will be eighty-six years and for a woman ninety-three years.[1] Increased life expectancies pose numerous questions regarding what tips the scale from cognitive wellness into epochs of cognitive vulnerability. Think about these questions:

- What separates cognitive wellness from cognitive decline?
- Is cognitive loss a condition we will realize is transpiring or are the losses so insidious that they will be under our radar?
- When is cognitive slippage a concern and when is it just a momentary glitch of insignificance?
- Is it possible to stave off decline?

I often say, "Without brain health, we do not have health." The brain is the most vital organ to everyday-life functioning, and it is just as essential to measure and monitor your brain fitness as it is to measure and monitor your physical fitness. Being proactive is key to building healthier cognitive function, and significantly more needs to be done to achieve a brain health span that more closely aligns with our body's new life span. The potential to increase the number of years you have with maximum brainpower is here and now. Take advantage of it.

The majority of the population thinks that only a tiny window of time and opportunity is available to focus on and encourage optimal brain development. In fact, we focus almost exclusively on early childhood in terms of brain health development. This, of course, is a crucial life stage. However, it is too narrow a focus. Just as we have learned about the lifelong need to stay physically fit, **brain fitness requires lifelong efforts.**

> Create the foundation for prime brain function and build cognitive reserves.

A Benchmark for Brain Health

Six important discoveries about the brain are making us increasingly aware of the importance of keeping our brain in good operating function.

1. Our brain continues to make new cells every day we live.
2. The brain can form complex connections throughout life.
3. The connections between neurons can be strengthened against weakness.[2]
4. There is no time limit to brain repair. Previously, it was believed that the window for brain recovery was at most one year after injury; my research has shown that the brain can be repaired months and years after injury if higher-level demands are placed on frontal lobe skills.[3]
5. Restorative brain training practices share commonalities across diseases, injuries, and age related declines.[4-5] For example, thinking beyond the surface-level meaning of information can help build new or strengthen old connections after traumatic brain injury, stroke, in normal aging, and even in a progressive brain disease such as Alzheimer's.
6. Advances in sophisticated brain imaging technology allow us to view changes in the activation of brain regions that occur over the very moments we acquire new knowledge.[6] The changes in brain regions suggest there is more activation during learning. Brain regions work harder (thus requiring more glucose) when acquiring a new skill. As one begins to master the skill, these same brain regions show less activation because the brain does not have to work so hard to carry out the same heavy mental load.

I predict that preventive medicine will put brain health benchmark evaluations at the top of the list of best practices very soon. A brain health benchmark establishes a cognitive index of brain performance to determine current level of function and identify strengths and weaknesses. It allows you to monitor changes in your cognitive function and keep tabs on the stability or fragility of your cognitive fitness as you age. There is also a proactive element to having a benchmark, since it allows you to strengthen areas of weakness and continue to build resilience to guard against cognitive decline. In short, a cognitive assessment will help you better understand how your brain works, what it needs to be more fit, and ideas about how to achieve higher brain performance.

> A benchmark is needed to identify baseline performance as a metric to maintain cognitive brain health.

Presently, no simple test exists that has widespread acceptability to provide a benchmark of brain health. In fact, a simple assessment is not what we should be seeking; a *simple* test will never be sensitive or informative enough to index early failings in the complexities of our brain's capacity. An out-of-state group of talented doctors, who deliver an exceptional two-day comprehensive annual assessment of the body's overall health, came to me asking for advice in adding a brain evaluation component to their protocol. They said they needed something that would take no longer than thirty minutes because the checkup was already too long and cumbersome. I said, "Fortunately for each of us, the complexity of our brains does not lend itself to a simple thirty-minute assessment."

The Known versus the Unknown

> Fear is the greatest culprit to maintaining and strengthening brain health.

Fear of Alzheimer's disease keeps the majority of people in a perpetual state of dread and anxiety about seeking information regarding their brain status. However, when it comes to other health matters, we are often quick to act: checking our cholesterol for fear of heart attacks, watching our diet and exercising to maintain optimal physical health, avoiding sugars and high fat foods to prevent type 2 diabetes. When it comes to matters of physical health, **the known provides the necessary impetus to establish life-saving habits.**

In my research with returning war veterans, one Navy SEAL said, "We spend time doing everything possible to keep our bodies in the highest level of fitness. We would do anything to increase our body's performance edge. As I hear you talk, I am stunned that we have ignored the brain so much in our high-performance training. I want to be the first to get a brain health benchmark. I want to know what can be done to increase my clarity of thinking." And another Navy SEAL said, "Brain performance is the last frontier of human performance. How can we claim to be elite performers if we don't put the focus on the brain?" You, too, can make your brain health a known.

Establishing a brain benchmark is critical. If weaknesses are identified, there are proactive steps to regain cognitive ground. Doing so will strengthen these cognitive frailties early and support independent thinking for vital life decisions for years to come. Unfortunately, the knowledge that something can be done to improve brain health is not widely known. People still believe that if they get bad news about their brain, it is just that—bad news without hope.

> Increasing brainpower can elevate performance and lead to higher return in brainomics.

As you become a brain health advocate, you can become part of the movement to change this outdated and wrong information. **Brain science is revealing there are many ways to fight against brain decline.**[7-14] Optimal cognitive health is a desirable goal, since healthy brain function will be the greatest boon to our personal lives and our national productivity across the life span. But the first step is having a benchmark by which to measure improvement or decline. My team sees individuals for brain health benchmarks with so many different perspectives: (1) those who are excited to know as much as possible about their brain, (2) those who are anxious and do not really want to know, and (3) those who have benefited from establishing a benchmark before brain injury or brain disease.

Like many of the people who visit me, sixty-three-year-old John first made an appointment for a brain health benchmark because he was having memory troubles. Since memory is the most tangible part of the brain, it is this common struggle that lights the fire under individuals to check in on their brain's health. John confessed that his concern stemmed from a history of Alzheimer's disease in his family. Upon assessment, John demonstrated robust cognitive function, innovation capabilities, and creative insight into complex issues. He did struggle with detailed information and strategic attention, saying, "I'm a big-picture guy."

To address his minor weaknesses, my team recommended that he continue to capitalize on his ability to recognize the important ideas. He was then advised to write down specific details that were critical to remember, so he was not constantly worrying whether he would remember those particular facts or not, which could serve to overload his mental workspace and contribute to mental fatigue. He should not be trying to keep track of such information in his working memory space when he could refer to it where he wrote it down. We also encouraged him to assimilate and synthesize new ideas into bigger concepts based on the significant input to which he was exposed in meetings, from substantive emails, or from lengthy documents he had to read. Extracting meaning from complex data is one of the best ways to strengthen frontal lobe connections.

John wrote me after his assessment and follow-up, saying, "I feel invigorated and armed with the knowledge I need to 'mind the gap' and ramp up my brainpower." He commented that due to his family history of Alzheimer's, every time he forgot something, his fear and anxiety would skyrocket. He felt his worry was making his wife very concerned. He was beating himself up about letting so many details fall through the cracks that he was missing the mark on maintaining and even continuing to challenge his innovative thinking capacity. John was relieved when he learned that he did have memory problems, but the cognitive capacities that matter more were intact. He was now able to distinguish between what was a real worry versus what was a vulnerability. Armed with the tools to compensating for his vulnerabilities, John regained his intellectual confidence. He thanked my team for the enlightening, positive experience and said his only regret was that he had waited for so long in a worried state of mind.

And then there's fifty-nine-year-old Mary, a successful CEO, who did not seem to be tuned in to her cognitive slippage. It was not clear whether she was in denial or truly not cognizant of the changes that others could see. Mary was strongly encouraged to establish a brain health benchmark by a colleague who had observed some worrisome loss in her day-to-day performance. When she reported for her brain health checkup, Mary seemed unaware and oblivious to any problems and did not report any concerns about her brain function and current thinking capacity. However, she did report that she often had difficulty remembering people's names and recalling information associated with them—though nothing unusual or worse than any of her friends.

Unconcerned as she completed the assessment, Mary put forth good effort on each cognitive task, but she struggled on every one. She demonstrated significant difficulty on all three key domains of frontal lobe functions (strategic attention, integrated reasoning, and innovation). She exhibited problems in blocking irrelevant data, synthesizing information, and remembering key ideas. Despite this overall low performance, Mary remained unmindful of her cognitive losses and to date has not heeded any of my team's recommendations. Since this was Mary's first brain health assessment, it was unclear how much slippage had occurred, but due to her level of achievement, clearly significant change had taken its toll on her brain's capacity.

Without insight, individuals may not make the necessary changes to take healthy steps to slow cognitive decline—just like with any health concern, whether it be diabetes and sugar or obesity and dieting. When I see clients like this, it causes me to work harder to increase public awareness before it's too late and too much loss has been incurred. What if Mary could have strengthened her cognitive functions earlier? Is it too late to ramp up Mary's cognitive capacity now? It's hard to know for sure and most likely some gains can be made, but one trend I do see is that when people lack insight into their problems, they rarely put in the effort required to make a difference. Sometimes lack of insight is a problem with frontal lobe function. Remember Phineas Gage in chapter 2, who was unaware of his deficits as a result of his brain injury? Change in insight capacity can also signal early signs of progressive brain concerns.

As we think about our brain's future, we need to adopt a comprehensive approach to brain health that is more thorough, more informative, more accurate, and more sensitive to establish a benchmark of brain health. You can join my movement to inspire your circle of influence to actively promote their cognitive brain's health. Everyone you inspire will be the biggest beneficiary.

Brain scientists have been working tirelessly to explore and discover the most sensitive and consequential measures of cognitive decline indicative of progressive brain diseases. Many of the widespread screenings are too low-level and superficial, asking questions such as:

• What day of the week is it?
• What season are we in?
• Who is the president? The vice president?

When you have problems with these questions, almost everyone knows, including the person questioned, that they have crossed the threshold from normal to disease. What if you were asked questions such as these?

• Explain what this saying means and apply it to a real-life circumstance: The long way home is often the fastest.
• Tell me about a complex project you recently completed and what actions you would change if you had it to do over and what you would do exactly the same. What are two things you added that have never been done before?
• Give me three specific ways you would improve health-care coverage and weigh how those changes would impact costs.

Leading-edge scientific teams have contributed significantly to our understanding of early symptoms of dementia and have focused largely on establishing measures to predict and detect Alzheimer's disease. What they have found is that cognitive measures are more sensitive than brain imaging or cerebrospinal fluid markers in predicting who would be most likely to develop Alzheimer's disease,[15-18] at least for now. My goal is not to focus solely on the brain in a state of injury or disease, but to apply the findings we have learned from these discoveries to healthy aging individuals like you to delay decline to the greatest degree and longest time period possible.

Utilizing complex cognitive measures and sophisticated brain imaging, my team and I have developed and tested measures to index the brain's strengths as well as areas that can be improved. Our cognitive assessment is called the BrainHealth Physical. Performance results are used to guide individuals on how to:

• Increase productivity
• Decrease brain fatigue
• Achieve higher levels of work efficiency
• Identify weaknesses in strategic attention
• Focus and stay on task

- Increase flexibility in thinking
- Be aware of habits that drain the brain
- Identify areas of strong mental reserve
- Recognize ways to strengthen core areas of vulnerability
- Increase brain energy

The BrainHealth Physical is a unique assessment of cognitive fitness that examines vital higher-order thinking abilities, such as strategic attention, integrated reasoning, innovative thinking, and mental flexibility. It is not an IQ measurement. It is not a brain scan. It is a mental stress test that measures cognitive abilities that can be enhanced and should remain robust as we age in the absence of progressive brain disease.

> Wouldn't you like to know what drains your brain's energy and regain energy instead of feeling brain exhaustion each and every day?

Clients are comforted by the amount of insight gleaned from their BrainHealth Physical. Jerry Hoag, the executive director of The University of Texas at Dallas School of Management Leadership Center, partnered with BrainHealth and offered BrainHealth Physicals to managers of the world's top corporations to give them an advantage on how to improve their leadership by understanding how to strengthen their own brain capacity. Mr. Hoag said, "So many tests administered to business executives do not inform them as to how to change their behavior."

After taking the BrainHealth Physical, the managers were given exercises to help them improve in areas that are vulnerable. The individual experienced what impacts his or her own brain health first. Then they learned how their leadership style could be either building or robbing their teams' highest brain performance.

We take better care of our cars than our brains by getting regular tune-ups. It is false to assume that the majority of individuals will no longer be able to make their own decisions due to a relentless loss of cognitive function. You can alter this downward course of events if you implement brain health practices now. Take the challenge to maintain and show gains in brain vibrancy in your core frontal lobe functions. Knowing where you stand now is the first step to building cognitive resilience.

Robust brain health **does not** equal high IQ.

There are three main areas of informative metrics to monitor as we age in order to maintain robust cognitive function. You will learn more about each in the following three chapters. These include:

1. **Strategic Attention**—How proficient are you at strategically evaluating information? How efficiently do you decide what information is important to know versus what information should be ignored? Blocking information and avoiding distractions have become increasingly more difficult and a weakened cognitive skill in this day of information overload. How can we tell? Twenty- to thirty-year-olds, whom I refer to as the Finders, are the lowest performers of practicing strategic attention. The frontal lobe skills involved in strategic attention are pivotal as they are some of the leading predictors of a high-performing brain.

   Check out your strategic attention:

   • Can you walk/jog outdoors without music or other input through earphones?
   • Can you hold off for one-hour intervals to check email or phone messages?
   • How many people do you interact with during the day where you are "present" in the conversation without distractions—either doing another task or attending to thoughts in your head? Track the times it occurs—it is rare.

2. **Integrated Reasoning**—What is the status of your current capacity to apply new information across situations? How often do you absorb new content and quickly synthesize the meanings for a vast richness of generalized applications? To succeed in a competitive work environment, one must have knowledge of facts and an ability

to appropriately apply ideas and content at a more global context to strategically direct key changes in course and actions, and an ability to dynamically switch between the two. Switching, or quickly shifting focus between details at hand to bigger issues, is essential to successful brain function whether in the workplace, service of others, or home environments. Believe it or not, those older than sixty-five are best at this skill—despite our current belief that we are the most cognitively robust in our twenties.

Check out your integrated reasoning skills:

- How often do you finish an important phone call and synthesize your viewpoint and ways it converged and diverged from the person you were speaking with?
- Do you prepare bold challenge statements to kick off conversations—even at routine gatherings?
- Do you create subject lines that entice others to read your emails?

3. **Innovation**—How strong is your ability to engage in novel thinking? How ingenious are you at identifying and generating multiple innovative solutions to a problem by seeing different options and appreciating others' perspectives, especially those that differ from yours? Innovation requires novel thinking at every age and involves being nimble in our thinking, keeping our ideas fluid, and staying creative when it comes to problem solving. The Thinkers, or baby boomers, are on top of the pyramid in this skill, at present. But every generation can ramp up their creativity and innovation skills. I will tell you different ways to do so, but you have to first start by understanding that you have untapped potential to be more creative.

Check out your innovative thinking skills:

- How often do you go to the same restaurant and order the same food?

- How often do you pick up and read periodicals or sections of the newspaper you have never read before?
- When someone disagrees with your point of view, how often do you find a few reasons why he may have a differing but sound experience base?
- Do you do something novel each day?

Why do these three areas—strategic attention, integrated reasoning, and innovation—matter so much? These cognitive areas are the foundation to achieve brain efficiency, ensure mental productivity, and maximize brainpower. **These brain processes are the key ingredients for robust brain function and independence late in life.**

> "Vulnerable to aging" is a warning to do something, not a pessimistic edict proclaiming the unstoppable and inevitable.

As you learned in the last chapter, research shows that frontal lobe functions, in general, and reasoning, in particular, are vulnerable to aging.

This progression of cognitive vulnerability has naturally unfolded in many older adults who have not had the benefit of focused attention to improve their brain health. It is time to change the course for each of us. The good news is that you can.

To think about your brain health, you must go beyond the two cognitive skills that we often hold in highest esteem—speed and vast memory capacity.

1. **Speed:** How quickly do you complete a task such as completing a crossword puzzle, finishing a report, preparing a presentation, or cleaning out a closet?
2. **Vast memory capacity:** How would you rate yourself at remembering facts, such as all the medication and various doses you are taking, the major turning points of the Cold War, the names of all the people at an event recently, the names of your high school teachers, the capitals of all the states, or the elements in the periodic table?

We put too much value on speed and memory. Remember, speed of responding and vast memory capacity does not equate to best outcome, nor do they correspond to high brain performance. Early in my research career, I learned that these two prized cognitive assets might not be the pinnacles of brainpower that we all seemed to hold dear. I continue to see this lesson reinforced. In my first aging grant funded by the National Institute of Aging almost twenty-five years ago, I adopted the pervasive view that advanced aging and early dementia were not distinct entities but rather on a continuum, a perspective that is still widely espoused today.

> Speed and quantity do not determine peak brain health.

That is, I hypothesized that adults between eighty and ninety-five would overlap considerably with younger adults (sixties and seventies) with early stage Alzheimer's disease. As often happens in scientific studies, my results were not at all what I expected. Yes, memory and speed of thinking in the cognitive healthy old-old adults, eighty to ninety-five years of age, were significantly lower; similarly, individuals with early-stage Alzheimer's disease in their sixties and seventies showed significant decline in these two areas. What I had not anticipated was that the old-old group were as cognitively capable as healthy adults in their sixties and seventies and even outperformed college students on measures of integrated reasoning and abstracting meanings. For example, when I asked my participants to interpret a long written text, older adults generated more responses and higher levels of generalized statements from a broader perspective than younger participants. To be quite honest, I was mildly shocked.

In contrast, individuals with very mild Alzheimer's disease were significantly impaired in the ability to convey abstracted meanings from complex content. Numerous studies have continued to reveal that higher-order synthesis of complex information is a vital cognitive skill that can be preserved, if not elevated to new heights, in healthy brain aging.[19–21]

Test yourself:

- Interpret as many meanings as you can from your favorite song lyrics.
- Practice devising a newspaper-

> Age is not an accurate predictor of decline in integrative thinking.

like heading to capture the essence of what you experienced during an evening out.

The key is to constantly push your cognitive performance to construct something novel and abstract. By doing so, you will begin to feel your brain energized and ramp up your brainpower.

Imagine the fifty- and sixty-year-olds and sixty-five-and-up participants outperforming the thirtysomethings at the cognitive skill of integrated reasoning. I would wager that the gap is widening each year. Today the young Finders (twenty- and thirty-year-olds) may be starting off at a weaker point when compared to other generations. Whereas Finders may be the strongest in areas of speed and quick recall of more facts, they do not have the accumulated experience and knowledge base to lead in integrated reasoning. Part of the problem is likely due to growing concern that the Finders are reading approximately 60 percent less than the Thinkers (fifties and sixties) generation. On the other hand, Finders may be taking in as much information—perhaps even more—just through different channels. Cognitive brain health depends not on how much information a person takes in but rather how deep the person is reinterpreting and creating new meaning from information.

Findings from my BrainHealth research team have shown that we can change the conversation of doom and gloom to one of hope and cognitive gain at each stage of life. **What's more, we can improve brain function in core areas that matter in the young and the old. But it all starts with awareness and benchmarking.**

Ask yourself these questions:

- How strategic are you in blocking extraneous input? How often do you make your brain do work in a noisy environment, when you could be working in a quieter context?
- How often are you reflecting on how to rethink a project—even when you cannot redo it?
- How often are you figuring out new ways to do things?

Just as the 1960s aerobic exercise movement got our bodies moving, efforts to motivate the public to get our brains in gear will have major payouts. We need to engage the frontal lobe in cognitively challenging activities that involve higher-order reasoning to strengthen and preserve cognitive capacity—regardless of age.

MIND THE GAP

"Mind the gap" is a warning that was coined in London in the late 1960s to warn Tube (or, underground) passengers of the potential danger in the gap between the station platform and the train door. Metaphorically speaking, nearly all of us possess brain gaps, or areas of cognitive function that are not performing to their optimal potential. If we do not mind our brain gaps continually every single day, the expanse between our lifespan and brain health span will grow wider—an overall gap that becomes increasingly more difficult to close. Just as passengers riding London's underground tunnel system are reminded to mind the gap between the train and the platform, you too want to heed this warning in terms of your brain and its performance. Tend to your cognitive gaps every day to build the most robust brain possible.

Think of your brain as a bank; you need to build your cognitive reserves, much as you would contribute to a savings account. This allows you to guard against cognitive decline. **Cognitive reserves are how much cognitive capacity you have built up or saved at any point in time to counter brain pathology either due to disease, injury, or age-related losses.** Research has proposed that the more cognitive reserve you accrue over the years, the more likely you are to be able to functionally stave off decline and guard against brain loss in terms of mitigating degrees of impairment. This explains why higher levels of education seem to be consistently associated with more protective cognitive capacity. How much is in your brain bank to counter the effects of brain loss? It is never too early or too late to start making deposits to your brain bank. For example, how often do you hear a fascinating interview on public radio or a talk show and share the meaningful messages you gleaned that are unique to you? To build reserves, you want to keep stretching your mind to extract big principles, not try to be a scribe of someone else's ideas. Stretch yourself to take on new mental challenges you have a natural affinity toward.

> Avoid challenges that drain your passion.

Though a real phenomenon, cognitive reserves are currently more of a theoretical construct than one that can actually be indexed. The term was conceived to help explain why people vary greatly in terms of the relationship between the degrees of brain damage and cognitive loss. For example, the same degree of Alzheimer's pathology may produce little cognitive impairment in one person and produce major cognitive impairment in another person. Similarly, my research in traumatic brain injury measured individuals with minimal brain damage who showed major cognitive problems as well as the reverse pattern.[22-25] That is, I evaluated those with severe brain damage who were able to recover high levels of cognitive functionality. So why is it that some brains experience minimal damage with major consequences? Whereas others suffer major injuries, and within months they are back to high functionality? Both may have similar pre-injury IQ but different cognitive reserves.

The lack of reliable correspondence between brain damage and cognitive performance has prompted researchers to explore this concept of cognitive reserves. Cognitive reserves mitigate the amount of brain loss that has to occur before evidence of cognitive impairment is manifested on measures or subjectively recognized by significant others in a person's life.[26-27]

The more cognitive reserves you have built up, the more protection you have for staving off decline resulting from the brain culprits that directly or indirectly damage the brain, e.g., chemotherapy, chronic stress, brain injury, stroke, or forms of dementia. When a person has lower levels of cognitive reserves stored, their cognitive capacity will likely be vulnerable to even small degrees of brain insult. In contrast, with higher reserve levels, the symptoms will appear later and be milder as compared to those with low

> Keeping your mind mentally active makes your brain's neurons healthier, longer.

reserves and similar degrees of brain insult. How do you build up cognitive reserves? By constantly engaging in complex mental activity.

You must decide today if you want to give your brain the best chance to rebound from injury or other brainpower thieves to be the strongest possible each day. You cannot wait a day to start actively working your brain. In fact, researchers find that people who are more cognitively active over their whole brain span have less amyloid buildup, an abnormal brain deposit associated with Alzheimer's disease.[28-30] If people wait to get their brain charged on challenges, the gains are less robust. Do you want to let your brain go backward? For the majority of people that is exactly what is happening.

Thus the higher levels of cognitive reserve you possess and build,

    1. the longer you will be able to stave off cognitive decline.
    2. the less severe the cognitive decline will be.

My research efforts over the past decade have focused on identifying brain-training regimens that can lengthen optimal cognitive functioning in meaningful ways critical for everyday life functions.[31-38] My findings are adding to the healthy brain evidence that fluid intelligence and higher-order thinking capacity can be improved into late life if we implement the ABCs of brain health.

> Your brain is your most important organ and deserves your attention.

- A = **Awareness** of personal brain performance—strengths and vulnerabilities
- B = **Benchmark** of cognitive brain function as the starting point of a cognitive fitness plan
- C = **Conditioning** to conscientiously engage in complex and personally motivating mental challenges that draw upon the vast frontal lobe networks.

As mentioned earlier, one of the most overlooked aspects of performance is our brains' health. One of my clients, Steve, commented that he had always prided himself in being able to keep up with all the demands that were handed to him. Not until his brain benchmark had Steve realized the high cost of the stress he was under and information overload on his brain performance. He was having memory problems, unable to keep a coherent train of thought, and slipping in terms of his previous innovative thinking. He was motivated to turn things around and regain his cognitive losses. With specific strategies in place, Steve was determined to change his brain habits and recapture his brainpower potential through conditioning and practice.

Know that your brain is one of the most modifiable parts of your whole body. As the most important aspect of your health, it should be delegated a prominent position front and center. It is up to you to either be a lackadaisical brain athlete or an elite Olympic-level performer. With a healthy brain, longevity will be a boon to society and to our economic bottom line. In the next chapters, you will learn the necessary steps to maintain your brain function and improve its health so that the brain you have at seventy-five or ninety-five is even more robust than it is today.

For additional tools and tips visit www.makeyourbrainsmarter.com.

Know Brainers

1. Without brain health, we do not have health.
2. Get a benchmark of your brain's fitness level as soon as possible to make sure you rebound and maintain your cognitive capacity as long as possible.
3. The complexity of our brain core processes requires a sophisticated measurement of fluid intellectual capacity.
4. Continual learning and education builds protective cognitive reserves.
5. A brain health benchmark is perhaps more important than a physical checkup because it is the first step toward maintaining and strengthening capacity.
6. Brain health habits are vital at all ages; each stage of life has different cognitive challenges and potentials.

SECTION II

MAXIMIZE YOUR COGNITIVE PERFORMANCE

CHAPTER 4

STRENGTHEN YOUR STRATEGIC BRAIN HABITS

How strategic is your thinking?
What is the upside and downside of multitasking?
Are you a gatekeeper or do you crave data downloading?
Why is access to more information not making us smarter?
Learn how improving your brain health can be as simple as remembering none, one, and two.
　　Brainpower of None
　　Brainpower of One
　　Brainpower of Two
How can you take advantage of silence to increase your insightful problem-solving capacity?
How can you advance your strategic task prioritization?

Your brain contains more than 10 billion neurons with more than 10 trillion connections, or synapses. The numbers are staggering, representing the most amazing and complex network imaginable. Your genetic makeup plays a key role as the architect of this intricate labyrinth; your brain, in general, and your frontal lobe, in particular, support unparalleled computational thinking, which, to be quite honest, no computer can come close to matching.

A thirty-five-year-old male client of mine announced to me, "More, more, more—the more I have access to helps me make better decisions." Joe, a highly successful professional who is actively involved in the community, attends every single meeting in and outside his office or town, seeks and keeps massive amounts of data constantly, and acts as the primary contact for many projects. He does not prioritize. He mistakenly thinks that **more is better.**

When asked if he had any concerns about his brain performance, he confessed, "My kids think I have a memory problem." Halfway joking and halfway not, he conceded, "I am having a little trouble. I feel like my brain is fried at the end of long days. I can't even keep their names straight, and I only have two kids!"

After our conversation, I assessed that his problem was not his memory. Joe, like many other high-achieving individuals, was pressing his brain to take in and manage as much as possible. Unfortunately, his relentless pace and info-craving habits were zapping his brain energy.

What is a strategic brain? When you use your brain strategically, it filters information by deliberately sorting input and output. The approach is two-pronged: (1) attending to necessarily essential information while (2) filtering out extraneous data that is less critical to the task at hand. In contrast, a nonstrategic brain takes in all information.

Despite the brain's immense processing capacity, it cannot take in every piece of input—it does have its limitations. Our brain is built to work dynamically and efficiently; by design, it is smart. It is not built to be a massive information storage processor. We need to stop and ask ourselves if we want to use up our brain's limited resource capacity by focusing on trivial and poorly vetted information. **Which type of brain are you building? A strategic or nonstrategic brain?**

Even if our brains could store and process endless amounts of information, you would not want to sort through it all. I am reminded of how Sherlock Holmes describes himself to Watson in *A Study in Scarlet.*

You see, I consider that a man's brain originally is like a little empty attic, and you have to stock it with such furniture as you choose. A fool takes in all the lumber of every sort that he comes across, so that the knowledge which might be useful to him gets crowded out, or at best is jumbled up with a lot of other things so that he has a difficulty in laying his hands upon it. Now the skillful workman is very careful indeed as to what he takes into his brain attic. He will have nothing but the tools which may help him in doing his work, but of these he has a large assortment, and all in the most perfect order. It is a mistake to think that that little room has elastic walls and can distend to any extent. Depend upon it, there comes a time when for every addition of knowledge you forget something that you knew before. It is of the highest importance, therefore, not to have useless facts elbowing out the useful ones.

Boost your brainpower: What are some take-home messages from this passage about Sherlock? By thinking about these, you will boost your brainpower.

For me, one thing is clear: you need to be selective and keenly strategic in terms of what you store in your brain's attic. Of course, knowing at the point of entry whether a piece of information will be useful is not always possible, but you definitely need an effective triaging system than most currently employ.

Do you ever stop at the end of a day to reflect on all the impressive feats your brain helped you achieve? You should. With seemingly little effort, the brain typically responds and carries out the many demands you constantly make of it. Therefore, it is often taken for granted. Instead of marveling at its magnificence, individuals tend to remember the glitches more often than not. Everyone thinks back on that day when they could not recall an individual's name, or walked into a room and forgot what they were there for, or the time when they had a brilliant idea or question but lost it when it was their turn to speak.

The immense power of your brains' intricate cognitive capacity is so much more sophisticated than a memory system. Still, people place an extraordinary value on memory. In a survey of five hundred adults, I asked for the number one thing they wish they could improve about their brainpower. More than 80 percent said they would wish for a better memory, even a perfect memory, if that could be achieved.

> The wish for perfect memory may be more of a curse than a blessing, if granted.

When a wish becomes reality, it may not be what you truly want at all. King Midas wished that everything he touched would turn to gold. His wish was granted, and he was exuberant until he touched his beloved daughter, who turned into a gold statue. If you were granted a perfect memory, it may be your greatest stumbling block in terms of brain health and higher-level thinking.

Your brain is updated moment by moment and hour by hour. In essence, you frequently get a new processing system. **Indeed, you have the potential to change your brain with everything you do that has some level of challenge, novelty, or variety.** My research has found an interesting paradox: when one focuses on remembering the minute details, it may ad-

> Everything is a trade-off. The more you focus on details, the more difficult it is to decipher big ideas to take into your brain bank.

versely affect the ability to engage in more strategic abstract thinking.[1-2] In essence, trying to remember as many details as possible can actually work against being selective about what you let into your brain's attic. This pattern helps explain why access to more information is not, on its own, making us smarter. More likely, quite the opposite is true. Exposure to large volumes of information steals and freezes your brainpower. However, my research has also shown that when focused and engaged more in strategic, abstract thinking, it becomes easier to remember the details.

> Strive to build a strategic brain; a strategic brain is a brain changer and life changer.

Adults are pushing their brains so

hard to solve and complete more tasks than ever before. Produce, produce, produce is a familiar refrain heard in our own thoughts, in school, in the workplace, and at home. But to build a healthy brain, you must stop your brain drinking from a fire hose that is spewing vast amounts of information. What you need to dedicate yourself to is building a strategic brain.

For Linda, a high-level executive at a Fortune 500 company, interruptions are her biggest hurdles to overcome. "Interruptions, people stopping by my office, phone calls, and an exponentially increasing number of emails—each with a new response expected instantly—are robbing me of my productivity. I often leave the office feeling like I can never catch up no matter how hard or how long I work."

Yes, being and feeling overworked is a prevailing hazard of the workplace. My BrainHealth team trained Linda in specific ways to take back control and harness the full frontal capacity of her brainpower. Retaking control requires daily prioritization of one or two predominant tasks, rather than jumping back and forth from one distraction to another. Task jumping is an all too common practice that is failing to advance the most crucial tasks and hinders strategic working and deeper thinking. Read on to see how Linda changed her beliefs and habits about what being mentally productive means.

One of the biggest obstacles to brain health is that our belief system about productivity is inaccurate. We all too often measure our productivity by how quickly we respond to emails and phone calls, juggle countless demands each day, and cross off item after item on our long to-do lists. The problem is, most tasks are done quickly without thoughtful processing— and instead almost with mind-numbing automaticity. Our quick responses make us feel like we are moving forward at the speed of light—as if we are keeping our daily bicycle moving forward. But are we running over pieces of glass or nails that may flatten our tires into mental exhaustion, making us lose our brain balance?

For some, there is a sense of guilt when they don't respond immediately to interruptions.

I remember when a client of mine, Paul, asked me: "What if it's your boss who is demanding immediate responses? If I fail to be timely, I will not

> Openness to distractions is keeping your brain off balance.

be looked upon favorably. It's easy for you to tell me to stall rather than respond quickly, but you better let my boss know or I'll be coming to you when I fail to get promoted."

I replied, "You are absolutely right. There must be buy-in at all levels—especially management. Leaders are some of the leading offenders—causing the state of constant distractedness and shooting themselves in the foot by reducing their team's productivity."

The guilt you feel from not responding instantly spurs you into action but does not pay off in terms of brain efficiency. For many, your competitive nature makes you your own worst enemy. We think we can do everything well, in record time, regardless of task.

Take Jim. A middle-level manager, he once told me, "I feel like I'm in a competition with myself and my team. It makes me feel worthy and important to know the answer and to be the first to send the answer out." But a polar opposite of Jim is Carmen, a woman I recently worked with who noticed the following: "I've found that if I don't respond immediately or engage in knee-jerk reactions, most of the problems solve themselves. Instead of a flurry of emails trying to solve a problem instantly, I let the problem take its course (if it's a nonemergency) and strategically select when to attend to it. By that time, eighty-five percent of the problems are solved and no response is necessary."

Dorie Clark, in a *Harvard Business Review* article titled "Five Things You Should Stop Doing in 2012," recommended that people stop responding to email like a "trained monkey."[3] She commented on how responding to email was becoming like a "slot machine for your brain"—with variable interval reinforcement. In fact, few of our emails require immediate responses. As Clark writes, "A 90-minute wait won't kill anyone, and will allow you to accomplish something substantive during your workday." I couldn't agree more.

Through my research, I've found that more than 87 percent of professionals report that they are interrupted more than 80 percent of their day, making it difficult to take even five minutes to deeply ponder the important work needed to be accomplished or thinking through ideas that would advance major conference calls concerning key problems. Much effort is wasted because we have not allowed space and time to ponder. **The unfiltered, massive influx of new information competing for your consideration and the constant interruptions from cell phones chirping, emails**

dinging, and in-person intrusions rob you of clear, strategic, insightful thinking. Constant interruptions are depleting your productivity. These interruptive expectations and environments are increasing rather than decreasing, causing a higher incidence of interruptions. The result is lower performance, more errors, and greater stress.

Rather than being strategic about how we use our brain time, we nurture and pride ourselves on how many emails and phone calls we receive and respond to each day. Rather than trying to fend off our addiction to being continuously available, we are reachable at all times, day or night, at work or at home. Until now, brain science had not discovered that such rapid exchanges of communication hinder rather than help your brain's competitive edge.

Nathan Zeldes, a former IT principal engineer at Intel Corporation and now principal at Nzeldes.com, wrote an article in 2007 titled "Infomania: Why We Can't Afford to Ignore It Any Longer."[4] Zeldes and his colleagues, David Sward and Sigal Louchheim, define "infomania" as the mental state where one is addicted to information downloading—an insatiable quest for additional information. This addictive habit is tough to break despite the continuous stress and distraction caused and, in essence, this infomania is detrimental to our brains.

> Our addiction is an insatiable craving for and an inability to be separated from technology. Our ability to constantly access more information may be the very thing that is contributing to our sickness.

Over time, your cognitive ability to focus and think deeply about one or two reputable information sources may be diminishing as a result of your habits. The brain's ability to inhibit how much information reaches its sphere of attention is weakening, meaning that the frontal lobe may become faulty, unreliable, even disrupted. In short, you may be reprogramming your brain to be exhausted, unfocused, and constantly responsive to interruptions. You are putting your intellectual capital at risk—daily.

> A voracious addiction to information is toxic to your brain's productivity.

"Each day I can feel my blood pressure rise as new information and an influx of new action items from emails, meetings, and conversations are thrown my way," Linda, the Fortune 500 company executive, said before her BrainHealth Physical. "I force myself to absorb volumes of information."

Are you able to strategically attend to tasks at hand?

Ask yourself these questions to determine how vulnerable or how robust your strategic attention is:

- Do you allow frequent interruptions (three to four per hour) when you are working on your main tasks?
- Do you jump to a new task when immediately asked rather than making good progress on the major goal of the day?
- Do you multitask more than twice a day when you're working on a major project or work with background noise that your brain may actively have to block out?
- Do you work past your regular bedtime two nights or more a week to solve complex problems or complete major assignments?
- Do you have difficulty knowing when you have saturated your capacity to think clearly and work effectively?
- Do you recognize when there are strains on your task performance?

If you answer yes on two or more of these questions, your strategic attention requires an overhaul.

Whose fault is it that you remain in a constant state of distractibility? Is it due to your rapidly changing world, your boss, or yourself? **It seems adults today literally strive to be distracted, unable to allow a solo entry of input for even brief lengths of time.**

Microsoft researchers studying productivity taped twenty-nine hours of people working in a typical office, and found that they were interrupted on average four times each hour.[5] Additionally, 40 percent of the time, the person did not resume the task they'd been working on before the interruption. The more complex the task, the less likely the person was to resume working on it after an interruption.

Boost your brainpower: Track yourself. How often do you spend more than ten minutes on one task at home or at work?

In addition to being continuously ready for any distractions (email chirping, texting, pinging), if you are like many adults, you have a strong attraction and bias toward overstimulation and massive data downloading. The immense information downloading is taking an insidious toll on each of us, and yet we falsely believe we are thriving on infomania. And on a personal level, these consistent and ever-increasing interruptions are related to **elevated stress levels,** i.e., increased cortisol, frustration, more sickness, and hampered creativity.

Do you often feel your brain is extraordinarily fatigued at the end of the day? You may be failing to develop and strengthen strong frontal lobe strategies to hierarchically organize the information to which you must attend and the information you can throw out. It is like staring at the sun and being unable to see it because of the brightness. There is no way your mind can remember everything. Information overload is blinding your mind.

Strategic attention involves removing yourself from information absorption to solve problems. It is the ability to block and filter distractions while focusing on a central task. Focus is not just concentrating on the context at hand but, more important, it is about knowing when to step away and when to close off your mind from distractions. As Kenny Rogers would say, "You gotta know when to hold 'em, know when to fold 'em." That is exactly what we must do to improve our strategic attention: know when and what to regard versus when and what to disregard.

> "Know when to hold 'em, know when to fold 'em."

Improving Strategic Attention

Your frontal lobe acts as your gatekeeper—letting in certain information while blocking out the rest. If you work hard to attend to as much information as possible, the brain gets overwhelmed and fails to reach its potential.

Science is revealing ways to maintain and strengthen your brainpower and improve your strategic attention, leading to increased productivity and overall well-being. **One key way to revolutionize the way you learn, energize your imagination, and ignite a deeper level of thinking is to be more strategic about how much information you take in at one time and how much effort you spend blocking out distracting information.**

> Strategic attention is based on the brain principle that less is more.

When you improve your strategic attention, you will develop habits to take back control of your time versus being controlled by your to-do list. You can take advantage of the vast potential of frontal lobe networks by sculpting your strategic attention habits.

Strive to develop and bolster strategies to enhance your strategic attention. How do you do it? You need to proactively and consciously establish core habits to prioritize goals and extract the goal-relevant ideas or features from the massive input you face.

Boost your brainpower: Practice strategically attending to a core task for a minimum of fifteen minutes at a time without interruptions.

With practice, the brain has amazing potential to filter out much of the superfluous information flooding our senses. But the problem is that we are engaging in hypervigilance—focusing on everything. Tony Schwartz, president and CEO of the Energy Project and author of *Be Excellent at Anything,* wrote an article for the *Harvard Business Review* on the importance of doing one thing at a time.[6] He warned that our major problem today is that we have lost our stopping points, finish lines, and boundaries. He warned that we are spending too many continuous hours juggling too many things at the same time. I agree. It has gotten so bad, we do not even believe we can do one thing at a time—nor do we want to. After reading this book, one of the biggest takeaways and easiest habits to implement is doing one thing at a time. Once you see how much more productive you are, you will not go back.

Track your own multitasking. For three days do the following:

- Chart the length of time per day you are able to focus on one and only one task without doing another single thing at the same time.
- Note how many tasks you work on longer than fifteen minutes without interruption.
- Note how many sidesteps arose because you were multitasking or allowing yourself to be pulled off task by distractions.
- Be aware that one of the major culprits to multitasking is the abundance of thoughts that fill your mind while you are doing something else.

We are forcing our minds to stretch their limited resources to actively ignore and simultaneously focus. As a result, we are doubly punished. This explains why clear thinking seems to be getting harder, regardless of age. But thinking doesn't have to be so arduous if you make just a few adjustments.

We often work in cluttered, noisy environments that push our brains to put forth an inordinate amount of effort just to actively block information. No wonder many of us are overworking and fatiguing our brain! Now that you realize you are having to work extra hard to block out stimulation, will you rethink your environment?

Scientists are working hard to develop markers to show brain efficiency in selecting and inhibiting information. It's just as essential to block information that's unimportant and irrelevant as it is to selectively attend to necessary information. When

> Your brain has to work hard to ignore and filter information just as it works hard to focus on information.

> In the near future, a brain biomarker could determine one's frontal lobe integrity by measuring the brain's capacity to inhibit and its ability to attend.

people say, "I wish I could improve my concentration and my ability to focus," I advise them it may be more productive to improve their ability to ignore—and then their ability to focus will be sharpened.

I have determined that there are at least four different profiles into which individuals can be categorized, determined by the characteristics of their strategic attention.

Strong Strategic Attention

1. **Strategic attenders:** Individuals who fall in this category learn over time and practice to employ strategies to improve their performance.
2. **Quick studies:** Quick-study performers adopt strategies immediately and continue to improve their performance as well as show generalized benefits to improving basic memory span.

Inefficient Strategic Attention

3. **Strategy-less:** These individuals try to remember everything without applying a strategy, failing to focus on particular information while ignoring other less relevant information.
4. **Faulty gatekeepers:** These individuals not only try to remember everything, but they also let the gates open too wide so that irrelevant information, even information that was never presented, intrudes on their learning and thinking.

What would your profile be?

Thirty-seven-year-old Doug does not practice gatekeeping. Even during his BrainHealth Physical, where he was asked to complete one task at a time, he was multitasking. Like many, Doug's chief multitasking distraction was taking place inside his own head. His internal thoughts were keeping him from being present. As a small business owner, Doug is involved in both strategy development and tactical execution at his company. However, his inability to attend strategically to important information while blocking out unimportant information is limiting his brain potential. No wonder he is struggling to move to a higher level of strategic planning.

Jane, a thirty-year-old communications professional, recently went through a BrainHealth Physical. She reported difficulty focusing on one task for an extended period of time, partly due to the nature of her job. With constantly changing circumstances and a pressure to respond to

> Stop blinding your mind. Step away and stop the flow and gluttony of information overload.

phone calls and emails quickly, she struggled to maintain strategic attention. In addition, Jane felt pressured to gather as much information as possible to form a well-grounded point of view to lead her clients down the correct path toward increased third-party credibility.

With a full explanation of strategic attention and recommendations to enhance the necessary cognitive process, she now practices ways to strategically attend to what is important and eliminate what is not. The result is a more efficient brain, increased creative thinking, and higher productivity. Specifically, Jane was given the following recommendations to reduce her brain fatigue:

1. Identify an issue/task each day for which she would like to find a better solution than the current practice and step away to take time to reflect on possible solutions. Within the week, offer her insights to her boss to show her independent and strategic thinking.
2. Practice interval training with email communications. Set regular times to attend to email and stop when time is up—for example, schedule twenty minutes three times a day. Only work on emails at that time—not simultaneously trying to do another task. The email messages will be more thoughtfully conveyed, standing out to recipients as being more thought-filled rather than reactionary. Do not spend your best brain hours deleting emails as it is a major time gobbler and gives a false sense of forward progress.
3. Reduce exposure to the amount of information she is being inundated with each day so that she can focus on one or two of the most important sources.

There are three strategies you can implement in your daily life to enhance your strategic attention. You will learn about these three core strategies below:

- **Brainpower of None**
- **Brainpower of One**
- **Brainpower of Two**

The Brainpower of None

How often do you work harder and harder to solve a problem? What if the brain solves problems best by taking a break from the matter? Have you ever noticed that when you struggle to solve a problem, you sometimes receive the answer just before you go to sleep or right when you wake up in the morning? Connections are built when brain activation slows, and even when our brain is at rest.

> Sleep is good for strategic thinking.

Brain scientists are beginning to show that when the mind quiets down and brain activity slows, we are able to connect the dots in new ways. When we are in a frenzy, frantically searching for answers, we do more to handicap our minds than to actually solve the problem; we are pushing our brains to the limits, failing to discover fresh insights.

Think back to when you could not remember the name of the person walking toward you; instantly you were embarrassed because you were well aware of all the facts about them, such as how you knew them, where they lived, and even their children's names. But your mind was frantically searching for that person's name, to no avail. Then somehow—out of the blue—

> Brain Paradox: Your brain works smarter when you make it slow down.

when you were no longer trying, perhaps on your drive home from the encounter or when you were brushing your teeth, the person's name came to you, clear as a bell. Why it could not come to your mind when you needed it demonstrates a glitch in the brain's search-and-rescue mission of immediately retrieving desired information that exists in your memory storage system. This simple example shows how you recall data when your mind is at rest.

Many report that they find themselves doing their best, most insightful thinking when they're half asleep, in the shower, or on an airplane—when they have been removed from their habitual hectic life context, precisely when they quit trying so hard. Now that is a mind marvel!

Solving problems or searching for an answer is not just about focusing and blocking distractions; it is also about stepping back to let the mind rest. Science suggests that a calm brain is more apt to trigger creative ideas and stimulate breakthrough thinking to solve complex problems when we hit a mental impasse. Joydeep Bhattacharya, a professor at Goldsmiths University of London, found that he could predict when people would solve insight puzzles based on their slowed EEG activity.[7] How? Steady alpha waves were seen on the right side of the brain, which is associated with a relaxed brain.

> Our brain works for us when we quit working it to the max.

Even more intriguing about how our brain works is that when participants in Bhattacharya's study showed strong gamma rhythms (as contrasted with alpha waves) after requesting clues to help solve problems, their brains seemed to be less open to using the clues to solve problems. Bhattacharya went on to suggest that when the brain is working hard to solve a problem, it basically froze the adults in their ability to benefit successfully from the additional clues they were given. Their minds seemed to get stuck and were not able to identify new options to solve the problem in front of them as opposed to being mentally nimble and flexible in seeing new possibilities. Although how alpha and gamma patterns predict brain states is still a bit controversial, brain scientists speculate that a relaxed brain allows the frontal brain regions to connect seemingly disparate and distant information to create novel solutions (see chapter 5 on integrated reasoning).

In his *New Yorker* article titled "The Eureka Hunt," Jonah Lehrer vividly described the real-life story of Wag Dodge, a man caught in the middle of a major fire in Montana while leading his team of fifteen firefighters to battle an out-of-control blaze in 1949.[8] Dodge saw the fire coming very close, and he did something very much against natural human instinct. He stopped. In that moment of pause, he had a flash of insight that saved his life. He lit a match that quickly set the slope around him on fire, then wet his kerchief and lay down amid the smoldering surrounding ground. Thirteen firefighters died trying to outrun the fire, but Dodge came away untouched. He could not explain how or where the idea came from, but in taking pause, a life-saving solution came to mind.

> Searching for more information to make a decision? Stopping the search may make you smarter and more decisive!

I refer to this as the **brainpower of none**. Big ideas often come when the brain stops frantically trying to solve the issue at hand. The brain thinks more clearly when it is seemingly doing nothing or is in a calmer state (since the brain is really never at rest—thank goodness!). We often experience major aha moments when we stop trying and clear our minds.[9] Often when we are practicing the brainpower of none, our brain's frontal lobe continues to search, change strategies, and start thinking in new ways.

Aha moments, or episodes of insight, are recognized as:

- A breakthrough after feeling like you were hitting a mental wall
- Seeing new ways to solve problems that did not seem to exist before
- Having a feeling of certainty that an idea will work
- Engaging in bigger-view thinking more than rationale thought

When we solve issues, we are often surprised we could not see the solution before. Does this mean you should not work hard to solve problems or complete tasks? Absolutely not! But you have to know when to practice the **brainpower of none**, giving your brain rest to allow new insights to emerge. Your frontal lobe works for you in creative ways when you step back.

> Use silence to think deeply, see things differently, and solve perplexing issues.

It is becoming increasingly rare to find times when people truly practice the brainpower of none. Instead, individuals constantly fill their thought-space with added stimulation. Take Patti, for example. She said her best downtime was when she was running. I said, "Terrific. Tell me about your running regime—do you observe nature or have music in your ears?" She said, "Oh, I definitely use an iPod with my favorite tunes when I run." I responded, "Having to actively block music from your mind, your brain is working rather than being freed up to make new connections. Therefore, running with an iPod is not downtime for the brain."

Others suggest driving in the car as their downtime. Again, many cannot stand the quiet. Try finding a time when your environment is truly quiet without any background stimulation to have to block out. When do you actively make time to have the **brainpower of none**? Incorporating time windows of silence in your hectic schedule will advance your complex thinking capacity.

Practice the **brainpower of none**, when you experience:

- Brain fatigue
- Information overload
- A major decision without clear direction
- A dead end to an issue
- Frustration and negativity

Boost your brainpower: Take time away and allow your brain to rest. To have your next aha moment, don't overthink it.

The Brainpower of One

Can you imagine a life without multi-tasking? With technological advances, we are readily able to do more; in other words, we are expected and addicted to doing more at once. Résumés from recent grads that come across my desk

Take your mind off your old thinking to discover a new way of thinking.

often include the words "efficient multitasker" or "ability to multitask" in a list of notable skills. With a constant connection to email, a cell phone, and the Internet, we have trained people to believe that multitasking is the key to success; we take pride in the ability of how much both others and ourselves can do at the same time.

Whenever I give a lecture on strategic attention and the **brainpower of one,** I often begin by raising my right hand and saying, "Hi, my name is Sandi, and I'm a recovering multitaskaholic."

It's true. I spent the first stage of my career juggling multiple tasks at the same time, thinking I was accomplishing everything at lightning speed and with the greatest efficiency. However, with more experience and knowledge of how the brain works, I learned that multitasking was one of the most toxic things I was doing to rob my brain of energy and high mental performance.

> Are you a multitaskaholic?

Yes, there are seemingly positive benefits to multitasking:

- Immediate access to massive amounts of information
- Greater input from multiple sources
- Ability to work faster
- Enhanced capacity to respond to more people in less time
- Being allowed to do more at the same time

But we have to stop and ask ourselves: What is our addiction to multitasking costing us? I asked myself this question years ago, and the answer I found changed my life forever.

Research has shown that if we counted all of the time we spend doing various tasks simultaneously, we'd actually be working an impossible forty-six-hour day and a 322-hour week, instead of our rampant 24/7.[10] No wonder we are so brain fatigued all day! Multitasking is bad for your brain and actually weakens your higher-order thinking capacity. Cognitive testing and brain imaging research reveals that multitasking causes

> Do you find yourself stretched to a breaking point? Do you often have trouble sleeping?

- shallower and less focused thinking;
- increased errors; and
- a dramatic negative decrease on mental processing.

Think about the impact of multi-tasking and frequent interruptions to task performance:

> Multitasking diminishes strategic attention.

- High mental productivity requires periods of single-minded tasking.
- The concept of doing one thing at a time is not being rewarded in the workplace, at home, by individuals, or by bosses.
- On average, we work for a total of only three minutes with laser focus, with no multitasking or interruptions.
- Once interrupted, it takes, on average, twenty minutes to return to the original task.
- In total, adding the time we are distracted and the time it takes us to return to the original critical task to complete it equals 2.1 hours! If only we could recoup all that time!

The lost time is not the only major cost. Multitasking actually makes us sick. It leads to a buildup of cortisol, the stress hormone that decreases our memory and contributes to increased brain cell death. Some scientists have even suggested that a buildup of stress and elevated cortisol levels is a major contributor to pathological conditions such as dementia.[11–13]

Our brain could have fooled most of us into thinking we are superior multitaskers! When asked, most people believe they are just as proficient when doing two things simultaneously. This is not true. We are wearing down our brains— literally fatiguing them with our constant demands to attempt two activities at the same time. The brain's frontal lobe has to quickly toggle back and forth while performing the two tasks. Your brain is built as a single channel action system with limited capacity; it bottlenecks when trying to do more than one thing at a time, except in very rare cases.

> Simply put: your brain is not wired to do multiple things at once.

When you superimpose a second

or even third task on top of doing something else, you saturate your mental capacity.[14] You are working your frontal connections harder to fight off interference from the flow of information. When pursuing a single goal, your frontal lobe works efficiently. When pursuing two goals concurrently, your frontal lobe power is divided and decreased.[15] If you add a third task to your attention dashboard, your errors increase dramatically, as much as tripling. This huge increase in errors reveals the severe limitation of our human cognition task overload. The debit to your intellectual capital is costly.

> What is on your brain's dashboard at this very moment?

People who are addicted to multitasking always want to challenge this finding. They say, "Maybe most people cannot, but I know I can multitask." And they are absolutely right. There are exceptions to the impossibilities of multitasking. When one or more of the tasks we are trying to complete are automatic (i.e., requiring less controlled thinking), it is possible to do two things precisely at the same time. For example, think of when you have folded laundry and held a conversation at the same time. Marcel Just and his colleagues at the Center for Cognitive Brain Imaging at Carnegie Mellon studied whether people could drive in a simulated driving task while having their brain scanned as they listened to spoken sentences and judged whether they were true or false.[16] The researchers were trying to mimic talking on the cell phone while driving, but admitted that judging sentences was not equivalent to deep conversation between the driver and the person on the other end, making it a more automatic task.

> Heavy multitaskers are building inefficient brains. Multitaskers have difficulty blocking out irrelevant input from their environment.

Nonetheless, in 2008 Just and colleagues still found a significant deterioration in driving accuracy (i.e., more driving errors) when research participants were processing sentences. Moreover, there was significantly less activation in the brain area (parietal lobes) devoted to the spatial processing necessary for driving ability—as much as a 37 percent reduction. The researchers suggested that their failure to find differences in frontal lobe activation as identified in other studies during multitasking might be due to more automaticity in both of their experimental tasks. For the brain, the task of processing sentences while simulating driving is not exactly comparable nor as challenging as dealing with all the life-threatening factors competing for our attention when driving in dense traffic on superhighways.

Now, all this is **NOT** to say that you should stick to one task for extended hours on end. **Your brain gets bored if fixed on one task too long.** Clearly, task toggling has its rewards. It helps to refresh one's mind. You may find that you are more mentally energized when you return to a complex task after a break to work on a separate issue. You just need to strike a balance between these two.

Boost your brainpower: instead of multitasking, perform tasks sequentially and remember the brainpower of one—focus on one task at a time, even if only short segments of time.

The Brainpower of Two

To-do lists are great and absolutely necessary so you're not forced to repeatedly remind yourself of the things you need to accomplish—a brain drain in itself. We have been trained to use to-do lists to organize our days. But, all too often, we have too many to-dos without any reflection of prioritization, leaving us feeling overwhelmed just by the sight of the list. They also fail to reflect a looming deadline and very often lack the necessary precision to tell us where to start and what to do here and now. Looking at an endless list of tasks freezes our minds.

More often than not, to-do lists consist of simple tasks to move the ball forward on a project such as the following: email so and so, call this person, check in with that person, or complete a specific document. If you're like most when looking at a massive to-do list, you choose to do the easiest things on the list, or tasks that can be completed in a measurable amount of time, so you can have the satisfaction of crossing something off the list. However, this process saves the difficult tasks that require more strategic thinking for later, when your brain is more tired. We are working and attending to distractions immediately and continually functioning well below our brain's potential. With the constant state of fragmented focus, our brainpower is kept at a very superficial level.

Remember Linda, the principal at a Fortune 500 company? After becoming more aware of her brain health and the importance of sequential tasking and not multitasking, she allowed herself the freedom to engage in continuous deep thinking on main tasks at certain time intervals. She intentionally assigned and gave the majority of her time to her highest priority and top-ranking tasks, investing wisely in her intellectual capital.

> To increase the return on investment in your intellectual capital, you need to focus on the highest priority task, and not invest time in a wide range of "junk" investments.

Linda explained the difference to me. "Professionally, improved strategic attention has helped me change how I allocate my time at work. I have forced myself to change my habits of instantaneous responding to most every interruption by practicing interval training with laser-focused blocks of work time. I no longer allow myself to be constantly interrupted, even by my own thoughts of the next small thing to do. Focusing on my major projects and not allowing time-gobbling constant disruptions has helped tremendously. I now set aside designated slots of time devoted to email and returning phone calls rather than being available all day long. I cannot believe the difference it has made to allow me to be more 'present' in each of the activities I'm involved with throughout the day."

She continued, "Becoming aware and doing something to strengthen my strategic attention relieved my stress by showing me that I really could take back control of my out of control schedule and still be highly productive and responsive."

> As T. Boone Pickens would say, "When you're hunting elephants, don't get distracted chasing rabbits."

Boost your brainpower: When you write your to-do list, focus on the two things—your elephants—that will have the most impact, require the most attention, the most rested brain effort and strategic thinking.

Don't get distracted chasing rabbits down endless trails all day long. Start using your copy of the elephants and rabbits **brainpower of two** to-do list at the end of this chapter. Identify your one or two elephants for the day—those are your top priorities. Be aware that rabbits should not turn into elephants; they truly are less important tasks.

Linda agrees with this approach. "Instead of constantly multitasking and crossing off less-essential items from my to-do list, I now concentrate on my pivotal goals for the majority of my working hours. When I need a break, I take care of some rabbits. I constantly reassess my schedule to make sure I am spending the largest chunk of my time tending to my elephants—the most important and vital tasks to being productive that day. I now realize if I neglect my elephants, they may run over me. Not so for my rabbits; they keep coming back. Learning about my brain health and how I was being inefficient with even the scheduling of my to-do list has had a major impact on my productivity and, in fact, has led to even stronger work output. I am even designing a sign to post on my closed door: 'Do not disturb—taking care of elephants!'"

To be mentally smarter, we must constantly reevaluate and identify one or two top priorities that demand the bulk of our energized brainpower, not the leftover, burned-out energy. Even in the midst of doing an activity, we should ask ourselves: "Is the task that is currently consuming my brainpower the activity that I need to devote my longest attention to because it will have the greatest impact?"

Boost your brainpower: Strategically attend to your two most important tasks every day.

To boost your cognitive function, you must harness the power of strategic attention and build a brain that filters and focuses. Doing so will increase your productivity and lead to improved well-being. Strategic attention alone is the most action-oriented step to maximizing your cognitive potential, but it cannot be done alone. Learn more about the important brain process of integrated reasoning in the next chapter.

Know Brainers

Brainpower of none: When you hit a mental wall, quiet your mind to regain brain energy and find fresh solutions. Learn to use silence to solve perplexing problems and think deeply.

Brainpower of one: Work on one thing at a time. Sequential-task instead of multitask. Secondly, strategically block a large percentage of incoming information and consciously know what to select.

Brainpower of two: Every day identify and dedicate the majority of time to your two most important "elephant" tasks.

Make Your Brain Smarter

makeyourbrainsmarter.com

CHAPTER 5

ENHANCE INTEGRATED REASONING TO ACCELERATE PERFORMANCE

How does complex mental activity rewire your brain to be healthier?

Why does continually engaging in integrated reasoning make your brain more efficient?

In what ways does engaging in complex mental activity, such as integrated reasoning, improve the biological health of the brain?

When and why should you transform incoming facts into abstracted ideas?

How do challenging integrated reasoning activities keep your fluid intelligence from going backward?

What activities and contexts provide rich opportunities to expand your integrated reasoning capacity?

How can the principles of integrated reasoning be exploited to energize meetings and inspire email communications?

What are ways to improve integrated reasoning capacity to accelerate strategic leadership skills?

Do you feel that those around you are able to:

- Express an idea you had been thinking, but say it with weighty impact and perfectly worded?

- Write emails that express ingenious thinking that garner positive traction?
- Interact on conference calls with comments that have lasting and strong influence?
- Generate promising solutions that others start immediately deliberating over?

Integrated reasoning is a rich, multifaceted, ubiquitous, and impressive mental capacity that, if regularly practiced, can revolutionize your brain health habits and your mental intellect.

You think you might have as much potential as any person does, but then you are not sure. Is it confidence? Is it social wherewithal? Or is it that such individuals have taken advantage of opportunities and expended the effort to be an entrepreneur of ideas? Have they developed regularly practiced habits of complex mental processing? I would wager the case is the latter. Remember the opening story of this book? We have long believed (the majority still believe) that we are either born smart or not. **Discard this outdated conventional wisdom today, this very minute. There is nothing you cannot get better at doing.**

Whereas it may seem that it comes naturally to others, well-formed innovative ideas are more typically the by-product of long-standing, effortful, dynamic thinking habits and content processing patterns. This mental habit can improve integrated reasoning levels regardless of age. Its expansion requires time and effort. To improve your skills in the bulleted points above, think deeply, and integrate those thoughts in your communications throughout your day. Even use silence to free the mind to imagine possibilities. Take the challenge to engage in complex mental activity daily by practicing integrated reasoning and you will advance your personal skills as a CEO, aka Cognitive Entrepreneur Officer.

Integrated reasoning is your brain's platinum cognitive asset. Really. Integrated reasoning is fundamental to all major goals you strive to achieve, decisions you make, projects you orchestrate, and major life changes and choices. This platinum asset requires continual fortification. On the upside, you can elevate your integrated reasoning capacity immediately. Do not be stuck and squelch your potential based on what others have told you at some point along your life path. You have immense potential to excel whatever your stage of life. On the other hand, if you perceive yourself as being relatively strong in integrated reasoning, cautiously remember that strong at one stage will not hold unless regularly practiced. Integrated reasoning is a skill that atrophies relatively quickly without practice.

Integrated reasoning is represented by these mental activities:

- Generating synthesized ideas
- Reconciling and updating novel ideas within the context of your rich knowledge base
- Extracting and altering broad principles from complex input
- Creating broader and new ways of thinking and acting
- Dynamically changing old practices by cultivating original thinking
- Reflecting on and discontinuing outdated old principles that are stifling entrepreneurial thinking

Integrated reasoning is transformative thinking. When you become astutely aware of the distinction between when you employ integrated reasoning habits of thinking versus insidious rote thinking patterns, you will see and experience a brain gain in a relatively short time period. Integrated reasoning is the fundamental principle for your brain's lasting resilience that ensures you do not lose ground. It is imperative to continue to exercise your integrated thinking muscle daily. See in the chart on page 85 some differences in integrated reasoning and insidious rote thinking on important tasks.

> What does it mean to synthesize ideas: to construct novel, generalized thoughts? To synthesize meaning requires taking in facts, filtering the meanings, and transforming these into abstract concepts by drawing upon the rich experiences and knowledge that come from your uniquely built mind.

Activity	Integrated Reasoning	Rote Thinking
Meeting Planning	Set novel goals, write desired outcomes; have each attendee abstract their take-home message; determine next best steps	Write out schedule, who is speaking, topic to discuss
Asking for a promotion	Write a vision statement for yourself in the current job; synthesize the major hurdles you have overcome; abstract three principles as your value-add	List all job duties, describe how you completed each, outline your next major projects assigned

Integrated reasoning is the most cost effective method to advance your fluid intelligence at any age. There are no fees, no particular amount of time to set aside for practice. Integrated reasoning can be incorporated in your daily activities as a way of thinking to extract and express ideas.

Integrated reasoning will energize your thinking as well as increase the biological well-being of your brain. **Simply put, you are promoting your integrated reasoning intellect when you actively synthesize new meanings continually.** What this means is you construct new meanings from the vast data you are consuming, then you update ideas constantly by reconciling, interpreting, and converting these concepts, ideas, approaches, and solutions within the context of your vast existing experience and knowledge. Integrated reasoning is a dynamic cognitive brain habit where ideas are rarely static. You are exercising your integrated reasoning when you:

- form uncommon ideas.
- identify new problems.
- generate and revise workable solutions.
- reject or accept possible directions.

Integrated reasoning requires that you pool information from a handful of reliable sources, combine the key ideas, and condense the core meanings to their bare essence. Note that I say "handful," because often too many sources are perused, but only at a shallow level. For frontal lobe strengthening, It's better to go deeper when processing a few meaningful sources than shallowly processing many sources.

In relaying transformed information to others, do not start with the minutiae—from the bottom up. You will lose their attention if you have them go through the same arduous process of sifting through the large volumes of data. Start with the big ideas instead; it is more mind captivating for you and for those with whom you are communicating.

Being a CEO (Chief Entrepreneur Officer), you want to lead by example. Show others how big ideas, new solutions, and new opportunities are created, generated, and pervasively incorporated at multiple levels of communication. How many times have you left a meeting and thought it was the biggest waste of time? Or hung up from a conference call and been

> Transformative thinking does not start from nothing. For novelty to emerge, new ideas are rooted in old ones.

exhausted by fast-fire exchange of undirected, low-level ideas with lack of meaningful takeaways or best next steps? Or gone to a lecture or community service meeting with high expectations but leaving in frustration due to the lack of a clear message?

Reflect on your entrepreneur of ideas status:

- Look at your sent email (or text messages) and locate ten that you wanted to send and receive back meaningful messages. What percentage are formulaic and predictable in the messaging and what percentage show high-level integrated reasoned messages? Is the message noticeably written by you, or could it have been written by anyone? Does it bring together ideas that were previously discussed with new concepts? Is it perfunctory or inspiring? Now rewrite one message you wish you had sent. From this point forward, take the time to write abstract, meaningful messages when it matters. This is one easy way to regularly practice constructing big ideas.

- Think back about a gathering of friends you recently attended and whether or not you had a meaningful conversation with a single person there or if it was all scripted at a superficial level of engagement. Now, for an upcoming outing, make a concerted effort to discuss some topic in detail, particularly if you and the other party may have differing views.

- Do you daily share something you read or heard on the news and give specific ways that you would improve the situation? I hear all the time how much people disagree with this point of view or that point of view. But individuals rarely voice the rationale for their stand because they have not taken the time to get to a deeper level of understanding.

Integrated Reasoning: A Comparison

Contrast the two stories of Mark and Wesley below to gain a better handle on why integrated reasoning is the significant groundwork necessary for increasing brain edge.

Case 1: Mark, a competitive individual with ample integrated reasoning capacity

Mark started a new career at age sixty-three, an age when many of his friends were either retired or certainly thinking of retiring. His bold move into a new job summoned different knowledge and responsibilities from the skill sets of his previous jobs, requiring major readjustment and on-the-job training. A year into his new job, he decided to get a cognitive checkup, a BrainHealth Physical, not because he was worried, but because he was curious about what a benchmark of his core cognitive areas (i.e., strategic attention, integrated reasoning, and innovation) would tell him about his brain's function. Plus, he prided himself in proactively being in the know and was always seeking ways to challenge and improve his high-performance edge.

The outcome of his assessment revealed that he excelled on measures of integrated reasoning.

- Mark synthesized complex information into novel ideas. He absorbed and processed new, unfamiliar content and constructed original ideas that were not explicitly stated.
- Mark showed a rich capacity to efficiently encapsulate multiple rich interpretations and applications from complex information.
- Mark actively constructed new thoughts and meanings by linking ideas from his rich experience and knowledge to the new skills.
- Mark was not stuck in the concrete data, words, and ideas as explicitly presented, nor was he blocked or overwhelmed by the abundant unfamiliar data he was being asked to absorb.

Mark's high level capacity of integrated reasoning likely accounts for why he quickly rose to a pivotal national leadership position and was able to take on great challenges in his new career. Within a year after the job shift, he was energized and contributing new ideas and ways of thinking to his colleagues. He was able to dynamically employ strategies to blend his rich knowledge and experience base with new on-the-job responsibilities. He put into practice the habit of utilizing frontal lobe processes to continually synthesize vast information into new, broader ways of approaching critical decisions and tasks. Mark actively added to his intellectual savings account.

His brainpower was a **major** contribution to his Fortune 500 company and supports a potentially positive side of **brainomics,** the economic benefits from brain gain. Mark's brain was being strengthened and the corporation's bottom line was likely boosted.

Case 2: Wesley, a competitive individual but with fledgling integrated reasoning capacity

When I saw Wesley, he was a fifty-two-year-old executive who had been a stockbroker. Wesley's performance on integrated reasoning tasks during his BrainHealth Physical was well below average. His primary way to absorb content entailed condensing and rearranging the content, paraphrasing the same ideas into his own words, and repeating the key points. He did not transform information into novel or generalized ideas other than those already conveyed. Although Wesley was skillfully competent at reducing the vast information he was given, he did little to change and construct broader perspectives.

Wesley had lost his job due to restructuring and was struggling to find a path to translate his old skills to a new job. Even though he was extremely bright, hardworking, and competitive, he was unable to create ways to reframe his vast expertise and knowledge to fit a changing, demanding environment.

On the surface, one might quickly conclude that Mark is smarter than Wesley. I would argue that this is not the case; in fact, they are both well above average intelligence. Mark, however, has used his brain dynamically to make it work smarter, which has paid off and will continue to pay off in the long run. Wesley, on the other hand, needs to ramp up his integrated reasoning capacity; it takes concerted effort, increasing challenges, and regular practice. Mark has continued to build this pivotal brain function at each decade. Wesley has not fully activated and harnessed his brainpower.

> Become a masterful synthesizer; don't remain an apprentice.

Our brain is designed to be a great synthesizer, but it requires effort to keep this amazing feat fine-tuned. Our brain is expertly capable of boiling down massive input streaming in and transforming ideas into generalized, abstracted essences of new meanings, new directions, new patterns of operating. The worrisome trend is that despite our brain being preferentially biased to extract meaning from the continuous, immense input; its synthesizing adeptness is rapidly losing ground.

> Ramping up your integrated reasoning will increase your brainpower. Exploit your capacity to design new knowledge, unveil new discoveries, chart new paths, and even invent new ways of thinking about old issues.

The problem is individuals are spending less and less time building, strengthening, and maintaining this platinum brain asset of integrated reasoning. Ramping up your integrated reasoning will increase your brainpower. We are weakening our brain's capacity to be a great synthesizer by overwhelming it with too much data and distracting information. We are constantly besieging our brain with information through all sensory inputs—visual, auditory, olfactory, tactile, and kinesthetic. As we take in, manage, and appraise vast amounts of information from every information platform possible—from conversations to computers to phones to television to newspapers, magazines, and books—we are incessantly processing thousands of stimuli and ideas, little to which we should pay conscious attention.

> Without practice, integrated reasoning capacity does not thrive or even survive regardless of how smart you are.

Catapult your Brain Plasticity: Utilize Your Complex Mental Capacity

Breakthrough brain discoveries reveal strong evidence as to what:

- Drives brain fitness
- Derails brain fitness

The answers lie largely in utilization issues. A common theme throughout this book is that **you control the destiny of your brain health.** Now consider this: how you use or fail to use your frontal lobe's complex thinking capacity of integrated reasoning drives whether you achieve and maintain higher levels of brain fitness or, conversely, whether you lose and regress to lower levels, at any age.

The following findings will hopefully give you the fuel you need to commit to a brain health exercise program this very day so you don't lose one more day of your brain's potential. In a randomized study of the effects of complex mental activity on brain and cognitive plasticity, my team and I found that engaging in integrated reasoning for a relatively short period of time was associated with **significant brain changes:**[1]

- Increases in brain blood flow by as much as 12 percent. This news alone should arouse you to invest in your brain by adopting complex thinking workouts daily. A healthy brain's total blood flow **decreases** each decade beginning at age twenty. The evidence of increasing brain blood flow with complex mental activity indicates that not only can you increase the total blood flow to build a healthier brain, but you can also prevent the inevitable reduction. When you engage in complex thinking, your brain's neurons demand glucose and oxygen, which therefore increases blood flow. Bottom line: the earlier you start and the longer you continue to engage in complex mental activity, the more you are likely improving your brain's health.

- Strengthening of communication between vital brain regions—specifically the left hippocampal region in the temporal lobe, which is linked to memory and learning, and the left inferior frontal lobe, which is linked to higher-order reasoning and problem solving.
- Structural brain changes that connect the parahippocampus region to the frontal lobe region of the brain.
- Marked improvements in frontal lobe cognitive functions, both those trained as well as many that were not specifically trained.

> Your brain may be sleepwalking through your days when you use your mind as a massive storage bin. Take the brain challenge to continually engage in complex mental activities.

The results are powerful. After six to twelve weeks of engaging in complex integrating reasoning, research participants demonstrated (1) cognitive gains, (2) increased brain blood flow, (3) improvements in brain efficiency, and (4) structural changes in white matter connections. This scientific evidence clearly shows that you can and do neuroengineer your brain by how you use it. Do not take this responsibility lightly. Make increasing your frontal lobe power your mission right now.

Brainomics Movement and You

My goal is to motivate you to join a brainomics movement to engage in complex mental activity. Why? Complex mental activity:

- reduces cognitive declines and losses.
- reverses degenerative brain changes.
- builds cognitive reserves.
- makes neurons healthier, at a molecular and cellular level.
- creates a smarter, longer-lasting brain.

The impact of weakened integrated reasoning capacity will dramatically increase the cost burden as generations age, thus negatively impacting brainomics. Weakened integrated reasoning is slowly robbing our intellectual capital, personally and societally.

> You cannot afford to let your integrated reasoning capacity atrophy.

How to Enhance Integrated Reasoning

Refocus your brain and sharpen your integrated reasoning capacity. The sooner you start, the better for long-term brain health. You can take advantage of the brain's smart design to create new ideas and tackle tough, never before experienced problems. Knowing practice makes perfect, expend major efforts toward building your brain's software to flexibly move from the known to the unknown, extracting the core messages. A high-performance brain can quickly combine seemingly disparate pieces of information to produce generalized principles while knowing expeditiously what to ignore.

Brain science and your prefrontal cortex guides you in reviewing the issues of each day, as well as problem finding—not just problem solving. Integrated reasoning calls upon the prefrontal cortex to combine existing experience with new happenings to search out and identify problems before they happen. Much of what your brainpower allows you to achieve is futurist thinking—not just reactionary thinking.

> Regardless of age, you can be a synthesizer and generator of new ideas and issues to be solved—energizing your brain.

Think about talking with your boss, brainstorming at a board meeting, seeking medical advice from your doctor, or probing for wiser investment practices from a financial advisor. What if you only absorbed the ideas you heard exactly as they were presented, without reprocessing to discern how it fits with your personal knowledge, biases, and experiences? You would be like a senseless brain guppy, taking in information without adding any insight or putting the new input into the perspective of your unique point of view. Not surprisingly, the chances of retaining information in this un-combined, rote way are very low—not to mention it is a wasted brain investment.

A better brain habit to adopt is to practice synthesizing ideas into one or two abstracted statements when presented with information. Ask probing questions that push the envelope on deeper thinking and action. For example, before going in to a meeting with your colleagues, boss, or volunteer organization, ask yourself: What changes do I want or what crucial issue do I need their help solving? What do I want them to consider? What are desired outcomes from this discussion? After a meeting, write down consolidated ideas, asking yourself: What are some new take-home messages? How does my thinking before the meeting compare with my thinking afterward? How can I use new information to redirect and reset goals? Write a synthesized brief of the meeting in three to five sentences and send it to those you met with to let them know you were listening and that the ideas and time they contributed made a difference. In doing so, you take pause and strategically engage your frontal lobe to reason continuously. Pushing your brainpower of integrated reasoning will be a boon to your brain health and your brain efficiency. It will help you think smarter, not harder.

Boost your brainpower: Stretch and challenge your mind to construct deeper-level, thought-filled ideas when presented with any type of information (magazine articles, movies, books, television shows, lectures, sermons, songs, political speeches, physician reports, comic strips, jokes, emails, etc.).

Extensive brain practices will help you:

1. ask probing questions about the unknown.
2. offer new possibilities to advance ideas and projects.
3. determine new paths that fit with your life changes.

A client exercised his integrated reasoning skills when he told me this new insight he gleaned after a talk I gave: "Your message of the importance of a deeper level of thinking—to find the pearl in what one is hearing, reading, seeing, etc.—was *profound*. I have always wanted to learn the details so I could be accurate. Now I realize that has kept my thinking at a fairly superficial level. Not good for a healthy, stimulated frontal lobe! Thanks for the eye and mind opener."

Integrated Reasoning Exercises

Integrated reasoning is a brain habit that should become your blueprint to absorb and repurpose content. The more often you practice this habit, the more intellectual capital you will build.

The best ways to practice integrated reasoning are to:

- take in the new meanings and quickly move away from the literal meanings conveyed.
- adroitly combine the diverse ideas with previous experiences.
- generate novel interpretations that few would have conceived.
- combine concepts—new with old—to help you harness your highest level of integrated reasoning capacity.

Try improving your fluid intelligence and increasing your intellectual capital in the integrated reasoning practice tasks below.

Practice Task #1:
Read this T. Boone Pickens quote: *"If you're going to run with the big dogs, you have to get out from under the porch."*

1. Give three explanations for what this saying could mean.
2. Relate one or two events in your life to this principle.

When you begin to think of how to encapsulate and convey your thoughts into higher-level concepts, your messages will be more meaningful. Being able to translate complex ideas into simple examples represents one of the highest levels of intellectual thinking.

Practice Task #2:
Think back on one of your favorite movies or books from the past year.

1. Generate five to eight different take-home messages that could be gleaned from the movie or book.
2. Moving forward, which lesson would influence your life the most and why?

Instead of simply retelling the plotline of a movie or book, practice your integrated reasoning skills. Brainstorm with others who also saw the movie or read the book and share your ideas. This builds deeper-level thinking. We have libraries full of books in our homes and oftentimes cannot remember whether we have read a book or not because we read it superficially. **Reading as an isolated activity without deeper processing will not build brainpower.**

The above activities challenge your mind and boost your brainpower. Practicing constructing high-level, generalized, and abstracted meaning allows you to move beyond the details to the bigger picture. Pushing your mind to constantly synthesize meanings is a lot of work, but the cost in effort pays off increasing your brain's robustness and the power of your frontal lobe functions. The more you make such mind stretching a habit, the easier it will become over time.

Integrated reasoning helps you identify key messages to inspire different groups or audiences, reduce complex material down to its memorable essence, relate current and future broad impact issues, and tune in to insightful generalizations to chart new directions.

> To build brainpower requires integrated reasoning to increase intellectual capital.

There are three strategies that will help you enhance your integrated reasoning, thus improving your frontal lobe function and brain efficiency. They are:

- Zoom In
- Zoom Out
- Zoom Deep and Wide

The Brainpower of Zoom In

It is a false belief to think that you are either a big-picture thinker or a detail-oriented person. You cannot be a big-picture thinker without knowing the supporting facts or else you would be an empty suit. **The brainpower of zoom in** requires attending to facts, content, and the situation at hand. Gathering facts and using them to support a novel approach is essential to enhancing integrated reasoning and deeper level thinking. However, it's a delicate balance of knowing when to gather more information and knowing when to stop looking for more facts to develop a point of view. **The key is to toggle back and forth from the immense raw details to form high-level ideas.** It is not enough to understand all the facts; it is highly critical to fit them into a larger schema.

> The whole is more than the sum of its parts.

The Brainpower of Zoom Out

We often cannot see the forest for the trees. We listen to political or graduation speeches and may remember funny one-liners or embarrassing moments shared, but we often fail to appreciate any meaningful or generalized messages that are typically conveyed. To be able to glean synthesized messages requires the **brainpower of zoom out,** to see a broader perspective, to appreciate the big picture. It is important to harness the **brainpower of zoom out** and lift off to a helicopter view, assessing pieces of data and disparate viewpoints from above, merging them into the major themes, core concepts, and broad principles. Consolidating facts and opinions into big ideas and perspectives is necessary to cultivate creative thinking and problem solving. **The brainpower of zoom out helps avoid silos of isolated or static thinking.**

The Brainpower of Zoom Deep and Wide

The **brainpower of zoom deep and wide** is the cognitive strategy of incorporating the major principles and generalized lessons learned into broader applications. This is cognitive strategy transfer at its best. **The brainpower of zoom deep and wide requires the deepest level of thinking where you apply novel developments from one area to other issues, other problems.**

Zoom deep and wide represents:

- Synthesized topics to guide effective meetings and gatherings
- Generalized applications to mentor new trainees, colleagues, and family members
- Intellectually energized writing in emails, speeches, and projects

The dynamic ability to assimilate information from multiple sources to apply to diverse, novel, and complex issues requires the integrated reasoning strategy of zoom deep and wide. It is critical to solving new problems that have ambiguity or arise unexpectedly almost daily. If you immediately knew the answer to a problem, then that situation would not be defined as a problem. Fine-tuning integrated reasoning capacity through practice equips individuals with the cognitive tools to discover and develop improved solutions to emerging problems, including analyzing information that may not even be available to them based on prior learning.

Practice Task #3:

Exercise your integrated reasoning talents by synthesizing the following quote from Steve Jobs. Use the brainpower of zoom deep and wide.

A lot of people in our industry haven't had very diverse experiences. So they don't have enough dots to connect, and they end up with very linear solutions without a broad perspective on the problem. The broader one's understanding of the human experience, the better design we will have.

The cognitive finesse involved in increasing aptitude in **zooming deep and wide** is exceptionally complex and requires heavy brain lifting. Most people easily give up and only identify the generalized ideas from specific readings or meetings—failing to creatively adapt these new concepts to inform new ways of thinking and acting. High performers know their area of expertise, build on it, and efficiently engage this knowledge to advance innovation across domains. Think of it as a mathematic equation.

$$A + B = Ø$$

**A=incoming content, B=knowledge/experience,
Ø = meaning converted into a new, transformed approach or product**

Practice Task #4:

Planning for an upcoming important meeting based on previous gatherings requires dynamic toggling across all three brainpowers of zooming—**zoom in** to the issues at hand; **zoom out** to the broadest perspectives to see vast solutions and potential directions, and **zoom deep and wide** to figure out new framing for old problems and novel applications to proven practices.

1. Write and distribute ahead of time the target topics to discuss or problem solve from the previous meetings.
2. Before the meeting takes place, think through what success would look like when the meeting is over.
3. Identify what topics attendees should think about or papers to read before the meeting. Have the meeting members consider the abstract ideas—not just give silos of opinions. The more prepared they are, the more they will be brain engaged in the discussion.
4. Lead from the bottom up. Let attendees take active thought-roles, as it will help to challenge and hone their frontal lobe skills as opposed to when the leader is always in charge of the meeting.

5. Identify and challenge new perspectives (zoom out) and rationale (zoom in) for high level goals, not information downloading.
6. Develop novel approaches to solve the primary key problems and apply proven practices to new contexts.

Meetings are one of the greatest brain drains in the workplace. Think of the number of people attending, their salaries, and the cost when nothing or next to nothing is accomplished. Practicing the skill of integrated reasoning will help create meetings that stretch the minds and build the brains of those attending and increase individual and corporate intellectual capital.

Practice Task #5:

Read the "Great Balls of Fire" text below to complete this next exercise. I want you to see how different it feels if you read it with two different goals in mind. First, I want you to read it with the idea that you will be tested on how many of the facts you can recite back after reading it.

Reading for the details will keep you in a mind-set focused on the pieces of information without thinking of how the pieces of information might be connected to more than that conveyed by the text.

Second, read "Great Balls of Fire" with the goal of formulating which of its lessons are still relevant today. The more knowledge one has, the easier the second reading becomes. Whatever the age, when you engage the brain to be open to constructing new meanings, you will always be more turned on to learning than when requiring the brain to be a robotic absorber and recorder of mass content.

"Great Balls of Fire" by Abul-Fazl*
(Accessed from *Lapham's Quarterly*)

Superficial observers look upon polo as a mere amusement and consider it only play, but men of more exalted views see in it a means of learning promptitude and decision. It tests the value of a man and strengthens the bonds of friendship. Strong men learn in playing this game the art of riding, and the animals learn to perform feats of agility and to obey the reins. Hence His Majesty Akbar the Great is very fond of this game. Externally, the game adds to the splendor of his court, but viewed from a higher point, it reveals concealed talents.

When His Majesty goes to the field in order to play this game, he selects an opponent and some active and clever players, who are only filled with one thought, namely, to show their skill against the opponents of His Majesty. From motives of kindness, His Majesty never orders anyone to be a player, but chooses the pairs by the cast of the die. There are not more than ten players, but many more keep themselves in readiness. When twenty-four minutes have passed, two players take rest, and two others supply their place.

His Majesty is unrivaled for the skill which he shows in the various ways of hitting the ball; he often manages to strike the ball while in the air and astonishes all. When a ball is driven to a goal, they beat the kettledrum, so that all who are far and near may hear it. In order to increase the excitement, betting is allowed. The players win from each other, and he who brought the ball to the goal wins most.

His Majesty also plays polo on dark nights, which caused much astonishment, even among clever players. The balls which are used at night are set on fire. For this purpose palás wood is used, which is very light and burns for a long time. For the sake of adding splendor to the games, which is necessary in wordly matters, His Majesty has knobs of gold and silver fixed to the tops of the polo sticks. If one of them breaks, any player that gets hold of the pieces may keep them.

*Abul-Fazl, from The Institutes of Akbar. Abul-Fazl served as a historian and secretary to Emperor Akbar, reforming Islamic theological practices and becoming a military commander of southern India in 1599. Following a rebellion by Akbar's son, Abul-Fazl was ordered back to court but was intercepted and assassinated en route. In addition to his historical works, the author is said to have translated the Bible into Persian.

Now that you have read the "Great Balls of Fire" two times, answer these queries:

1. What are ten major themes you deciphered from "Great Balls of Fire"?
2. How many generalized messages can you generate?

3. Apply those meanings to three different current world situations.

Some of you may be thinking, "This seems like being in school again. I do not want to think that hard." But what is vital to keep in mind is that if you desire to stretch your brain years to more closely align and match your life span, then these brain habits can and will make a difference.

Some themes from "Great Balls of Fire" might be:

- Compassion
- Fairness
- Encouragement
- Motivation
- Competition
- Excellence
- Inclusion
- Passion

Some generalized messages might be:

- Team building around freedom.
- Games are a way to bring joy to dark times.
- Recognize physical and mental limits.
- Competition amplifies talent.
- One must lead by example.
- Preparation and chance provide an opportunity.

When you challenge your brain to synthesize individualized interpretations from incoming information, you will be building stronger frontal lobe networks—networks important for staying brain fit longer and building brain reserves at every age.

> You can rewire your frontal lobe connectivity by constantly thinking in challenging, complex ways.

The goal is to optimize the core mental processes of strategic attention (as discussed in the previous chapter), integrated reasoning, and innovation (see the next chapter) for a sustainable brain future that supports your ability to make vital decisions every day. The more frequently you push your brain to absorb meaning by using the brainpower of zooming in, out, and deep and wide, the more efficiently your brain will work.

Boost your brainpower: Make a concerted effort to transform your hundreds of thoughts each day to the highest level of thinking as possible.

The brainpower of zooming is not a trivial skill; it is recognized as a vital cognitive skill that has not been easy to assess. A recent survey of 740 business faculty worldwide revealed that they believed incoming business students needed to assimilate, interpret, and convert data, evaluate outcomes, and listen—key skills for twenty-first-century students and future leaders in business.[2] Armed with that data, the Graduate Management Admission Council (GMAC) reformatted and added a new section to the Graduate Management Admission Test (GMAT). The title of the new section: "Integrated Reasoning."

According to the announcement from GMAC, which leads the development of the GMAT, "The new integrated reasoning section of the GMAT will be a microcosm of today's b-school classroom." Dave Wilson, president and CEO of GMAC, went on to say, "These questions will provide critical intelligence to schools about the ability of prospective students to make sound decisions by evaluating, assimilating or extrapolating data."

Integrated Reasoning Linked to Strategic Leadership

Integrated reasoning is one of our most complex and forceful thinking capacities that can be enhanced. As such, this skill is associated with decisive and strategic leadership.

William Duggan shares his definitions of three kinds of intuition—ordinary, expert, and strategic—in his book *Strategic Intuition: The Creative Spark in Human Achievement*.[3] He defines each type of intuition:

- Ordinary intuition is a gut instinct.
- Expert intuition is a snap judgment that is done at rapid speed, based on experience.
- Strategic intuition is a slow, thoughtful way of solving a problem.

I can see the parallels between intuition and integrated reasoning. Precisely,

- Zoom out is a quickly abstracted idea. This is similar to a gut instinct, a vague notion of the key points and directions.
- Zoom in corresponds to the power of knowledge where one can make a very quick, snap judgment or decision based on extensive facts and expertise.
- Zoom deep and wide is a process that is not fast, but it is deliberate. It involves an effortful, integrative process of reflective thinking through all the possibilities. Strategic leaders will use this type of cognitive process to prime new ideas and advance lines of thinking, as well as rethink past misdirection. This is the foundation for entrepreneurial and innovative thinking that is discussed in the next chapter.

When honed, the benefits of integrated reasoning and strategic global thinking spill over to many frontal lobe and other brain functions. The ability to harness this global perspective is fundamental to creative thinking, problem solving, and energizing productivity.

Remember Linda, the high-level executive at a Fortune 500 company who was interested in maximizing her cognitive performance? For her, learning and applying the brainpowers of zooming to her everyday life, both personally and professionally, has led to increased productivity. "Zooming in, zooming out, and zooming deep and

Brain value of integrated reasoning

- Become a mastermind of information
- Create fresh and bigger ideas rather than crank out rote facts
- Chart unique insights by combining new data with rich experiences and knowledge

wide has advanced my brain potential. Zooming deep and wide is a skill I had not cultivated to any degree, but now I'm finding that using it leads to better work, particularly on the most challenging assignments like strategy development. The statements I prepare are more thought filled and forward thinking than the ones I prepared last year."

The brainpower of zooming encourages deliberate, reflective thinking, not just a snap judgment or acting on a gut reaction. Using this strategic approach to understanding information in your daily life requires dynamically shifting from what is in front of you to a global view and transcending the literal surface to construct novel and deeper levels of meaning in contexts you never before experienced. Integrated reasoning is a platinum cognitive asset that you absolutely can enhance to increase your performance and boost your intellectual capital.

Integrated reasoning allows you to identify and group important details into condensed, global meanings; thereby efficiently limiting the massive amounts of information one has to manipulate, comprehend, encode, and recall. My research has shown that when individuals improve their ability to assimilate and synthesize information, they experience a direct beneficial effect on brain health fitness.[4-5] There is an added bonus to keeping the frontal lobe skill of integrated reasoning in shape: if exercised and maintained into late life, integrated reasoning significantly improves and spills over to other executive cognitive functions that were never trained, achieving gains in higher memory for details and faster speed of processing.

> Practice the brainpower of zooming to strengthen integrated reasoning continually to make your brain think smarter—longer.

Benefits of integrated reasoning intensive workouts	
↑ Mental productivity	↓ Brain fatigue
↑ Brain energy	↓ Brain boredom
↑ Idea innovation	↓ Rote repetition

Move out of a rote-mill way of idea processing to churning out newly created ideas. Integrated reasoning alone does not maximize your cognitive prowess, but it is fundamental to creative thinking, problem solving, and energized productivity. Learn more about the brainpower of innovation and mental flexibility in the next chapter to build even more cognitive capacity.

Know Brainers

1. Harness the dynamic brainpowers of zooming
   - Zoom In:
     Get the facts.
   - Zoom Out:
     Transform literal facts into bigger ideas, diverse perspectives, and global themes by combining new input with existing knowledge.
   - Zoom Deep and Wide:
     Formulate broader novel applications with bold, deep, more strategic thinking.
2. Rewire your brain's frontal lobe connectivity by deeper level thinking.
3. Transform your habitual thinking and acting by constantly synthesizing and constructing abstracted meanings that are useful—not random.
4. Recognize when you are engaging in rote versus riveting communication of ideas or planning something that is original.
5. Mentor your team members to become CEOs (aka Cognitive Entrepreneur Officers) of their own thinking, contributing new ways to change current practices on their own by exploring new concepts, modifying, transforming, extending, and even rejecting current thinking patterns.
6. Knowledge is power when it is not static but when it is constantly being updated by combining new possibilities with rich experiences.

CHAPTER 6

INNOVATE TO INSPIRE YOUR THINKING

Do you want to be smarter and more creative?
What limits your innovative thinking capacity?
What tasks inspire creativity and which ones just need to be completed?
What is the fuel to engage your brain's strongest creative power?
Can you train your brain to be innovative and imaginative?

As a society, we believe that we are able to innovate best during youth, a fertilized and frenetic life stage when creativity is encouraged. However, as we age, imaginative thinking is all too often ignored, fatigued, and underdeveloped. It is incorrect to think that not much can be done to increase your creative prowess. So when does innovation and creativity peak?

Our complex frontal lobe networks are the creative epicenters of our brains as well as the command centers of our lives. Everyone has the potential to break new ground, to be more inventive at any age. One obstacle to our doing so is receiving an early label that inaccurately frames our brain and robs us of our confidence. A second is the widely held belief that limits the age expectations of when we can be creative geniuses.

Definition: Innovation is the ability to generate and exploit new ideas to solve problems; to seek, devise, and employ improved ways of dealing with unknown and unfamiliar contexts; or to create something that is original and valuable.

- Innovation is about improving upon and changing old ways of doing things through novel thinking.
- Innovative thinkers practice mental flexibility—stretching their creativity and imagination.
- Ingenious thinkers are open to experimentation to rethink practices and are at ease with ambiguity.
- Innovators are not beaten down by failure, rather, they constantly ask what they can learn from their mistakes.

"Imagination is more important than knowledge. Knowledge is limited. Imagination encircles the world." —Einstein

An Innovator

Clint Bruce is an innovator. He owns his own company, started a successful non-profit, and is a former Navy SEAL. In any meeting, conversation, or communication with him, your mind will be stretched—as he challenges you to think about new ideas and new ways to approach situations that were not even on your radar or in your repertoire of thoughts. Was he born this way? Or was his innovative mind built because of his experience as a Navy SEAL whose team's survival depended on his ability to quickly see reality and make the impossible happen?

When I first met Clint, he complained that his brain was firing so rapidly that he could not slow it down. After brain health training, Clint is armed with the strategies he needs to implement in order to constantly solve new problems, to explore new possibilities. Clint's innovative training regimen is simple. My team challenged Clint to strengthen his already stellar innovative capacity. With every task put before him, whether with his family, at the office, or when consulting across the country, Clint seeks, devises, and employs improved ways of dealing with unknown and unfamiliar con-

texts. He thrives on tough problems to solve. When you have a conversation with him, you can see his prodigious brainpower of innovation in action.

Are you an innovator?

You can ramp up your innovative capacity.

The destiny of your innovative thinking capacity is largely in your hands. Your innovative capacity is limitless, and your only enemy is yourself. We often think our most imaginative years are behind us. Some believe you either have it or you don't. Others think creativity has to be nourished by a certain age or else it's too late. And others still think it's in your genetic code.

You can spark creativity in your brain and stoke the smoldering fire of your imaginative capacity at any age. Innovation can be fostered and developed no matter your life's work; creativity can be trained and regained if you practice and unlock its immense capacity to create and innovate.

Creative versus Smart

Research reveals that people who are smart or have high general intelligence are not necessarily the same as those who are highly creative.[1–2] Of course, the question of whether you would wish to be smarter or more creative is a bit of an esoteric academic exercise. But we often place a demarcation between being smart and being creative as if they are separate entities. This separation insinuates that if you are smart, you may or may not be creative and vice versa.

Webster's Thesaurus has very different synonyms to describe the two. Synonyms for "creative" include:

clever . . . inspired . . . inventive . . . ingenious . . . prolific . . . visionary . . . stimulating.

Synonyms for "smart" consist of words like:

adept . . . . apt . . . brilliant . . . knowing . . . sharp . . . shrewd . . . wise

The difference in meanings conveys a sense that being smart is a *state,* and being creative is an *action.* For me, these words can be used synonymously, and I will use these words interchangeably throughout this book. All too often we think of "creative" in the context of the arts and innovation in science—which is a major mistake. **Innovation and creativity matter at every life stage, for every walk of life.** You can experience an increase in brainpower when you constantly practice being an entrepreneur of ideas.

I have polled people to find out their beliefs on how they value creativity by asking: "Would you rather be smarter or more creative?" Think about the question for yourself. What would you rather be? I've asked many individuals of different ages, genders, and backgrounds. The responses are fascinating.

> *One young executive said, "Well if they are mutually exclusive, then I would rather be smart to allow myself to make better life and business decisions. The term 'starving artist' must be at least partially based in reality."*
> *A thirtysomething female said, "Being creative leads to being smart since creativity leads to new thoughts, truths, and ideas."*
> *When I asked my twentysomething son, he said, "You need a level of smart to be creative. There has to be a balance in levels of creativity and smartness. If you are very creative and not very smart, you might not have direction."*
> *A female from the boomer generation responded saying, "Knowledge or smarts is good, but being able to apply or talk about what I know in a creative way is what can inspire, motivate, and educate. I want to be more creative!"*
> *A fortysomething male responded by saying, "I'd rather be more creative. I already have a high IQ, but I'm too concrete at times. I'd rather think out of the box more easily."*

In actuality, both creative capacity and smartness work hand in hand to energize the brain. The ability to continually engage in innovative thinking is likely a key indicator of who will retain their smart capacity, the ability to acquire and build new knowledge.

Knowledge is part of the creative equation; we cannot go to the next level without knowing the basic facts. However, innovative thinking should work synergistically with analytical and practical thinking for the best results. Often we take in information as truth rather than pondering what we do not know. Nor do we consider how we can add or modify that knowledge or practice.

> *"Creativity is not just a matter of thinking in a certain way, but rather it is an attitude toward life."*
> —**Robert Sternberg, a leading American psychologist and researcher**

Your Innovative Capacity

However, innovation as a skill becomes paralyzed from lack of use, limited challenges, and fear of failure. Do not let your innovative capacity go dormant and weak from not being properly exercised. Below are innovation's greatest enemies:

- A brain on automatic pilot
- An avoidance of new challenges
- A belief that your best and most creative work is behind you
- An opposition to being renewable, adaptable
- A strong separation from those who have radically different viewpoints
- An evasion of collaborations on major projects

Innovation, creativity, and imagination require practice, just like staying proficient in a foreign language you once learned to speak. You are well aware that the less you use the second language, the weaker it gets. With total neglect over a span of years, you have to almost start from scratch to build the expertise to speak a foreign language fluently. The same is true for being innovative.

> Your brainpower of innovative thinking should be exercised daily.

If you have not been stretching your innovative skills, then now is the time to jump-start this immense brain capacity. How often do you:

- figure out ways to deal with new circumstances?
- adapt quickly and adeptly to novel challenges?
- shake up regular meetings that tend to drain the brain?
- break with past habits?

Reflect on your own capacity to be innovative in everyday tasks or ask someone who knows you well. I recently asked my son if he thought I was relatively smarter or more creative. He was too naive to realize this was a loaded question and answered instantly, "You are higher on the smart than creative scale, without question."

After I licked my wounds, he said, "I guess you didn't like my answer." I responded by explaining that I had to be innovative to do what I do and by always modifying and updating the research initiatives I encountered—always going in new directions. This immediately changed his mind, and he went on to say that he thought I had grown more creative over the past decade as I created and retooled the vision and expansion of brain discoveries at the Center for BrainHealth. I think he is correct; as a young adult, I was more interested in acquiring knowledge. Now I am energized by creating knowledge.

> Innovation drives national economic growth and well-being.

Innovative Thinkers Invent Again and Again

Dr. Alan Leshner, CEO of the American Association for the Advancement of Science and executive publisher of *Science* magazine, wrote an editorial titled, "Innovation Needs Novel Thinking."[3] He challenged funders to foster innovative research by encouraging scientists through the support of creative pursuits, instead of the already-know-the-answer line of research that is commonly practiced. I would elaborate on this to say **we need to train people—at every stage of life—to ignite their highest level of novel thinking.** This brain competency predominates as a key investment to enhance your intellectual capital.

You may be thinking to yourself: "Gee, I'm too old to start ramping up my innovative capacity now," or "Why should I start now when I just retired?" The greatest hindrance to enhancing your capacity of innovative thinking is your own self-limiting brain habits. We often desire that all days and projects be clearly delineated, in an almost cut-and-paste routine with as little deviation as possible. We get distressed rather than inspired when asked to rethink a project or action or mistake. My goal is to inspire you to break these brain-draining habits.

Many conceive brain aging as a relentless decline. Brain imaging studies support this view with evidence of age-related declines in the medial prefrontal cortex and deep brain structures. Corresponding with these brain losses are documented cognitive declines in innovative thinking and mental flexibility.[4] Does this sound like an impossible course to correct?

> The downward spiral of innovative brain decline can be changed, but it requires your commitment.

Frontal Lobe Connectivity Supports Innovative Thinkers

A neuroscientific team from Japan was among the first to document that individuals with higher innovative thinking scores also show increased structural connectivity between the frontal lobe and the corpus callosum—a deep portion of the brain that links both hemispheres. This research supports my view that the frontal lobe is positively related to pivotal dimensions of creativity—specifically cognitive flexibility.

Studies of brain efficiency are shedding light on the concept that more brain activation versus less is associated with more learning as a novice. When your brain becomes an expert, it works more efficiently. That is, those with higher expertise, perhaps associated with greater practice, perform the task more efficiently, with less brain activation.

> A more efficient brain does not have to work as hard.

Brain plasticity studies offer high promise that the declining brain capacity can be positively altered in the healthy brain by exercising innovative thinking. Findings show that the process of learning or creating something new is linked to changes in brain structure.[5] Stop and think for a moment: learning or creating something new is linked to changes in brain structure!

Your brain can be changed by how you use it, by how you activate it every day—no matter your age. Be astonished at what a powerful role you play in changing your brain.

Open up your thinking to devise new ways of doing things.

All of the core brainpowers—strategic attention, integrated reasoning, and innovation—require hard work. We falsely think we are either gifted in an area or not. But you can become more innovative if you take the challenge to heart and open your mind. You can become more creative and inventive with practice. You just need to recognize and fully embrace that you have the capacity to increase your genius.

The success of keeping your brainpower fully engaged throughout your life span depends largely on attending to and strengthening our immense innovative capacity. Each of us can strive to build an innovative brain, one that seeks ways to uncover the maximum number of possibilities. You need to use and therefore design your brain to move from the known to the unknown—but with foresight about the risks and opportunities that are changing at the speed of light.

Transformative Thinking

In my work with executive and high level management, I have found significant gains in innovative thinking after only six hours of concentrated brain training. Ninety-two percent of those trained showed improvements in generating new ideas. Before the training, their flexibility in deriving new ideas was restricted, concrete, and automatic. You might be thinking, "Of course they improved, you trained them!" However, the training was not dedicated to practicing this critical skill. The training provided the high level executives with the strategies needed

Become an entrepreneur of ideas.

to innovate. The bottom line: every individual has greater creative potential than they are currently achieving.

Nowhere has the significance of innovative thinking been more apparent than in the study of the brain. If cognitive neuroscience had not continued to challenge and seek alternative explanations for why some people show tremendous brainpower until late life while others seem halted in their early adulthood, we would still believe that decline is the only path our brains can take as we age. If scientists had not pushed to discover more about our most astonishing organ, we would not know that the brain can grow, change, and repair connections throughout life.

> Innovative brain building: Brain networks strengthen in response to new challenges or wither with status quo thinking at all ages.

I acknowledge that we are still unclear on exactly how to apply the knowledge from vast brain discoveries to real-life settings. But we do know enough to adopt better habits that will help our brains as we age. Remember, you have 100 billion neurons and trillions of deep brain connections working for you, waiting to be called on to strengthen your brainpower.

Take Advantage of Neuroplasticity

Your road to increasing innovation is rarely a straight line. Innovation and creativity are brain potentials that can be nurtured or stunted throughout life; they are lifelong processes, not a single stage or a goal reached.

Innovation has little to do with:

- How many hours you work
- How much information you absorb
- How many classes you take
- How many major tasks you design and complete
- How quickly you learn

> When imagination stalls, you are like the walking dead with little energy day by day.

So, how do you know if you are innovative or not? It's a matter of adopting nimble brain habits to energize your inner genius.

Building creativity requires continually exercising habits throughout your day, not simply every so often. Incite innovation daily when you:

- Seek to broaden and revamp your perspectives, to view life differently, by reading different types of books, exposing yourself to different types of people, changing routine work presentations, etc.
- Dismantle old linkages of information to allow new thoughts to brew
- Ponder free-flowing ideas
- Consciously and dedicatedly convert ideas into deliberate change
- Recognize there is no road map to get you there
- Reflect and learn from mistakes—quickly

However, it's not that you need to innovate at every moment, in every instance. Rather, you need to choose critical issues or messy problems to apply these abilities toward.

**To revolutionize your brainpower,
seek to be a change maker—now.**

Work, passion, and a sense of purpose are the best nourishments for healthy brain function and innovation. As I have said before, our brain is remarkable. We exhaust it each day, yet every morning we awake with a recharged battery, ready for the next challenge. And even though you can build your brain depending on how you use it every day, you must neuro-engineer it in the most engaging ways to stay inspired.

Remember Linda—the fiftysomething high-level executive of a Fortune 500 company? Linda was inherently very talented and an innovative thinker. She quickly broke through the glass ceiling at a very young age. Her insightful and innovative ways of thinking were obvious to all who worked with her. However, after years of climbing the ladder, she thought that she'd hit a plateau. "I felt frozen," she told me. The roadblock in her case was not her own inability to exercise innovative thinking but rather the environment in which she found herself. Her work environment championed and rewarded knowledge and constant output. Linda's environment was literally suffocating her creative power.

Boost your brainpower: Step back and take note of how your environment is stifling and constraining your imagination. Instead of complaining—imagine, create, and develop potential solutions.

Innovative ideas are created out of fragments of information. Good, creative, and novel ideas are a composition of knowledge, experience, and new exposures fused in different ways.

Expand your extraordinary capacity for innovation by exercising the:

- Brainpower of infinite
- Brainpower of paradox
- Brainpower of unknown

A bored brain is a brain in decline.

Brainpower of Infinite

Innovative ideas are created out of pieces of seemingly random data, recombined in such a novel way that the whole that was comprised of the pieces does not even look the same. There are infinite possibilities of how information can be connected in new ways to innovate. There is not a single answer or only one way to do things. Challenge your innovative capacity by practicing the **brainpower of infinite** strategy.

Practice Tasks:

1. Create novel and innovative topics in your email subject line.
2. If you give a lot of presentations or lead meetings, change the message and make it fresh each time. A stale talk will bore you the speaker/leader, and the audience will feel the zestless message.
3. In this tough economy, think of at least ten new ways you can cut your monthly budget by 30 percent. All too often, we complain but do not break new ground by breaking old habits to create a new modus operandi.
4. Mentor and encourage small teams to be inventive problem solvers on crucial projects.
5. Think of family gatherings that fall flat with the same old discussions. Stretch family members to engage in new ways they never have before, e.g., meet in new venues, discuss fascinating people of substance, or talk about current ethical dilemmas.
6. Buying the perfect gift for someone requires creativity and innovation. Watch what their preferences are and connect the observations to what you think they would want.

Brainpower of Paradox

Innovation and mental flexibility require embracing and learning from mistakes and challenges—overcoming insurmountable odds. Paradoxically, the tenacity to not get stopped or stuck by failure is the fuel that leads to the greatest advances in these areas. The **brainpower of paradox** is enhanced when one reflects on a completed task and perceives the holes, and then dynamically and flexibly reworks and reinvents for a better product/output. The mental flexibility required to reflect on, revisit, and seek better solutions engages the frontal lobe, optimizing learning, which leads to transformative new insights and fresh ways of approaching outdated tasks—large and small.

Practice Tasks:

1. Reflect on a meeting that was essentially a time waster. Think about how to re-engage the issues to bring about mutually beneficial solutions. Attempt to garner more participation and idea sharing to make gatherings more meaningful to attendees.
2. Rethink a project, presentation, or event that you think went well. Brainstorm at least five ways it could have gone even better and how it could be improved if you had another opportunity tomorrow.
3. Remember back on a happening that seemed like the worst possible turn of events for you at the time and list at least five good things that eventually arose from that challenge.
4. Identify your favorite mistake weekly and see what you can now learn by looking back.

Brainpower of Unknown

The **brainpower of unknown** requires valuing curiosity and asking, "What if?" We are born with an unparalleled capacity to explore. As we age, we often set our brains on default mode until they become paralyzed in familiarity. This is a choice, not a necessity. **A highly innovative person is never satisfied with the status quo (the known) and is always looking for ways to move to the unknown, where things are constantly improving, changing, growing, and expanding.**

Practice Tasks:

1. Volunteer to direct something you have never taken the lead on before; you will feel stretched with new ways of thinking.
2. When a new opportunity approaches you, think of ways it will teach you something new if you spend the time to be innovative.
3. When you are feeling overwhelmed by a new position or

major responsibility where 75 percent of what you are doing is unknown, practice earlier brainpowers:

   a. Brainpower of two (see chapter 4)—identify your two most important tasks to learn to make the greatest difference in your new position in the next month.

   b. Brainpower of zooming (see integrated reasoning, chapter 5)—step back to appreciate how the important task you identified above fits into a bigger picture while continually breaking down important new learning tasks into doable steps.

As you expand your inventiveness, write how you have or will attempt to manifest each high-powered skill to increase your intellectual capital.

- Cause new things to happen:

   _____

- Switch to novel modes of thinking:

   _____

- Energize out-of-the-box thinking:

   _____

- Construct ideas that relate to the future:

   _____

- Imagine how things can be beyond the situation:

   _____

- Seek ways to improve processes and products:

   _____

- Become an agent of peace in a difficult conflict within your sphere of influence

   _____

Remember: when you are hunting your elephants (see chapter 4) on your daily to-do list, note one thing each day that you want to revisit, rethink, and reinvent. It is best if the one thing you revisit is an elephant and not a rabbit. Your brain will be energized as you begin to practice and amplify your fuller innovative potential.

> As you age, your brain gets better at envisioning and making the impossible happen—if you keep your inventiveness well-tuned.

Innovative thinking is pivotal to the upside of **brainomics**—the economic gains possible from advancing innovative thinking. Are you motivated to start today to practice and strengthen your innovative thinking?

Know Brainers

1. Your brainpower of innovation can be enhanced every year of your life.
2. Your brain is inspired when you seek as many diverse new ways to do old things.
3. Challenge your brainpower and increase your intellect by devising a wide array of original solutions and interpretations regularly.
4. Innovative thinking is like speaking a foreign language—it must be practiced to stay strong and become more dependable.
5. Your brain's connectivity is enhanced when you engage in mentally innovative thinking.
6. If you never thought of yourself as an innovative thinker, it is never too late to start and improve by incremental degrees.
7. Even small incremental improvements in innovative thinking could contribute to your bottom line.
8. Your innovative capacity is limited primarily by you.
9. The more you push yourself to identify and apply diverse strategies to solve problems, the more likely you will transfer this skill to other areas of your brain function.

SECTION III

MAKE YOUR BRAIN SMARTER AT ANY AGE

The frontal lobe fitness needs of the millennial generation vary from those of the traditionalist generation. Baby boomers require still different frontal lobe practice as they begin navigating through their fifties and sixties. Building effective and efficient brain health levels across the life span requires an understanding of the basic needs of each one. Chapters 7 through 10 give specific case illustrations and tips based on cutting-edge neuroscience research for each generation.

CHAPTER 7

THE IMMEDIATES, 13–24 YEARS OF AGE

You are an ImMEDIAte if you are currently between thirteen and twenty-four years of age. If you are an Immediate, your life blood is your *media*. I labeled this generation the ImMEDIAtes because you crave immediate access to your social network and are constantly satisfying your perpetual need to be connected.

Why is now the most vulnerable brain stage of your life?

What are the pros and cons of your amazing ability to stay hyperconnected?

Why is the Immediate generation slower to emerge into adulthood than earlier generations?

What is robbing you of your intellectual potential as an Immediate?

How can you conquer the obstacles that are slowing, perhaps even stalling, your frontal lobe fitness?

How do you catapult your brainpower to take advantage of your current stage of rapid frontal lobe development?

Can you unlock your creative potential when you are being trained "to do," rather than encouraged "to think"?

ImMEDIAtes represent the youngest generation discussed in this book and are the adolescent-plus generation who range in age from the teen years to early twenties. Your best pal is your phone—so much so that you panic if you are separated from your phone even briefly. It knows more about you than your parents or your friends. You keep it so close to your side that you even sleep with it. But oddly enough, you rarely use it as a phone; instead you use it for texting and logging on to social media outlets for immediate access to answers and to massive networks of people.

> As an ImMEDIAte, your attachment to your personal communication device is as integral to your being as eating and breathing.

A recent report found that one in three college students considers being able to connect to the Internet as important as fundamental resources like air, water, and shelter.[1] If this constant dependence on technology sounds like an addiction, in some instances, it just may be, says Dr. Nora Volkow, director of the National Institute on Drug Abuse. Dr. Volkow explains that just the emotional surge experienced when you receive an unexpected text fires up the dopamine cells in the brain. Dopamine is a neurotransmitter positively associated with pleasure, but it also plays a role in reinforcing addictive behaviors. In essence, you get high just thinking about who is texting you or what the message might be.

As an Immediate, you interact primarily through media; it is the main channel for how you initiate, keep, and terminate relationships. It is how you network with your friends, teachers, parents, and most everyone who wants to be in touch with you at all times of the day and night. Even passing between classes, you would rather text a friend than meet up to have a two-minute face-to-face conversation. Immediates thrive on sharing and knowing where "friends" are at any point in time and what their views are on any and every topic—ranging from the most trivial to the tragic to the triumphant. In fact, your connections are not limited by proximity or geographic boundaries. Your connections are far and wide—even continents away.

Technology is rewiring your brain daily so that you are becoming addicted to being distracted. One report showed that one in five college students say they are interrupted six times or more every hour when doing their homework—an average of at least once every ten minutes.[2] What's more, the same report noted that one in ten students said they lose count how many times they are interrupted while they are trying to focus on a project.

Boost your brainpower: Take your own tally of how often you are interrupted when doing your next project.

Certain habits are taking a toll on development of critical reasoning skills and innovative thinking in Immediates. Social networking and information overload may be major thieves stealing your brain performance. **Technological progress is obstructing individual creativity and failing to inspire your generation's capacity to think for yourselves.** The detrimental effects of technology on your generation's brain prowess are happening worldwide and are issues for concern. You can change your habits and alter your path to one of innovation, weighed reasoning, and deeper thinking by knowing when and when not to let your technology rule your thinking.

Boost your brainpower: Take on the challenge of not allowing yourself to be constantly interrupted and see how much faster you get your homework done or how much better you perform on a school or work-related assignment.

With instant access to the Internet through laptops, iPads, and cell phones, Immediates always have massive amounts of information instantly available at their fingertips. By posting and updating information through your social media channels, you rapidly influence available knowledge. However, there is a downside. Beware of your media's drawbacks. **You may be developing a blind trust in technology, and a large percentage of the information you are bombarded with is inaccurate, incomplete, and unqualified by valid facts.** You are perhaps unknowingly letting computers do the bulk of your thinking. You habitually and deftly retrieve information and rapidly recall an amazing quantity of facts and details from topics that interest you and even from topics that do not. As an Immediate, you are building a brain that knows how to store and retrieve facts with a speed that is hard to match or beat.

Though your generation is scoring perfect or near perfect scores on the SAT, ACT, GRE, MCAT, LSAT, and GMAT, many of you who are making the highest scores on entrance exams and achieve the highest grades in your classes are all too often failing to harness your full brain potential. **Top marks in school and on exams do not predict who will make the best doctor, teacher, parent, innovator, scientist, lawyer, business executive, or any chosen career expert.**

Why is this the case? **Your intense search for the immediate, correct answer does not necessarily lead to expanding curiosity and enhanced capacity to solve the complexity of problems that may plague your generation for the next decades.** In other words, the emphasis on speed of information access may be weakening your brain fitness at a time when you should be strengthening your brain's strategic and deeper thinking capacity.

And still, there are other Immediates who may have low grades or low scores on IQ or SAT tests. These tests are rigid, though rigorous, measures of fact-based learning and often incorrectly and detrimentally ascertain an Immediate's potential. **The momentous principle to remember is that performance on these structured tests does not define your potential.** These tests do not evaluate the entire range of fluid thinking that comes from deeper processing and practical problem solving that awaits you if you work daily to unlock your full potential.

A portion of the blame can be directed at how the education system is focused on test performance rather than training students how to generate new ideas; however, **a large degree of responsibility is on you** and the way you depend on quick access to knowledge as the way to learn. Current education practices are not elevating your brain health fitness and perhaps are even contributing to its decline. The causes of the downward trend in cognitive fitness of reasoning and critical thinking are multifactorial, but many are pointing not only to the continual distractions you actively seek, but also to the overemphasis on high-stakes standardized testing and teaching to the test.

> Immediates taught in a mechanistic, rote style of stuffing away facts for a test will build very different brains than those trained to abstract, synthesize, and connect meaning to their own world and other vast knowledge sources.

Sir Ken Robinson, in his updated edition of *Out of Our Minds: Learning to be Creative,* warns that we are not educating youth to take their place in the economies of the twenty-first century.[3] The current system of education was designed for a different age, namely the Industrial Revolution, where public education did not exist and youth had minimal access to information. What motivated students years ago to go to school may no longer work today. In the name of education, schools are slowly diminishing student capacities to excel in divergent thinking on tasks such as coming up with as many ways as possible to interpret a question.

For years parents and educators have preached, "The more you know, the better." The system has been building, training, and rewarding Immediates for spouting off numerous facts, leading you to value the rote memorization of data, a skill that stymies creativity. **One lesson to embrace now and throughout your life is: the more you learn, the more you will be humbled by how little you know and have yet to learn.**

Think about thinking—not knowing. Brain science is revealing that access to massive amounts of information is not making any of us smarter, regardless of age.[4] The Immediate generation is living in an era when being exposed to too much data and vast numbers of choices is your daily bread. But what if this voluminous cafeteria of options is hindering your brain's ability to adequately weigh the pros and cons to make healthy choices? Because your brain's frontal lobe is developing this lifelong powerful capacity during your current life stage, too many choices are actually stalling the development of decision making in your brain.

Just imagine when you were first learning to talk. Instead of learning your first words by being exposed to one, maybe two languages, imagine being exposed to ten languages all at once and simultaneously learning to talk. That enormous exposure to many diverse languages would make learning to talk harder, not easier. Similarly, information overload is crippling your development in making wise choices.

Another obstacle to achieving your brain potential is a falsely held belief that being exposed to more of the adult world sooner is making you grow up faster. Physically, you look more grown up earlier, but the brain's frontal lobe maturation is not happening faster. In fact, the opposite may be

> Less is more for brain development of sound decision making.

happening. All of this no-holds-barred access is making the Immediate generation mature slower. One key reason for this stalled development is that the immense number of opportunities stalls and overwhelms your choice making. In essence, your Immediate brain is almost frozen by the many choices in front of you.

So how do you handle it? Oftentimes you do not make a choice because the rapidly changing and yet immature stage of frontal lobe development makes decision making very undependable. **Your brain's maturation is at a vulnerable developmental crossroad, when rational judgment is unfolding and dangerous choices are real options.** You are better equipped to make sound choices when faced with one or two alternatives—such as places to meet your friends, colleges to apply, or even where to eat.

As an Immediate, you will learn sound judgment and weighed decision making by seeking advice from adults whom you trust—your parents, teachers or mentors. You will be often faced with some of the toughest life issues at an early age that necessitate even more guidance than when you were younger and did not have such risky options at your doorstep. The more you seek wise counsel, the more you will help yourself maximize the brain potential of your frontal lobe development.

There is obviously a delicate balance between being allowed to make the majority of your own decisions versus controlling how those decisions and judgments are made. If there is too much adult control, you will be at greater risk for not developing adult-level sound decision making. *If you do not have safe and stable boundaries, you may find yourself in deep trouble because you lack the skills to reason your way back to healthy choices.* Practicing frontal lobe skills and pushing the boundaries of decision making, planning, and having to suffer the consequences—however grave—seem to be prerequisites for adequate frontal lobe development.

> Parents and guardians: do not act as your Immediates' frontal lobe in every instance nor remove consequences—this will stall your Immediates' cognitive development.

Whereas you are at a vulnerable life stage, you are also at a very creative stage in your life. Rote memorization of information stifles your desire to learn and become an innovator. Moreover, information is turning over so quickly, much of it at your fingertips through the Internet, that you fail to see the point in learning something for a test, knowing you'll forget the information shortly afterward. You are more motivated to create new ideas than learn facts that you can readily access. As an Immediate, your brain is primed to be challenged to develop deep-thinking capacity in order to expand frontal lobe function and to maximize intellectual capital. You need to take this challenge seriously because it matters now and for the rest of your life.

Never has our country been more worried about the future brain health of the young, particularly the way your minds are developing (or perhaps not developing). Alarms are sounding across the nation and around the world about the failure to maximize the brainpower of your generation. **As an Immediate, do not let the system limit your potential. You have control over your brain destiny, but it takes persistence and dedication.** Do not let circumstances limit your potential.

Take Philip, a senior in high school, whose teachers and parents were concerned about his lackluster school performance, which had become increasingly mediocre over the past two to three years. They were worried that his performance would end up hurting his chances to get into a good college. His parents reported that he read and researched on the Internet and worked on assignments for hours, but did not know how to translate all of those efforts into completed course projects. Philip's teachers suggested to his parents that he likely had attention deficit/hyperactivity disorder (ADHD). He didn't sit still for long, had been labeled lazy, and often failed to turn in homework assignments. Though he was producing excellent work in some classes, he was failing two others.

Philip's performance on all three core frontal lobe domains of strategic attention, integrated reasoning, and innovation were significantly below what he should be capable of given his high intelligence. He had not learned how to maximize his intellectual brain worth. His brain was quickly overwhelmed by the amount of information he was trying to absorb and he shut down, lost confidence, and no longer put forth effort. He was having significant difficulty in his history classes because he had to memorize a vast number of dates and places. He said, "I am all about the present and the future. Besides, I can look up all the old dates if I need to know them."

With regard to integrated reasoning, Philip was particularly deficient at being able to use knowledge to create new ideas. He had not learned to engage his advanced reasoning capacity and was stuck at a literal level in his ability to understand and absorb content. He was unable to combine concepts and synthesize meanings to advance his higher-order thinking ability.

Lastly, Philip's innovative performance was stilted as he could only squeeze out one or two ideas—not pushing himself to generate more—and thought that was sufficient.

Do you relate to Philip as a powerful representative of your Immediate generation? Do you feel like you are failing to reach your full intellectual potential? Philip is highly intelligent but is not adequately developing frontal lobe strategies to engage in dynamic thinking to prepare for the future. He needs to become adept at using knowledge to enhance his creativity. Right now Philip is experiencing information overload, and his ability to think for himself is stalled, thwarting his capacity to generate innovative ideas. He does not think of himself as being smart and is losing his confidence as a learner. The system is failing to inspire his brain-building curiosity.

According to *Lost in Transition: The Dark Side of Emerging Adulthood* by Christian Smith[5] adolescents are now:

- slower to emerge into adulthood.
- taking longer to graduate from college, if they graduate at all.
- depending on their parents longer.
- marrying later.
- struggling to find jobs.
- failing to work at stable jobs for any extended length.

All of these responsibilities are mediated by frontal lobe brainpower. Immediates as a group are struggling because their significant influencers are failing them, and Immediates themselves are struggling to properly engage their strategic thinking during a critical stage of development, **thus inadequately developing mature frontal lobe capacity. This does not have to be your story,** if you take steps now. You can become a brain fitness buff by establishing brain habits that strengthen your fluid intelligence skills. These are the skills that are necessary to flexibly use your mental resources to:

- identify problems that need to be solved.
- envision a major goal to achieve and determine the steps to get there.
- sort out what is enhancing and what is blocking forward progress.

- figure options to get out of life ruts.
- become more than completers of tasks.
- have confidence to innovate new approaches.

As an Immediate, be inspired by knowing that you are at a life stage where you have immense potential for brain expansion, if you take advantage of it. The sooner, the better. The brain undergoes more changes during these years from adolescence until midtwenties than in any other time except for the first two months of life. The changes can be seen dramatically in the frontal lobe, the area responsible for planning, reasoning, decision making, and other high-level cognitive functions. The Immediate years are a critical time for developing the fundamentally necessary strategic-thinking skills to guide you for a lifetime, because your brain's frontal lobe is primed to undergo rapid development. The caveat is that it now appears that this higher-level cognitive capacity does not unfold on its own but requires proper stimulation, exposure, and training to fully develop. Working to improve strategic thinking skills lays the foundation for the advanced reasoning that should be continually refined in complexity and maturity throughout adulthood.

Frontal Lobe Brainpower of Immediates

Frontal brain networks undergo dramatic expansion and remodeling during the Immediate stage of life. Education is neglecting the fourth "R" of education—reading, 'riting, 'rithmetic, and now *reasoning*.

Embrace this stage with all the gusto you can muster. As an Immediate, you are at a life stage where your brain is particularly primed to acquire the abilities that comprise the foundation of integrated reasoning (see chapter 5). You have probably heard your parents tell you the age when you learned to walk, talk, and read, because deeply ingrained developmental milestones exist for these skills. But there is controversy over whether or not critical reasoning skills can be taught, acquired, and applied across a wide variety of contexts.

Research has shown that some degree of reasoning may evolve on its own with the maturation of the frontal lobe, given proper environmental opportunities.[6] However, it appears that reasoning training may be necessary now more than ever since the vast majority of youth (upward of 75 percent) are failing to develop advanced reasoning even in the best environments. One key question is: Can individuals be taught how to *think about thinking* in such a way that it will provide a road map of strategic learning that could transfer across course content areas? Or is it a skill that if you have difficulty, you will always struggle with being a strategic and deep thinker much as if you were dyslexic and would struggle with reading? In this case, it is never too early or too late to develop strategic and innovative thinking skills. Your brain will be energized when you take them on, especially during the Immediate years.

Janet is an extraordinarily bright Immediate, a tenth grader, but the tragic news is that she is suffering immensely and not able to maximize her intellectual potential. She is driven to make high grades in every class. She stays up until the wee hours of the night overcompensating to overlearn everything so she can ace her tests. She has developed a very poor self-image and has been told that she is lazy, unmotivated, and stupid compared to others. She exhibits signs of anxiety and depression and is developing sleep problems.

Janet's performance on the core frontal lobe measures revealed extremely low strategic attention performance. Not only does she not block out information that does not need to be learned, she adds extraneous information. She is showing a pattern of **faulty gatekeepers** (see chapter 4). She is trying to remember everything and lets the gates open too wide so that irrelevant information, even information that was never presented, intrudes on her learning and thinking. She's a miserable memorizer, but that's how she is being judged as smart or not.

Her frontal lobe cognitive strength shone through in her advanced capacity to creatively combine separate ideas into synthesized meanings, indicating a high level of performance on integrated reasoning. Janet's ability to generate a number of innovative ideas, however, was very limited and narrow compared to what would be expected based on her integrated reasoning capacity. Her classroom training and testing was focused on getting the correct answer—that approach was clearly stifling her creative capacity to generate novel ideas. She was trying to please her parents and her teachers, but she was completely bored by the monotony of school, and all the facts she had to learn verbatim were causing her to **lose confidence in her own thinking.** The distressing paradox is that Janet is a creative thinker, not a rote, robotic learner. She is not being challenged to expand and stretch her fluid intelligence potential. In fact, just the opposite is happening, and she is paying the price.

In this period of information overload and constant distraction, as an Immediate, you will need to think more strategically about how to extract deeper meanings from complex information, apply them to your life issues, and develop study habits that focus on advanced reasoning and generating new ideas from what you are learning. **When you feel mentally stifled or when your brain feels frozen, it may be that you are approaching learning as a masterful memorizer.** Consider whether or not you're trying to superficially scan too much information with not enough time, rather than taking time to process smaller chunks of information more deeply and creatively.

You have the power to take control of how to ask new questions, not just try to answer a finite issue. Sure, education needs to be revamped to inspire your immense advanced reasoning and innovative thinking capacity. But you can be the instigator or agent of change by becoming part of the paradigm shift in showing how you transform rote facts into futuristic ideas. Surprise your teacher and your parents. Surprise your boss and mentors. Surprise yourself with your ability to stretch the boundaries of your imagination.

If properly enlisted, the brain can be mobilized to catapult you to a new level of thinking, of creating, helping to develop the prerequisite smarts and creativity to build a productive life. During the Immediate years, take advantage of:

- One of the richest epochs of brain modifiability
- The primed capacity of the human mind to think critically, which can be fine-tuned during adolescence and the twenties
- The emanating ability to synthesize meaning from complex information
- The brain fuel that arises from motivation and enables you to be innovative and think in novel ways

Brain Health Fitness

To think that you are building an unhealthy brain, unfit to solve the complexities of your early adulthood and beyond, is startling. Whatever the factors, as an Immediate you may not be developing the three core frontal lobe skills—strategic attention, integrated reasoning, and innovation—at the same rate and level as previous generations at your age. Some of the problems are outlined below:

Strategic attention: the ability to filter and focus on vast information (defined in chapter 4).

You are continually attending to everything at all times due to hypervigilance to your social media alerts. The ability to suppress unwanted information is a developmental cognitive process that should improve during the Immediate life stage if properly exercised. Blocking information is an active cognitive process, and when it works, the brain shows increased activation in the frontal lobe combined with reduced activation in medial temporal lobe regions.

Often you are asking your brain to work harder to focus because it has to actively block out extraneous background noise and switch back and forth between constant interruptions, hindering its efficiency. As a result, your brain is developing a faulty and inadequate filtering system. My team and I are currently looking into what percentage of Immediates has significant difficulty with strategic attention, but we estimate it to be upward of 75 percent. This could explain why large numbers of your generation are being diagnosed with attention deficit/hyperactivity disorder.

As a general rule, you are not building or strengthening your ability to sift through information and decide what's important versus unimportant. You might counter that it's because you do not have the knowledge base to separate the wheat from the chaff, but this deficiency is present even when knowledge is within your expertise.

Boost your brainpower: See if you have difficulty blocking what is irrelevant when you read something. Can you mark through the less important information, omitting at least 50 percent or more? Just imagine how hard it is to learn when every statement on the page seems to be of equal importance.

Thirty-five percent of Immediates drop out of school because of academic challenges, and many of you feel you do not want to, nor can absorb, all you're being asked to learn.[7] This push to memorize what can readily be looked up may be squelching your brain curiosity; there is too much low-level information for the brain to learn or to be inspired to innovate.

Think about this: you are keeping your brain in a continual state of vigilance to distraction. As a result, your brain stays too overtaxed and overwhelmed to promote deeper-level thinking and learning. **Left in this state of mind, you will be a robotic, unthinking consumer of information instead of a dynamic, flexible, creative thinker prepared to launch into a productive adulthood.**

> Without the gating mechanism to filter unnecessary information out, the heavy load of information, which the mind is trying to handle, is too much.

Integrated reasoning: the ability to synthesize disparate pieces of information to form novel ideas, solutions, and directions (described in chapter 5).

New evidence indicates that the ability to synthesize meaning through integrated reasoning is declining in normally developing Immediates despite strong recall of the facts and details.[8] The studies reveal a stall in development of this capacity with as many as 85 percent failing to reach expected criteria.[9–10] Although our brains are intricately designed to be great synthesizers, the skill of integrated reasoning must be acquired. Through research at the Center for BrainHealth, my team and I have now evaluated integrated reasoning in Immediates across all socioeconomic levels.[11] At benchmark testing, the news is bleak. The Immediates we have assessed show dramatic deficiencies in the ability to think on their own and create multiple abstract answers to issues. We are actively searching for ways to empower youth, to transform classrooms into a rich context of inspired brain building, and to solve this crisis through cutting-edge research and training protocols. You will see how later in this chapter.

Innovation: the ability to solve new problems encountered; the ability to design and offer novel ideas and new directions at work or in academic learning (chapter 6).

Okay, this is not good news. You, at this young Immediate age, are already manifesting deterioration in your innovative thinking compared to what you could do even five years back. A longitudinal study indicated that divergent thinking (the ability to see multiple sides of issues or to generate large numbers of interpretations) peaks in primary school and gradually diminishes through early adolescence.[12] It's alarming that higher-level abilities are declining even at your young age, since we know that the immense power of the frontal lobe is just beginning to take off during this life stage.

How could the frontal lobe capacity of Immediates already be in a state of decay—going backward—before its time? A major contributing factor is that in the current education system, **Immediates are being trained to think of each question, first as if it had only one answer, and second, that the answer will never change.** This is a tragedy for the goal of increasing your human cognitive potential because the current situation is restricting the scope of your fluid intelligence.

> In essence, your brain may be losing capacity despite being in a life stage where brain potential should be increasing.

Enhancing Immediates' Brain Potential: Getting SMARTer

In this world, where information is being turned over at lightning speed, brain training practices of teaching what to learn will build out-of-date brains. Think about how you are trained to take college entrance exams. Since the questions are constantly changing, it is more about a strategy of test taking and less about the answers.

The extensive growth of the brain during the teen-plus years makes this an optimal time to train reasoning and higher-order creative thinking skills. One way to train higher-order creative thinking skills is through a unique and scientifically proven program called Strategic Memory Advanced Reasoning Training, or SMART. Developed at the Center for BrainHealth, SMART is based on cognitive neuroscience principles of how to best exercise the rapidly developing frontal brain networks.[13] SMART teaches Immediates to improve brain efficiency through organization, synthesis, abstraction, and constructing unique and novel ideas and approaches to doing things. Brain science has shown that constructing novel, generalized meanings is how the brain best learns. The SMART program teaches Immediates *how* to strategically think rather than *what* to learn.

SMART teaches Immediates techniques for deeper processing of information and critical innovative thinking, enabling longer-lasting understanding, better grasping of generalized significance, and inspired novel and creative applications of knowledge. The focus is on the three core frontal lobe functions, including strategic thinking, integration, and innovation.

- **Strategic attention:** Immediates learn how to focus with laser precision on the tasks and decisions that matter.
- **Integration:** Immediates learn to synthesize ideas from complex information across diverse multimedia and engage in futuristic thinking.
- **Innovation:** Through the SMART program, Immediates learn to construct insightful interpretations, imagine potential problems, identify multiple solutions, create novel directions, and view issues from diverse perspectives.

Helping students think SMARTer

Immediates become engaged in classroom discussions as they are challenged to think strategically and respond to readings with fresh, self-generated ideas. When you push yourself to think about content beyond the literal facts, you will glean insightful meanings and new applications to lessons. Moreover, as you begin to construct novel generalized meanings in one class, research at the Center for BrainHealth reveals that you can transfer this strategic approach across contexts such as science, history, math, and reading. When you continually challenge yourself to synthesize and create your own meanings, you brain performance skyrockets. Yes, you can rewire your brain at this young age.

My research shows:

- You will experience gains across core content areas, such as social studies, reading, math, and science, when you apply

generalized strategies to absorb and transform meaning (see chapter 5).
- Your love of learning will be reignited when you are encouraged to think and engage in lively interactions beyond answering specific questions with a single correct answer.

Research also discovered that Immediates at all levels of proficiencies showed gains—from the lowest performing to those with the most potential:

- 78 percent of the lowest-performing Immediates showed improvement after SMART.
- High-potential Immediates (like Philip and Janet) showed gains to superior range of advanced reasoning.
- Results showed dramatic gains in integration reasoning as well as generalization to other untrained areas.
- Statewide assessment scores for math, science, reading, and social studies show doubling of commended performance (the highest performance possible) after SMART (see graph below).
- Hispanic and African-American students demonstrate gains in reasoning ability similar to Caucasian students.
- All income levels make comparable gains in reasoning ability after SMART.

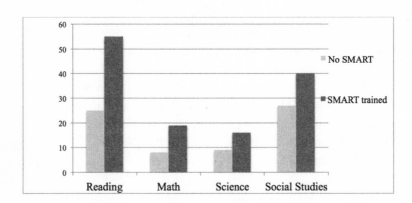

Building the core frontal lobe capacities to acquire new knowledge will be one of the most powerful brain training regimens you can adopt for life. It will help you apply old knowledge in novel contexts, chart new and insightful directions, specify unidentified problems and approaches, flexibly extract meaning from various sources, construct new abstract ideas, and cultivate futuristic thinking. **Brain science has shown that constructing novel, generalized meanings is how the brain best learns.** You will be ready for a futuristic workplace—one that does not even exist today.

Boost your brainpower: Try this when you are studying for your classes. Read the assignment and concoct your own abstract meanings in your notes. You will enhance your independent thinking capacity and also reinforce your ability to learn and apply the fundamental facts to boot.

By practicing the habits of formulating generalized principles and meanings, you will look forward to classroom discussions. Your brain is invigorated when you challenge it to compose new ideas and reasoning instead of regurgitating precise facts. **Take the strategic thinking challenge to see if you can transform yourself into an enthusiastic learner as you interpret content in new ways.**

Basic fact retrieval is boring when contrasted with the soaring pleasure of creating new knowledge. Creating makes learning worth it.

Real-Life Improvements in Advanced Reasoning

Below is a true story that represents the life-changing effects that are possible when the pivotal window of Immediate brain development is advantageously engaged.

Thirteen-year-old Cole had always been successful in school, making mostly As. In fact, he was in the talented and gifted classes through seventh grade. In middle school everything began to decline—his school performance, his self-confidence, and his peer relationships. His tests and class project grades began to drop, some even to failing level. His parents were repeatedly talking to his teachers to try to get at the root of his learning decline. They took him out of public school and put him in a private school to see if smaller classes would help. Cole continued to fall behind even more and began to think of himself as a poor student. He was completely overwhelmed by every assignment and felt he could never master the massive amounts of information he was trying to learn.

At pretesting, Cole's Test of Strategic Learning revealed that he was attempting to learn everything verbatim. After ten sessions of brain training he learned how to engage in top-down processing (such as identifying themes, abstracting ideas, and giving interpretations) instead of bottom-up learning (isolated facts). At post-testing, Cole was able to combine separate concepts into abstracted, self-created ideas. He was able to more quickly process the content from academic assignments. He showed a dramatic increase in ability to generate rich interpretations from readings. Moreover, his ability to remember the basic facts significantly improved.

Cole, his parents, and his teachers observed the benefits of the training. His study time went from six hours per assignment to about forty-five minutes when he began to think about and learn bigger ideas first (top-down processing), rather than memorize isolated facts. Cole was no longer failing and instead was at the top of his class in most courses.

"After training, I felt so much smarter—like I knew exactly how to learn and think for myself. I felt inspired at school when I stopped trying to remember everything exactly as it was printed. I am much more creative."

"After the training, Cole became a confident and efficient learner," his father Joe said. "His conversations even showed more depth of thinking. He now feels there is no goal he cannot achieve and has for the first time set high expectations for his future."

Dramatic progress can be made by enlisting your frontal lobe to maximize your brain potential. By engaging the frontal lobe networks to think strategically, you will be transformed into innovative and inspirational leaders.

Parents: How do you help your Immediate?

A time of extraordinary promise and vulnerability, this critical life stage merits larger-than-life attention from parents, brain scientists, educators, policy makers, and economists. Encouraging brain health fitness will set the stage for a productive life.

- It is important to teach Immediates to conceive of their own unique interpretations of movies; political discussions; local, national, and worldwide tragedies; unsettling school issues; bullying situations; or interpreting their own art creations to stimulate their frontal lobe brain function.
- Encourage them to be problem finders and designers of solutions for the context above or others that arise daily, using their new knowledge.
- Engage Immediates in discussions and reward reflection and imaginative thought grounded in reality instead of just listing the facts.
  * Ask your teenager to give you a "message" from a movie rather than a long-winded retell.
  * Have them interpret the lyrics of their favorite song from positive and negative perspectives.
- Encourage curiosity and train selective attention—the ability to focus on one object, voice, or thought—and to ignore or suppress nonattended or competing inputs.
  * Have them develop their own experiment to study uninterrupted, in a quiet environment on one course, versus studying with normal interruptions as usual on another course. Have them evaluate their own performances with their own rating scales as well as by their class grades.
- Inspire creativity and push for a multitude of answers to a question or problem versus seeking the "right" answer.
  * Have them imagine as many new phone apps as possible that would help to make usable reminders of things to do.
  * Share an ethical dilemma you are dealing with and have them advise you with as many good responses as pos-

sible, such as someone at work is sneaking out early continually at a cost to coworkers.
* Watch their favorite television show and share in an exchange about different take-home messages for the different characters.

Brainomics of the Immediates

The worst-case scenario for brainomics is dramatically unfolding in the Immediate generation. Lifetime habits are being set in motion at this pivotal development stage that will have lasting ramifications on later economic productivity and health of individuals. I first conceived the notion of brainomics to capture the consequential relationship between educational achievement and economic well-being in the teen generation. Though this relationship may be most vividly portrayed in this generation, I subsequently realized that it applies to all stages of life.

It is becoming more apparent that the ability of any developed country to maintain a competitive edge in the global economy will depend on the competency of reasoning and critical thinking skills of your generation—the Immediates. Yet the current stats on achievement of your age group reflected on cognitive tests are staggeringly bleak:

- Reasoning, creative innovation, and critical thinking skill are stagnating in the United States.
- In a recent Programme for International Assessment (PISA) study, the United States ranked seventeenth out of twenty-seven participating developed countries in critical thinking and reasoning.[14]
- The United States ranked twenty-third out of twenty-seven in math, and seventeenth out of twenty-seven in science, as compared to other developed countries.
- More American teens are dropping out of high school than at any time in history. It is estimated that one teen drops out every twenty-six seconds, resulting in an average one million dropouts each year.
- Almost one-third of all public high school students fail to

graduate from high school with their class according to John Bridgeland, president and CEO of Civic Enterprises, whose research, *The Silent Epidemic: Perspectives of High School Dropouts,* was published in 2006.[15]

- Roughly two-thirds of U.S. teens, including those who graduate from high school, are unprepared for college work.
- Educators, public policy experts, and cognitive neuroscientists recognize the pervasive crisis of adolescents failing to thrive academically and personally as they transition from secondary and tertiary schools to real life but are unsure of the solutions to this dilemma.

Investing in the creative cognitive capital of your generation now can have a significant positive force on major economic growth, particularly in the long haul. **Enhancing brainpower will have an exponential benefit on economic growth. Our human cognitive capital is our greatest natural resource and yet we are letting it lay barren. How we teach students to become innovative, independent thinkers and train young professionals will be the strongest predictor for our economic well-being for the short term and future.**

Economists show that cognitive gains, achieved through transformations in innovative educational practices, are closely associated with long-run economic growth potentials.[16] If the United States were to contend with the highest performing countries (such as Finland and Canada) in educational levels in math, reasoning, and science, the cost benefit would be an estimated $100 trillion dollars. As Eric Hanushek, from the Hoover Institution at Stanford University, and Ludger Woessmann, from the University of Munich's Ifo Institute for Economic Research, warned in their 2011 article that appeared in *Economic Policy,* we cannot underestimate the high economic cost of low educational attainment.[17]

> The dynamic interaction between human brainpower and economic growth is a wake-up call to find viable ways for Immediates to achieve their optimal brain edge—our future demands it.

Hanushek and Woessmann clarify that improving education is not about throwing more money or more regulations at schools. In fact, there is **not** a significant relationship between more funding and better student outcomes. Instead, educational reform needs to be directed at enhancing deeper level thinking and innovative brainpower of Immediates—especially at this critical developmental stage for advanced reasoning.

As I said earlier, adolescence and early adulthood represents one of the most optimal yet vulnerable stages for cognitive development supporting imagination and innovation. Critical reasoning and strategic thinking skills typically undergo rapid expansion during adolescence and are refined in complexity and maturity throughout adulthood. The failure to engage Immediates in strategic thinking and innovative reasoning is happening across socioeconomic levels.

Every year that we fail to train strategic and inventive thinking and advanced reasoning in Immediates, we fail to invest in the future of our human cognitive capital. Elevating brainpower in impressionable Immediates is imperative to promoting independent and creative ways of living. Sparking your imagination can truly make a difference for all of us. You are the future of your family, your city, your state, and this nation.

What kind of brain do you want to build? Now is the prime time to start construction on and commitment to your foundational healthy brain habits. You will want to deeply mine your creative capital, the richest, more renewable natural resource you will ever own. This gain will be the difference in making the world a more sustainable place.

Know Brainers

1. Immediates are at greater risk for developing addiction than at any other stage in life.
2. The brainpower in Immediates requires different educational strategies than previous generations to prepare them to solve the complexities of future problems.
3. Creative thinking is already declining in Immediates, but proper training can reverse the downward spiral.
4. Frontal lobe capacities of strategic attention, integrated reasoning, and innovative thinking are core areas that

Immediates need to be strengthening during this critical stage of brain development.

5. Being allowed to make tough decisions as an Immediate is necessary for healthy frontal lobe development.

6. Thrill seeking is an important aspect of this developmental stage.

7. In every single aspect of your life, you are being exposed to more choices, which are contributing to a freeze or stall in your brain's development. Seek guidance from parents and mentors and face the consequences of your choices.

8. The Immediate brain is being neuroengineered to have faulty strategic attention due to the immense sensory overload from all the information competing for their attention.

CHAPTER 8

THE FINDERS, 25–35, AND THE SEEKERS, 36–45 YEARS OF AGE

In this chapter, I consider the current status and future potential to increase intellectual capacity in two groups—the Finders and Seekers. The Finders, ages twenty-five to thirty-five, are tasked with "finding" the answers and taking care of routines. The Seekers, ages thirty-six to forty-five, are "seeking" their place of value in the leadership ranks.

Questions relevant to Finders and Seekers include:

Once the frontal lobe is developed at age twenty-five to thirty, what mental activities improve your frontal lobe capacity?

Why does making top grades in college not readily translate to rapid advancement in the workplace?

How can you move from knowing how to quickly gather facts to knowing how to think creatively to invigorate your work satisfaction?

How does the work environment enhance or impede brain productivity?

How is Google changing the way we learn and remember?

Are you aware of when you are in trouble with information overload?

What are ways you can determine when to stay the course and when to be an agent of change in terms of healthy brain development?

Finders

Finders, those in their midtwenties to midthirties, crave and are addicted to finding. You are the point-and-click generation, accustomed to fulfilling your incessant need for information and answers to questions with a simple entry in a search bar.

Take Molly, a young, seemingly bright twenty-eight-year-old. She was at the top of her class throughout high school and college, and after graduation she landed a highly sought-after position as the assistant to the CEO of a company that makes eco-friendly products. For six years she received small incremental annual raises but was never given more responsibility.

> Finders have been trained to find the correct answers since grade school and are always searching for "the" right response.

She consistently recorded enormous amounts of information, writing everything down almost verbatim. She produced well-organized technical reports of meetings and set forth next steps based on exacting precise recommendations from attendees. None of these amazing feats of information management required self-generated, novel ideas.

When I met Molly she said she loved the company for which she worked but admitted that **she was bored and felt that her mind was stagnating in a *cut-and-paste* routine.** She felt appreciation from her boss but was limited in opportunity. She did not know how to move up, over, or out. Molly was not provided the opportunities she needed to neuroengineer her brain into one that could be innovative and solve the complex problems of the organization. She was quite literally stuck.

Think of the negative impact on **brainomics.** Imagine the kind of brain Molly was building in her robotic job responsibilities. After education is completed, the work environment is the major shaper and contributor to advancing further intellectual development. How was her brain being neuroengineered and how were the

> Searching for "the" answer does not maximize innovative brainpower.

limited work-related brain challenges impacting her bottom line now and for the future? Sure, she was in an all-knowing position, aware of and carefully documenting copious amounts of information related to the organization's pivotal projects. **What an economic loss to the company for which she worked by their failure to mentor and more thoughtfully advance her creative brainpower!**

Frontal Lobe Brainpower of Finders

As reported in the Immediates chapter, recent discoveries in brain science indicate that the brain undergoes dramatic changes beginning in the teenage years and continuing through the twenties up until the early thirties. I think it is imperative to repeat this powerful piece of brain news since you are at a life stage, i.e., a transformative window of brain development, where your brain is primed for maximizing its inherent capacity to advance high-level decision making, innovative thinking, and strategic reasoning for sound judgment needed for life. This cognitive stage is happening in parallel with dramatic remodeling in the complex frontal brain networks. This brain development requires an ability to move from collegiate book learning to on-the-job learning—where you are set on identifying new approaches to almost everything.

For many reasons, your frontal lobe brainpower is underdeveloped and may even be stalled. Vital time and effort are spent stimulating learning and cognitive development throughout college to build strong language, literacy, and historical perspectives on societal issues, basic scientific knowledge, and computational skills. However, brain science has shown that similar efforts are needed to build foundational strategic reasoning and innovative thinking skills.

Evidence of this cognitive brain stall is emerging more and more, which means it is even more critical to take full advantage of your brain potential now. Training these critical skills is paramount to prepare your brain for the future. When you were in school or college, you could lay the blame on the education system. Now it is up to you to crack open the door to achieve your highest brain performance. Will you look to be told what to do, or will you discover things that need to be done?

BrainHealth Physical in Finders

Strategic Attention

Strategic attention is the easiest cognitive function to enhance through practical applications in daily life. Finders almost instantly report back a substantial brain gain when they follow the Brain Powers of strategic attention: None (make time for down time), One (sequential tasking), and Two (identifying their elephants or big tasks). Reread chapter 3 to review how to incorporate these Brain Powers into your life. One element that has a critical impact on this function is technology.

I saw the negative effects of technology in two Finders I worked with recently. Both scored low on measures of strategic attention, and it was evident that instead of thoughtfully processing information, these two Finders showed their naiveté and demonstrated a great memory but an inability to strategically select and block information they were presented.

It is quite challenging for you to sort through all the information that inundates your daily life. Indeed, **your greatest deficit is being unable to block information from your attention. You try to process all the information presented instead of blocking 50 percent or more of what confronts you.** Because you, as a Finder, are accustomed to searching for and finding information, your knee-jerk reaction is to survey as much information as possible, typically through Internet searches. However, this detrimental habit bores your brain and overloads intellectual capacity.

> "The thing about technology is that it has made the world of information ever more dominant."—Jaron Lanier, computer scientist and author from UC Berkeley.

Integrated Reasoning

Evidence reveals that the more choices a person has, the less likely he is going to make a rational decision or even make a decision at all. The brain appears to get overwhelmed and even frozen with the burden of too much information.[1] This overload is preventing Finders from engaging in deeper, more strategic and innovative thinking.

Is it possible that more information is making us less smart—perhaps even stupider? There is not a straightforward answer. Roddy Roediger, a professor of psychology at Washington University in St. Louis, suggests that the gradual increase in IQ scores identified over the past hundred years may result from our information-rich environment.[2]

However, I warn that just because you are information rich and because we have seen a dramatic increase in IQ does not mean that fluid thinking has increased. Remember, IQ is an outdated, out-of-touch index of dynamic thinking (see chapter 1). Fluid thinking is exactly what you need to be smart in the future. This was incredibly evident in the two Finders I mentioned earlier. On measures of integrated reasoning in their BrainHealth Physical assessment, these Finders demonstrated a sophisticated vocabulary. However, the praise stopped there. They failed to exhibit dynamic and flexible thinking as manifested by inadequate utilization of the Brain Powers of Zooming (see chapter 5). They failed to zoom out from the details to derive bigger ideas and were unable to think of broader applications, instead being stuck in the literal information as presented. They simply skimmed the surface and retained superficial information instead of deeply processing what was presented.

> Finders are addicted to the need for speed.

You have grown up with modern, easily accessible technology. When people ask me if technology is good or bad for the brain, I say emphatically— "YES!" Inquisitive minds stare at me for a minute, but then the message is clear to them. Technology has been both good and bad for our brain development.

I would never go back to a time without technology. I can remember when I was working on my dissertation—it would take me two, sometimes three months to get access to certain research articles or books. Now, with technological advances, you have just about any article you want at your fingertips within minutes. This immediate access to information is a dream come true to a researcher and to most any business with rapidly changing schemas.

A recent study shows that Google has caused our whole memory systems to become revamped.[3] If we know we can look it up later, we don't recall information nearly as robustly as we would if we thought that we might not have access to the information online. In essence, individuals are able to remember the folder where the information was stored, but not the information. You no longer need to learn and remember facts—you just need to store data and know how to find it quickly.

At a recent speaking engagement, Jaron Lanier, a computer scientist guru who is best known for popularizing the term "virtual reality," asked his audience not to blog, text, or tweet while he was speaking. He was trying to stop the pervasive multitasking efforts that preclude people from being present and in the moment. His point of view: "The most important reason to stop multitasking so much isn't to make me feel respected, but to make you exist. If you listen first and write later, then whatever you write will have had time to filter through your brain, and you'll be in what you say. This is what makes you exist. **If you are only a reflector of information, are you really there?**"[4]

Finders have a laborious time taking notes in meetings beyond what is said verbatim. You report difficulty knowing how to conceive bigger ideas in real time. And often you fear that if you wait to write things down, you will forget the message. However, science shows that if you wait, you will process the information more deeply and integrate it through your own perceptions.[5] Doing so will change the hard-to-remember rote-meaning into something more personal and memorable, increasing your frontal lobe brainpower.

> Are you a reflector or a processor? Think about how you approach information.

As a Finder, you have been rewarded for accuracy in how precisely you remember information as it was delivered, thus reinforcing a detrimental brain habit. As you learned in earlier chapters, **rote learning does not build the core frontal lobe skills that are indispensible for the fluid, dynamic intellect** necessary in a constantly changing world. For too many, the highest goal is accumulating information rather than generating new ways of thinking and innovative problem solving. However, effortful, thoughtful processing is key to healthy brain development. **Remember, complex thinking makes your brain healthier** (chapter 5). Pushing the limits of your brain function will not only be a boon to your personal brain development but will benefit the companies for which you work as well as the economy of our nation as a whole.

Innovation

As Finders, you have the opportunity to become visionaries more than any other generation, using social networking for brain gain rather than drain. But you have to guard against following the crowd blindly. In Jaron Lanier's book *You Are Not a Gadget: A Manifesto,* he claims that social-networking sites like Facebook and Twitter encourage shallow interactions.[6] He suggests that he hopes to revive the development of software to allow people to be creative. I suggest that this means technology has made the Finder generation, your generation, more robotic.

So, Finders, what does this mean for you? When I asked a group of Finders recently about when they felt their brain was/is or will be at peak performance, the majority answered that now is when they are maximizing their potential. While I am thrilled that these Finders did not think their best brain years were behind them, I was hoping they would realize that while they feel their brain is operating at a high level of performance, they still have an opportunity to go even higher. You have the ability to build your own brain by how you use it every day. Build a brain health plan to help you reach your brain fitness goals.

How are you going to increase your strategic attention, enhance your integrated reasoning, and increase your innovative capacity?

One Finder I recently worked with named Abby put the following brain health plan into place:

To improve her strategic attention:

- While on the phone, avoid checking emails or looking online and vice versa.
- Stop checking email and text messages at night before bed to limit overactive thought at night.

To enhance her integrated reasoning:

- Skim presented material once, but then go back through and spend time synthesizing the main takeaways and formulating big ideas from material.

To increase her innovative capacity:

- Mull over thoughts, contemplate ideas, and envision solutions instead of just immediately responding with the first thing that comes to mind.
- Carve out a small project rather than taking on more tasks, and develop visionary plans of action to achieve goals.

The possibilities are boundless now that you have the necessary strategies needed to boost your brainpower. The power is truly in your hands, or your head, to be exact, so take control and reach your maximum cognitive potential.

Brainomics of the Finders

Clearly, our general economy is suffering major current and future losses due to unrealized brain attainment. **How can you become prepared to solve minor and major national and world crises if your brain is primarily trained to always *find* an answer?** The answers you are striving to find probably do not even exist yet, and even if the answers were available, they would be too complicated to find in a point-and-click search in a source that is rarely validated. Finders need to move to the next stage of life where you have the responsibility to identify the core issues to be solved and generate the answers, rather than solely searching for data and explanations that already exist.

Indeed, Finders are failing to meet basic expectations as critical thinkers because you are not adequately harnessing and exploiting your own brain potential. You may have strong qualifications on paper, but if your intellectual capacity remains static, we will all suffer economic loss in the not too distant future.

Current leaders need to rethink how Finders' brains are being trained; it is up to those in charge of bringing on and cultivating new talent to capitalize on the potential brainpower of young adults. The potential is there but old ideas of productivity are repressing the developing fluid intelligence of the Finders by failing to

Nurture versus nature: brainpower must be nurtured so that it's not a victim to the nature of our environment.

nurture their core frontal lobe functions of strategic attention, integrated reasoning, and innovation.

One place to enact change is in the workplace. Work environments provide the perfect life-laboratory where brainpower can be advanced or stymied in major ways. Corporate executives constantly approach me, saying, "We do not know how to integrate the smartest and brightest twenty- and thirtysomethings into our workplace. They are smart, have high GPAs and impressive résumés, but they cannot solve problems or even think what to do each day without being told exactly what to do. They need and want to be given a list of exactly what to achieve. They feel anxiety if they are left on their own to try to figure new ways to advance their work output and increase productivity."

One reason: the pervasive use of cubicles. Cubicles impede and are toxic to your brain health and stifle brain development. Ponder how the very nature of cubicles works against strategic attention and integrated reasoning. The whole concept was deliberately conjured up to spawn and foster more collaborative work habits that inspire innovation. Certainly, cubicles increase crosstalk among individuals considerably; however, the jury remains out as to whether this environmental design has been a boon or a disadvantage to innovative thinking. For sure, it has elevated cross-hearing where no such thing as a private conversation exists in a cubicle setting. Think of the cost to strategic attention—how hard the brain has to work to block out ambient conversation just to focus on the task at hand.

One Finder, Jeremy, told me that he did not know if he had ADHD or if he was just having a hard time blocking out all the stimulation from his surrounding coworkers in close cubicle spaces. He said that he suffered from migraines and wondered if the work environment was contributing to his brain drain. All of us know how hard it is to be productive when in pain. I advised him to talk to his boss about finding a quiet office space to work for short intervals, especially when it was a major project that demanded more focused attention. Jeremy reported back that this simple modification made a big difference in his brain energy and efficiency. His migraines dwindled as well.

> You are primed to develop your brain function and expand your innovative potential.

I recently worked with Julie, a

thirty-three-year-old marketing professional. At first glance, she seemed apathetic, disengaged, and disinterested in the day-to-day tasks of her job. She confessed, "I feel like I'm doing the same thing day in and day out; I rarely feel challenged and want more from my professional life." Indeed, her performance on her BrainHealth Physical revealed that she struggled with abstracting new ideas and rarely, if ever, applied innovative thinking to create solutions or different outcomes. She was stuck in concrete mode, searching for one clearly defined answer. She was not bridging meaning from what she was learning and observing with previous experience to generate new possibilities. Thus, her brain's generator, which was recycling information rather than combining separate ideas in creative ways, was easily bored and burned out.

Failing to engage in novel thinking and critical reasoning is detrimental to your brain and the advancement of thinking smarter—not harder. This failure is happening across all careers and all fields regardless of whether you are a high achiever or underachiever. Every year we fail to incite and arouse strategic novel thinking and advanced reasoning, we fail to invest in the future of our human cognitive capital.

Seekers

When I first developed my ideas for this chapter, I had lumped the ages from twenty-six to forty-five together as one generation. But as I began to talk to individuals in the *thirty*-six to forty-five age range, you told me that you were very different from the Finders. I stepped back and realized that even though there were many commonalities, there were striking differences between the two age groups.

Seekers are between a rock and a hard place in life. You are seeking to:

- Identify your place in society
- Figure out where you best fit in
- Determine where your growth potential resides

The Thinkers, or those between age forty-six and sixty-five, are your mentors and managers and are not readily turning over the reins to you in the foreseeable future. In fact, Thinkers seem to have balanced things out nicely. They can be the big-picture visionaries while Seekers, who report to them, can be the make-it-happen, detail-oriented group.

Couple this gray zone of leadership potential with the evidence that in the majority of countries the Seeker age group is the unhappiest. Why is this the case? The results have been interpreted to suggest that happiness dips in the Seeker years due to elevated stress, worry, and the complications of managing families—especially young teenagers.[7-8] Stress could be attributed to being stuck in jobs with no ability to see future growth.

Ted definitely feels stuck. He is a forty-two-year-old Seeker who came from out of town to find out if there was something more he could do to increase his mental productivity and leadership skills. He was:

- a chronic multitaskaholic,
- an information downloading junkie, and
- working long hours but getting less done.

He overcommitted himself, believing it would help him get an edge up on a promotion. The problem, as he described it, was that he reported to two people—both who were in the Thinker generation. Neither had any plans on retiring. The thing that frustrated him the most was that he felt his superiors had switched to an automatic pilot mode of operating and that he was carrying more of their load but getting paid much less. He felt he was a more strategic thinker, more expressive contributor in meetings, and more tuned into where the company should be going but was not.

I see Ted's situation in other people over and over again. He really is between a rock and a hard place because he does not know where to turn. He cannot go complaining to his boss.

Seekers: you are not climbing the corporate ladder at the same speed Thinkers did when they were in their thirties and forties. Twenty years ago, CEOs were commonly in their thirties and forties, but this is rarer now. Ted is looking for a new job where he can sprout his wings to lead. What a major loss it will be for his company and the leadership team. **The work environment is stalling his ability to increase his intellectual capital; brainomics is losing in this situation.**

Another Seeker, Shirley, is a different story. She is forty-one and has been promoted, currently serving as CEO of a national corporation with multiple businesses. However, she came to see me because she had some concerns. She felt:

- her high level performance declining.
- loss of motivation.
- excessively distracted.
- growing unhappiness with her work.

On her BrainHealth Physical, she exhibited inefficient strategic attention with her ability to apply strategies to focus and filter information getting worse with repeated trials. Her brain was quickly overwhelmed with information. Her integrated reasoning was extraordinarily low given the high complexity of the cognitive demands of her job. She excelled in innovation, being able to think fluidly and creatively with a multitude of interpretations. For Shirley, her intellect was being drained. She was definitely intelligent, but her brain energy was being depleted. One of the key areas I recommended that she improve was in prioritizing her efforts. She was trying to do it all, and giving everything the same level of attention. It's not possible for a brain to push wildly day in and day out. She did not know where her elephants were.

Finders and Seekers: here are some key ways to advance the core frontal lobe skills of strategic attention, integrated reasoning, and innovation:

1. **Strategic attention:** Use your elephant and rabbit to-do list pad from chapter 4 daily. Do not let your rabbits (low-priority tasks) turn into elephants (major objectives) so that you pay less attention to the assignments that will make the most difference daily.
   a. Practice sorting the essential from the trivial.
   b. Recognize which decisions require the greatest attention and which ones can be relegated to less effort.
   c. Train how to get the important decision right.

2. **Integrated reasoning:**
   a. Gain intellectual capital by mentoring others to rely on their executive decision making.
   b. Hone your skills in recognizing when your knowledge seeking is enhancing your deeper thinking and when it is freezing your mind from synthesizing higher-level ideas.

    c. Develop the brainpower of zoom deep and wide and combine your expanding expertise with newly emerging ideas and criticisms.

3. **Innovation:**
   a. Engage in seeking new directions.
   b. Develop novel ideas.
   c. Reflect on where things may go in the future and how to stay ahead of the game.

Finders and Seekers are nearing a recipe for disaster because your environment is not building the type of brainpower that will ensure you are leaders of tomorrow. Small changes can make all the difference and brain growth can be impressive. It will take some flexibility and understanding on the part of Thinkers and Knowers who manage you to make sure they are harnessing the power of the next generations.

Know Brainers

1. Use technology to your advantage to manage information.
2. Strengthen your resolve to change your habits away from overloading and downloading data that is causing mind-freezing from the deluge of data.
3. Continue to challenge frontal lobe proficiency by blocking unimportant information, thereby letting the most important ideas take greater precedence.
4. Instead of searching to find the answer, spend time thoughtfully combining concepts to generate new ideas and solutions.
5. Consult only a limited number of information sources and think deeper about how the ideas can impact your team. (Make sure the source is credible.)
6. Mentor and be mentored to strengthen executive function skills to orchestrate new projects.
7. Advocate for yourself to receive training to make leadership decisions and take leadership

responsibilities to strengthen your frontal lobe
networks.

8. Reflect on how your environment is inspiring or
deflating your brain innovation at the end of each
day.

9. Decide if you are afflicted by infomania (addicted to
rapid communication responding) and if so, stop the
rapid back-and-forth barrage that is taking its toll on
your mental productivity.

10. Help develop a more efficient way to be focused
and mentally present in meetings and on conference
calls by making these oftentimes brain drains more
inspiring and engaging for innovative exchange of
ideas.

CHAPTER 9

THE THINKERS, 46–65 YEARS OF AGE

If you are between forty-six and sixty-five years of age, you are part of the Thinker generation, otherwise known as boomers. I labeled your group Thinkers as you tend to view yourself as thinking from a very unique and different viewpoint from the generations that came before. You did not necessarily go along with the thinking of the time, instead becoming an independent thinker who had the courage to take a stand counter to the popular views of the time. As a Thinker, you are part of one of the most optimistic generations and genuinely expect the economic opportunities and realities to improve with time. You are part of the healthiest and wealthiest generation, and you feel that with hard work you can change the world and your standard of living.

Questions relevant to Thinkers include:

Why do you worry about memory problems more than other diseases?

Are your best brain years behind you?

Are you working out your brain or burning it out with the daily mental challenges you take on?

What is robbing you of your brain value?

Can you keep from going backward in your brain performance levels?

How can you slow the rate of losses in your brain performance?

What can you do to make sure your intellectual reserves will last throughout retirement years?

Michael, a sixty-year-old Thinker and entrepreneur, explained when he felt that his brainpower and decision-making capacity were at their prime levels: "I think I am able to make better decisions now than ever before. For me, it's the difference between *learning* and *thinking*." He went on to say, "I may not learn as fast as I did when I was younger, but I can certainly think a whole lot better now. And even when I learn, I know how to do it better. I love to problem solve—the more complex the task, the higher the buzz I get from the challenge. The challenges I am now tackling would have eluded and overwhelmed me earlier in life."

Michael's sentiments vividly portray why I call the boomer generation the Thinkers. Thinkers have spent the majority of their adult lives relying on themselves to change and invent things and be entrepreneurs of ideas, companies, and solutions.

Maybe you've heard the story about the very self-important college freshman, or Immediate, seated next to a Thinker at a football game. The freshman had just explained to the Thinker why it was impossible for his older generation to understand his generation.

"You grew up in a different world, actually an almost primitive, unconnected one. My friends grew up with email, unstamped cards, texting, iPhones, iPad, iPods, cloud storage—even electric cars. We can be with our friends anytime, day or night, without being with them. We have wireless connections and high-speed computers that can think faster than you can blink."

When he paused to take a swig of beer, the Thinker took the opportunity to say, "You're right, son. We didn't have those things when we were young . . . so we INVENTED them. Now, you arrogant little tweeter, what are you doing for the next generation?"

Though not exactly a true story, it clearly illustrates my point that brainpower does not have a preference for a young brain. The latest challenge for Thinkers is to continuously maintain your highest level of performance as a CEO of your brain—Cognitive Entrepreneur Officer.

How Much Savings Are in the Thinkers' Intellectual Account?

Thinkers are a paradox. You are working nonstop—you stay connected at all hours to family and your professional life. You are addicted to working toward your goal: to retire as early as possible and maintain the comfortable lifestyle to which you have become accustomed.

Now, as a Thinker, you are faced with two dilemmas. The largest is that you may need to work longer since much of your financial nest egg has disappeared due to bad investments and a weakened global economy. The second is that you are anxious about losing your mental edge. **According to a recent MetLife study, your number one health concern is memory problems.**[1] In fact, for the first time in decades, you are more worried about memory loss—a potential harbinger of dementia—than you fear other health concerns such as heart disease, stroke, or diabetes. In one of my recent surveys of hundreds of Thinkers ages forty-six to sixty-five, 86 percent indicated that their memory was not as good as they would like and is often unreliable.

It is intriguing that memory is the key area Thinkers want to improve. **Memory grabs our attention because we experience glitches throughout our day** as vivid reminders that our mind is not a digital camera whose data can be quickly retrieved exactly as it happened with the push of a button. Are memory problems the big kahuna for Thinkers?

> We rarely stop to take inventory of all the things our brain remembered at the end of the day—instead we remember the few things that we forgot. Fascinating that we *remember* what we *forget.*

Build BrainHealth Fitness

When asked what kind of brains Thinkers would create for themselves if they could do some rewiring or what they wish their brains could do that they do not do now, I get responses like:

- Not deteriorate with time
- More memory capacity

- Ability to learn faster
- Learn with less effort
- Faster processing
- Faster search and recall
- Ability to turn off brain
- Improved analytical ability
- Photographic memory
- Manage stress effectively
- Remember names
- Not wander with thoughts
- More technically minded
- Exact replica of mine now, but faster
- Better retention

Thinkers are actively striving to test the limits of staying youthful longer—both physically and in terms of brainpower. The sixties are the new fifties—maybe even the new forties. Advertising is playing into this ego perspective. Infomercials scream, "If you buy this product, it will take five . . . ten . . . maybe fifteen years off your brain."

With age, it is natural to value youth in appearance. **Now this "stop aging" bias is carrying over to how you think about your brain.** There are valid reasons and scientific proof supporting the idea that as a Thinker, you believe your best brain years could be in the past. But don't put too much faith into this viewpoint—remember how fast I said brain facts are getting upended? Nonetheless, let's consider the evidence before I dispute it.

For example, look at the dismal current data indicating cognitive decline status in the figure below.

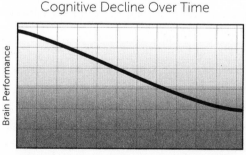

Cognitive Decline Over Time

Brain Performance

Age

Are Thinkers losing their intellectual capital at too rapid a
rate to avert the brain drain?

The downward spiral of cognitive decline resembles the Dow Jones average curves in periods of severe economic depression. If it were true, as a Thinker, you could be losing your intellectual capital at a faster rate than you can fend off! As measured, the peak years on select cognitive domains are around the late twenties to thirties. This young age of brain peak performance is precisely the period when the rich frontal lobe networks are reaching adult-level maturity.

Thinkers are aghast when I show the sharp decline in cognitive skills graph. Their moans are loudly audible. They are taken aback by the large body of research asserting that they are losing and becoming less efficient at engaging their brainpower.

A large number of studies from cognitive scientists, indeed, show that basic cognitive capacities begin to decline in our forties—earlier than the youngest members of the Thinker generation.[2-3] That such continual and unstoppable losses will accrue over time is *not* the type of news Thinkers will take sitting down—especially at such an early age—given that life expectancies are now reaching all-time highs. But these declines in cognitive performance are backed up with brain changes. Data from brain imaging studies support significant changes in brain structure and function in Thinkers and Knowers (those who are older than sixty-five) that could account for cognitive losses.[4-5] The frontal cortex, which is pivotal to higher-order thinking skills, shrinks and loses gray matter beginning at a relatively early adult age with a peak in our twenties to thirties. Indeed, prefrontal brain regions show decreases in brain volume, brain blood flow, and metabolism with increasing age.[6]

Studies investigating brain change in aging populations elegantly analyze large volumes of imaging data from MRI brain scans to try to offer explanations for different patterns of brain response. Some believe that Thinkers-plus may have to work their brains harder to achieve the same levels of performance as younger adults. People may use more mental effort, effectively using more "brain muscle" to maintain performance levels.

Researchers propose that younger adults use their brains more efficiently than older adults.[7] That is, they use less brain to accomplish the same task where older adults activate more regions. This shift is interpreted to indicate that perhaps the Thinkers' age group is restructuring how they use their brain networks to compensate for brain loss and cognitive decline. If this foreboding of cognitive loss were the whole story, why would I call a group whose brain is going down the drain the Thinkers?

I often ask those over fifty, **"Could you do what you are doing now, say, twenty years ago, even ten years ago?" Most, like Michael, honestly say they could not solve the complex issues they deal with today.** What would your answer be?

> Most leadership positions are held by Thinkers.

If such cognitive decline were the whole story, I would have dubbed this group the Relinquishers—giving up brain capital. Whereas the data is real, I believe the interpretation is defective and requires reconsideration and fuller examination.

I make my case by asking: "If you think brain performance in twenty- and thirtysomethings is at peak performance, have you spent much time with Immediates or Finders lately?" Please understand that I am not meaning to insult the younger generations who have immense potential; I just want us to rethink how we objectify intellectual brainpower. Society's conceptualization of what is smart is obsolete (chapter 1). I repeat this several times throughout the book so you'll take heed. IQ testing was established to make sure children with learning problems received the necessary intervention. Now the interpretation of IQ measurement has been blown out of proportion, its importance exaggerated, and the limitation of such testing has stifled how we envision the immense potential for the human mind. From my perspective, IQ testing may do more harm than good. As Sir Robinson states in his book *Out of Our Minds,* the popular notion of intellectual abilities has become dangerously narrow and other intellectual abilities are either ignored or underestimated. Using intelligence in a traditional sense may fail to capture the musings and innovations of the mind that get stronger with rich experiences and vast exposure to new complexities of life.

The discoveries about brain efficiency and the disparity profiles between age groups are in relatively early stages of exploration and need to be interpreted cautiously.[8] Indeed, in some studies more focal activation of the brain is interpreted as deficient and in others it is thought to indicate enhancement. For example, studies show that when adults move into early stages of dementia called mild cognitive impairment, their brain shows significant increases in activation.[9] When these individuals are compared to those who officially meet the criteria for dementia, the brains of the dementia group show considerably less activation when compared to either normal groups or those with mild cognitive impairment. The point is: arguments saying less brain activation is either better or worse depend largely on a number of individual factors.

> More brain activation may be either good or bad; the direction is not absolute.

A second major caveat to blindly accepting that Thinkers' brains are in a stage of decline rather than growth has to do with the data being collected largely from cross-sectional studies rather than longitudinal studies.[10] Whereas longitudinal studies follow the same individuals over time, cross-sectional studies compare age groups at one point in time. Imagine the mistakes we could make by comparing functionality across Immediates, Finders and Seekers, and Thinkers and Knowers in the year 2020. Given the fact that a brain is neuroengineered by how it is used at any age, you can just begin to imagine the immense differences and experiences that separate each generation.[11-13] Variables other than age contribute significantly to these differences. Consider how the use of technology for the present generation is building a very different brain compared to past generations.[14]

My BrainHealth team and others are upending the views of a brain in decline with age to recognize and build the fuller potential—the full frontal potential. Think about the amount and type of information to which a Thinker has in his or her knowledge repertoire versus what a Finder (twenty-six to thirty-five years of age) has to help them solve problems. Few would disagree that Finders have much less facts and experience stored up for expansive use. It is highly plausible that a higher data-rich brain could activate more brain regions as it has access to immense associations stored across brain areas.

Dr. Gene Cohen, the first chief of the Center on Aging at the National Institute of Mental Health and the first director of George Washington University's Center on Aging, Health & Humanities, once commented that an older brain may represent a more fully networked brain. As such, the Thinker's brain may actively integrate elements across diverse regions and between hemispheres to perform tasks. The Thinker's brain, with more elaborate content and widely distributed information brain networks than younger brains, could be a partial explanation for this. Thinkers engage more brain regions of activation than Immediates and Finders on select tasks.

With age, there is increased risk of adults having coexisting brain complications that can impair thinking that go beyond such aging changes as dementia. Researchers suspect that past studies on cognitive aging may have included participants who were in very early stages of dementia (where brain cell loss is rampant even though symptoms are not yet overt). Investigations must carefully screen out and exclude complicating brain conditions in adult populations. Otherwise the findings can lead to the wrong interpretations regarding the rich potential for brain gains even in advanced aging.

> A normal aging brain does not have to lose connections in the prefrontal cortex related to using knowledge and expertise.

Good News Is Growing

A team of scientists from Mount Sinai School of Medicine found that a certain type of brain connection responsible for engaging long-term knowledge and expertise was unaffected by normal aging.[15]

Take Betsy, a sixty-two-year-old president of a large investment firm. She is concerned about her mental decline and has been for the past eight years because Alzheimer's disease runs in her family. Betsy complains that her memory troubles her, and she is frustrated by the inordinate amount of time it takes her to absorb content. She reports that she has to read information five to six times just to get the key ideas.

Like many, Betsy is not the only one concerned; her colleagues and family have also brought her memory shortfalls to her attention. Betsy said, "I have always had problems. But now, my problems seem to be more blatant because of how much I have to read and the slowness I experience in gathering the most meaningful ideas. I feel at a disadvantage compared to my colleagues who can recall facts on a whim, but I still excel in my analytical ability." She asserts that she is "holding [her] own and still able to competently sort through the chaff and wheat to extract the core issues from meeting briefings at a level even better than five years ago." In fact, Betsy is recognized for her astuteness in culling out the critical issues.

So, what are the results of her BrainHealth Physical? On standardized cognitive testing, Betsy's memory is quite worrisome, falling three standard deviations below normal. Her speed of processing, concentration, and attention are all also significantly lower as compared to the norms.

In sharp contrast to these extremely low performances on lab tests, Betsy's performance on the three core frontal lobe domains of strategic attention (chapter 4), integrated reasoning (chapter 5), and innovation (chapter 6) were notably impressive. On the strategic attention measure, her profile was that of a Strong Strategic Attender—Quick Study (profiles described in chapter 4). She was able to immediately adopt an efficient strategy on the very first trial and continued to use it on the third trial. In fact, she was 100 percent efficient in recalling the high-priority items and completely blocking the low-priority items for trials one and three. **To employ this high-level filter-focus strategy so early and effectively was intriguing in the context of low memory performance.**

The strategic attention measure also evaluated her immediate memory span. Betsy's memory span was significantly lower than most Thinkers. Even still, she was above the majority, showing a perfect frontal lobe strategy for gating information from the beginning. That is, she exhibited a proficient ability to work around her memory problems at the highest level possible, spontaneously adopting a strategy to remember the most important items from the first try. Betsy's high level of strategic learning surprised even me, given her severe memory problems.

In regard to integrated reasoning, Betsy demonstrated an average ability to read new information and construct synthesized meanings by interpreting new information within the context of her rich repository of wealth of knowledge. In addition to stellar performance on strategic attention, Betsy also showed impressive innovation skills as reflected in generating a multitude of diverse high-level creative interpretations across three tasks. Her ability to answer specific probes on data retrieval was extremely low, again consistent with real memory problems.

Betsy's question to me was: "How can my horrible memory that I suffer day in and day out exist side by side with a high capacity to engage in the complex strategic thinking skills required in my job?" She continued, "I never fail to extract the best next steps in executive meetings; in fact, my team looks to me to come through on the big ideas. However, I do not keep up in remembering the point-by-point details of what had happened previously even close to others at our meetings. Still, I feel that I am at the height of my brain functionality in decision making."

I must confess I have not seen a person with such contrasting high functionality on our three core frontal lobe measures in the same context of such low memory functioning. My recommendations were surprisingly not directed toward increasing her memory span aside from trying to get someone to take high-level notes during meetings that she could review when thinking about next steps.

Rather, I gave Betsy specific strategies on how to strengthen her high aptitude for successfully linking disparate ideas for best next steps. I also suggested that she take time to step away to take advantage of her brainpower during silence to cultivate her higher-level strategic thinking capacity and to generate, thought-filled original ideas to lead discussions in upcoming briefings. Based on published research findings, I told Betsy that if she strengthened her integrated thinking, I expected the gains would likely spill over to enhance her memory as well. I recommended that we monitor whether or not she rewired her synthesized thinking capacity to a higher performance level and also check for gains in memory function at the same time. Additionally, I found that she had not made time for active exercise in the past few years; thus, I strongly encouraged her to exercise aerobically at least three times per week for approximately one hour. My team and I have found significant improvements in memory function and increased brain volume in brain memory areas in Thinkers who exercise regularly.

Thinkers' Intellectual Capital

As a Thinker, you seek to be the first to know what to do to increase your brainpower. What should you avoid to make sure you are not spending

> Keystone cognitive capacities can be retained and even strengthened with age.

unnecessary effort on less consequential areas? What is happening to your frontal lobe functions? What can you do to exploit and invest in your greatest asset and natural resource—your brain?

Certain cognitive functions obviously decline with age, but now we're identifying core cognitive assets that can be retained, regained after losses, and even strengthened.

Thinkers want to know:

- How much intellectual capital have you built up?
- What are the best brain investments—which areas are the most profitable?
- How can you best hedge your bets to make sure your intellectual savings represent a balanced brain portfolio to protect against the potential doom and gloom losses versus preventable decline?
- What mental activities are time wasters instead of brain savers?

Increasing Intellectual Capital in Thinkers

Thinkers, do not despair. New findings reveal that you have immense potential to be as sharp as or even sharper than you were decades earlier on dynamically complex cognitive processes. What age do you think most CEOs of major corporations are? **If mental capacity peaked in early adulthood, then CEOs predictably should be young adults—right?**

> The peak age of CEOs for Fortune 500 companies are in the Thinker age group. Conversely, there are nearly zero CEOs forty and under.

The steep downward slope in cognitive losses[16] does not correspond to real-life abilities to reason and deal with crises. The cognitive tests used in the majority of cognitive aging studies do not capture the intellectual capital or the potential required to be successful in the complexity of responsibilities that increase with age. My team and others are revealing that **age alone,**

if one remains healthy, explains only a very small proportion of what is changing cognitively.

I am not surprised that in accounting for cognitive ability, Timothy Salthouse, a renowned expert on cognitive aging at the Department of Psychology, University of Virginia, proposes that age contributes only 20 percent at most to cognitive losses. Supporting a newly arising view of cognitive growth with age, I found that Thinkers rate their peak performance as being right now—not in the past—on the complex cognitive processes necessary to tackle everyday responsibilities.

Check out your perception of your peak performance on key issues relevant to high-level cognitive functionality. Fill out the following questionnaire we developed in partnership with the MetLife Mature Market Institute to assess how people view their brain status.

Check the time when you were/are/will be at peak performance in the following areas:

	In the past	Now	In the future
A. Taking time to think about possible good and bad outcomes of situations			
B. Using information from different areas to come up with new ways to solve problems			
C. Working toward a common goal despite opposing viewpoints			
D. Actively acquiring knowledge to make complex decisions			
E. Orchestrating the steps required to carry out a vision			
F. Feeling confident in your decision making			

Now compare your responses to a group of recently surveyed Thinkers (ages forty-six to sixty-five) who responded to an online survey sponsored by MetLife Mature Market Institute,[17] conducted in 2011—the first year the boomers were turning sixty-five.

Overall (All Boomers)

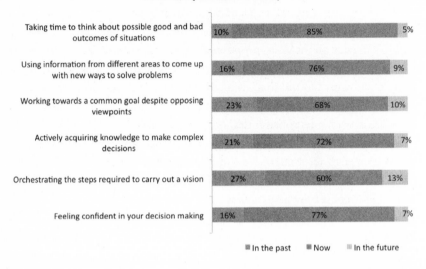

	In the past	Now	In the future
Taking time to think about possible good and bad outcomes of situations	10%	85%	5%
Using information from different areas to come up with new ways to solve problems	16%	76%	9%
Working towards a common goal despite opposing viewpoints	23%	68%	10%
Actively acquiring knowledge to make complex decisions	21%	72%	7%
Orchestrating the steps required to carry out a vision	27%	60%	13%
Feeling confident in your decision making	16%	77%	7%

■ In the past   ■ Now   ■ In the future

As you can see from the graph above, a majority of your group perceive their dynamic fluid thinking capacity to be optimal now—or expect it to improve in future years. Few believe your best brain years to be behind you in younger days. The items were selected to elicit personal reflections about how Thinkers view their peak performance on keystone frontal lobe functions of reasoning, learning, planning, adapting, and confidence in decision making. You can see an obvious omission about memory. In earlier studies at the Center for BrainHealth in more than six hundred adults, Thinkers always responded that their memories were better in the past. **Memory is important, but how a person strategically manipulates information is more vital than how much one remembers.** Would you rather be able to quickly remember an obscure date or know how to talk to your parents' doctor to help them receive the proper medical care?

As a Thinker, you are a bit conflicted. When asked what age your brain was the sharpest, you typically say at least ten to twenty years ago, suggesting your best brain days are behind you. On the questionnaire above, many of you said now. And then you go on to characterize your younger decision-making days in these ways:

- Rarely taking the time to weigh the pros and cons of actions when younger
- Not thinking much about how things went to consider new solutions
- Not thinking through where others might be coming from
- Not really thinking about mistakes except to feel bad—not how one could learn from them

Only a very small portion of your group felt your peak performance to be in the past. When I compared the younger boomers/Thinkers (ages forty-seven to fifty-three years) to the older boomers/Thinkers (sixty to sixty-five years), there was a significant difference in the query about "orchestrating the steps required to carry out a vision." Approximately 40 percent of the older boomers/Thinkers felt their peak performance on this dynamic ability of envisioning and completing a goal to be in the past, when they were younger. I can see why that might be true—with increasing age, we may become less inclined to attend to the tedious aspects required to make the big things happen. Perhaps we get used to delegating and lose confidence in making sure all the necessary steps are completed, for good or bad.

In sum, the responses from more than a thousand boomers/Thinkers argue against the view that the majority of your generation feels you fall short in dynamic reasoning and problem-solving aspects related to everyday life. You appear confident in your cognitive abilities to:

- deal with novelty.
- effectively accumulate new knowledge that requires more than manipulating old learnings.
- flexibly weigh consequences from either potentially positive and negative outcomes.
- make competent decisions.

Despite these relatively high ratings for adequate brainpower, it is important that as a Thinker you do not slough off and become satisfied with the status quo of your brain function. Like Jim Collins, a leading American business consultant, author, and lecturer who wrote the book *Good to Great*, says, "Good is the enemy of great" as applied to business practices where companies fail to transition to great as they become complacent with status quo of good enough.[18] **Nowhere is the saying "Good is the enemy of great" more applicable than in brain functionality.** The goal is to push beyond adequate brain capacity, continuing to recognize and act on the need to strengthen and increase your intellectual capital regularly.

Strength Assessment in Intellectual Capital

For years you have maintained annual physician visits, and according to a 2008 report from the Institute for the Future, the baby boomer generation holds the status of the healthiest generation in American history.[19] The word "aerobics" was coined during the Thinkers' early pivotal years. This health obsession has focused mostly on physical health because we have not been long aware that much, if anything, could be done to increase brain health and intellectual capital.

> A Thinker's idea of fitness stops at the neck.

As a Thinker, you are always the first to ask questions and say you want to know everything about what you should be doing for your brain's health. On the flip side of that, you are also slow to follow through on getting new information, mainly due to the *fear* that resides in your mind of what memory concerns could mean. Plus, you hold on to the belief that what you don't know won't hurt you. You still widely believe your intellect is largely fixed and immutable, but that is a false concept that has been held far too long to the detriment of those who have been told they are average at best.

Instead of being frozen by fear, you should start investing daily in your brain's health. The news is comforting and compelling. Based on Brain-Health Physical results, we find Thinkers' cognitive performances to be holding up well on the three core cognitive areas of:

- Strategic attention
- Integrated reasoning
- Innovation

On the domain of strategic attention, the Thinkers' performance is superior to the Seekers (younger adults) and the Knowers (older adults). They spontaneously adopted the strategy to block out information to make their learning efficiency higher. But all three groups learned to efficiently apply strategies to improve learning with repetition.

Let me also interject that not all Thinkers are equally at the top of their brain game. Some brains hold up better than others. Group data obscures and both under- and overestimates performance by individuals. Approximately 30 percent of the Thinkers had vulnerabilities on strategic attention. Similar group profiles of cognitive stability were also identified for integrated reasoning and innovation in Thinkers. That is, Thinkers seem to maintain the ability to synthesize meaning and to create a large number of novel interpretations. For both domains, 30 percent had lower performance, but individuals who exhibited lowered capacities were not all the same across all three domains. As expected, memory performances were lower than core frontal lobe abilities. Identifying which areas can and should be boosted with investment capital will inform brain health practices and training development.

Brad is a perfect example of a talented Thinker who may need to rebalance his brain health portfolio. Brad is a fifty-five-year-old entrepreneur who received his MBA from Columbia and has launched and mentored more than twenty new ventures and businesses. He commented that his concentration powers had changed in that he could not concentrate as long as he used to, but he felt his depth of reasoning was better than ever. He judged that he was able to extract the necessary business details to determine whether he felt different ventures were viable businesses. Once he had carefully thought out the bigger strategies, he was able to adeptly conceptualize the steps to carry out the vision.

> Are your cognitive investments in frontal lobe assets as strong as they need to be?

On the BrainHealth Physical, he exhibited some interesting patterns on the three core frontal lobe functions. On strategic attention, he performed almost at the highest level possible on the first two trials. He selected predominantly the most important items and blocked out the irrelevant data. But on the third trial, his performance completely broke down and he was no longer strategic. He was equally selecting important and irrelevant items to recall. He went from being a Quick Study–Strong Strategic Attention pattern responder to a Strategy-less Inefficient Strategic Attention responder (individuals who try to remember everything without applying a strategy, failing to focus particular information while ignoring other less relevant information). It is unusual to see someone's performance slip so abruptly, but Brad obviously had overloaded his working memory. As he himself admitted, his ability to concentrate had shortened over the years, but when it was good, it was very good. To combat this deficiency, it was recommended that Brad take frequent breaks when engaging in strategic thinking activities to maintain high levels of performance.

On integrated reasoning, he relied more on the literal input than on constructing novel synthesized ideas from his wealth of expertise and prior knowledge. This frontal lobe asset was vulnerable and likely needed fine-tuning to make sure no more slippage occurred. In contrast, Brad was an impressive performer on innovation. He exhibited flexibility of thinking, offering multiple solutions and rich interpretations. Brad can continue to strengthen his brain investment by being tuned in to when his filter was being breached and stepping away to let his brain rest.

Balancing the Brainpower Portfolio

One of **the greatest assets of your Thinker generation is your deep repository of learned information and experiences that accrue extensively each year if you stay mentally engaged.** This yearly brain gain builds and protects your intellectual assets.

Hedging Your Bets

Cognitive neuroscientists are on the cusp of more fully recognizing how Thinkers can increase their mental astuteness. These discoveries will help identify the steps Thinkers can take to make the best investments that will pay off in terms of increased cognitive brain fitness.

Look at Bill Gates, Condoleezza Rice, and Bill and Hillary Clinton—all of these Thinkers are still climbing to reach the peak of intellectual power. Indeed, as a group, your brainpower as a Thinker can continue to be cultivated and nourished to maintain healthy cognitive function for years to come.

Thinkers, take notice: You can nurture and improve your mental productivity by strengthening frontal lobe power—powers that were

difficult, even next to impossible, to master at younger ages. Frontal lobe functions are a promising path to increasing intellectual capital.

Human frontal lobe functions may be modified in both good and bad ways as you age. The trick is that these networks must remain exercised and challenged to retain high levels of competence. The more you engage these rich information associations, the more likely you are to retain and increase higher brainpower and strengthen the complex brain network. The saying "A brain that rests will rust" applies to frontal lobe functions.

Thinkers: Change the course of your own brain health, build cognitive reserves, regain losses, and even stave off what you may deem inevitable cognitive decline if you practice healthy brain habits regularly—daily.

Increasing Investment in Strategic Attention Capacity

Let's face it: memory becomes more fragile as you age. You cannot learn or remember everything—nor should you. What forms of learning build more resilience and be longer lasting? As a Thinker, you can increase their intellectual capital by continuing to master your strategic attention capacity. With age, adults should become increasingly proficient at knowing what to remember and what to discard. Thinkers should actively strive to strategically gauge what to learn and what to block. Improving performance in this domain will make your brain more efficient at learning and remembering.

Take Yvette, a fifty-seven-year-old top executive of a nonprofit company. She scored high on measures of integrated reasoning and innovation. In terms of integrated reasoning, she demonstrated robust function during her benchmark assessment. She was able to synthesize and apply meanings from new content to broader contexts. And on innovation, she showed very strong brainpower and was able to develop innovative, novel ideas.

But her strategic attention was not up to par with her other frontal lobe functions. She needed to boost her brainpower in strategically gating information. She was frying her brain trying to absorb everything possible as she had been able to accomplish when she was younger. Now the overwhelming amount of information she was trying to absorb was robbing her brainpower. In contrast to Betsy, described earlier in the chapter, Yvette's memory span was above normal. Her problem was that she was trying to take it all in and not triage any information out. She had difficulty blocking irrelevant information. By training Yvette on the three brainpowers of strategic attention (see chapter 4)—the brainpowers of none, one, and two—she was able to strategically attend to critical information and block out unimportant information, an essential skill needed for success in the high-stress environment in which she works. She was surprised to find how energized she was after making this change.

Increasing Investment in Integrated Reasoning

As a Thinker, you often over-obsess about annoying memory glitches. In Betsy's case, her concerns were beyond bothersome, but fortunately they were not impacting her decision making, at least not at the moment. To increase intellectual capital, certain core aspects of memory can be retained and even increased if properly invested. People want to immediately know what part of their memory can get better. Your brain is most efficient at remembering abstracted big ideas and less efficient when it tries to remember lower-level details. These global ideas—deeper, synthesized meanings—are more robustly stored and retrieved.

People value photographic-like memories, which are more precise when we are young, but these exact memories do not correspond to CEO brainpower. That is, **the more you know does not make you a more effective leader.** Thinkers may not solidly remember the specific details of meetings, readings, or speeches, but they should get better and better at remembering the bigger thoughts and directions.

> Thinkers are better at constructing generalized, synthesized meanings than ImMEDIAtes, Finders and Seekers, and Knowers.

One of my Thinker friends, a partner in a successful law firm, recently shared his take on the difference between the young brain and older brain:

"I am so glad you clarified what is happening to me and my brain. I was getting so down on my mental capacity. I used to be able to remember every single data point and decision on legal cases—now I cannot remember them to save my life. Our firm is hiring these crackerjack smart young attorneys, and they can take reams of documents home and come back the next day and give me every piece of information I could possibly need. They are remembering circles around me."

Then I asked him, "But can they write a brief to make the case like you?"

He jerked his head back with a knowing look in his eye and replied, "You've got to be kidding! Not even close! They do not even know where to start in making the case arguments. They cannot take the prior cases and abstract the relevant points."

Case closed! Thinkers are able to extract the big ideas and know what details are needed to support the major points. This is not yet true for the younger developing minds. As a Thinker, you will continue to get smarter if you invest in complex thinking.

Remember Betsy, who had horrible memory but strong integrated reasoning ability? Based on my research, I recommended that she work to increase her intellectual capital, not by increasing her weak basic memory, but by strengthening and building her high aptitude in applying knowledge, flexibly synthesizing new learnings, and extending to innovations. As these strengthen, I fully expect her memory to improve. Additionally, I said one of the most effective ways to improve memory is to write down the key things you need to remember in a consistent place.

And then there's Roger, a late-forties middle-level manager. Roger was relatively unconcerned about his cognitive brain function, but he wanted to know if there was some area he might need to improve. He reported a few brain glitches when I first met him, explaining that perhaps they were due to a "constant state of mental overload at work." His days were filled with meeting after meeting and he had a hard time keeping track of all of the information being thrown his way.

Roger gave a solid performance on his brain benchmark assessment in the areas of strategic attention. He was able to block out distractions and focus on important information. But in terms of integrated reasoning, Roger had difficulty going beyond the literal facts to synthesize abstracted meanings. As I encouraged him to take a more global perspective, his ideas became more superficial—a sign of a brain on automatic pilot. He was unable to zoom out or zoom deep and wide (chapter 5). With practice and concerted effort of heavy brain lifting, Roger could change his track. I have not yet seen Roger back for his reassessment to see if he is taking the challenge—perhaps this is not a good sign.

Just like body fitness, you do not have to be in trouble to take steps to increase your brain fitness. The three core frontal lobe domains of strategic attention, integrated reasoning, and innovation require regular practice to stay in top working order.

Increasing Investment in Innovation

Although individuals tend to believe that you either have innovative capacity or not, you learned in chapter 6 that you have great potential to become more innovative every year. Thinkers, however, are most guilty of letting creative thinking fall by the wayside instead of continuing to sharpen this critical skill.

> As a Thinker, boiling your problems down to memory issues may make you miss the real culprits robbing your brain value.

Take Mary, a sixty-two-year-old who travels two to three days every week for work. When I first met her, she described her memory as "okay" but was concerned that deficits were detrimentally affecting her ability to carry out her daily tasks. She was beginning to lose her enthusiasm for a job she once coveted and felt energized by. Upon assessment, she demonstrated robust function in strategic attention and integrated reasoning. In these two domains, Mary's brain was operating as a superstar. In contrast, her innovative thinking was abysmal and stilted. Environmental factors were drowning out the creative thinking that fuels the brain. Overloaded by stress, her brain was fried. With a constant flow of information, increasing responsibilities, nonstop travel, and the drastic time difference she had to manage with projects all over the world, her brain was taxed; she was on overdrive and automatic pilot. Mary struggled to come up with new ideas and ingenious ways to interpret approaches beyond what was already in practice. She has stopped stretching her innovative spirit to change things up, as she was using up all her energy just to survive her strenuous schedule. We will continue to advise her, providing strategies to help her regain her innovative brainpower. The potential could be dormant or it may be temporarily weakened (aka a "stress fracture").

These cases demonstrate the difference in brainpower under varying circumstances. Each individual had the capacity but did not know how to tap the well of the brain to maximize his or her potential.

In a recent randomized study of brain training versus physical training for Thinkers, my team and I found that innovation was the area that experienced the greatest gains in brain training. We also found that innovation improvements added to the confidence the participants felt in their cognitive ability and diminished depressive symptoms even in the absence of clinical depression.

> Increasing innovative thinking will be one of the most promising investments to increase intellectual capital.

Will the Intellectual Reserves Hold Out Through Retirement Age?

The majority of Thinkers live in fear that their bodies will outlive their minds. The stats for onset of dementia are frightening, given that an estimated one of two who live to be eighty years and older are likely to develop some form of dementia. Thinkers have seen their parents struggle with loss of mental function in growing numbers, witnessing firsthand the high economic costs of loss of brainpower. Thinkers have had to step in to make the complex decisions for their parents. In some cases, Thinkers' financial resources are burdened or even depleted due to the costs of elderly parents whose cognitive resources fall short.

The Brainomics of Thinker Brainpower

The brainomics of longevity are an immense concern to individuals and public policy experts. Will there be enough money to support the massive numbers of Thinkers who are reaching retirement age, especially if their brain health does not allow independence and personal decision making?

Thinkers have been satisfied living as fully in the present as possible, taking advantage of all the amazing opportunities before them. The world has truly been your oyster as you achieve educationally, travel internationally, rapidly climb the business ladder of success, reinvent yourselves in terms of job and life skills, and even embrace relocating. These vast prospects of growth and change were rarely attainable or sought after in earlier generations.

Only recently are you beginning to think about your future and its sustainability. Your concerns have focused largely on whether you will be able to retire as young as you had hoped, typically on or before the age of sixty-five. That is, you have been most anxious about whether you have the financial wherewithal to maintain the lifestyle to which you have become accustomed.

Whatever our age, our human cognitive capital is our greatest natural resource if properly mined (chapter 7). Thinkers spend little time pondering whether they have the brainpower to sustain their functional independence and personal decision making. Mainly this void exists because you believe you were born with the level of brainpower or intelligence you would always possess. If you believed it possible to improve, you would be all over it.

> Brain concerns for Thinkers should supersede money matters since the latter can be solved if you pay attention to the former.

Thinkers also experience the personal **brainomics** of the high economic costs of stalled brainpower development in your children. You are often referred to as the sandwich generation, as you are not only having to support aging parents but also your children who are taking more years than ever to graduate from college. With college tuition at all-time highs, there are large costs to educating your children. Today our young adult children are returning home after college in record numbers because their brainpower and a dismal job market are not leading to self-sufficient employment or life sustenance.

Thinkers have always felt mentally competent. Consequently, you have not stopped to realize that your own brainpower may require your immediate and constant attention. You may not be building the necessary reserves for a sustainable brain future. The **brainomics** of Thinkers is rapidly diminishing. That is, Thinkers' own insidious cognitive brain decline may become an even costlier reality than what you have been doling out for your parents and children combined.

Take Bart, a fifty-two-year-old recently widowed dad, working full-time as an attorney and serving as primary caregiver to three children. When I met him, he reported living in "overdrive" and consistently "pushing to the limit."

He said he had difficulty sleeping and only averaged two to four hours a night. To combat consistent fatigue, he downed eight cups of coffee a day! Although he found time to exercise every day and followed a moderately healthy diet, his daily grind took its toll. Lack of sleep combined with personal and professional stress caused emotional problems such as depression, anxiety, and panic attacks.

Before his BrainHealth Physical, Bart reported poor memory for day-to-day information and had difficulty concentrating and organizing his thoughts and words into clear communication. What we found during his assessment was an ability to identify the main ideas of information, but his ability to communicate those ideas was fragmented and lacked sufficient supporting information, making it difficult to understand his meaning.

For Thinkers, now is a vital time to build your brainpower. Doing so will not only improve your brain's function now but will also contribute to your cognitive reserves to stave off cognitive decline. Reread chapter 5 to more fully recognize and embrace your potential and the immense brain health gains from regularly engaging in complex mental activities such as integrated reasoning. You will strengthen and maintain high brain performance; your overall brain will be healthier with promises of increases in brain blood flow, increased communication between brain regions and strengthened synapses.

Good brain health habits to adopt:

1. Take inventory of all that goes on in your life and figure out ways to take control of your brain function. Figure out what makes you inefficient and drains your brainpower and come up with ways to mitigate things that take their toll.
2. Exercise your gatekeeping skills on a constant basis. Each day, prioritize and find ways to delegate or eliminate tasks.
3. Despite your drive to respond to inquiries and communications in a timely manner, it's important to consider that efficiency can be the enemy of excellence. Take your time when processing information and composing responses to emails. Allowing complex decisions to simmer over time leads to better outcomes.
4. Try to focus on one thing at a time, especially when you're

dealing with complex issues. A chaotic environment is counterproductive for remembering detailed information and for the deeper-level processing that is required for creative problem solving and troubleshooting.

5. Take time to think about information and synthesize it into the most important ideas. Make sure what you write is a balance between high-level ideas and relevant detail. Writing down important and big ideas can be helpful when considering the sheer volume of information with which we are exposed, and this is also true for the important detail-level information you receive. Not every detail is important, but the ones that are critical are worth documenting, especially when you have to keep lots of balls in the air.

What are you waiting for? You alone have considerable control over the destiny of your brain's health. If you are a Thinker, you will be motivated to ramp up your brainpower today.

Know Brainers

1. Thinkers will reap the greatest investment gains when you invest in your frontal lobe assets more than your memory capacity.
2. Thinkers are losing capacity to quickly process new information and to store and retrieve data.
3. Thinkers have increased potential to become effective cullers of unimportant and irrelevant information by recognizing the most salient concepts.
4. Thinkers can avert the brain drain of memory decline by expanding your ability to synthesize bigger ideas from massive input.
5. Innovation should be stronger in the Thinkers' generation than younger generations if this capacity is continually exercised.
6. Thinkers represent the largest age group of Fortune 500 CEOs.
7. The Thinkers' idea of fitness should focus on brain fitness as much as or more than physical fitness.

CHAPTER 10

THE KNOWERS, 66–100+ YEARS OF AGE

If you are older than sixty-five years of age, you are part of the Knower generation, otherwise known as traditionalists. I labeled your group Knowers because you have the greatest breadth and depth of knowledge and experience. You are able to discern what to quickly know and what to forget or, even better, never to encode. You are more than wise, you have the capacity to take advantage of well-practiced habits of strategic thinking, weighed reasoning, and immense creativity to expand your brainpower and to mentor others. As a Knower, you frame and remember life events in a more positive perspective than when you were younger. The span of Knowers is growing in numbers as life expectancy is increasing.

How will your brain perform at age sixty-five? At age seventy-five? At age eighty-five? At age ninety-five?

What does retirement mean for your brain?

What cognitive areas are requisite for independent decision making and should be strengthened by training?

What mental activities should you practice to maintain, improve brain performance, and even stave off dementia?

How do you capitalize on your intellectual capital from now until the end of your life?

In what areas is your brain capacity outperforming a younger brain?

Ruth continues to lead an active life, both personally and professionally. Despite a number of brain setbacks—chemotherapy and numerous surgeries where she was placed under general anesthesia—she has built the necessary cognitive reserves to continue to innovate effectively.

Ruth demonstrated her robust cognitive capabilities during her brain health fitness assessment. She was able to adopt a strategic plan for many of the tasks to complete them with ease. On the strategic attention measures, she showed a pattern consistent with having **strong strategic attention** as a person who was able to learn over time and to employ frontal lobe strategies to improve her selecting and blocking skills with practice. She performed well on the BrainHealth Physical on measures of integrated reasoning and innovation, showing an impressive depth of processing complex messages. What may surprise you is that Ruth is nearly ninety years old!

Estimates show that Knowers are the fastest growing population worldwide. By the year 2050, nearly one in every six persons is projected to be sixty-five years of age or older.

When most would consider their best brain years behind them, Ruth exemplifies just the opposite. She is the perfect example that the brain can improve and dynamically perform no matter numeric age. She considers her brain to be in its prime, despite physical frailty.

As people age, the inevitable happens. There is a loss in vitality, dimming of eyesight, fading of hearing, thinning of hair, and increase in wrinkles—not to mention mental sharpness declines in:

- Speed of thinking
- Ability to efficiently utilize new understandings
- Memory
- Quickness in disambiguating

However, it is not all bad news.

In his book *Lastingness: The Art of Old Age,* Nicholas Delbanco, one of America's most revered writers and thinkers, describes the work of great artists and change makers who exhibited remarkable and lasting intellectual talent into late life.[1] Examples are rich. Renoir, despite being severely crippled with arthritis from midlife, painted the very day of his death at the age of seventy-eight. Einstein discovered the theory of relativity in his twenties but did not know what it meant until his seventies. You may remember Mike Mansfield, the longest-serving majority leader of the United States Senate, who was politically active in various capacities until his nineties. Right now these individuals tend to be exceptions rather than the rule.

> As a Knower, you can maintain and even increase your creative capital with continued mental stimulation if you keep your brain fit and are fortunate enough to avoid Alzheimer's.

The idea that retirement is not the golden glory days of daily joy and meaningfulness is gaining traction by some of the world's richest people who are refusing to retire. In a recent global survey of two thousand high-net worth individuals by Ledbury Research, more than 60 percent are not quitting their professions.[2] The good news is that retirement is not just about economic productivity, but also about how individuals can contribute in meaningful ways to society. Daniel Egan, head of behavioral finance for Barclays Wealth Americas, keenly observed that many people make their wealth doing something they love. So why give it up? He calls them "never-tirees." Link that idea with the fact that individuals who work the hardest, are successful in their careers, and love what they do also live the longest, as discovered by Howard S. Friedman, a professor at the University of California, Riverside, and one of the authors of *The Longevity Project*.[3]

Whereas brain scientists disagree about aspects of cognitive function that can be preserved or vulnerable to decline, most all agree that knowledge can be maintained and potentially increased with age. That possibility alone is exceedingly exciting. **What is even more provocative is that older adults are more proficient at picking and choosing what knowledge to store and what to disregard** as compared to younger adults who store more needless stuff—only later to discard. That is, as a Knower, you are selective about what you add to your storage bin, restricting the clutter in your brain's attic.

Despite the capacity to maintain knowledge, as a Knower, you do experience more difficulty recalling particular knowledge at the instant you want it. Nonetheless, the surprising realization is that the memory has not disappeared with advanced aging; it just takes you longer to call it up. The sought-after item or name is usually found, just not timely enough for that usage. Fascinatingly, you remember what you forgot, so it's really not gone—it's just hiding.

Not only does the capacity to hold on to and expand experience and knowledge remain stable with advancing age, the memory for the positive side of events increases with age as well. That is, as you age, you often fail to even encode the negative aspect of events. Against the stereotype of getting more and more negative with age, we, in fact, tend to pay less attention to the negative side of things and are much more likely to remember the good of a situation or context. Cognitive studies show that older adults (at least those not suffering from progressive brain disease) are less likely to dwell on information that has a negative valence—instead showing a much higher preference for positive-valenced information. Moreover, older adults are less likely to display destructive social behaviors such as shouting or name calling[4] in tough emotional exchanges. Negative moody periods are shorter lived in older adults than in young adults. If those are not enough positive trends for you as a Knower, add one more: older adults reconstruct earlier life events in a more positive light than what actually happened.

> Our memory becomes more positive with increasing age.

So when would different age groups say they would be the happiest? This perception of happiness across the age span is exactly what studies by both Laura Carstensen, director of the Stanford Center on Longevity and a professor of psychology, and Peter Ubel, a professor of medicine and psychology at the University of Michigan, tested.[5] They asked a group of Finders (thirty-year-olds) and a group of Knowers (seventy-year-olds) this question. To no one's surprise, both groups solidly picked the thirty-year-olds to be happier. The twist came when they asked both groups to rate their own happiness. The Knowers rated themselves happier by far.

Think about these brain states—*enjoyment, happiness, sadness, worry,* and *stress.* Enjoyment and happiness peak in Knowers. Sadness, worry, and stress are the lowest in Knowers. Who knew that with aging comes increased happiness? Who would have suspected this? The added benefits of Knowers being on the higher end of the happy scale are that happiness has two additional gains: (1) happier people are healthier and (2) happier people are more productive.

Of course, age alone does not explain it all. Individual happiness varies. Consider these questions:

- Do unhappy people die sooner?
- Do older people have more money and therefore worry less?
- Do unsettling teens who have left the house help lighten the Knowers' moods, emotions, and daily burdens?

None of these factors account for the major differences in happiness between groups. Does one give up striving to be something they are not likely to become—skinnier, younger, richer, and happier? Perhaps older people are more relaxed with who they are. As stated above, as a Knower, you tend to have fewer blowups, but even more interesting is that you devise better and more solutions to conflicts. Knowers can definitely be the **more innovative thinkers** in conflict resolution.

> The grayer the world gets, the happier it becomes.

Brainomics of Knowers

Nowhere is the issue of the high costs of brain drain more relevant than in the Knower generation. The truth is, aging is costly. The majority of health-care costs are expended during the last few months to year of life. The longer we live, the more likely we are to suffer cognitive, physical, and/or financial hardships. No matter how positive I paint the potential, there is a reality to aging that is costly.

Alzheimer's disease alone is predicted to double every five-year epoch beginning at age sixty-five. Though we are all going to die, the key to health is to stay as mentally and physically fit as possible and to be prepared for the time when we aren't.

As a Knower, you can expect to live for decades enjoying relatively good physical health—and stronger physical health than any generation before. **Your major concern is of cognitive decline, where your mind does not outlast your body.** Many health-care professionals hold the view that the functional capacity of the brain to engage in sound decision making diminishes relentlessly with advancing age. Supporting this view, some scientific research has shown that decision-making abilities peak in the early fifties—years before retirement, according to David Laibson, an economist and professor at Harvard University.[6] This diminishing decision-making capacity would not be good news for you as a Knower if you view it as an unmodifiable outcome of a long life. Instead, it should motivate you to do as much as possible to improve your odds of reversing these trends.

Robert Wilson, a neuropsychologist at Rush University in Chicago, and his colleagues reported that seniors who were more actively engaged in mentally stimulating activities such as reading newspapers, books, and magazines, playing challenging games like chess, or visiting museums were more likely to retain their intellectual investment.[7] Knowers need to upend the widespread aging bias by taking immediate actions to make a concerted effort to reverse and counteract unnecessary cognitive decline. For you to prosper and flourish as a Knower in our rapidly aging and changing world, you must exploit your greatest assets—your intellectual capital and brain health.

Your brain, as a Knower, retains immense capacity to be strengthened by your efforts. Now is the time to take advantage of your brain's inherent plasticity (chapter 1). Don't let your potential go to waste for a single day. You can lead your cohort of friends to implement the necessary steps to maximize your higher brain performance now. Ignoring this is neither a workable nor a sound long-term solution. In fact, a number of corporations say that many of their Thinkers, i.e., boomers, and Knower-age employees have put their minds on automatic pilot and no longer contribute to corporate strategic thinking. Older Thinkers turned Knowers seem to be viewed (and even perceive themselves) as having little to contribute when it comes to novel and innovative thinking. This frame of mind is off—way off. Time is of essence for Knowers to turn the positive index up to focus on their intellectual potential.

> Age itself is not the major cause of intellectual loss; it is more your failure to remain mentally active.

One of my goals is to raise awareness of the brain's potential with advancing years. **As a thriving society, we must change the negative framing of brain aging and instead harness the full frontal potential of our brain's capacity throughout life (where more wrinkles on the brain, by the way, are** a good thing since brain wrinkles indicate a larger cortex—gray matter!) and more fully strive to achieve the brain potential that is yet to come.

What Does Retirement Mean for Your Brain?

In the new millennium, four generations—Finders, Seekers, Thinkers, and Knowers—are working side by side in the workplace for the first time in our nation's history. Although about 95 percent of Knowers are retired, many are not retiring as young as earlier generations did. Instead, Knowers are seeking to continue to work, often with reduced work hours, according to Lynne Lancaster and David Stillman, authors of *When Generations Collide.*[8] More Knowers want to work longer; the limitation is the lack of jobs in tough economic times and some have not kept their skills relevant to the changing workforce demands. **Knowers who do continue to work tend to enjoy their job and are valued by employers because they are hard workers and extremely loyal,** according to Sally Kane, an attorney and writer of hundreds of career-related articles.[9] Many employees are slowly changing attitudes and policies against forced retirement and instead are hiring and keeping older workers. Nonetheless, some Knowers are certainly working in uninspiring jobs only to pay the bills.

For the most part, as a Knower you are continually pondering when you will retire or should retire if you haven't already done so. "Retirement" is an interesting word—particularly when you think closely at what it might mean for brain health. Some definitions of the word are the "withdrawal from service, office, or business; the act of going away, going into seclusion."

When Knowers begin to think of retirement, they all too often put their brains on retirement mode. Each day is a Saturday, where they rarely tackle tough, novel situations and often are not challenged to offer advice on complex issues and problems in new ways, instead staying quietly on course. While a month of Saturdays can sound like a dream—especially when a fast-paced life has run out of steam—Knowers are now living as retired for

> Retirement is associated with concepts like leaving, quitting, abandoning, exiting, separating, taking off, bowing out, escaping.

longer periods than ever before, and many have cautioned that it's not good for vital brain health.

A 2010 study published in the *Journal of Economic Perspectives* showed that "data from the United States, England and eleven other European countries suggest that the earlier people retire, the more quickly their memories decline."[10] A RAND Center for the Study of Aging and the University of Michigan published a study showing that cognitive performance levels drop earlier in countries that have younger retirement ages.[11] Why is this the case? Retirement often takes you away from an engaging social environment, and social interaction is necessary to increase cognitive reserves. Second, once individuals retire, they are often less motivated to participate in mentally challenging and complex problem finding and solving dilemmas.

In fact, when we look at graphs and the research on cognitive losses— some noticeable declines occur right around the time of retirement. This is when Knowers are beginning to focus on having fun and enjoying the things they couldn't take part in while working. But what if you do not have the mind capacity to plan and orchestrate the things that you want to do for the remainder of your years?

> The retirement age of sixty-five was set when the average life span was sixty-three.

Discoveries now show that your brain retains immense capacity to be modified and strengthened into late life. Unfortunately, habits that build healthier brain function may not be fully realized and adopted, especially with the lack of regularly scheduled work or community service demands that have kept the brain engaged mentally and socially. However, this word of caution does not mean that you have to be working in the traditional sense to avoid mental decline. A brain-healthy lifestyle requires constant cognitive challenge and upkeep to maintain high-level function, but certainly this cognitive challenge can take place with reduced work hours or community service or mentoring opportunities after retirement.

Your mind can be stretched in leisure- as well as work-related activities. These two should not be viewed as mutually exclusive. When you retire from service or business, whether as a Knower or Thinker, you can do much to keep your brain active. It is not only imperative but will add life to your brain and excitement to your life.

Knower BrainHealth Fitness

The brain typically is at its maximum weight around age twenty. For many of us, we wish our body's weight maxed out at twentysomething, instead of the gradual increase of two pounds or more every year. For the brain, more or less weight does not necessarily relate to higher or lower levels of cognitive reasoning or decision-making skills. Over our lifetimes, the brain is constantly being hit with insults or changes that can cause the loss of neurons. The brain circuitry in Knowers, just as with other generations, is continually changing. The brain never stays the same. Some scientists argue that aging causes the atrophy of neurons; others go further to implicate the actual loss of neurons may be our own doing.

Not all the hits to the brain are widely understood. Some of the culprits include hormonal influences, chemotherapy, immune system dysfunction, or general anesthesia, to mention a few.[12–13] Think about Ruth—who was treated for breast cancer with chemotherapy and experienced the foggy aftermath of general anesthesia lasting more than a year post-surgery. She continues to challenge her brain to take on new problems to solve and complex information to learn. Her high-level thinking capacity and independent decision making is decidedly robust and impressive to all who know her.

> As a Knower, you may be recruiting your brain networks in different ways than you did when you were younger.

Despite widespread belief that Knowers are at a stage of insidious brain decline, brains of individuals at this life stage do not manifest widespread loss of neurons as compared to that observed in Alzheimer's disease, brain injury, or stroke.

Brain science dictates that all of our complex, goal-oriented behavior is dependent on a healthy brain and how well its different regions talk to one another—especially the frontal lobe networks. **What cognitive skills the Knowers lose in speed and quantity of learning capacity, they make**

> When thinking power depends on previously learned knowledge, as a Knower, you can excel if you keep your brain fit.

up with rich knowledge, experience, and wisdom. Indeed, Knowers potentially could supersede the Thinkers and Finders in terms of frontal lobe brainpower related to deeper level strategic thinking. The reason that this is not what is currently unfolding is that you **as a Knower may be failing to make the effort to capitalize on your vast brain potential.**

Not Warren Bennis, one of the nation's leading business advisors. Currently in his late eighties, he continues to stretch his intellectual capital. He is an active distinguished professor of management at the University of Southern California and has recently authored a book on leadership, *Still Surprised: A Memoir of a Life in Leadership.*[14] He has published vast pearls of wisdom that say you can challenge your intellectual capital by stretching your mind to interpret or counter. Try these examples:

- Leaders must encourage their organizations to dance to forms of music yet to be heard.
- People who cannot invent and reinvent themselves must be content with borrowed postures, secondhand ideas, fitting in instead of standing out.
- Becoming a leader is synonymous with becoming yourself. It is precisely that simple, and it is also that difficult.
- Taking charge of your own learning is a part of taking charge of your life, which is the sine qua non in becoming an integrated person.

Capitalizing on Knower Brainpower

Rapidly expanding evidence heralds the potential of the remarkable brain plasticity of your brain as a Knower to counteract and prevent the cognitive consequences of brain aging. It will require consistent practice and challenges in deeper thinking. You have immense potential to continue to neuroengineer your brains through new learning and by how you use your brain daily.

Strategic Attention
Knowers typically have the deepest storage of knowledge and they are ahead of the Thinkers in knowing what to ignore at the earliest trial—what is best

not to even learn as well as what to learn. In other words, Knowers know what should be tossed out with the trash and not stored in the brain's attic at all—more so than do Immediates, Finders, and Seekers. As a Knower, with practice you can actually increase your performance as superior selectors and inhibitors. One caveat consistent with extant evidence is that your memory span is the lowest as compared to younger generations. But as I have said before: for intellectual capital to grow, it is not how much you know but how you strategically use what you know. That is where your Knower brainpower can excel.

Integrated Reasoning

Steven Spielberg, the acclaimed director of Academy Award–winning movies, has just turned into a Knower. He is busier than ever making new films, TV series, and being with his family. His products represent a perfectly challenging and fun brain-training activity, as they are always thought provoking and his talents contribute a great deal to brainpower by the nature of movies he directs. He says:

> The magic of movies is that everybody sees them differently. I am always so excited when someone tells me what a movie means to them.

That is integrated reasoning at its core. How many different ways can you synthesize meaning off the screen to apply to real life? Try it—for movies such as *Schindler's List* or *War Horse*. This is one of the three-core frontal lobe processes that Knowers get better and better at.

It is even more meaningful to me that Steven Spielberg collects Norman Rockwell paintings. I have used Rockwell paintings for the past thirty years as rich stimuli in my research because of the deep meaning that each painting portrays.[15] The lessons depicted are ageless, and my team and I have utilized many of these illustrations to examine brain activation when a person is processing the abstract meaning versus the isolated detail. Guess what? Older people show preserved patterns of brain activation when processing synthesized meanings.

Knowers in their eighties and nineties show remarkable preservation in integrated reasoning. We have also shown longitudinally that this ability stays remarkably robust—even in the midst of declines in detail memory that grow larger with age. My research was the first to reveal that cognitively healthy adults eighty years and older demonstrate a remarkable adaptive brainpower to derive a central or deeper meaning in the form of an abstracted interpretation that is maintained in memory over long delay periods.[16-17] This pivotal brain capacity has been shown over and over again to be stable, if not enhanced, in Knowers when they stay mentally active.

Our minds, at any age, but particularly as Knowers, decline when you think like robots—information in and information out without reprocessing and reconciling the new input with what is already known. As a Knower, it is vital for you to continue to create new meanings from contexts or readings. If not, your mind will become almost frozen or lose ground.

> As a Knower, embrace your wisdom and seek to be a master of one or two things rather than a jack-of-all-trades.

Knowers, you will find that you can and do think deeper about areas and contexts in which you are an expert. You make wiser choices about how you spend your mental energies rather than shifting willy-nilly to new areas. The latter course of action, where one learns a little bit here and there, builds fragile and short-lived brain connections. It is your disciplined thinking as a Knower that strengthens your brain capital to prevail over the culprits that could diminish your brainpower in pivotal frontal lobe areas.

Be inspired as a Knower because you can maintain and increase your capacity to engage in integrated reasoning and push yourself to never be satisfied with the status quo. This desire to always be creating something new is a boost to brain health.

Innovation

One viewpoint that needs to be retired is that younger brains are more likely to be innovators.

Take Larry, who at seventy-two started a new company—his fifth, to be exact. Moreover, he launched a major foundation to help advise, mentor, and fund promising new entrepreneurs. Think of the brainpower that will be stimulated in Larry as he evaluates newly emerging high-tech companies. As he is a collaborator, he has of course hired a team to help gather all the information, conduct many of the interviews, and narrow the field.

When he took his first BrainHealth Physical approximately four years ago, he was at the top in strategic attention and integrated reasoning. The one area where he showed preserved but average ability was in innovation. Larry took this news to heart—well, really to brain training. He constantly pursued multiple solutions and ideas every chance he got. Four years later his performance on innovation has almost doubled.

Larry is a Knower and a wildly successful entrepreneur. The age of entrepreneurs has been increasing over the past decade. In fact, according to the Kauffman Foundation, the highest rate of entrepreneurship in American has shifted to Thinkers, extending into early Knowers.[18] Older entrepreneurs have higher success rates than younger high-tech start-ups. What accounts for this age-up shift? Perhaps with age comes:

- Greater accumulated expertise in their fields
- Deeper knowledge of customers' needs
- More years of network supporters, increasing access to financial backers as friends

Knowers have the continued capacity to innovate, envision novel ideas, and make them a reality. A slow brain death comes from ritualistic and mechanistic thinking, no matter the age. Creating novel ideas is the best source of energy for the brain. Creativity, productivity, and innovative thinking thrive much later in life than anyone previously thought.

Cognitive neuroscientists at the Center for BrainHealth are advancing the knowledge of how the brain can continue to be innovative early and late in life. Keeping the mind curious matters immensely at both ends

> Novel thinking can improve, not diminish, with aging.

of the age spectrum, especially at the upper end. I often ask older adults if they could do the work they are doing now thirty, twenty, or even ten years ago. Most know they could not. With age and experience comes richer thinking.

Brain-Training Exercises

Knowers' brains retain the potential for neuroplasticity (capacity for the brain to change) in response to how one engages or fails to engage brain networks during mental tasks—either positively or negatively. Individuals across the life span who have higher levels of engagement in complex cognitive activity show a concomitant reduced rate of hippocampal atrophy in the medial temporal lobe, an area of the brain critical for memory.[19] On the downside, disuse of cognitive skills has been implicated in age-related brain atrophy.

My goal is to inspire Knowers about the many ways they can make their brains smarter—longer. Optimal cognitive training for Knowers entails continual engagement in activities that exert mental challenge that is within the range of cognitive capacity, but is neither too easy nor too difficult. Science offers persuasive and mounting evidence that complex mental activity enhances brain health and reduces risk of dementia. Read back over all the good news about gains from active mental stimulation to enhancing brain health in chapter 5. Guess what? About 50 percent of the research participants were Knowers. Get your mind moving!

> By changing your habitual way of thinking, you will experience your best brain years ahead of you throughout this Knower generation.

Before, the public and health-care professionals did not have a good handle on the best ways to engage the brain. I ask Knowers some of the things they do to keep their mind sharp. They report that they partake in the following:

- Playing bridge
- Learning vocabulary from different languages
- Working on crossword puzzles or sudoku
- Learning to use a computer
- Reading constantly
- Listening to music
- Staying busy
- Trying not to overschedule

- Trying new things
- Looking up topics of interest
- Trying to understand new topics on an elementary level
- Doing crafts

The important idea to recognize is that you will get better and better at whatever you practice, regardless of age. There is nothing a Knower cannot do better with one hundred hours of practice. The limitation to most tasks and activities is that practicing specific tasks makes the person primarily better at the skill practiced, but the brain gains rarely generalize to other skills.

One of the key principles to engage and strengthen frontal brain regions is to make sure the cognitive challenge level is fine-tuned in terms of effort expended. When the challenge exceeds capacity to a large degree, Knowers become overwhelmed, discouraged, and may fail completely and withdraw. When the cognitive challenge is effortless, individuals operate almost on autopilot, which does not appear to be the best approach for maintaining brain health fitness.

Coupled with the fact that each Knower's brain is uniquely designed, prescribing a one-size-fits-all program is challenging. The nature of mental stimulation essential for helping Knowers to become smarter for longer varies from person to person due to the increasing levels of individual differences in baseline cognitive function with advancing age.

My research has shown that for Knowers, the brain responds to the complex mental activity involved in integrated reasoning within a relatively short time.[20–22] By training them to engage their frontal lobe during deeper thinking activities, Knowers report and show improvements in brain and cognitive function. The fascinating feature is that no two Knowers' brains are alike, so perhaps it's not surprising that different patterns of response to brain training would be discovered. Knowers' brains exhibit greater variations from one another than do the brains of of any other generation. That is, as we age, we get more different—not more similar. This increasing diversity is due to the vast differences in experiences that build our brains—no two people have the same life experiences—even identical twins.

It is fascinating that as a Knower you can experience not only stability but also vitality in your brain health throughout your life, if you actively practice the core frontal lobe functions. You will also need to continually seek social and environmental stimulation to maintain cognitive stability with increasing age.

I am actively examining how much brainpower can be attained and regained with brain training. In one study, we considered the cognitive gains of integrated reasoning training in a group of seniors whose mean age was seventy-four. After eight hours of training over a one-month period, the Knowers showed training gains in the integrated reasoning ability—the ability to synthesize meaning—a skill relevant to everyday life and decisions. More important, the findings revealed that the brain-training benefits generalized to untrained measures of other frontal lobe functions, including strategic attention, innovation, and cognitive switching.

Two patterns emerged from this study. First, the Knowers with the lowest baseline ability showed the greatest gain in integrated reasoning. Second, those that were already high performers showed spill-over benefits to other cognitive areas of fluid intelligence. The results are being confirmed in a clinical trial where the participants are randomly placed in either a physical training group, a brain-training group, or a wait-list control group.

The early results show that brain training and physical exercise contribute very different gains to intellectual capital. Again, our brain training showed gains in the three core frontal lobe domains as contrasted with memory gains in the physical exercise group. We are looking at changes that look promising for both training groups, but in distinct brain areas. Just think about how little time and effort was required to produce significant brain gains. The problem is that the brain habits likely need to be maintained to keep the benefits. Once you stop complex thinking habits, your brain is at risk for decline.

As you age, ask yourself if your frontal lobe functions are what they should be and what they optimally could be. As a Knower in your seventies or older, take the brain challenge to guard against the notion that cognitive brain decline is inevitable. The brain does change with normal aging, but the changes are not all bad, and with proper focus you can make your brain even better in pivotal cognitive domains than in its younger days.

A Knower's brain has the potential to continually increase its capacity to get better at formulating an informed, experienced position or opinion because of our rich experiences and knowledge. Knowers can also grow to know what questions to ask to prove or disprove a position. Finally, Knowers have the greatest degree of insight into how best to interpret the answers with the greatest positive gains. That is wisdom. It is a brain thing that matters.

Know Brainers

1. Your brain gets more positive as you get older.
2. Knowers can maintain core frontal lobe functions of strategic attention, integrated reasoning, and innovation given continual challenges.
3. Engaging in complex mental activities will likely be associated with considerable gains in neural health and higher cognitive performance.
4. Knowers who are at the top of their mental game should continue to challenge their thinking to keep from going backward.
5. Retirement from work does not have to be a brain loss, but maintaining brain function in retirement will require a concerted effort to pursue social connectedness and cognitive complexities.
6. Knowers can get better and better at solving conflicts due to positive-bent and broad perspectives.
7. Knowers must maintain active mental lifestyles to extend their brain spans to more closely match their life spans.

SECTION IV

MIND THE GAP IN INJURY AND DISEASE

Most consider only the negative of a brain injury or brain disease, but it is also important to remember that injury or disease does not necessarily mean drastic changes or the end of life as we know it. It is vital to keep the brain active in areas of preserved cognitive function and slow cognitive changes. The brain's incredible ability to grow, change, rewire, and repair itself throughout our lifetime offers hope where little existed before.

CHAPTER 11

REBOUND AND REWIRE YOUR BRAIN AFTER INJURY

What is a brain injury?
How is the brain affected by a brain injury?
Why is a concussion considered to be a brain injury?
Can the brain heal after injury?
What is the time window when the brain can be repaired?
Is a brain injury in a child the same as one in an adult?

Thirty-one-year-old Charlie suffered debilitating brain damage because of a car accident. A husband and father of three, he was left unable to think or talk clearly. His doctors told him that he needed to realistically accept that his employment capabilities were low. Discouraged and disappointed, Charlie worried about how he would provide for his young family.

After little progress over eighteen months, Charlie joined one of my studies. After testing him, I discovered that though his language was significantly impaired, his mental capabilities were remarkably strong. To help him achieve optimum brain recovery, I encouraged him to enroll in college classes to ensure that he was continually cognitively stimulated. To his surprise, Charlie surpassed everyone's expectations. Charlie not only received his diploma but also earned magna cum laude honors.

How can such a complex organ like the brain be repaired after injury?

I am frequently asked this very question when I tell Charlie's story during a lecture or public talk. The repair is not the result of a surgical procedure or a medication. It is not a product of a single effort. The astounding ability of the brain to grow, change, heal, and restore cognitive capacities is due to its remarkable plasticity in response to complex mental challenges such as those exemplified in chapters 4, 5, and 6. Yes, these same strategies work in the presence of a brain injury. Acknowledging and taking advantage of this extraordinary ability after injury will not only boost the personal well-being and financial bottom line of those directly affected by injury, it will also positively contribute to the community and nation as a whole.

> We can harness our brain's inherent plasticity to rewire it after injury.

To understand how the brain can repair and restore after injury, you must first understand what constitutes a brain injury.

What Is a Brain Injury?

Brain injury is the loudest silent epidemic. It is alarmingly the number one cause of disability and death in our country and across most other developed countries. It is a leading cause of disability, affecting the lives and livelihoods of nearly two million people in the United States every year.[1-2] It is referred to as silent because you cannot see a brain injury. For the most part a person looks perfectly normal— they walk, they talk—but inside they feel the difference.

> Brain injuries are known as invisible injuries.

- Children who have suffered brain injuries have said they often feel overwhelmed by information.
- Young adults who had injuries earlier in life say they cannot absorb content as fast as their peer group despite feeling as smart as others.
- Older adults often complain that their thinking is just not the same.

- Retired professional athletes talk about feeling like they're in a fog all the time.
- War veterans reflect how often they feel that their minds fail them, leaving them unable to quickly scan and assess the complex environments in which they operate.

What Happens to the Brain in a Brain Injury?

> No head injury is too severe to despair of, nor too trivial to ignore.
> —Hippocrates

Our Brains: Vaulted but Vulnerable

Our amazing brain controls everything we do—our thinking, decision making, ability to make and maintain friendships, capacity to problem solve and figure out best next steps, and more (see chapter 2). All regions of the brain work in concert, like a world-class orchestra, to produce the simplest and most complex activities with seemingly little exertion. When you think about the brain's daily accomplishments, it is literally mind-boggling.

By design, the human brain inhabits a uniquely protective environment; it is hidden away in a vault. To understand a brain injury, it helps to know a bit about how the brain is encased for safety but also how that design is easily breached, and often violated. The vaultlike protection in which our brain thrives has three layers of protection:

- A tough membrane-like cellophane wrap (the dura mater) covers the brain.
- A closed chamber of fluid (the cerebrospinal fluid) surrounds the brain.
- A one-quarter-inch thick bony surface (the skull) encapsulates the brain.

Unlike most other organs, the brain:

- is not fixed in place.
- floats in fluid inside the skull surrounding it.

• is restrained to a small degree by being attached to a long stem—the spinal cord.

Picture a flower floating in the wind. As the wind blows, the delicate flower rotates, changing direction effortlessly. The brain is similar in that it is free to rotate and move about at the end of a stem. But there is a difference. The brain's movement is constrained by the space it inhabits within the skull.

> The brain paradox: The three-layer, vaulted, protective design of our brain makes it vulnerable to injury.

Just imagine the brain safely sloshing within your skull as you partake in the following activities:

- Getting out of bed
- Standing up from the sofa
- Turning your head to look for cars behind you
- Walking down stairs
- Jumping over a water puddle in your path
- Throwing back your head in uproarious laughter, or
- Bouncing on a mountainbike down rugged terrain

With each movement, your brain moves in its fluid encasement.

Next, imagine an egg enclosed in a small jar full of water, moving back and forth, bumping softly against the sides of the jar as you walk along. Sounds pretty safe. Although it's benignly bumping against the walls of the jar, the egg is still intact.

Think what would happen to the egg if you ran at full speed into a wall. The egg would undergo an extreme jolt. You, and the glass jar, would quickly stop moving, but inside, the egg twists and reverberates violently even if the glass jar does not break. What are the chances of the egg coming out unscathed, unbroken without a chip? Slim to none.

Now imagine that egg is your brain.

An Injured Brain

There is horrific jarring of the brain when bodies collide, vehicles crash, heads crush against hard surfaces, or explosive forces propel bodies hard to the ground. Picture a brain when:

- Heading a soccer ball
- Tumbling off a person pyramid at a sporting event
- Being bumped abruptly in your car from behind by someone driving while talking on cell phone. (It is now estimated that more than 80 percent of collisions happen within three seconds of being distracted, typically by cell phone use.)
- Falling from a standing position without catching oneself. (Falling is the number one cause of brain injuries in older adults.)
- Being tackled by a three hundred and fifty-pound linebacker running at high speed, causing the head to be slammed against hard Astroturf
- Being thrown against hard surfaces in blast-related injuries—from improvised explosive devices (IED), rocket-propelled grenades, or mines

Brain scientists are only beginning to appreciate the full extent to which external forces internally injure the brain, allowing a more precise characterization of brain injuries. When the brain is slammed into a hard, bony skull, it rotates and spins. These rotational forces cause shearing and tearing of many nerve fibers that connect near and far brain regions. This stretching and tearing disrupts and cuts off the ability of different brain regions to communicate effectively. Recollect the far-reaching impact across large communities when electrical wires or telephone wires are cut after a devastating storm. That is comparable to what is going on inside the brain of someone who has suffered a brain injury.

A brain can be injured without either the individual or the people nearby realizing it. Nonetheless, the person may still be able to carry out basic functions. How is that possible? The brain has considerable redundancy built into its complex design, allowing multiple areas to take over new functions when others have been damaged.

For the most part, the wide dispersion of random stretching and tearing across brain connections cannot be detected by commonly used brain scan methodologies and technologies widely available in clinical practice today, especially in milder forms of brain injury. But this insensitivity to concussive brain trauma is likely to change in the near future. Already, new imaging techniques, such as diffusion tensor imaging (DTI), are allowing us to document the major shearing of brain fibers in moderate to severe injuries. In the DTI, scans below, image A shows the corpus callosum fibers that connect both hemispheres in a normal brain.[3] In image B, you can see the severe loss of fibers in an individual who has suffered a severe brain injury. The tiny hemorrhages from the blood vessels may show up on computed tomography (CT) scans taken later as small deposits of iron called hemosiderin (iron from an earlier bleed) appear.

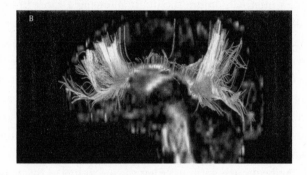

The cascading effects from a brain injury can include some of the following:

- Brain swelling (edema). Swelling can cause brain herniation where the brain is trapped and squeezed against the fixed, hard, bony skull. Brain herniation can potentially cut off

blood supply to parts of the brain causing rapid death, even after seemingly mild injuries
- Increased intracranial pressure
- Seizure activity
- Medication-induced low blood pressure to reduce the high blood pressure and combat threatening brain swelling
- Hematomas (collection of blood in brain)

These forms of brain disruption can happen in brain injuries of differing degrees of severity—from the very mild to the most severe.

When the connections deep within the brain are severed or weakened by tearing, the communication between brain regions is cut off or short-circuited. As a result, almost all complex tasks that require integration across multiple brain regions are damaged. Things that were once automatic now become much more effortful and brain draining.

What are the consequences of a brain injury?

The public has only recently become aware that a concussion *is* a brain injury, not a benign bruise or bump on the head. Concussions need to be taken seriously because potentially grave consequences may arise as a direct result of such an injury. **Knee and shoulder injuries receive more medical attention than brain injuries, yet nothing has more lasting ramifications than an injury to the brain.** The evidence is clear that persistent cognitive and behavioral deficits increase exponentially when the brain is not given time to heal before enduring another concussion.[4] Repair can be elevated given proper cognitive training even years after the injury.[5]

> The frontal lobe is the most vulnerable brain region in brain injury.

True or False? When a concussion occurs, the person is knocked out momentarily, losing consciousness.

Most individuals believe this to be true. This perception is what has guided regulations for removing athletes from play and then returning them to play for all sports—football, hockey, lacrosse, soccer, basketball, cheerleading, and even baseball. In reality, rarely does a concussion cause a person to lose consciousness—whether on the playing field, battlefield, or field of life.

Though the misfortune of a concussion or brain injury is bad, the aftermath is far worse. Throughout my career, I have heard hundreds of gut-wrenching stories of children, teens, adults, and seniors who have experience brain injuries. In each case, **the individual's life as they knew it was dramatically altered in a split second—a change that often has dire ramifications for an entire lifetime.**

A concussion *is* a brain injury.

Perhaps one of the most **detrimental aspects of a brain injury is that the frontal lobe is the most vulnerable to being damaged,** especially the prefrontal cortex.[6-7] The temporal lobe is the second most commonly injured region. These two regions are the most likely to be injured because the skull areas surrounding these regions have sharp, protruding inner surfaces that act like weapons of destruction as the brain rams against them. Also, the frontal lobe is particularly vulnerable in brain trauma because they have extensively rich long and short connections across and within the deep brain regions. Thus, any stretching and rotating of the brain is likely to disrupt connections to the frontal lobe.

And because of the intricate design of the brain and the command center–like function of the frontal lobe, the rich cognitive strategies a person once had ready for **negotiating and figuring out the complexities of daily life events now become more unpredictable after an injury.**[8] Individuals with mild to severe brain injuries may experience and report symptoms, but health care providers lack the necessary tools or knowledge to detect these complex and debilitating symptoms. **Research reveals that widely used cognitive measures are insensitive to the high-level cognitive deficits in traumatic brain injuries.** In fact, performance on many standardized measures can return to normal or near normal levels of functioning. Individuals are often falsely told the problems should resolve, given time, when they leave the hospital or rehabilitation facility.

My team and other brain scientists are discovering that many may not recover, despite their potential, due largely to:

- premature cessation of training.
- insufficient monitoring.
- ineffective, low-level training protocols.

The traumatic brain injury patient may seem like he or she has returned to normal from the outside—at least when in a familiar, unchallenging environment. **However, after an injury, brain breakdowns erupt unpredictably. When there is a change of expectations or new problems to negotiate, the individual will experience significant cognitive challenges that lead to discouragement and will perplex others.**[9–10] One common outcome is agitation after not being able to overcome the brain inconsistencies.

Despite the return of general normal intellectual capacity in the majority of individuals who suffer a brain trauma, the more lasting consequences of the brain injury will appear as:

- Poor strategic attention to the task at hand in a distracting environment
- Reduced ability to see the big picture to make sound decisions
- Impaired ability to make or initiate a new plan
- Inability to think of solutions beyond the obvious
- Difficulty establishing steps to take from extensive instructions
- Inactivity because one cannot devise multiple solutions to solve a crisis
- Overwhelmed brain when faced with massive input
- Resistant to changing directions
- Inadequate ability to anticipate consequences

If all this sounds like the frontal lobe functions discussed in chapter 2, that's because they are. **Individuals with brain trauma will struggle significantly in dynamically employing frontal lobe functions, as these intricate pathways may be short-circuited and malfunctioning.**

Ryan is a perfect example of a teen who seemed to have recovered from a brain injury. At the age of thirteen, Ryan's life was forever changed when he was hit by a car while riding his bike and was thrown fifteen feet into the air, landing on his head.

Ryan's devastating accident caused dozens of microscopic shearing tears throughout his brain. What may surprise you is that his brain scans did not show any signs of injury. **Ryan and his family were told he would fully recover** from his injuries within months. But a year after his accident, he was still experiencing problems with learning new things. Ryan was having trouble in school and at home. Most research only follows children with traumatic brain injury up to a year after their injuries, but I have been able to document a neurocognitive stall, or a halting or slowing in later stages of cognitive, social, and motor development beyond a year after brain injury. **A pediatric brain injury can be a lifelong process due to the nature of the developing brain.**

The public health issue of how we assess, monitor, and train those with brain injuries will hopefully change rapidly. Research indicates that **many individuals will later show emerging deficits from earlier brain injuries.**[11-12] **I propose that individuals with brain injuries should be monitored on a yearly basis, just like children and adults with a cancer such as leukemia.** Training could be implemented as soon as complex cognitive functions are stalled or later emerging deficits detected in order to ensure that the person "stays in remission" to keep cognitive losses at bay.

The frontal lobe cognitive functions are the most pivotal in terms of supporting our ability to become and remain productive in life. Frontal-lobe-mediated, cognitive-control functions are also the very ones that are most vulnerable to all severity levels of traumatic brain injuries, from mild to moderate to severe.

Repair and Rebound to Get an Edge

After an initial concussion, it's important that the brain heal completely to regain maximum brain performance. Cognitive rehabilitation following a traumatic brain injury traditionally focuses on strengthening specific cognitive skills, such as memory. Doctors and therapists also aim to retrain specific daily functions, such as cooking or driving, through a drill and practice method as well as the use of compensatory tools, such as memory books or planners. Although these training approaches improve targeted skills in acute stages of recovery and are beneficial for short periods, they seldom have a significant impact on the quality of life. With many doctors and therapists providing a bleak long-term prognosis, few programs exist that dramatically improve the lives of those with traumatic brain injuries.

> The chances are high that a large proportion of people today will experience a concussion sometime in their lives.

As one Navy SEAL I recently worked with stated, "Today if cognitive functioning is increased by 10 percent after an injury, it is considered a success. I argue that a college graduate reading at a third grade level after an injury is not a success; it's an absolute failure. Our men and woman in the military put everything into what they do, sometimes giving their lives for the sacrifice. The organizations responsible for these people spend millions of dollars building, training, preparing them to go into battle. Sadly, no efforts have gone into a focused training regiment for the brain."

It was previously believed that the window for brain recovery was at most one year after injury; my research has shown that the brain can be repaired months and years after injury if the right interventions are applied.[13–15] **Never have I been more optimistic about the potential of the human mind to be repaired**—not only in the short term but, even more impactful, years even decades after suffering brain trauma.

To achieve brain repair at later ages and stages of life, effective treatments and training need to be implemented so individuals can take advantage of restorative brain training now. Unacceptably, the hundreds of thousands who have suffered brain injuries are living with less than their personal best, not rebounding to their maximum, high-performance potential.

The knowledge that the brain can continue to be repaired and strengthened years after injury is not widely appreciated, despite the fact that this information appeared in scientific journals more than a decade ago.

The Power of Plasticity

It has taken so long a time for us to get to this stage for three key reasons:

Technological

Brain imaging technology has improved dramatically over the past ten years, but brain scientists have only recently been able to utilize sensitive brain imaging techniques to measure brain change and brain activation patterns in response to treatments, whether pharmacological or cognitive training. Being able to visibly measure regions of the brain as they start communicating again is extremely encouraging.

Short time windows for brain repair

Widely held tenets of brain repair had previously been limited to only one-year post–brain injury, with the greatest extent of recovery taking place within the first three months. This evidence has provided the guideline to define insurance coverage. At present, most medical coverage runs out within three months after injury, with rare cases extending benefits up to six, maybe twelve months at most. These coverage time intervals have been defined by falsely held brain repair assumptions of limited recovery after one year.[16] The new brain science must be translated and insurance must be revamped and lengthened to achieve higher levels of recovery and long-term productivity.

Training regimens largely ignored rebuilding frontal lobe functions

Most treatment protocols were focused on specific cognitive processes to achieve basic functions, such as memory or attention. Results of these programs improved the specific skills trained but failed to show significant degrees of transfer to complex skills needed to orchestrate the intricacies of life work and to maintain healthy relationships both within the family unit and beyond. **Until recently, little focus was given to training the dynamic fluid thinking of frontal lobe skills because the mainline thinking of brain repair experts was that training had to start from the bottom to rebuild skills.** *Evidence has mounted in present years that basic bottom-up training has not worked. This low-level training focus does little to make sure the individual achieves his or her personal best.*

A focus of my team is to advance brain health and high performance for all individuals who have suffered brain injury. In the near future, we plan to capitalize on new technology platforms to provide virtual diagnostic evaluations and episodic, long-term training wherever the individual is injured or resides—allowing all to be monitored long term and to receive the best training possible by the most talented experts.

Most exciting are the discoveries that significant degrees of brain rewiring and repair can be achieved after training that engages frontal lobe cognitive control processes.[17] Remember Ryan? He participated in training where we taught him how to more effectively assimilate, manage, and utilize information—skills that are crucial for academic success and overall brain function in daily life. We were able to train and monitor his recovery of important cognitive, social, and emotional functioning abilities months after his initial injury.

After training, Ryan showed improvements in several areas, including his ability to interpret and express important ideas from what he was reading, as well as his ability to use critical thinking skills to abstract the deeper-level meanings from complex information. His mother also reported improvements in areas that we did not train specifically, including emotional control, initiation, working memory, planning, and organizational abilities. These are major life improvement gains.

As has happened over and over in my career, the amazing people with whom I work inflame my mind to continuously update my research goals. Scientists at the Center for BrainHealth are searching for ways to:

- increase human cognitive potential.
- enhance brain edge and high performance.
- develop and test new frontal lobe training regimens.
- repair and restore cognitive brain health after injury.
- ensure that those with brain repair achieve their personal best throughout life.

The mechanisms of plasticity can be harnessed to bring about neuronal changes, many of which are beneficial and some of which may not be. The changes are seen at the neurotransmitter level as well as at the most complex level of how different regions of the brain work together to make things happen—including intracellular signaling, cell birth, alterations in dendritic and axonal structures, and more.

The complete answer as to how exactly the brain rewires with use remains to be explored, but we know that it happens and that it takes different routes. Some of the possible ways include these:

- Sometimes the **injured brain region heals;** the function of that region returns to the same brain area.
- At other times, **the areas surrounding the injured area take over** that skill set.

• Another possibility is when **the opposite side of the brain begins to play** an integral role in taking over the functions previously performed by the injured networks.
• It is also plausible that almost new or completely new combinations of brain pathways start to work to support the cognitive processes that have been disrupted.

The brain has immense plasticity to rewire and reorganize. One great example of this is in the research of brain rewiring in persons with deafness.[18] Areas of the brain devoted to hearing were shown to become actively involved in visual processing in deafness. It was revolutionary to discover that a person with severe hearing loss would reorganize his or her brain such that the auditory cortex, no longer actively engaged for hearing purposes, would be called upon to process complex visual spatial patterns—more commonly processed in the visual cortex. Although this explanation is oversimplified, the immense plasticity of the brain is richly illustrated.

Cognitive scientists around the world are actively researching and developing specific approaches to build stronger brain function not only in health, but also in brain injury. Science is investigating ways to substantially advance brain repair through brain training or drugs either used alone or in combination. I expect great gains in the next decade to define ways to measure and achieve cognitive improvements and the underlying brain mechanisms that support these gains.

The rewiring of a brain depends on the degree to which the brain is challenged, just as it does for those with uninjured brains. The power of brain plasticity, especially at stages one year and longer postinjury, depends on the complexity level of the mental challenge and the relevance of the activity to real life. In later years after the injury, the majority of spontaneous brain repair mechanisms have halted or significantly slowed. If a person with a brain injury is trained using predominantly low-level thinking tasks, those are the connections that will be rebuilt. As individuals with brain injury are trained to practice advanced thinking and reasoning, based on our evidence we expect they will rewire frontal lobe networks to support those functions. As the cognitive brain levels are challenged, the brain will rewire networks and make headway in regaining lost or weakened skills.[19]

John Prigg was one of the top high school wrestlers in Texas when he suffered a severe head injury. "John fell underneath the other opponent, hit the side and then back of his head on the wood floor outside the mat. It was an accident. It was devastating," John's father said. Immediately John, his family, and the medical staff caring for him knew his memory had been affected. "It was just a heart-sinking feeling when your son doesn't even know he's a wrestler when he's in a wrestling meet, in his wrestling uniform. That's pretty devastating," John's father told me.

His mother noticed something else, too. "People who did not know my son, they did not know that he was very outgoing—the first one with a practical joke, the first one with a hug, a pat on a back, a little wrestling move. After his accident, he just seemed like a very quiet, shy, withdrawn teenager, and that was not my son."

John underwent extensive therapy to relearn basic activities such as eating and showering. He struggled completing and coherently communicating his thoughts, but he was determined to improve his thinking abilities, to move past his injury and on with his life.

After twelve hours of intensive training five years after his initial injury, John was able to better convey his thoughts and communicate his ideas. As John said, "I feel like I can problem solve and organize my thoughts to achieve a goal." John's scores after training demonstrated his success. His strategic thinking and organizational skills improved by 50 percent. The transformational program provided life skills for improved quality of life, helping John and others like him with traumatic brain injuries think smarter, not harder.

> The time window for brain repair may be limitless except in very severe cases.

Brainomics

The high economic cost of brain loss in injury is exorbitant since we have failed to rebuild stronger brain capacity. The loss is greatest in those with the mildest forms of injury because they:

- are the most likely to return to pre-injury cognitive levels.
- represent the largest proportion of brain injured (approxi-

mately three in four have mild brain injuries). Our research indicates that about 30 to 40 percent of these will go on to have persistent or later-emerging deficits.

• possess a high potential to have a productive life given timely training.

The Brain Injury Association of America reports that "while a price can't be put on the cost of the emotional and physical issues that arise as a result of a brain injury, a price can be put on the financial burden that results from a brain injury. The monetary cost of brain injuries varies significantly—it's estimated that a mild head injury costs $85,000; a moderate injury costs $941,000; and a severe injury costs $3 million. Overall, it is estimated that the cost of traumatic brain injuries in the United States weighs in at $48.3 billion annually."[20]

According to the Centers for Disease Control and Prevention (CDC), acute care and rehabilitation of brain injury patients in the United States costs about $9 billion to $10 billion per year.[21] This does not include the indirect costs to society as well as to families, including the costs associated with lost earnings, work time, and productivity, as well as those linked to providing social services. While costs vary according to the extent of the injury and its specific long-term effects, it is estimated that the cost of caring for a survivor of severe traumatic brain injury is between $600,000 and $1.875 million over a lifetime.

Individuals with concussions and other more severe forms of traumatic brain injury are at risk for not being able to achieve a productive life independently. A survey of traumatic brain injury needs across fourteen states reported that one-third required significant assistance when taken one year post-injury.

It's hard to fathom the widespread degree of stalled brain potential that has occurred from past injuries, not to mention the unacceptable years of of future loss of brain potential if brain training protocols to help victims recover are not converted to everyday practice and brain care. The prior lack of effective long-term treatment offerings was not because the brain could not be repaired. **Rather, the void was a result of the pervasive false perspective that the brain was a rigid organ with limited potential to birth new neurons**—much less new brain connections after injury. The brain was conceived as a fixed black box—instead of an organ with an amazing capacity to continue to change, be modified, and be repaired into late life given proper degrees of cognitive challenges.

Even small incremental gains in brain performance would make significant cost reductions and, even better, ensure that those with injury continue to be productive in life.

In 2008, Stanley Francis was "pretty banged up" in a motorcycle accident. While wearing a helmet, he was tossed thirty feet into the air, landing face-first. After several hours in the ER, doctors assessed his physical injuries (several broken ribs) and made sure there was no severely acute trauma to the brain. Discharged and thankful to be alive, Stanley went home, and within weeks, back to work.

It was at the office that Stanley first noticed changes in his cognitive function. "I had always been able to keep everything mentally cohesive, but after the accident I struggled with completing thoughts and following through," he said. "I first took note of my struggle with personal interaction during a conference call with a client. I was asked a question that I should have answered diplomatically and thoroughly, but instead I just abruptly brushed it off and changed the subject."

"Immediately after that phone call, one of my colleagues suggested that I look into the long-term effects of traumatic brain injury. His daughter had similar struggles after an injury, so he was knowledgeable about both the effects and treatments," Stanley said.

"After the accident, we focused on getting Stanley's physical ailments healed," his wife, Carol, told me. "It was a full year before any other issues were noticed. Stanley was always gifted in analyzing information, digesting it, and presenting a summary in a very logical manner. Suddenly it seemed that instead of going from point A to point B in a straight line, he would start, then wander around in circles, maybe never arriving at point B at all. Even more, his usual mild-tempered personality was now vacillating between passive and aggressive."

After an initial appointment with a clinical neuropsychologist, Stanley was referred to the Center for BrainHealth, where researchers employed strategies with a goal of teaching participants how to better enhance strategic attention, integration of information, and innovation. The methodology and strategies are designed to improve frontal lobe flexibility and function.

"I was very skeptical at first," Stanley said. "The processes we were learning seemed, to me, too simple to have an effect. But after the second session, they began to work."

In just eight sessions, Stanley began to notice improvements in how he was thinking, his depth of responding, and his problem-solving skills in both his personal and professional lives. Since completing the study, he has made the strategies integral parts of his daily routine. "It's been profound," he said.

Stanley continued, **"I didn't want to be defined by my traumatic brain injury,** and if I had not completed the program, I wouldn't have the strategies I need to manage my daily life."

If you have experienced a brain injury recently or years ago, here are a few tips to help you take advantage of your brain's capacity to rewire:

1. **Keep a balanced level of brain stimulation.** When your brain has been injured, active mental stimulation is required to continue to recover lost cognitive functions and to repair the brain. A word of caution is that the mental challenges should not be too low or too high, otherwise your brain will shut down with boredom or agitation. The tasks need to be ratcheted up a notch constantly to achieve brain rewiring.

2. **Strengthen strategic attention.** When the brain has been injured, some abilities are particularly degraded and compromised. To compensate:
   * Keep background stimulation as low as possible. The brain has to work harder to comprehend and quickly process input while simultaneously actively blocking out extraneous distractions. The brain after injury tires quicker especially when you do not minimize stimuli intruding on your thinking.
   * Avoid trying to do two things at once. This is more difficult after a brain injury, so focus on one task at a time.
   * Identify your top two tasks; get help if needed. The brain gets quickly overwhelmed when given a long to-do list.

3. **Practice integrated reasoning.** After a brain injury, the brain

quickly shuts down when it has too much detailed information. Practice restating or writing down your big ideas. This provides experience in synthesizing meaning continually. This practice will increase levels of brain repair and mental productivity. Integrated reasoning will also likely transfer to higher levels of functionality in everyday life.

4. **Never give up.** Your brain can continue to rewire for the rest of your life. Keep looking for new ways to challenge your mind to repair and to reach higher levels of recovery.

5. **Expect new breakthroughs each year in brain repair.** Keep researching to stay in touch with new scientific discoveries that may promote brain rewiring. **Reach out to experts who can offer advice as to the next steps** to take. In the near future, my vision is to have a Virtual Center that will reach people who have had a brain injury regardless of **where they live, the severity of their injury,** or the number of years post injury. One of my goals is that everyone has access to the best experts for their case to advise on how to achieve the highest level of mental and life productivity. This level of access may be achievable through technological advances in the next few years.

Brain injury is deeply bothersome because it involves extraordinary misery juxtaposed with a _tremendous unrealized potential for brain repair._ Unfortunately, this potential is typically untapped. Think of the boon to brainomics if we significantly reduce the costs of the number one cause of disability in our country. One of the most productive ways to reduce costs from brain injuries is to prevent them altogether. Brain injury is one of the few preventable catastrophic epidemics. Prevention and restoring brainpower are achievable.

Know Brainers

1. A concussion is a brain injury.
2. The frontal lobe is the most vulnerable brain region in brain injury.
3. A brain must be allowed to recover after a concussion to achieve the highest level and long-lasting recovery.

4. Lasting deficits may be hard to detect, but the person injured and those around them usually realize the victim is not the same as before the injury.

5. Tremendous efforts should be directed at mitigating the problems, rewiring the brain, and getting the person back to a productive livelihood.

6. The effects of a brain injury may emerge years after the injury.

7. Recovery from a brain injury is a lifelong process and needs to be regularly monitored to make sure the impact stays in remission, similar to how health-care providers continue to follow cancer patients.

8. The brain can be repaired years after the injury given proper levels of brain training.

CHAPTER 12

STAVE OFF DECLINE IN ALZHEIMER'S

I am hungry for the life that is being taken away from me through misperception of my abilities. I am a human being. I still exist. I have a family. I hunger for friendship, happiness, and the touch of a loved hand. What I ask for is that what is left of my life shall have meaning. Give me something to live for! Help me to be strong and free until my last day.

—Unknown person with Alzheimer's

How do you know if it is normal brain glitches or something more worrisome?

Is cognitive and intellectual stimulation protective against dementia in general?

What are the advantages of early detection, since getting bad news without a cure can be devastating?

How can the rate of cognitive decline be slowed down in a progressive brain disease?

Is Alzheimer's the same in men and women?

Does keeping a person with dementia mentally engaged help or frustrate them?

The public and personal image of Alzheimer's disease is a devastating one. It conjures up awful possibilities:

- It steals your identity, your sense of self, your memories, and your ability to experience joy.
- It abducts your ability to think and recognize those you love.

Alzheimer's is a major brain disease that is viewed in the end stage at the very time of diagnosis. After a diagnosis, it is common to focus even more on diminishing abilities and what can no longer be performed rather than reframe abilities to appreciate the things that are still possible, perhaps with a little assistance or initial help. Individuals are often humiliated by the diagnosis because they think they will embarrass themselves or someone else due to being too forgetful. *Preserved abilities become obscured and ignored,* and the whole family begins to cease the lives they once lived.

And yet it is individuals diagnosed with Alzheimer's who taught me profound lessons of the brain and changed my career forever. I still remember the day I met Dave Fox. He walked into my office unannounced, without an appointment. He had been there several weeks before when he'd visited one of my team members. David had undergone comprehensive assessments by a neurologist, a neuropsychologist, a brain imaging expert, a cognitive neuroscientist, a speech-language pathologist, and a psychiatrist in an attempt to find the root cause of his increasing struggles with word finding.

Now in his early sixties, Mr. Fox was a bigger-than-life gentleman whose list of civic, business, and political accomplishments could fill a book. He was chair of the National Republican convention, a county judge, one of the largest home builders in the nation, the first major inner-city developer in a large metroplex, and he even rebuilt the State Fair of Texas. But today, he was coming to discuss a problem. He told me that he had just been diagnosed with Alzheimer's and needed my help.

My eyes got as big as saucers as I tried to think how to help this hero of my city deal with such a dreaded, horrific disease. But I said exactly what I was thinking—that I didn't know how I could help him—and explained that Alzheimer's is a progressive brain disease and that there was nothing we could do to make him better beyond the medications he'd been prescribed.

But he went on to say that our

> Alzheimer's is regarded as a disease without hope. But we have found hope in the midst of this devastating illness.

institution helps people with brain problems and since his brain was still working, there must be something we could do. Never before had I thought of a progressive brain disorder as a disease I could slow or halt, much less improve his brain fuction.

Years earlier I had reluctantly added Alzheimer's disease to my research domains to identify the similarities and differences between cognitively healthy older adults and those in the early stage of this disease.[1-3] I was hesitant because I didn't think I could handle working with individuals with relentless cognitive decline. *I had specifically chosen a field of cognitive brain health in which I could discover ways to strengthen brain capacity rather than watch it disappear. I did not want to go down a hopeless path.*

But on this day Dave Fox changed my perspective on brain health forever. I teamed up with one of my graduate students and worked with Dave for the next three to four years. The three of us made a significant impact on his ability to remain intimately engaged in his life's work longer. He was able to work through and achieve daily goals in the midst of severe word finding problems, major memory deficits, and other complex thinking problems. He inspired many professionals to rethink dementia—especially me. He motivated me to seek grant funding to systematically address whether and how much we could stave off cognitive decline to maintain daily function and quality of life in people with progressive brain disease.

Working with adults with dementia has been one of the most inspiring experiences of my life. **I have learned more about the positive possibilities from people with Alzheimer's disease than from any textbook or article I've read.** Instead of focusing on the limitations, I can now choose to focus on what can be done to cognitively stimulate those diagnosed with Alzheimer's.

Alzheimer's Disease: The Basics

Alzheimer's is the most common form of dementia, a general term for memory loss and other intellectual abilities serious enough to interfere with daily life. Alzheimer's is a progressive disease, meaning that the dementia symptoms gradually worsen over a number of years. In its early stages memory loss is mild, but in the later stages individuals lose the ability to carry on conversations and respond to their environment. Those with Alzheimer's live an average of eight years after their symptoms become noticeable to others, but survival can range from four to twenty years, depending on age and other health conditions.

> Alzheimer's is the sixth leading cause of death in the United States.

Alzheimer's is not a normal part of aging, but the majority of people with Alzheimer's disease are sixty-five and older. However, dementia and Alzheimer's disease are not always diseases of the elderly. One in ten people diagnosed with Alzheimer's disease is younger than sixty-five. Some cases have been diagnosed in patients as young as their midtwenties and early thirties.[4]

> Alzheimer's disease accounts for 50 to 80 percent of dementia cases.

Brainomics of Alzheimer's and Related Dementias

Alzheimer's is one of the **world's** fastest growing diseases. Millions more have other types of dementia, which refers to brain disorders that cause visible worsening forgetfulness, deteriorating behavioral changes, and progressively more decision-making errors.

As the Thinker generation is aging, they are voicing greater concern over memory problems than cancer and worry about what these memory problems could signify later on down the road (chapter 9). Treatable versus untreatable cognitive decline is one of the most widely shared and feared public health concerns today.

Alzheimer's has a wide-ranging impact on an individual's functionality and quality of life, and it dramatically burdens both families and whole societal infrastructures—emotionally and economically. **Some have estimated that if we can stave off the onset of dementia by two years, it will reduce the prevalence by an estimated 50 percent,** since Alzheimer's is a disease of aging. Just think of the major cost savings.

> Estimates indicate that Alzheimer's disease, a leading cause of cognitive impairment in older adults, will afflict fifteen million Americans by midcentury.

According to the Alzheimer's Association, the average lifetime cost per patient is $174,000.[5] Those dollars quickly add up, with an overall cost of health care, long-term care, and hospice estimates to be $200 billion in 2012. Projected costs for 2050 are at a record $1.1 trillion.

Since there are presently no cures for Alzheimer's disease, how do we stave off dementia? In chapter 3, we discussed the importance of getting a BrainHealth Physical for healthy people to detect early vulnerabilities so that these areas can be regained and re-wired and intact areas can be strengthened to maintain cognitive wellness. This is what we call staving off— avoiding unnecessary and preventable decline. In irreversible dementias, all the active cognitive stimulation in the world will not prevent the disease. We just want to try to take advantage of the cognitive capacity that remains as long as possible. In that sense, we should try to discover ways to:

> In 2010, nearly $203 billion was spent to care for individuals with Alzheimer's disease and other dementias.

- Forestall or thwart
- Slow the rate
- Avoid or fend off

Why Early Detection Is Important

Everyone is worried about memory loss and what it means. Currently, Alzheimer's treatment options are most effective when initiated sooner rather than later. Medical professionals and researchers refer to this early stage as mild cognitive impairment. Individuals with mild cognitive decline include those with minor memory problems, those who experience difficulty extracting the core message of conversations or reading material, or those who see changes in complex decision making.

Alzheimer's can be very frustrating for both the person and his significant other. This is especially true when you have a seemingly meaningful and co-

> Worrying does nothing more than add to the fear.

229

herent conversation either in person or on the phone, only for the person with dementia not to recollect an important idea an hour later. I know one man with Alzheimer's told me that his spouse was very demeaning and "lost it" by yelling at him. When I asked him how he was coping with the public display of frustration, he poignantly said, "I cannot blame her. It's not her or me that's the problem. **It's the disease that is the perpetrator.** It doesn't

> **The disease is the perpetrator!**

hurt me as I know she's raging at the disease—so am I." This is another message of wisdom from a person with moderate Alzheimer's who demonstrates intact cognitive capacity.

Changing the Conversation About Dementia

Our genes are certainly a factor in the development of Alzheimer's, but we also play a major role in the healthy habits we adopt or ignore. Extant evidence points to the benefits of continued education, exercise, staying mentally active, and maintaining strong social ties in staving off symptoms of dementia.[6–8] Whereas there is **considerable controversy as to the benefits of available medications for Alzheimer's, strong evidence supports the view that adults should adopt lifelong habits of engaging in mentally and physically challenging activities to help the brain resist dementia to the largest degree possible.** Even if the gains are small for some, there is no downside; not to mention the additional bonus that actively engaged lifestyles mitigate loneliness and depression.

More than a decade ago, I set out to scientifically validate whether individuals with early to moderate stages of Alzheimer's could benefit from active mental stimulation when coupled with a commonly prescribed drug for the disease. The trial included individuals with confirmed diagnoses of Alzheimer's who were randomly assigned to either a group receiving mental stimulation plus drugs or to a group just taking the drug alone.

> We cannot choose our future but we can choose our habits. Our habits define our future. Choose brain-healthy habits wisely.

My results revealed a ***slower rate of decline*** in communication, functional ability, and emotional well-being in those individuals who received both mental stimulation and pharmacological intervention as compared to the drug-only group.[9] Those who were randomly selected to receive mental stimulation showed less apathy and irritability and improved quality of life.

This was one of the first studies to suggest that active mental stimulation could be a factor to exploit to maintain or potentially slow the rate of decline in early stages of progressive brain disease.

Patients with Alzheimer's rarely receive treatments or strategies beyond medication. The benefits from medication alone have not been overwhelming. Some outcomes may have negative effects or even show adverse effects. It seems that at our current state of knowledge, we should be paying attention to combined treatments of pharmacology with just as strong attention to lifestyle factors such as exercise and diet as related to cardiovascular health as well as staying cognitively active.

> It is amazing that we can neuroengineer our brains by choosing habits that use our minds even in the midst of a progressive brain disease.

As at every stage of my research career, I continuously learn the most meaningful lessons from the individuals whose lives constantly inspire my work. One individual with early-onset dementia who was younger than sixty-five advised me:

> You know what the worst part of AD is? That people have a predisposition to make certain assumptions and prejudices about me now that I have been diagnosed with Alzheimer's. It is as though diagnosis and dementedness is a single event. My common failings that would be readily dismissed in "normal" people are now given intense scrutiny, given new meanings, and are assigned new values— all of which feel dehumanizing. If I had a stroke, people wouldn't get mad if I couldn't move my arm. When I cannot remember, everyone seems to get down on me—especially me.

If medical treatments extend a terminal cancer patient's life by one or even two years, the achievement is fully celebrated. I know this because my first husband survived only six months after being diagnosed with leukemia. I would have given anything for another year or two. The potential to extend brain capacity by one year or perhaps two by active mental stimulation plus medication in Alzheimer's should be embraced as a similarly major achievement for individuals and their loved ones. These efforts can be implemented now to improve lives and to complement the major efforts to find improved vaccines or pharmacological or genetic treatments for later generations.

Stark Club for Young-Age Onset Dementia

My team and I realized that lives could be dramatically changed for the better when hope is instilled, backed by scientific research. The evidence from the cognitive training trial motivated our researchers to expand efforts in Alzheimer's disease and related dementias and launch the Stark Club, a support group for those diagnosed with Alzheimer's and their families. Named for one of the founding members, Temple Stark, this club has grown to more than fifty members over its seven years of operation. They have forged new ground as spokespersons for Alzheimer's with a steadfast determination to change attitudes about the disease and those afflicted with it.

In Audette Rackley's heartwarming book, *I Can Still Laugh,* positive changes were documented as the group members participated in an intervention program.[10] The training taught a number of ways those with Alzheimer's disease could still participate in the activities they valued while helping others at the same time. One clearly learned life message was that most individuals with Alzheimer's, given the opportunity, share the same desire as those without the disease: they longed to continue to contribute to life in meaningful ways.

> "The disease is NOT the culprit that robs us of who we are but the people around us who shun or diminish us by their pity." — Bill Tuel, Stark Club member

"We're not sitting around waiting for life to end, we're finding ways to bring more to it."

Whereas many felt wounded at the time of the diagnosis, Stark Club members found a deeper meaning in life, more than they ever expected. Focusing on using their abilities, Stark Club members volunteered in a variety of activities, including reading to children in a Head Start program, building wheelchair ramps for people's homes, delivering Meals on Wheels, serving as nursing home ombudsmen, stocking a food pantry, and serving as greeters at a senior center.

Believing that the sum of the parts was greater than the whole, under the leadership of Audette Rackley, the Stark Club undertook writing a book to share the lessons they learned. They hoped to inspire others to keep their brain edge in the midst of a diagnosis. Since being involuntarily drafted into the fight with Alzheimer's disease and other dementias, the club members knew strategies to deal with combating and overcoming the battle scars of dementia.

Pearls of Wisdom from the Stark Club

The Stark Club members and their caregivers immortalized their positive experiences in dealing with dementia, providing real-life illustrations on how not to become overwhelmed by desolate despair upon learning of the diagnosis. Here are a few pearls of wisdom from the Stark Club that are more completely conveyed in their book:

- **"Tune into changes in memory and functioning and don't just write things off."** Bill Tuel never failed at anything, but at age sixty he began having difficulty at work. As a solutions architect for a Fortune 500 company, his work required high-level mental abilities, and he was now having problems doing a job in which he'd typically excelled. He struggled to solve high-level business problems and give client presentations. Even routine tasks were becoming intermittently difficult. Doctors felt his problems were due to stress. The last thing on anyone's mind was Alzheimer's disease. Bill and his wife, Carol, learned firsthand the importance of early diagnosis; the relief of knowing what they were facing overshadowed the devastation of learning he had Alzheimer's.

- **"The spirit can still soar though abilities may be changing."** You've never met an optimist until you've met Bob Eshbaugh. His smile and warmth is evident though semantic dementia, a form of frontotemporal dementia that has affected his ability to express himself. His wife, Marie, tells a story she heard some time ago that she thinks captures Bob's spirit. As the story goes, there was a cave that only knew darkness. One day the sunshine invited the cave to come out and see its light. The cave enjoyed his day in the sun so much that he wanted to return the favor. He decided to invite the sun to come into his cave and see the darkness. The sun entered the cave, and wondered aloud, "But where's the darkness?" As Marie told the story, she said, "That's what I've learned from Bob. His approach to life is to get up in the morning and do what needs to be done that day. I've learned a lot from him in my life . . . and I'm still learning."

- **"Appreciate the simple things in life and remember every day is a gift."** Dawn and Stan Fedyniak and their daughter were devastated when they heard the diagnosis of Alzheimer's disease. Stan, a proud man, emigrated to the United States from Poland and proudly served in the United States Marines during Vietnam. He loved being an American and valued the closeness of his family. Dawn reflects, "Getting the diagnosis was so hard, but it seems we appreciate things like we never did before. Now we talk about the little details of the day and appreciate our time together more than ever. It reminds me that every day is a gift we should embrace."

The Stark Club members, their spouses, and families agree that a diagnosis of Alzheimer's disease, or other dementia, was the most challenging life event they had experienced to date; but they found resilience as they learned how to deal with new challenges. Do not get me wrong; they would quickly tell you that it was not an easy or desired life path. But being part of an active stimulation group—the Stark Club—changed their life course by helping them discover they could keep their minds active and even give back to others and not be just victims of the disease.

In the words of one of the caregivers, **"We're all looking for our purpose in life,** and our challenge is to accept our current circumstance as our purpose. When I remember that, it gives me peace. It's important to hear a message of hope and remember what really matters." Every lifetime offers countless opportunities to become more whole or to be torn to pieces. Most members of the Stark Club have now passed away, but they left us a lasting legacy by sharing their stories to give inspiration and courage for others to embrace life and therein find joy in the midst of a dreaded disease.

How Early to Seek Brain Training

As I mentioned in early chapters, keeping a brain-health fitness regime in place matters at every stage of life. It is of paramount importance that we have a benchmark against which to identify cognitive slippage and losses as early as possible. Early detection and aggressive treatment are critical to slow the rate of decline and hopefully stave off dementia in a large percentage of cases.

Even getting a diagnosis early may help to position the person in a more positive light. When one of the Center for BrainHealth's dearest friends brought her mom to our center, she said:

> 10–15 percent of individuals with mild cognitive loss go on to develop Alzheimer's each year.

> I have observed decline for the past few years. My mom is very smart and can still do almost everything, but I am worried that something is going on and it is getting to her. She is different. But whatever you find out, I warn you, you cannot tell her she has Alzheimer's disease. That news would devastate her.

Unfortunately, after all the assessments were done and her mom had seen my team and a neurologist, the news was what she had most dreaded. We told her that her memory problems were likely due to Alzheimer's disease. Although she received a painful diagnosis, her mom lived out the rest of her years with dignity and a sense of humor and style.

It is never too late or too soon to close the gap between what you could achieve and the level you are currently performing cognitively. I am actively researching the most informative and less concerning symptoms of mild cognitive loss and testing the effect of brain training to forge a meaningful brain health buffer to slow or even stop cognitive deterioration.

I am also examining how brains can be changed if brain training is given to at-risk adults. The goal is to follow individuals and see who is able to take a more positive course and who goes on to develop dementia. We are interested in using brain imaging to reveal differences in those who respond or fail to respond to treatments whether cognitive, physical exercise, pharmacological, or some combination. Cognitive decline can be improved in many, and we want to reach the most people possible.

Steps to Stave off Decline in Alzheimer's

Pursuing ways to continually engage brain stimulation and frontal lobe activity in particular is not the only tack to stave off Alzheimer's disease. Of all the clinical recommendations for preserving cognitive function, one habit that regularly comes out a winner is physical exercise. In a randomized control study of adults age fifty and older who had subjective complaints of memory problems, those who engaged in physical exercise showed gains across the board. They showed significantly higher global cognitive scores, better delayed memory scores, and less depression as compared to a control group who were provided healthy guidelines.

> Lifestyle habits may be our best option for reaching our maximum cognitive potential. Do not overlook their tremendous promise in healthy brain function.

Research on the benefits of physical exercise show comprehensive gains in increased brain blood flow in the hippocampus region[11–13] (the area supporting memory function), increased brain volume, improved delayed memory scores, and improved physical fitness as measured by VO2 max, a measure of maximum lung capacity. All of these gains potentially impact patients with any stage of dementia.

How to help a loved one diagnosed with Alzheimer's disease

When diagnosed with Alzheimer's, most fast forward and only consider the negative, but it is also important to remember that this does not necessarily mean a complete halt to life as you once knew it. It is vital to keep the brain active in areas of preserved cognitive function to slow cognitive changes.

When you see somebody with Alzheimer's disease very anxious or agitated, it's typically because they are in an environment that is either over- or understimulating. Figuring out the optimal cognitive level at which the person with Alzheimer's is currently functioning will help to set appropriate tasks and responsibilities for them. The tasks need to be somewhat challenging to keep them motivated. I recommend the following to stave off decline and maintain the built-up cognitive reserves in the earliest stages of dementia:

- Keep working as long as possible, which may in fact be years and not months and days, since we are diagnosing earlier and earlier.
- Nonetheless, once diagnosed, check out long-term disability coverage to make sure you do not lose much-needed benefits in case of job loss.
- Capitalize and highlight strengths.
- Delegate to supportive individual areas where the greatest vulnerabilities exist, such as moment-to-moment memory.
- Be sensitive to good and bad days; there is fluctuation in all brain diseases, so go with the flow. On good days, do more; on bad days, rest and avoid overly stimulating environments.
- Organize valuables, such as keys and wallet, so that they are always in the same place in order to avoid the frustration of constant treasure hunts.
- Write down or ask others to write down key information and appointments you need to know about in ONE place. Write enough to know what the time or name means.
- Tune in to minimize and avoid anxiety-producing situations.

- Do not try to do everything you were doing before; do less and you will do it better.
- Have communication with one person at a time, in a calm environment.
- Reduce distractions to the largest degree possible, since they merely add to the confusion.
- Don't hide. It takes a lot of energy to keep a diagnosis a secret. You don't have to tell everyone, but being honest with family and friends will relieve a lot of pressure and help you focus on engaging in life.
- Appreciate today. Enjoy what you have today instead of borrowing trouble from tomorrow. What you worry about may never happen and you'll have a better quality of life if you focus on what you can do now.
- Find other people with similar challenges for support. A network of people you can relate to helps, with one caveat: it is important to surround yourself with positive people.

Here are a few tips to stimulate the brain and maximize independence without pushing your loved ones past what the disease allows in more advanced disease stages:

1. **Have conversations, but give context.** Don't say, "We just talked about that," or, "Remember when?" Instead, give context. "Last year we went on a picnic at the beach . . . ." Memories will start to come together.
2. **Bring the person your dilemmas.** Ask, "What do you think about . . . ?" or, "What would you do?" People with Alzheimer's retain their wisdom during the early and moderate stages. They love to share it, and doing so helps their sense of integrity.
3. **Keep up hobbies.** The things they were good at before Alzheimer's are typically the things they'll be best at with Alzheimer's.
4. **Help them start tasks.** Getting started on everyday activities like eating and getting dressed is so hard for people with Alzheimer's. Their brains may preclude them from

SECTION V

FULFILL THE PROMISE

CHAPTER 13

FORGE A BLAZING TRAIL OR GO BACKWARD

Your brain never stops developing and changing. It's been doing it from the time you were an embryo, and will keep doing it all your life. And this ability, perhaps, represents its greatest strength.

—James Trefil, physicist and author

Achieving your current level of human performance **starts** with your brain.

Ultimate human performance *starts and ends with YOU.* Your level of commitment can optimize your brain's cognitive capacity. Every day you wait is a gamble with diminishing returns. **Your brain performance does not stand still—it either declines or improves.** The direction depends on you—the way and degree to which you challenge your core frontal lobe brainpowers. I know that you are not likely achieving your maximal cognitive potential. What brain value are you willing to lose this year? Or will you take the necessary steps to experience brain gain?

The Promise

My goal in this book was to deliver a promise. A promise that you learn to:

- Increase your intellectual capital
- Enhance your brainpower

- Build cognitive reserves
- Slow brain slippage

It is up to you to make these promises real. The assurances will not develop just by passively reading this book with wishful thinking, but by your efforts in taking immediate and continual actions. **You control the destiny of your human cognitive performance.** You can take countless steps forward instead of going backward. However, your brain gains will not come from simply knowing what to do; they will only come when you rigorously practice strategies to build the three core frontal lobe processes:

1. Strategic attention
2. Integrated reasoning
3. Innovation

Preventing brain decline is all about everyday healthy brain habits and healthy living. You are likely your own greatest stumbling block—letting your brain edge get dull. Instead of fulfilling the promise, are you:

- adopting unhealthy mind-stressing routines that do not optimize efficient brain performance, such as chronic multitasking or shallow downloading of massive amounts of new information in the belief that more and faster will make you smarter?
- waiting for a quick fix—a pill that will make you smarter, not a continual practice of deeper, more innovative thinking?
- falsely believing in the now debunked conventional wisdom that your basic thinking capacity is unchangeable? You still hear the old tapes of an early label that you were average or not smart enough to become_____ (you fill in the blank), and you have not challenged the wrong labeling or recognized that **no one but you can limit your potential.**

You are likely to live to be ninety and older. But will your brain span match your life span? We have been working off the wrong blueprint— thinking our brains would keep going strong even though we let them become mental couch potatoes or that working our brains harder will make us smarter. We are working our brains so hard that they are fatigued, burned out, and begging for mercy. Closing the gap depends on you. The greater effort you commit to reducing the gap, the greater the increase in brainomics—the high returns from brain gain.

If you want to become better at anything, what do you do? You practice over and over. There is nothing you cannot get better at with intensive workouts. By adopting the evidence-based guide spelled out in chapters 4, 5, and 6, your brain's capacity and human performance will be rekindled, reconfigured, reshaped, and reinvigorated—no matter your age. Starting at a high level rather than an elementary one will more fully engage the complex capacity of your frontal lobe. You will become a better problem solver and decision maker when you begin to practice synthesizing big ideas and embrace the capacity of your brain to think:

- Broadly
- Strategically
- Tactically
- In a focused manner
- Innovatively
- In a more integrated way

Everyone is smart and can be smarter. You have the potential to improve your personal cognitive performance—your greatest asset and utmost gift. For sure, the major lessons about the tremendous potential of the human mind come largely from those who have participated in my research. I have witnessed significant improvements in high performers and low performers. The shared ingredient is not the baseline level of performance, but a steadfast commitment to engaging in and exercising complex cognitive thinking patterns—continually.

Take elite military personnel. I have learned monumental lessons from these high performers who participated in my brain-training research. Without exception, every member of my BrainHealth training team was inspired by the dedication of retired service members such as Navy SEALs. They are not only dedicated to putting their life on the line to defend our freedom but, just as important, they are devoted to being in the best physical and mental shape at all times. Allowing slippage is not acceptable. As a group they display an extraordinary dedication to whole body fitness and welcome the opportunity to add promising brain training to their toolbox of high performance training.

Previously the majority of the investments were made in building and restoring their amazing physical fitness. With their partnership, a goal of mine is to add the optimization of their natural intellect to the training regimen. It is a know-brainer. As one clearly commented, "When we pull a hamstring, tear a muscle, or break a bone, we undergo intensive training to regain our strength and highest human motor performance level. We never stop training. The brain is like a muscle you use in your everyday life, so why wouldn't we work even harder to escalate our brain's performance potential?"

By learning and continuously adopting the nine brain power strategies outlined in this chapter, you, too, just like the elite military professionals I have worked with, will engage in an efficient process for:

1. new learning,
2. content absorption,
3. project design and implementation,
4. problem solving,
5. breakthrough thinking, and
6. sound decision making.

Will you make and receive the greatest return on investment or will you go backward? You have nothing to lose and everything to gain by trying these methods. This book focuses on your most important and valuable natural resource—your brainpower. **What will your brain habits become now that you have read this book? Test the science for yourself and see if in fact you can become smarter this next year. Your brain potential is limitless.**

It will not be enough to pick and choose which of these processes you build. As illustrated in the diagram on page 247, all three cognitive domains provide a process to continually employ synergistically to help you think smarter—not harder.

STRATEGIC THINKING
Learning to think smarter, not harder.

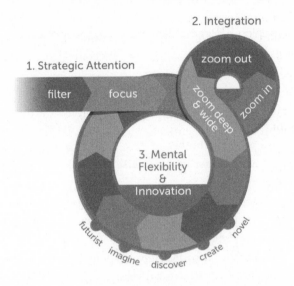

Quick Reference to the Nine Brainpowers Discussed in This Book:

Strategic Attention—Manage Brainpower
- **Brainpower of None**
  * Take advantage of silence to think deeply and solve tough problems.

    When you hit a wall mentally, quiet your mind to regain brain energy and find fresh solutions.
- **Brainpower of One**
  * Perform one task at a time even if for short intervals.

    Sequential task instead of multitask.
- **Brainpower of Two**
  * Isolate and escalate your top two daily imperatives.

    Every day, identify and dedicate the majority of prime brain time to your two most important tasks. When taking a break or needing a mental shift, fill in with your necessary, but less important, tasks. Do not let these less important priorities take over.

Integrated Reasoning—Harness Dynamic Brainpower of Zoom
- **Zoom In**
  - * Be in the know.

    Get the facts; know the logistics of what knowledge is needed.
- **Zoom Out**
  - * Be a strategic thinker.

    Identify bigger ideas, diverse perspectives, and global themes.
- **Zoom Deep and Wide**
  - * Be a tactical thinker, knowing when to apply knowledge and when not to apply.

    Formulate broader novel applications with bold, deeper, more strategic thinking.

Innovation—Harness Brain's Imagination
- **Brainpower of Infinite**
  - * Know that there are endless possibilities.

    Combine disparate ideas into a multitude of concepts, discussions, and directions.
- **Brainpower of Paradox**
  - * The tenacity to not get stopped or stuck by failure is the fuel that leads to the greatest advances in creativity and innovation.

    Reflect, reframe, and learn from mistakes. Mistakes are more informative than successes.
- **Brainpower of Unknown**
  - * Ask why and what if.

    Seek change, not a brain on automatic pilot. Keep your brain actively curious and leading from known to unknown.

You are the CEO of your brainpower, aka the Cognitive Entrepreneur Officer. You are in control of the ways in which you will neuroengineer your brain operations. You decide every single day if you will:

- increase your intellectual capital,
- hold it in reserve, or
- spend what you have until depleted.

Each day, ask yourself these questions:

1. Am I adding to my brain account?
2. Is the currency that I am adding of value?
3. Can I escalate my level of thinking capacity?

What you do has more influence on your potential brain growth than your genetic makeup, your gender, or your inherent smarts. Discoveries are taking place at an accelerated speed, but getting the science into practice is slow. **The evidence is compelling for you to become and remain committed to enhancing your brain's performance—today and every day.** You are the neuroengineer of this intricate machine that drives how you achieve your highest human cognitive performance.

Become an advocate, become a devoted adopter by proactively and continually engaging in complex mental thinking. Start reaping the rewards of your return on investment. Put your brain at the center of your health habits. For you, **meaningful gains in human cognitive performance are probable** outcomes of persistent efforts, not to mention strengthening your functional and structural brain networks.

You have been given the greatest gift and rich natural resource—the ability to think beyond the literal data and to make complex decisions. **Do not go backward.** Keep your brain fit to actualize your immense human cognitive capacity. The gains will be profound.

As Navy SEAL Morgan Luttrell asked in the Foreword:

How far can [you] take the ability of [your] brain if [you] actually focused on training it like [you] do [your] body?

For additional tools and tips visit makingyourbrainsmarter.com.

ACKNOWLEDGMENTS

This is a book I have long wanted to write. It is a book about harnessing the untapped potential of your brain to think smarter, longer; a book about cognitive brain health for all ages and all walks of life. As is usually the case, timing works out for the best. Many discoveries set forth in the previous chapters were not yet known or published even as recently as one year ago. That is how fast brain breakthroughs are happening.

My life's work is dedicated to maximizing human cognitive potential—always. Through the years, I have been deeply influenced and inspired by my family and friends, by my patients, by my team at the Center for BrainHealth, as well as other brilliant scientists from around the world. I face each day with renewed conviction to solve the immense challenge of enhancing brain performance for all: those who are stuck or losing ground in their intellectual capacity due to brain injury, those who have been diagnosed with brain disease, and still others who have limited their potential because of inappropriate labels or lack of knowledge that something could be done to increase their brain performance. I am thankful for those individuals who have continually revealed new lessons about the immense potential of the human mind.

For their particular roles in making this book possible, I am deeply grateful to my husband, Don Chapman, whose love and encouragement inspired me in every possible way to write this book; to my son, Noah Chapman, who always worried about whether I was burning out my brain by working so hard; to my sisters Shelia Schlosberg, who was instrumental in the formation of the Center for BrainHealth, and Sue McCart, who constantly encourages me and always adds a touch of humor. I am indebted to the amazing mind and spirit of Shelly Kirkland, who worked

ACKNOWLEDGMENTS

tirelessly editing our book. I am immensely thankful to Dr. John Hart, Debbie Francis, Sarah Schoellkopf, Jennifer Zientz, Audette Rackley, Molly Keebler, Jacque Gamino, Lori Cook, Raksha Mudar, Rebecca Peterson, and every scientist and research clinician at the Center for BrainHealth at The University of Texas at Dallas who has taken on the important work of translating brain health discovery to improving lives today. A thank-you is owed to Claire Gardner for her help gathering and compiling the necessary scientific references made within these pages.

Those close to me know that my deceased husband, Carroll Bond, played a major role in my steadfast pursuit of life-changing work, making me promise before his death to finish my doctorate and someday have a center focused on helping others. I am grateful to Dr. Hanna Ulatowska, my mentor, who taught me to see the lastingness of the aging mind through scientific study.

I owe a debt of gratitude to Jan Miller Rich and Nena Madonia at Dupree Miller & Associates for their insightful guidance and tenacity in taking this project to the best publishing partner, Dominick Anfuso, along with Sydney Tanigawa at Free Press. I would be remiss in not thanking Debbie Dunlop, who instantly went to work on introducing me to Jan when she learned about the vision for this book.

In closing, I especially want to thank our brave men and women who give their lives courageously fighting for our freedom and aspire to achieve the highest brain performance possible to become the next greatest generation. I am grateful for their encouragement to expand my vision for brain health.

NOTES

Introduction

1. Jaeggi, S. M., M. Buschkuehl, J. Jonides, and W. J. Perrig. 2008. "Improving fluid intelligence with training on working memory." Proceedings of the National Academy of Sciences of the United States of America 105(19): 6829–33.
2. Sternberg, R. J. 2008. "Increasing fluid intelligence is possible after all." Proceedings of the National Academy of Sciences of the United States of America 105(19): 6791–92.
3. Diamond, A. and K. Lee. 2011. "Interventions shown to aid executive function development in children 4 to 12 years old." Science 333(6045): 959–64.
4. Kuszewski, A. 2011. "You can increase your intelligence: 5 ways to maximize your cognitive potential." "Guest Blog," Scientific American.
5. Preusse, F., E. Van der Meer, G. Deshpande, F. Krueger, and I. Wartenburger. 2011. "Fluid intelligence allows flexible recruitment of the parieto-frontal network in analogical reasoning." Frontiers in Human Neuroscience 5(22).
6. Ramsden, S., F. M. Richardson, G. Josse, M. S. C. Thomas, C. Ellis, C. Shakeshaft, M. L. Seghier, and C. J. Price. 2011. "Verbal and non-verbal intelligence changes in the teenage brain." Nature 479(7371): 113–16.
7. Wilson, R. S., E. Segawa, P. A. Boyle, and D. A. Bennett. 2012. "Influence of late-life cognitive activity on cognitive health." Neurology 78(15): 1123–29.
8. Chapman, S. B., J. Zientz, M. Weiner, R. Rosenberg, W. Frawley, and M. H. Burns. 2002. "Discourse changes in early Alzheimer disease, mild cognitive impairment, and normal aging." Alzheimer Disease and Associated Disorders 16(3): 177–86.

9. Chapman, S. B., R. Anand, G. Sparks, and C. M. Cullum. 2006. "Gist distinctions in healthy cognitive aging versus mild Alzheimer's disease." *Brain Impairment* 7: 223–33.

10. Anand, R., S. B. Chapman, A. Rackley, M. Keebler, J. Zientz, and J. Hart. 2011. "Gist reasoning training in cognitively normal seniors." *International Journal of Geriatric Psychiatry* 26(9): 961–68.

11. Cook, L. G., R. DePompei, and S. B. Chapman. 2011. "Cognitive communicative challenges in TBI: Assessment and intervention in the long term." *ASHA Perspectives* 21(1): 33–42.

12. Gamino, J., S. B. Chapman, E. L. Hull, G. R. Lyon, G. R. 2010. "Effects of higher-order cognitive strategy training on gist reasoning and fact learning in adolescents." *Frontiers in Educational Psychology* 1.

13. Vas, A. K., S. B. Chapman, L. G. Cook, A. C. Elliott, and M. Keebler. 2011. "Higher-order reasoning training years after traumatic brain injury in adults." *The Journal of Head Trauma Rehabilitation* 26(3): 224–39.

14. Chapman, S. B., C. W. Cotman, H. M. Fillit, M. Gallagher, and C. H. van Dyck. 2012. "Clinical trials: New opportunities." *Journals of Gerontology Series A: Biological Sciences and Medical Sciences*: 1–13.

15. Chapman, S. B., S. Aslan, E. Kanter, R. A. Mudar, M. Keebler, and C. Gardner. (In process.) "Capitalizing on brain and cognitive plasticity with complex mental activity in adults." To be submitted to *Annals of Neurology*.

16. Horn, J. L. 1982. "The aging of human abilities." In B. B. Wolman, ed., *Handbook of Developmental Psychology*, pp 847–70 Englewood Cliffs, N.J.: Prentice-Hall, 1982.

17. Hanushek, E. A. and L. Woessmann. 2011. "How much do educational outcomes matter in OECD countries?" *Economic Policy* 26(67): 427–91.

18. Ulatowska, H. K., S. B. Chapman, A. P. Highly, and J. Prince. 1998. "Discourse in healthy old-elderly adults: A longitudinal study." *Aphasiology* 12(7/8): 619–33.

19. Valenzuela, M. J., M. Breakspear, and P. Sachdev. 2007. "Complex mental activity and the aging brain: Molecular, cellular and cortical network mechanisms." *Brain Research Reviews* 56(1): 198–213.

20. Anand, R., S. B. Chapman, A. Rackley, and J. Zientz. 2011. "Brain health fitness: Beyond retirement." *Educational Gerontology, International Journal* 37(6): 450–66.

21. Anand, R., M. A. Motes, M. J. Maguire, P. S. Moore, S. B. Chapman, and J. Hart. 2009. "Neural basis of abstracted meaning." *Neurobiology of Language*, Chicago, IL.

22. Roldan-Tapia, L., J. Garcia, R. Canovas, and I. Leon. 2012. "Cognitive re-

serve, age, and their relation to attentional and executive functions." *Applied Neuropsychology* 19(1): 2–8.

Section I: Discover the Frontal Lobe Frontier
Chapter 1 Your Brain, Your Productivity

1. Anand, R., S. B. Chapman, A. Rackley, M. Keebler, J. Zientz, and J. Hart. 2011. "Gist reasoning training in cognitively normal seniors." *International Journal of Geriatric Psychiatry* 26(9): 961–68.
2. Gamino, J., S. B. Chapman, E. L. Hull, G. R. Lyon. 2010. "Effects of higher-order cognitive strategy training on gist reasoning and fact learning in adolescents." *Frontiers in Educational Psychology* 1.
3. Roldan-Tapia, L., J. Garcia, R. Canovas, and I. Leon. 2012. "Cognitive reserve, age, and their relation to attentional and executive functions." *Applied Neuropsychology* 19(1): 2–8.
4. Chapman, S. B., C. W. Cotman, H. M. Fillit, M. Gallagher, and C. H. van Dyck. 2012. "Clinical trials: New opportunities." *Journals of Gerontology Series A: Biological Sciences and Medical Sciences*: 1–13.
5. Chapman, S. B., S. Aslan, E. Kanter, R. A. Mudar, M. Keebler, and C. Gardner. (In process.) "Capitalizing on brain and cognitive plasticity with complex mental activity in adults." To be submitted to *Annals of Neurology*.
6. Braver, T. S. 2012. "The variable nature of cognitive control: a dual mechanisms framework." *Trends in Cognitive Sciences* 16(2): 106–13.
7. Kruglanski, A. W., J. J. Belanger, X. Y. Chen, C. Kopetz, A. Pierro, L. Mannetti. 2012. "The energetics of motivated cognition: A force-field analysis." *Psychological Review* 119(1): 1–20.
8. Chapman, Aslan, et al. "Capitalizing on brain and cognitive plasticity with complex mental activity in adults."
9. Valenzuela, M. J., M. Breakspear, and P. Sachdev. 2007. "Complex mental activity and the aging brain: Molecular, cellular and cortical network mechanisms." *Brain Research Reviews* 56(1): 198–213.
10. Lewis, C. M., A. Baldassarre, G. Committeri, G. L. Romani, and M. Corbetta. 2009. "Learning sculpts the spontaneous activity of the resting human brain." Proceedings of the National Academy of Sciences of the United States of America 106(41): 17558–63.
11. Greenwood, P. M., and R. Parasuraman. 2010. "Neuronal and cognitive plasticity: A neurocognitive framework for ameliorating cognitive aging." *Frontiers in Aging Neuroscience* 2: 150.

12. Seeley, W. W., V. Menon, A. F. Schatzberg, J. Keller, G. H. Glover, H. Kenna, et al. 2007. "Dissociable intrinsic connectivity networks for salience processing and executive control." *Journal of Neuroscience* 27(9): 2349–56.

13. Hanushek, E. A. and L. Woessmann. 2011. "How much do educational outcomes matter in OECD countries?" *Economic Policy* 26(67): 427–91.

14. Roldan-Tapia et al. "Cognitive reserve, age, and their relation to attentional and executive functions," 2–8.

15. Kruglanski et al. "The energetics of motivated cognition: A force-field analysis," 1–20.

16. Preusse, F., E. Van der Meer, G. Deshpande, F. Krueger, and I. Wartenburger. 2011. "Fluid intelligence allows flexible recruitment of the parieto-frontal network in analogical reasoning." *Frontiers in Human Neuroscience* 5(22).

17. Seeley et al. "Dissociable intrinsic connectivity networks for salience processing and executive control," 2349–56.

18. Badre, D. and M. D'Esposito. 2009. "Is the rostro-caudal axis of the frontal lobe hierarchical?" *Nature Reviews, Neuroscience* 10(9): 659–69.

19. Christoff, K., K. Keramantian, G. Alan, R. Smith, and B. Madler. 2009. "Prefrontal organization of cognitive control according to levels of abstraction." *Brain Research* 1286: 94–105.

20. Stuss, D. T. 2011. "Functions of the frontal lobes: Relation to executive functions." *Journal of the International Neuropsychological Society* 17(5): 759–65.

21. Collins, A. and E. Koechlin. 2012. "Reasoning, learning, and creativity: frontal lobe function and human decision-making." *PLoS Biology* 10(3): e1001293.

Chapter 2 Frontal Lobe Fitness Rules

1. Braver, T. S. 2012. "The variable nature of cognitive control: a dual mechanisms framework." *Trends in Cognitive Sciences* 16(2): 106–13.

2. Collins, A. and E. Koechlin. 2012. "Reasoning, learning, and creativity: frontal lobe function and human decision-making." *PLoS Biology* 10(3): e1001293.

3. Mozolic, J. L., A. B. Long, A. R. Morgan, M. Rawley-Payne, and P. J. Laurienti. 2011. "A cognitive training intervention improves modality-specific attention in a randomized controlled trial of healthy older adults." *Neurobiology of Aging* 32(4): 655–68.

4. Gogtay, N., J. N. Giedd, L. Lusk, K. M. Hayashi, D. Greenstein, A. C. Vaituzis, et al. 2004. "Dynamic mapping of human cortical development dur-

ing childhood through early adulthood." Proceedings of the National Academy of Sciences of the United States of America 101(21): 8174–79.

5. Casey, B. J., N. Tottenham, C. Liston, and S. Durston. 2005. "Imaging the developing brain: What have we learned about cognitive development?" *Trends in Cognitive Science* 9(3): 104–10.

6. Diamond, A. 2011. "Biological and social influences on cognitive control processes dependent on prefrontal cortex." *Progress in Brain Research* 189: 319–39.

7. Keating, D. P. 2004. "Cognitive and brain development." In R. J. Lerner and L. D. Steinberg (Eds.), *Handbook of Adolescent Psychology* (2nd ed). Hoboken, NJ: Wiley: 45–84.

8. Badre, D. and M. D'Esposito. 2009. "Is the rostro-caudal axis of the frontal lobe hierarchical?" *Nature Reviews, Neuroscience* 10(9): 659–69.

9. Stuss, D. T. 2011. "Functions of the frontal lobes: Relation to executive functions." *Journal of the International Neuropsychological Society* 17(5): 759–65.

10. Goel, V. and R. J. Dolan. 2003. "Reciprocal neural response within lateral and ventral medial prefrontal cortex during hot and cold reasoning." *NeuroImage* 20: 2314–21.

11. Carlile, P. R. 2004. "Transferring, translating, and transforming: An integrative framework for managing knowledge across boundaries." *Organization Science* 15(5): 555–68.

12. Jung-Beeman, M., E. M. Bowden, J. Haberman, J. L. Frymiare, S. Arambel-Liu, R. Greenblatt, et al. 2004. "Neural Activity When People Solve Verbal Problems with Insight." *PLoS Biology* 2(4): 500–510.

13. Baltes, P. B. and U. M. Staudinger. 2000. "Wisdom: A metaheuristic (pragmatic) to orchestrate mind and virtue toward excellence." *American Psychologist* 55(1): 122–36.

14. Sandku, S. and J. Bhattacharya. 2008. "Deconstructing insight: EEG correlates of insightful problem solving." *PLoS ONE* 3(1): e1459.

15. Sternberg, R. J. 2008. "Increasing fluid intelligence is possible after all." Proceedings of the National Academy of Sciences of the United States of America 105(19): 6791–92.

16. Norman, D. A. and T. Shallice. 1983. "Attention to action—Willed and automatic-control of behavior." *Bulletin of the Psychonomic Society* 21(5): 354.

17. Eyrolle, H. and J. M. Cellier. 2000. "The effects of interruptions in work activity: Field and laboratory results." *Applied Ergonomics* 31: 537–43.

18. Mark, G., V. M. Gonzalez, and J. Harris. 2005. "No Task Left Behind? Exam-

ining the Nature of Fragmented Work." CHI 2005 | PAPERS: Take a Number, Stand in Line (Interruptions & Attention 1): 321–30.

19. Glascher, J., D. Rudauf, R. Colom, L. K. Paul, D. Tranel, H. Damasio, and R. Adolphs. 2010. "Distributed neural system for general intelligence revealed by lesion mapping." Proceedings of the National Academy of Sciences of the United States of America 107(10): 4705–9.

20. Dreher, J-C., E. Koechlin, S. O. Ali, and J. Grafman. 2002. "The roles of timing and task order during task switching." *NeuroImage* 17: 95–109.

21. Kuchinskas, S. 2008. "Multitasking is a myth: Your brain is actually rapidly switching focus from one task to another." *WebMD the Magazine*: 1–2.

22. Kruglanski, A. W., J. J. Belanger, X. Y. Chen, C. Kopetz, A. Pierro, and L. Mannetti. 2012. "The energetics of motivated cognition: A force-field analysis." *Psychological Review* 119(1): 1–20.

23. Cattell, R. B. 1971. *Abilities: Their Structure, Growth and Action*. Boston: Houghton-Mifflin.

24. Levine, B., I. H. Robertson, L. Clare, G. Carter, J. Hong, B. A. Wilson, et al. 2000. "Rehabilitation of executive functioning: An experimental-clinical validation of goal management training." *Journal of the International Neuropsychological Society*, 6(3): 299–312.

25. Sternberg. "Increasing fluid intelligence is possible after all," 6791–92.

26. Lewis, C. M., A. Baldassarre, G. Committeri, G. L. Romani, and M. Corbetta. 2009. "Learning sculpts the spontaneous activity of the resting human brain." Proceedings of the National Academy of Sciences of the United States of America 106(41): 17558–63.

27. Badre and D'Esposito. "Is the rostro-caudal axis of the frontal lobe hierarchical?" 659–669.

28. Diamond. "Biological and social influences on cognitive control processes dependent on prefrontal cortex," 319–39.

29. Carlile. "Transferring, translating, and transforming: An integrative framework for managing knowledge across boundaries," 555–68.

30. Burgess, P. W., E. Veitcha, A. L. Costello, and T. Shallice. 1999. "The cognitive and neuroanatomical correlates of multitasking." *Neuropsychologia* 38(2000): 848–63.

31. De Kloet, E. R., M. Joels, and F. Holsboer. 2005. "Stress and the brain: From adaptation to disease." *Nature Reviews, Neuroscience* 6(6): 463–75.

32. Clark, K. and R. Smith. 2008. "Unleashing the Power of Design Thinking." *Design Management Review* Summer: 8–15.

33. Clark and Smith. "Unleashing the Power of Design Thinking," 8–15.

34. Begley, S. 2007. "New research finds some brain functions actually improve with age. Our reporter on delayed retirement and how to stay sharp." *Wall Street Journal* online, W1.

35. Scardamalia, M. and C. Bereiter. 2008. "Pedagogical biases in educational technologies." *Educational Technology* XLVIII(3): 3–11.

36. Christoff, K., K. Keramantian, G. Alan, R. Smith, and B. Madler. 2009. "Prefrontal organization of cognitive control according to levels of abstraction." *Brain Research* 1286: 94–105.

37. Stuss. "Functions of the frontal lobes: Relation to executive functions," 759–65.

38. Goel and Dolan. "Reciprocal neural response within lateral and ventral medial prefrontal cortex during hot and cold reasoning," 2314–21.

39. Glascher et al. "Distributed neural system for general intelligence revealed by lesion mapping," 4705–9.

40. Saladin, K. 2007. *Anatomy and Physiology: The Unity of Form and Function.* New York: McGraw Hill.

41. Dumitriu, D., J. Hao, Y. Hara, J. Kaufmann, W. G. M. Janssen, W. Lou, et al. 2010. "Selective changes in thin spine density and morphology in monkey prefrontal cortex correlate with aging-related cognitive impairment." *Journal of Neuroscience* 30(22): 7507–15.

42. Grossmann, I., J. Na, M. E. W. Varnum, D. C. Park, S. Kitayama and R. E. Nisbett. 2010. "Reasoning about social conflicts improves into old age." Proceedings of the National Academy of Sciences of the United States of America 107(16): 7246–50.

43. Raz, N., A. Williamson, F. Gunning-Dixon, D. Head, and J. D. Acker. 2000. "Neuroanatomical and cognitive correlates of adult age differences in acquisition of a perceptual-motor skill." *Microscopy Research and Technique* 51(1): 85–93.

44. Miller, E. K. 2000. "The prefrontal cortex and cognitive control." *Nature Reviews, Neuroscience* 3(11): 1066–68.

45. Giedd, J. N., L. S. Clasen, R. Lenroot, D. Greenstein, G. L. Wallace, S. Ordaz, et al. 2006. "Puberty-related influences on brain development." *Mollecular and Cellular Endocrinology* 254–255: 154–62.

46. Diamond, A. and K. Lee. 2011. "Interventions shown to aid executive function development in children 4 to 12 years old." *Science* 333(6045): 959–64.

47. Kruglanski et al. "The energetics of motivated cognition: A force-field analysis," 1–20.

48. Kuchinskas. "Multitasking is a myth: Your brain is actually rapidly switching focus from one task to another," 1–2.

49. Burgess. "The cognitive and neuroanatomical correlates of multitasking," 848–63.

50. Ophir, E., C. Nass, and A. D. Wagner. 2009. "Cognitive control in media multitaskers." Proceedings of the National Academy of Sciences of the United States of America 106(37): 15583–87.

51. Ophir et al. "Cognitive control in media multitaskers," 15583–87.

52. Van der Linden, D., M. Frese, and T. F. Meijman. 2003. "Mental fatigue and the control of cognitive processes: effects on perseveration and planning." *Acta Psychologica* 113: 45–65.

53. Sternberg. "Increasing fluid intelligence is possible after all," 6791–92.

54. Valenzuela, M. J., M. Breakspear, and P. Sachdev. 2007. "Complex mental activity and the aging brain: Molecular, cellular and cortical network mechanisms." *Brain Research Reviews* 56(1): 198–213.

55. Begley. "New research finds some brain functions actually improve with age. Our reporter on delayed retirement and how to stay sharp," W1.

56. Gould, E., A. Beylin, P. Tanapat, A. Reeves, and T. J. Shors. 1999. "Learning enhances adult neurogenesis in the hippocampal formation." *Nature Neuroscience* 2(3): 260–5.

57. Gould, E., P. Tanapat, N. B. Hastings, and T. J. Shors. 1999. "Neurogenesis in adulthood: A possible role in learning." *Trends in Cognitive Sciences* 3(5): 186–92.

58. Cracchiolo, J. R., T. Mori, S. J. Nazian, J. Tan, H. Potter, and G. W. Arendash. 2007. "Enhanced cognitive activity—over and above social or physical activity—is required to protect Alzheimer's mice against cognitive impairment, reduce Abeta deposition, and increase synaptic immunoreactivity." *Neurobiology of Learning and Memory* 88: 277–94.

59. Gilkey, R. and C. Kilts. 2007. "Cognitive Fitness." *Harvard Business Review*: 1–9.

60. Sternberg. "Increasing fluid intelligence is possible after all," 6791–92.

61. Greenwood, P. M. and R. Parasuraman. 2010. "Neuronal and cognitive plasticity: A neurocognitive framework for ameliorating cognitive aging." *Frontiers in Aging Neuroscience* 2: 150.

62. Paavola, S. and K. Hakkarainen. 2005. "The knowledge creation metaphor—An emergent epistemological approach to learning." *Science & Education* 14: 535–57.

63. Horn, J. L. 1982. "The aging of human abilities." In *Intelligence: Measurement, Theory and Public Policy,* edited by B. B. Wolman, 29–73. Urbana: University of Illinois Press.

64. Hedden, T. and J. D. Gabrieli. 2004. "Insights into the ageing mind: a view from cognitive neuroscience." *Nature Reviews, Neuroscience* 5(2): 87–96.

65. Grady, C. L., M. V. Springer, D. Hongwanishkul, A. R. McIntosh, and G. Winocur. 2006. "Age-related changes in brain activity across the adult lifespan." *Journal of Cognitive Neuroscience* 18(2): 227–41.

66. Salthouse, T. A. 2006. "Aging of thought." In E. Bialystok and F. I. M. Craik (eds.), *Lifespan cognition: Mechanisms of change.* NY: Oxford University Press.

67. Salthouse, T. A. 2011. "Neuroanatomical substrates of age-related cognitive decline." *Psychological Bulletin* 137(5): 753–84.

68. Craik, F. M. and A. M. Schloerscheidt. 2011. "Age-related differences in recognition memory: Effects of materials and context change." *Psychology and Aging* 26(3): 671–77.

69. Lewis, C. M., A. Baldassarre, G. Committeri, G. L. Romani, and M. Corbetta. 2009. "Learning sculpts the spontaneous activity of the resting human brain." Proceedings of the National Academy of Sciences of the United States of America 106(41): 17558–63.

70. Greenwood, P. M. and R. Parasuraman. 2010. "Neuronal and cognitive plasticity: A neurocognitive framework for ameliorating cognitive aging." *Frontiers in Aging Neuroscience* 2: 150.

71. Mozolic, J. L., A. B. Long, A. R. Morgan, M. Rawley-Payne, and P. J. Laurienti. 2011. "A cognitive training intervention improves modality-specific attention in a randomized controlled trial of healthy older adults." *Neurobiology of Aging* 32(4): 655–68.

72. Ball, K., D. B. Berch, K. F. Helmers, J. B. Jobe, M. D. Leveck, M. Marsiske, et al. 2002. "Effects of cognitive training interventions with older adults: A randomized controlled trial." *Journal of the American Medical Association* 288(18): 2271–81.

73. Hartman-Stein, P. and E. Potkanowicz. 2003. "Behavioral determinants of healthy aging: Good news for the baby boomer generation." *Online Journal of Issues in Nursing* 8(2), Manuscript 5.

74. Acevedo, A. and D. A. Loewenstein. 2007. "Nonpharmacological cognitive interventions in aging and dementia." *Journal of Geriatric Psychiatry and Neurology* 20(4): 239–49.

75. Valenzuela, Breakspear, and Sachdev. "Complex mental activity and the aging brain: Molecular, cellular and cortical network mechanisms," 198–213.

76. Lewis, C. M. A. Baldassarre, G. Committeri, G. L. Romani, and M. Corbetta. 2009. "Learning sculpts the spontaneous activity of the resting human brain." Proceedings of the National Academy of Sciences of the United States of America 106(41): 17558–63.

77. Wilson, R. S., C. F. M. de Leon, L. L. Barnes, J. A. Schneider, J. L. Bienias, D. A. Evans, and D. A. Bennett. 2002. "Participation in cognitively stimulating activities and risk of incident Alzheimer disease." *Journal of the American Medical Association* 287(6): 742–48.

78. Ulatowska, H. K., S. B. Chapman, A. P. Highly, and J. Prince. 1998. "Discourse in healthy old-elderly adults: A longitudinal study." *Aphasiology* 12(⅞): 619–33.

79. Greenwood and Parasuraman. "Neuronal and cognitive plasticity: A neurocognitive framework for ameliorating cognitive aging," 150.

80. Mozolic et al. "A cognitive training intervention improves modality-specific attention in a randomized controlled trial of healthy older adults," 655–68.

81. Begley. "New research finds some brain functions actually improve with age. Our reporter on delayed retirement and how to stay sharp," W1.

82. Grossmann et al. "Reasoning about social conflicts improves into old age," 7246–50.

83. Guttman, M. 2001. "The Aging Brain." *USC Health Magazine* (Spring). http://www.usc.edu/hsc/info/pr/hmm/01spring/brain.html.

84. Guttman. "The Aging Brain."

85. MacMillan, M. 2000. *An Odd Kind of Fame: Stones of Phineas Gage.* Cambridge: MIT Press.

86. Rao, V. and C. Lyketsos. 2000. "Neuropsychiatric sequelae of traumatic brain Injury." *Psychosomatics* 41(2): 95–103.

87. Guskiewicz, K. M., S. W. Marshall, J. Bailes, M. McCrea, R. C. Cantu, C. Randolph, et al. 2005. "Association between recurrent concussion, mild cognitive impairment, and Alzheimer's disease in retired professional football players." *Neurosurgery* 57(4): 719–24.

88. Chen, A. J. W., G. M. Abrams, and M. D'Esposito. 2006. "Functional reintegration of prefrontal neural networks for enhancing recovery after brain injury." *Journal of Head Trauma Rehabilitation* 21(2): 107.

89. Bloss, E. B., W. G. Janssen, B. S. McEwen, and J. H. Morrison. 2010. "Interactive effects of stress and aging on structural plasticity in the prefrontal cortex." *Journal of Neuroscience* 30(19): 6726–31.

90. Anand, R., S. B. Chapman, A. Rackley, M. Keebler, J. Zientz, and J. Hart. 2011. "Gist reasoning training in cognitively normal seniors." *International Journal of Geriatric Psychiatry* 26(9): 961–68.

91. Gamino, J., S. B. Chapman, E. L. Hull, G. R. Lyon. 2010. "Effects of higher-order cognitive strategy training on gist reasoning and fact learning in adolescents." *Frontiers in Educational Psychology* 1.

92. Vas, A. K., S. B. Chapman, L. G. Cook, A. C. Elliott, and M. Keebler. 2011. "Higher-order reasoning training years after traumatic brain injury in adults." *The Journal of Head Trauma Rehabilitation* 26(3): 224–39.

93. Anand, R., S. B. Chapman, A. Rackley, and J. Zientz, J. 2011. "Brain health fitness: Beyond retirement." *Educational Gerontology, International Journal* 37(6): 450–66.

94. Chapman, S. B., H. K. Ulatowska, and C. Branch. 1994. "Successful aging: Depth of discourse processing and utilization of wisdom." Presentation given at the Conference of the Gerontological Society of America.

95. Kuszewski, A. 2011. "You can increase your intelligence: 5 ways to maximize your cognitive potential." *Scientific American Guest Blog.*

96. Carlile. "Transferring, translating, and transforming: An integrative framework for managing knowledge across boundaries," 555–68.

97. Levine et al. "Rehabilitation of executive functioning: An experimental-clinical validation of goal management training," 299–312.

98. Clark and Smith. "Unleashing the Power of Design Thinking," 8–15.

99. Paavola and Hakkarainen "The knowledge creation metaphor—An emergent epistemological approach to learning," 535–57.

100. Owen, A. M., A. Hampshire, J. A. Grahn, R. Stenton, S. Dajani, A. S. Burns, R. J. Howard, C. G. Ballard. 2010. "Putting brain training to the test." *Nature* 465(7299): 775–78.

101. Anand et al. "Gist reasoning training in cognitively normal seniors," 961–68.

102. Gamino, J., S. B. Chapman, E. L. Hull, G. R. Lyon. 2010. "Effects of higher-order cognitive strategy training on gist reasoning and fact learning in adolescents." *Frontiers in Educational Psychology* 1.

103. Vas et al. "Higher-order reasoning training years after traumatic brain injury in adults," 224–39.

104. Chapman, S. B., J. F. Gamino, and R. A. Mudar. 2012. "Higher order strategic gist reasoning in adolescence." In Reyna, V. F., S. B. Chapman, M. Dougherty, and J. Confrey (Eds.), *The Adolescent Brain: Learning, Reasoning, and Decision Making.* Washington, DC: American Psychological Association.

CHAPTER 3 A Checkup from Your Neck Up

1. Knickman, J. R. and E. K. Snell. 2002. "The 2030 problem: Caring for aging baby boomers." *Health Services Research* 37(4) 849–84.

2. Taubert, M., B. Draganski, A. Anwander, K. Muller, A. Horstmann, A. Villringer, and P. Ragert. 2010. "Dynamic properties of human brain structure: Learning-related changes in cortical areas and associated fiber connections." *Journal of Neuroscience* 30(35): 11670–7.

3. Vas, A. K., S. B. Chapman, L. G. Cook, A. C. Elliott, and M. Keebler. 2011. "Higher-order reasoning training years after traumatic brain injury in adults." *The Journal of Head Trauma Rehabilitation* 26(3): 224–39.

4. Seeley, W. W., V. Menon, A. F. Schatzberg, J. Keller, G. H. Glover, H. Kenna, et al. 2007. "Dissociable intrinsic connectivity networks for salience processing and executive control." *Journal of Neuroscience* 27(9): 2349–56.

5. Guskiewicz, K. M., S. W. Marshall, J. Bailes, M. McCrea, R. C. Cantu, C. Randolph, et al. 2005. "Association between recurrent concussion, mild cognitive impairment, and Alzheimer's disease in retired professional football players." *Neurosurgery* 57(4): 719–24.

6. Bassett, D. S., N. F. Wymbs, M. A. Porterc, P. J. Muchae, J. M. Carlson, and S. T. Grafton. 2011. "Dynamic reconfiguration of human brain networks during learning." Proceedings of the National Academy of Sciences of the United States of America 108(18): 7641–46.

7. Sternberg, R. J. 2008. "Increasing fluid intelligence is possible after all." Proceedings of the National Academy of Sciences of the United States of America 105(19): 6791–92.

8. Kuszewski, A. 2011. "You can increase your intelligence: 5 ways to maximize your cognitive potential." "Guest Blog," *Scientific American.*

9. Lewis, C. M., A. Baldassarre, G. Committeri, G. L. Romani, and M. Corbetta. 2009. "Learning sculpts the spontaneous activity of the resting human brain." Proceedings of the National Academy of Sciences of the United States of America 106(41): 17558–63.

10. Greenwood, P. M. and R. Parasuraman. 2010. "Neuronal and cognitive plasticity: A neurocognitive framework for ameliorating cognitive aging." *Frontiers in Aging Neuroscience* 2: 150.

11. Scardamalia, M. and C. Bereiter. 2006. "Knowledge building: Theory, pedagogy, and technology." In K. Sawyer (ed.), *Cambridge Handbook of the Learning Sciences.* New York: Cambridge University Press: 97–118.

12. Kramer, A. F. and K. I. Erickson. 2007. "Capitalizing on cortical plasticity:

Influence of physical activity on cognition and brain function." *Trends in Cognitive Sciences* 11(8): 342–48.

13. Willis, S. L., S. L. Tennstedt, M. Marsiske, K. Ball, J. Elias, K. M. Koepke, et al. 2006. "Long-term effects of cognitive training on everyday functional outcomes in older adults." *Journal of the American Medical Association* 296(23): 2805–14.

14. Sagi, Y., I. Tavor, S. Hofstetter, S. Tzur-Moryosef, T. Blumenfeld-Katzirand, and Y. Assaf. 2012. "Learning in the Fast Lane: New Insights into Neuroplasticity." *Neuron* 73(6): 1195–203.

15. Chapman, S. B., J. Zientz, M. Weiner, R. Rosenberg, W. Frawley, and M. H. Burns. 2002. "Discourse changes in early Alzheimer disease, mild cognitive impairment, and normal aging." *Alzheimer Disease and Associated Disorders* 16(3): 177–86.

16. Chapman, S. B., R. Anand, G. Sparks, and C. M. Cullum. 2006. "Gist distinctions in healthy cognitive aging versus mild Alzheimer's disease." *Brain Impairment* 7: 223–33.

17. Della Sala, S., G. Cocchini, R. H. Logie, M. Allerhand, and S. E. MacPherson. 2010. "Dual task during encoding, maintenance, and retrieval in Alzheimer's Disease." *Journal of Alzheimers Disease* 19(2): 503–15.

18. MacPherson, S. 2012. "Dual task abilities as a possible preclinical marker of Alzheimer's Disease in carriers of the E280A presenilin-1 mutation." *Journal of the International Neuropsychological Society* 18(02): 234–41.

19. Anand, R., S. B. Chapman, A. Rackley, M. Keebler, J. Zientz, and J. Hart. 2011. "Gist reasoning training in cognitively normal seniors." *International Journal of Geriatric Psychiatry* 26(9): 961–68.

20. Ulatowska, H. K., S. B. Chapman, A. P. Highly and J. Prince. 1998. "Discourse in healthy old-elderly adults: A longitudinal study." *Aphasiology* 12(⅞): 619–33.

21. Baltes, P. B. and U. M. Staudinger. 2000. "Wisdom: A metaheuristic (pragmatic) to orchestrate mind and virtue toward excellence." *American Psychologist* 55(1): 122–36.

22. Vas, Chapman, Cook et al. "Higher-order reasoning training years after traumatic brain injury in adults," 224–39.

23. Vas, A., S. B. Chapman, D. Krawczyk, K. Krishnan, and M. Keebler. 2010. "Executive control training to enhance frontal plasticity in traumatic brain injury." International Brain Injury Association's Eighth World Congress on Brain Injury, *Brain Injury* 24(3): 115–463.

24. Chapman, S. B., G. Sparks, H. S. Levin, M. Dennis, C. Roncadin, L. Zhang, and J. Song. 2004. "Discourse macrolevel processing after severe pediatric traumatic brain injury." *Developmental Neuropsychology* 25(1&2): 37–60.

25. Chapman, S. B., J. F. Gamino, L. G. Cook, G. Hanten, X. Li, and H. S. Levin. 2006. "Impaired discourse gist and working memory in children after brain injury." *Brain and Language* 97: 178–88.

26. Roldan-Tapia, L., J. Garcia, R. Canovas, and I. Leon. "Cognitive reserve, age, and their relation to attentional and executive functions." *Applied Neuropsychology* 19 (1): 2–8.

27. Foubert-Samier, A., G. Catheline, H. Amieva, B. Dilharreguy, C. Helmer, M. Allard, and J. F. Dartigues. 2010. "Education, occupation, leisure activities, and brain reserve: a population-based study." *Neurobiology of Aging* 33(2): 423e15.

28. Valenzuela, M. J., M. Breakspear, and P. Sachdev. 2007. "Complex mental activity and the aging brain: Molecular, cellular and cortical network mechanisms." *Brain Research Reviews* 56(1): 198–213.

29. Levine, B., I. H. Robertson, L. Clare, G. Carter, J. Hong, B. A. Wilson, et al. 2000. "Rehabilitation of executive functioning: An experimental-clinical validation of goal management training." *Journal of the International Neuropsychological Society* 6(3): 299–312.

30. Gilkey, R. and C. Kilts. 2007. "Cognitive Fitness." *Harvard Business Review*: 1–9.

31. Chapman, Zientz, et al. "Discourse changes in early Alzheimer disease, mild cognitive impairment, and normal aging," 177–86.

32. Chapman, Anand, et al. "Gist distinctions in healthy cognitive aging versus mild Alzheimer's disease," 223–33.

33. Cook, L. G., R. DePompei, and S. B. Chapman. 2010. "Cognitive communicative challenges in TBI: Assessment and intervention in the long term." *ASHA Perspectives, Division 2.*

34. Gamino, J., S. B. Chapman, E. L. Hull, G. R. Lyon, G. R. 2010. "Effects of higher-order cognitive strategy training on gist reasoning and fact learning in adolescents." *Frontiers in Educational Psychology* 1.

35. Vas, Chapman, Cook, et al. "Higher-order reasoning training years after traumatic brain injury in adults," 224–39.

36. Chapman, S. B., S. Aslan, E. Kanter, R. A. Mudar, M. Keebler, and C. Gardner. (In process.) "Capitalizing on brain and cognitive plasticity with complex mental activity in adults." To be submitted to *Annals of Neurology*.

37. Anand, R., S. B. Chapman, A. Rackley, and J. Zientz. 2011. "Brain health fitness: Beyond retirement." *Educational Gerontology, International Journal* 37(6): 450–66.

38. Chapman, S. B. and H. K. Ulatowska. 1997. "Discourse in dementia: Consideration of consciousness." In M. I. Stamenov (Ed.), *Language Structure, Discourse and the Access to Consciousness*. Philadelphia: John Benjamin Publishing Company: 155–88.

Section II Maximize Your Cognitive Performance
Chapter 4 Strengthen Your Strategic Brain Habits

1. Gamino, J., S. B. Chapman, E. L. Hull, and G. R. Lyon. 2010. "Effects of higher-order cognitive strategy training on gist reasoning and fact learning in adolescents." *Frontiers in Educational Psychology* 1.

2. Chapman, S. B., J. F. Gamino, and R. A. Mudar. 2012. "Higher order strategic gist reasoning in adolescence." In Reyna, V. F., S. B. Chapman, M. Dougherty, and J. Confrey (eds.), *The Adolescent Brain: Learning, Reasoning, and Decision Making*. Washington, DC: American Psychological Association.

3. Clark, D. 2011. "Five Things You Should Stop Doing in 2012." "HBR Blog," *Harvard Business Review*.

4. Zeldes, N., D. Sward, and S Louchheim. 2007. "Infomania: Why we can't afford to ignore it any longer." *First Monday* 12(8–6).

5. Czerwinski, M., E. Horvitz, and S. Wilhite. 2010. "A Diary Study of Task Switching and Interruptions." Microsoft Research, 1–8. http://research.microsoft.com/en-us/um/people/horvitz/taskdiary.pdf.

6. Schwartz, T. 2012. "The Magic of Doing One Thing at a Time," "HBR Blog," *Harvard Business Review*.

7. Sandku, S. and J. Bhattacharya. 2008. "Deconstructing insight: EEG correlates of insightful problem solving." *PLoS ONE* 3(1): e1459.

8. Lehrer, J. 2008. Annals of Science, "The Eureka Hunt." *The New Yorker*. 40.

9. Kounios J. and M. Beeman. 2009. "The Aha! Moment: The cognitive neuroscience of insight." *Current Directions in Psychological Science* 18: 210–16.

10. Burgess, P. W., E. Veitcha, A. L. Costello, and T. Shallice. 1999. "The cognitive and neuroanatomical correlates of multitasking." *Neuropsychologia* 38(2000): 848–63.

11. Bloss, E. B., W. G. Janssen, B. S. McEwen and J. H. Morrison. 2010. "Interactive effects of stress and aging on structural plasticity in the prefrontal cortex." *Journal of Neuroscience* 30(19): 6726–31.

12. Vedhara, K., J. Hyde, I. D. Gilchrist, M. Tytherleigh, and S. Plummer. 2000. "Acute stress, memory, attention and cortisol." *Psychoneuroendocrinology* 25: 535–49.

13. McCormick, C. M., E. Lewis, B. Somley, and T. A. Kahan. 2007. "Individual differences in cortisol levels and performance on a test of executive function in men and women." *Physiology & Behavior* 91: 87–94.

14. Van der Linden, D., M. Frese and T. F. Meijman. 2003. "Mental fatigue and the control of cognitive processes: effects on perseveration and planning." *Acta Psychologica* 113: 45–65.

15. Levine, B., I. H. Robertson, L. Clare, G. Carter, J. Hong, B. A. Wilson, et al. 2000. "Rehabilitation of executive functioning: An experimental-clinical validation of goal management training." *Journal of the International Neuropsychological Society* 6(3): 299–312.

16. Just, M. A., T. A. Keller, and J. Cynkar. 2008. "A decrease in brain activation associated with driving when listening to someone speak." *Brain Research*. Author Manuscript: 1–22.

Chapter 5 Enhance Integrated Reasoning to Accelerate Performance

1. Chapman, S. B., S. Aslan, E. Kanter, R. A. Mudar, M. Keebler, and C. Gardner. (In process.) "Capitalizing on brain and cognitive plasticity with complex mental activity in adults." To be submitted to *Annals of Neurology*.

2. Fairlie, R. W. 2012. "2011 Kauffman index of entrepreneurial activity." *Ewing Marion Kauffman Foundation*: 1–32.

3. Duggan, T. 2007. *Strategic Intuition: The Creative Spark in Human Achievement*. Chichester, West Sussex, UK: Columbia University Press.

4. Anand, R., S. B. Chapman, A. Rackley, M. Keebler, J. Zientz, and J. Hart. 2011. "Gist reasoning training in cognitively normal seniors." *International Journal of Geriatric Psychiatry* 26 (9): 961–68.

5. Chapman et al. "Capitalizing on brain and cognitive plasticity with complex mental activity in adults." (To be submitted to *Annals of Neurology*.)

Chapter 6 Innovate to Inspire Your Thinking

1. Ward, T. B. 2004. "Cognition, creativity, and entrepreneurship." *Journal of Business Venturing* 19: 173–88.

2. Sternberg, R. J. 2006. "The Rainbow Project: Enhancing the SAT through assessments of analytical, practical, and creative skills." *Intelligence* 34(4): 321–50.

3. Leshner, A. 2011. "Innovation Needs Novel Thinking." *Science* 332(6033): 1009.

4. Goel, V. and R. J. Dolan. 2003. "Reciprocal neural response within lateral and ventral medial prefrontal cortex during hot and cold reasoning." *Neuro-Image* 20: 2314–21.

5. Draganskia, B. and A. May. 2008. "Training-induced structural changes in the adult human brain." *Behavioural Brain Research* 192: 137–42.

Section III Make Your Brain Smarter at Any Age
Chapter 7 The Immediates, 13–24 Years of Age

1. Jones, S., L. N. Clarke, S. Cornish, M. Gonzales, C. Johnson, J. N. Lawson, et al. 2002. "The Internet goes to college: How students are living in the future with today's technology." Pew Internet Project Survey, Pew Internet & American Life Project. http://www.pewinternet.org/~/media/Files/Reports/2002/PIP_College_Report.pdf.pdf.

2. Jones et al. "The Internet goes to college: How students are living in the future with today's technology."

3. Robinson, K. 2011. *Out of Our Minds: Learning to Be Creative*. Oxford, UK: Capstone Publishing Limited.

4. Zeldes, N., D. Sward, and S. Louchheim. 2007. "Infomania: Why we can't afford to ignore it any longer." *First Monday* 12(8–6).

5. Smith, C. 2011. *Lost in Transition: The Dark Side of Emerging Adulthood*. New York: Oxford University Press, Inc.

6. Ito, M. 2004. "'Nurturing the brain' as an emerging research field involving child neurology." *Brain & Development* 26: 429–33.

7. Bridgeland, J. M., J. J. Dilulio, Jr., and K. B. Morison. 2006. "The silent epidemic: perspectives of high school dropouts. A report by Civic Enterprises in association with Peter D. Hart Research Associates for the Bill & Melinda Gates Foundation."

8. Chapman, S. B., J. F. Gamino, and R. A. Mudar. 2012. "Higher order strategic gist reasoning in adolescence." In Reyna, V. F., S. B. Chapman, M. Dougherty, and J. Confrey (eds.), *The Adolescent Brain: Learning, Reasoning, and Decision Making*. Washington, DC: American Psychological Association.

9. Gogtay, N., J. N. Giedd, L. Lusk, K. M. Hayashi, D. Greenstein, A. C. Vaituzis, et al. 2004. "Dynamic mapping of human cortical development during childhood through early adulthood." Proceedings of the National Academy of Sciences of the United States of America 101(21): 8174–79.

10. Giedd, J. N., L. S. Clasen, R. Lenroot, D. Greenstein, G. L. Wallace, S. Ordaz, and G. P. Chrousos. 2006. "Puberty-related influences on brain development." *Mollecular and Cellular Endocrinology* 254–255: 154–62.

11. Gamino, J., S. B. Chapman, E. L. Hull, G. R. Lyon, G. R. 2010. "Effects of higher-order cognitive strategy training on gist reasoning and fact learning in adolescents." *Frontiers in Educational Psychology* 1.

12. Diamond, A. and K. Lee. 2011. "Interventions shown to aid executive function development in children 4 to 12 years old." *Science* 333(6045): 959–64.

13. Gamino et al. "Effects of higher-order cognitive strategy training on gist reasoning and fact learning in adolescents."

14. Perkins, R., G. Moran, J. Cosgrove, and G. Shield. 2010. "PISA 2009: The performance and progress of 15-year-olds in Ireland." Summary report. Dublin: Educational Research Centre.

15. Bridgeland et al. "The silent epidemic: perspectives of high school dropouts. A report by Civic Enterprises in association with Peter D. Hart Research Associates for the Bill & Melinda Gates Foundation."

16. Perkins et al. "PISA 2009: The performance and progress of 15-year-olds in Ireland."

17. Hanushek, E. A. and L. Woessmann. 2011. "How much do educational outcomes matter in OECD countries?" *Economic Policy* 26(67): 427–91.

Chapter 8 The Finders, 25–35, and the Seekers, 36–45 Years of Age

1. Sparrow, B., J. Liu, and D. M. Wegner. 2011. "Google effects on memory: cognitive consequences of having information at our fingertips." *Sciencexpress*, 1–6.

2. Bonahan, J. 2011. "Searching for the Google Effect on people's memory." Science 333(6040): 277.

3. Sparrow et al. "Google effects on memory: cognitive consequences of having information at our fingertips."

4. Lanier, J. 2010. "The end of human specialness." The Chronicle of Higher Education, 10th Anniversary Review. https://chronicle.com/article/The-End -of-Human-Specialness/124124/.

5. Carlile, P. R. 2004. "Transferring, translating, and transforming: An integrative framework for managing knowledge across boundaries." *Organization Science* 15(5): 555–68.

6. Lanier, J. 2010. *You Are Not a Gadget: A Manifesto*. New York: Alfred A. Knopf.

7. McCormick, C. M., E. Lewis, B. Somley, and T. A. Kahan. 2007. "Individual differences in cortisol levels and performance on a test of executive function in men and women." *Physiology & Behavior* 91: 87–94.

8. McEwen, B. S. 2007. "Physiology and neurobiology of stress and adaptation: Central role of the brain." *Physiological Review* 87: 873–904.

Chapter 9 The Thinkers, 46–65 Years of Age

1. MetLife Mature Market Institute. 2006. "Memory screening: Who attends and Why—A Survey of Participants at National Memory Screening Day." http://www.alzfdn.org/Surveys/survey1.pdf.

2. Salthouse, T. A. 2011. "Neuroanatomical substrates of age-related cognitive decline." *Psychological Bulletin* 137(5): 753–84.

3. Smith, C. 2011. *Lost in Transition: The Dark Side of Emerging Adulthood.* New York: Oxford University Press, Inc.

4. Valenzuela, M. J., M. Breakspear, and P. Sachdev. 2007. "Complex mental activity and the aging brain: Molecular, cellular and cortical network mechanisms." *Brain Research Reviews* 56(1): 198–213.

5. D'Esposito, M., and A. Gazzaley. 2011. "Can age-associated memory decline be treated?" *New England Journal Medicine* 365: 1346–47.

6. Rajah, M. N., S. Bastianetto, K. Bromley-Brits, R. Cools, M. D'Esposito, C. L. Grady, et al. 2009. "Biological changes associated with healthy versus pathological aging: A symposium review." *Ageing Research Reviews* 8(2): 140–146.

7. Salthouse. "Neuroanatomical substrates of age-related cognitive decline," 753–84.

8. Salthouse. "Neuroanatomical substrates of age-related cognitive decline," 753–84.

9. Preusse, F., E. Van der Meer, G. Deshpande, F. Krueger, and I. Wartenburger. 2011. "Fluid intelligence allows flexible recruitment of the parieto-frontal network in analogical reasoning." *Frontiers in Human Neuroscience* 5(22).

10. Greenwood, P. M. and R. Parasuraman. 2010. "Neuronal and cognitive plasticity: A neurocognitive framework for ameliorating cognitive aging." *Frontiers in Aging Neuroscience* 2: 150.

11. Valenzuela et al. "Complex mental activity and the aging brain: Molecular, cellular and cortical network mechanisms," 198–213.

12. Braver, T. S. 2012. "The variable nature of cognitive control: a dual mechanisms framework." *Trends in Cognitive Sciences* 16(2): 106–13.

13. Keeter, S. 2008. "The aging of the boomers and the rise of the millennials." In R. Teixeira (Ed.), *Red, Blue and Purple America: The Future of Election Demographics*. Washington, DC: Brookings Press: 225-57.

14. Bonahan, J. 2011. "Searching for the Google Effect on people's memory." *Science* 333(6040): 277.

15. Dumitriu, D., J. Hao, Y. Hara, J. Kaufmann, W. G. M. Janssen, W. Lou, et al. 2010. "Selective changes in thin spine density and morphology in monkey prefrontal cortex correlate with aging-related cognitive impairment." *Journal of Neuroscience* 30(22): 7507–15.

16. Salthouse. "Neuroanatomical substrates of age-related cognitive decline," 753–84.

17. MetLife Mature Market Institute. 2012. "Transitioning into retirement: the MetLife study of baby boomers at 65." http://www.metlife.com/assets/cao/mmi/publications/studies/2012/studies/mmi-transitioning-retirement.pdf.

18. Collins, J. 2001. *Good to Great: Why Some Companies Make the Leap . . . and Others Don't*. New York: HarperCollins.

19. "Boomers: The next 20 years." 2007. Institute for the Future. Pamphlet available at http://www.iftf.org.

Chapter 10 The Knowers, 66–100+ Years of Age

1. Delbanco, N. 2011. *Lastingness: The art of old age*. New York: Grand Central Publishing.

2. Dana, R. 2012. "'Nevertirees': Elderly Americans who refuse to retire." *Newsweek*. Retrieved from http://www.thedailybeast.com/newsweek/2012/03/11/nevertirees-elderly-americans-who-refuse-to-retire.html.

3. Friedman, H. S. and L. R. Martin. 2011. *The Longevity Project: Surprising Discoveries for Health and Long Life from the Landmark Eight-Decade Study*. New York: Hudson Street Press.

4. Grossmann, I., J. Na, M. E. W. Varnum, D. C. Park, S. Kitayama and R. E. Nisbett. 2010. "Reasoning about social conflicts improves into old age." Proceedings of the National Academy of Sciences of the United States of America 107(16): 7246–50.

5. Coombes, A. 2007. "Happy days ahead." *The Wall Street Journal: Market Watch*. http://articles.marketwatch.com/2007-08-05/finance/30812757_1_younger-people-happy-days-laura-carstensen.

6. Lancaster, L. C. and D. Stillman. 2002. *When Generations Collide: Who They Are. Why They Clash. How to Solve the Generational Puzzle at Work*. New York: HarperCollins.

7. Kane, S. 2012. "The true recipe for workplace complexity." *BusinessDay Online.* http://businessdayonline.com/NG/index.php/work/33088-the-true-recipe-for-workplace-complexity.

8. Berns, G. S., D. Laibson, and G. Loewenstein. 2007. "Intertemporal choice—toward an integrative framework." *Trends in Cognitive Sciences* 11(11): 482–88.

9. Wilson, R. S., E. Segawa, P. A. Boyle, and D. A. Bennett. 2012. "Influence of late-life cognitive activity on cognitive health." *Neurology* 78(15): 1123–29.

10. Rohwedder, S. and R. J. Willis. 2010. "Mental Retirement." *Journal of Economic Perspectives* 24(1): 119–38.

11. Oz, M. 2011. "Why work is good for brain health: Studies show staying active is good for your body and mind." *AARP The Magazine* May/June 2011.

12. Vedhara K., J. Hyde, I. D. Gilchrist, M. Tytherleigh, and S. Plummer. 2000. "Acute stress, memory, attention and cortisol." *Psychoneuroendocrinology* 25: 535–49.

13. Chrousos, G. P. 2009. "Stress and disorders of the stress system." *National Review Endocrinology* 5: 374–81.

14. Bennis, W. and P. W. Biederman. 2010. *Still Surprised: A Memoir of a Life in Leadership.* New York: Jossey-Bass.

15. Anand, R., S. B. Chapman, A. Rackley, M. Keebler, J. Zientz, and J. Hart. 2011. "Gist reasoning training in cognitively normal seniors." *International Journal of Geriatric Psychiatry* 26(9): 961–68.

16. Chapman, S. B., J. Zientz, M. Weiner, R. Rosenberg, W. Frawley, and M. H. Burns. 2002. "Discourse changes in early Alzheimer disease, mild cognitive impairment, and normal aging." *Alzheimer Disease and Associated Disorders* 16(3): 177–86.

17. Ulatowska, H. K., S. B. Chapman, A. P. Highly, and J. Prince. 1998. "Discourse in healthy old-elderly adults: A longitudinal study." *Aphasiology* 12(7/8): 619–33.

18. Fairlie, R. W. 2012. "2011 Kauffman index of entrepreneurial activity." Ewing Marion Kauffman Foundation: 1–32.

19. Foubert-Samier, A., G. Catheline, H. Amieva, B. Dilharreguy, C. Helmer, M. Allard, and J. F. Dartigues, 2010. "Education, occupation, leisure activities, and brain reserve: a population-based study." *Neurobiology of Aging* 33(2): 423.e15.

20. Anand et al. "Gist reasoning training in cognitively normal seniors," 961–68.

21. Chapman, S. B., C. W. Cotman, H. M. Fillit, M. Gallagher, and C. H. van Dyck. 2012. "Clinical trials: New opportunities." *Journals of Gerontology Series A: Biological Sciences and Medical Sciences*: 1–13.

22. Chapman, S. B., S. Aslan, E. Kanter, R. A. Mudar, M. Keebler, and C. Gardner. (In process.) "Capitalizing on brain and cognitive plasticity with complex mental activity in adults." To be submitted to *Annals of Neurology*.

Section IV Mind the Gap in Injury and Disease
Chapter 11 Rebound and Rewire Your Brain After Injury

1. Rao, V. and C. Lyketsos. 2000. "Neuropsychiatric sequelae of traumatic brain Injury." *Psychosomatics* 41(2): 95–103.
2. Rehabilitation of persons with Traumatic Brain Injury. NIH Consensus Statement Online 1998 Oct 26-2816(1): 1–41.
3. Marquez de la Plata, C., F. G. Yang, J. Y. Wang, K. Krishnan, K. Bakhadirov, C. Paliotta, et al. 2011. "Diffusion tensor imaging biomarkers for traumatic axonal injury: Analysis of three analytic methods." *Journal of the International Neuropsychological Society* 17: 24–35.
4. Guskiewicz, K. M., S. W. Marshall, J. Bailes, M. McCrea, H. P. Harding, Jr., A. Matthews, et al. 2007. "Recurrent concussion and risk of depression in retired professional football players." *Medicine and Science in Sports & Exercise* 39(6): 903–9.
5. Chen, A. J. W., G. M. Abrams, and M. D'Esposito, M. 2006. "Functional reintegration of prefrontal neural networks for enhancing recovery after brain injury." *Journal of Head Trauma Rehabilitation* 21(2): 107.
6. Max, W., E. J. MacKenzie, and D. P. Rice. 1991. "Head injuries: Cost and consequences." *Journal of Head Trauma Rehabilitation* 6: 76–91.
7. Benson, R. R., S. A. Meda, S. Vasudevan, Z. Kou, K. A. Govindarajan, R. A. Hanks, et al. 2007. "Global white matter analysis of diffusion tensor images is predictive of injury severity in traumatic brain injury." *Journal of Neurotrauma* 3: 446–59.
8. Benson et al. "Global white matter analysis of diffusion tensor images is predictive of injury severity in traumatic brain injury," 446–59.
9. Vas, A. K., S. B. Chapman, L. G. Cook, A. C. Elliott, and M. Keebler. 2011. "Higher-order reasoning training years after traumatic brain injury in adults." *The Journal of Head Trauma Rehabilitation* 26(3): 224–39.
10. Vas, A., S. B. Chapman, D. Krawczyk, K. Krishnan, and M. Keebler. 2010. "Executive control training to enhance frontal plasticity in traumatic brain injury." International Brain Injury Association's Eighth World Congress on Brain Injury, *Brain Injury* 24(3): 115–463.
11. Chen et al. "Functional reintegration of prefrontal neural networks for enhancing recovery after brain injury," 107.

12. Benson et al. "Global white matter analysis of diffusion tensor images is predictive of injury severity in traumatic brain injury," 446–59.

13. Cook, L. G., R. DePompei, and S. B. Chapman. 2010. "Cognitive communicative challenges in TBI: Assessment and intervention in the long term." *ASHA Perspectives, Division 2.*

14. Vas, Chapman, Cook, et al. "Higher-order reasoning training years after traumatic brain injury in adults," 224–39.

15. McCauley, S. R., C. Pedroza, S. B. Chapman, L. G. Cook, A. C. Vásquez, and H. S. Levin. 2011. "Monetary incentive effects on event-based prospective memory three months after traumatic brain injury in children." *Journal of Clinical and Experimental Neuropsychology* 33(6): 639–46.

16. McCauley et al. "Monetary incentive effects on event-based prospective memory three months after traumatic brain injury in children," 639–46.

17. Chen et al. "Functional reintegration of prefrontal neural networks for enhancing recovery after brain injury," 107.

18. Lomber, S. G., M. A. Meredith and A. Kral. 2010. "Cross-modal plasticity in specific auditory cortices underlies visual compensations in the deaf." *Nature Neuroscience* 13(11): 1421–29.

19. Vas, Chapman, Cook, et al. "Higher-order reasoning training years after traumatic brain injury in adults," 224–39.

20. Max et al. "Head injuries: Cost and consequences," 76–91.

21. National Center for Injury Prevention and Control. 2003. "Report to Congress on Mild Traumatic Brain Injury in the United States: Steps to Prevent a Serious Public Health Problem." Atlanta, GA: Centers for Disease Control and Prevention.

Chapter 12 Stave Off Decline in Alzheimer's

1. Chapman, S. B., J. Zientz, M. Weiner, R. Rosenberg, W. Frawley, and M. H. Burns. 2002. "Discourse changes in early Alzheimer disease, mild cognitive impairment, and normal aging." *Alzheimer Disease and Associated Disorders* 16(3): 177–86.

2. Chapman, S. B., J. F. Gamino, L. G. Cook, G. Hanten, X. Li, and H. S. Levin. 2006. "Impaired discourse gist and working memory in children after brain injury." *Brain and Language* 97: 178–88.

3. Chapman, S. B. and H. K. Ulatowska. 1997. "Discourse in dementia: Consideration of consciousness." In M. I. Stamenov (Ed.), *Language Structure, Discourse and the Access to Consciousness.* Philadelphia: John Benjamin Publishing Company: 155–88.

4. Alzheimer's Association. http://www.alz.org/research/science/alzheimers_re search.asp.

5. Alzheimer's Association. "What is the economic impact of Alzheimer's disease?" http://alzheimers.factsforhealth.org/what/impact.asp.

6. Acevedo, A. and D. A. Loewenstein. 2007. "Nonpharmacological cognitive interventions in aging and dementia." *Journal of Geriatric Psychiatry and Neurology* 20(4): 239–49.

7. Eisler, R. and D. S. Levine. 2002. "Nurture, nature, and caring: We are not prisoners of our genes." *Brain and Mind* 3: 9–52.

8. Erickson, K. I., R. S. Prakash, M. W. Voss, L. Chaddock, L. Hu, K. S. Morris, et al. (2009). "Aerobic fitness is associated with hippocampal volume in elderly humans." *Hippocampus* 19(10), 1030–39.

9. Chapman, Zientz, et al. "Discourse changes in early Alzheimer disease, mild cognitive impairment, and normal aging," 177–86.

10. Rackley, A. and S. Dembling. 2009. *I Can Still Laugh: Stories of Inspiration and Hope from Individuals Living with Alzheimer's.* Charleston, SC: BookSurge Publishing.

11. Chapman, S. B., C. W. Cotman, H. M. Fillit, M. Gallagher, and C. H. van Dyck. 2012. "Clinical trials: New opportunities." *Journals of Gerontology Series A: Biological Sciences and Medical Sciences*: 1–13.

12. Erickson et al. "Aerobic fitness is associated with hippocampal volume in elderly humans," 1030–39.

13. Ruscheweyh, R., C. Willemer, K. Kruger, T. Duning, T. Warnecke, J. Sommer, et al. 2011. "Physical activity and memory functions: An interventional study." *Neurobiology of Aging* 32(7), 1304–19.

INDEX

ABOUT THE AUTHORS

Sandra Bond Chapman, Ph.D., founder and chief director of the Center for BrainHealth, is a Distinguished Professor at The University of Texas at Dallas in the School of Behavioral and Brain Sciences. Known for thirty years of innovative discovery, she is recognized as a leading thinker in transforming how people, young and old, can build a smarter brain. A cognitive neuroscientist with more than forty fully funded research grants, Dr. Chapman collaborates with scientists across the country and around the world to solve some of the most important issues concerning the brain and its health. Dr. Chapman's scientific study elucidates these issues and applies novel approaches to advance creative and critical thinking, to strengthen healthy brain development, and to incite innovation throughout life. She lives in Dallas with her husband, Don.

Shelly Kirkland, public relations director at the Center for BrainHealth at The University of Texas at Dallas, brings national attention to the cutting-edge research facility dedicated to understanding, protecting, and healing the brain. She lives in Dallas with her husband, Keith.